THE PEOPLES
OF THE USSR
An Ethnographic Handbook

THE PEOPLES OF THE USSR

An Ethnographic Handbook

Ronald Wixman

M.E. Sharpe, Inc. Armonk, N.Y.

146777

Library of Congress Cataloging-in-Publication Data

Wixman, Ronald.
The Peoples Of The USSR.
1. Ethnology—Soviet Union—Handbooks, manuals, etc.
I. Title.
DK33.W59   1984
947′.004
83-18433
ISBN 0-87332-203-7 (cloth)
ISBN 0-87332-506-0 (pbk.)

CIP

Printed in the United States of America

The paper used in this publication meets the minimum requirements of American National Standard for Information Sciences— Permanence of Paper for Printed Library Materials, ANSI Z39.48–1984.

MA (c)   10 9 8 7 6 5 4 3 2
MA (p)   10 9 8 7 6 5 4

Contents

Acknowledgments

I would like to express my gratitude to a number of people who helped in the preparation of this book. Without the suggestion of Paul Goble the book might never have been conceived. It was his idea that my original research, which centered solely on the North Caucasus, should be expanded to include all of the peoples of the USSR and be made widely available to scholars.

I would also like to thank Douglas Michael Leander, who helped in the compilation, alphabetizing, and cross-referencing of all entries. Very special thanks go to Stephen Reynolds for his information on the Baltic and Western Finnic peoples and on the religions of many of the peoples of the USSR. He also inserted the diacritical marks in the text by hand. In addition to all this, his numerous and valuable suggestions regarding style and format greatly facilitated the actual preparation of this work.

I am grateful to Marjorie Mandelstam Balzer for her editorial comments and for providing me with a great deal of information on the people of Siberia. Her contribution certainly increased the value and usefulness of this reference book. I would also like to express my gratitude to my editor, Patricia Kolb, for her suggestions and her patience, and for her help in the eventual publication of the text.

All cartographic work was prepared by my close friend Frederick Wilson, and I owe him special thanks for his personal support during the difficult period during which this book was completed. Similar thanks go to my very dear friends James L. Hardcastle, Todd A. Asay, Kenton Kullby, and Norman P. Frantzen. I could never overstate the importance of their support and encouragement.

My deepest appreciation also goes to Mary Alice Stander for the numerous hours of work she put in editing the many copies and versions of this text. Her constant support and encouragement were at least as important in the completion of this work as her technical help.

Most of all I want to thank the one responsible for my becoming a professor. No words can express the great debt of gratitude I owe to Stephen Lee Glaser, "the best friend of my childhood years." Without him and his special concern, patience, and encouragement I would never have gone to college or graduate school. He was not only my friend, but also my mentor. It is to him that I dedicate this book.

Preface

While a graduate student at the University of Chicago I was inspired by professors Alexandre Bennigsen and Chauncy Harris to work on the ethnic and social geography of the Islamic peoples of the USSR. This research culminated in my writing a book on the North Caucasus region (*Language Aspects of Ethnic Patterns and Processes in the North Caucasus*). While doing this research I came across numerous ethnonyms applied to the peoples of this region that are no longer in use. I found it extremely difficult to identify these peoples, to figure out their contemporary names, and in general to trace ethnic processes. It was frustrating to learn that there was no simple reference work, or in fact, any single reference work, in which to find this information. I began, therefore, to turn to various ethnographic, historical, and other sources to obtain such information and to record it in an index file. In this file I kept and cross-referenced data on self designations, Russian and other designations, location, language, religion, ethnic processes, literary language, official status, ethnographic divisions, etc. Without this file (which has over 200 entries on the North Caucasus alone) it would have been impossible to keep all these ethnonyms and groups straight—and the book would never have been completed.

I found, through this arduous task, that frequent mistakes were made by Western scholars when writing about numerically small and seemingly insignificant peoples. For example, sometimes the North Ossetians were described as Christians and the South Ossetians as Moslems (neither statement is correct). Frequently the Abkhaz were identified as being related to the Georgians, and often they were described as Moslems (again, neither statement is correct). It was also discovered that the usage of different ethnonyms, even by Russian scholars, has been inconsistent. The term Lezgin, for example, during the nineteenth and early twentieth centuries was used by different writers and at different times to mean all Moslem North Caucasian Mountaineers, all Dagestanis and Chechens, all Mountaineer Dagestanis, all southern Dagestanis, or simply the people today referred to as Lezgins.

Having found that no single source existed in which a Western scholar could find all of these names and groups, I undertook to expand the file at the urging of my good friend and colleague Paul Goble. This book is the result. In it, I have included all of the reference data I came across in seven years of research on the ethnographic groups of the Russian Empire and the USSR during the nineteenth and twentieth centuries.

Clearly this work is not exhaustive or complete and I do not claim that it includes every ethnonym that belongs here. I would like to apologize for any and all errors made. Since the sources on many of these peoples are so varied, and often give contradictory information, and since so many groups exist, the making of errors is inevitable. It would be greatly appreciated if readers knowledgeable in this field would inform me of any groups omitted and convey any additional information on the peoples listed but not adequately covered.

RONALD WIXMAN

Introduction

The purpose of this book is to be a quick reference for Western social scientists doing research on the peoples of the Russian Empire and the USSR. Basic information is provided on ethnonyms (self, alternative, Russian, and other), ethnogenesis and ethnic divisions, ethnic processes (including assimilation, consolidation, etc.), language (linguistic affiliation, literary status, alphabet reforms, etc.), population (according to the 1926, 1959, 1970, and 1979 Soviet censuses or other sources), religious affiliation, and location. It is not intended to be an encyclopedia and therefore does not include detailed historical, cultural, literary, or political information. Fifteen maps based on the Soviet publication *Atlas Narodov Mira* are provided at the end of this book. All maps were prepared by Frederick Wilson.

It is also beyond the scope of this work to attempt to establish "standard" spellings or designations for the various groups here included. Numerous transliteration systems exist, each with advantages and disadvantages. In addition, various scholars, fields, journals, etc. have their own preferred systems. One of the greatest problems is that the use of different ethnonyms or spellings frequently carries political or social significance. It should not be assumed that the use of a particular spelling or ethnonym in this book as the "main entry" is an attempt to force this form as a standard. This issue is further complicated by the facts that: (1) in general there are no standard English designations for the great majority of peoples included; (2) when an English designation does exist it often does not correspond to either the self designation or even the Russian one; (3) most often Western scholars use a transliterated, and often mutated, form of the Russian designation, which frequently corresponds neither to the sound of the Russian, nor to the self designation of the given people (nor might it have the same scope of meaning); (4) many peoples of the Russian Empire lacked ethnic self designations, and the ethnonyms provided them or used to refer to them were defined by outsiders (most often Russians) or neighboring groups; (5) ethnonyms frequently change over time; (6) over time specific ethnonyms have had different meanings (for example, the term Tatar has been used to refer to: any "oriental-looking" people; any Turkic-speaking people, any Moslem people, or some combination thereof; the Crimean, Volga, and Western Siberian Tatars, undifferentiated; or the latter three in differentiated forms); and (7) the English language lacks many sounds (or means of representation of those sounds) that occur not only in ethnic self designations but also in Russian forms.

When a commonly used English designation exists for a given people, that form is used as the main entry (for example, Russian, Ukrainian, Estonian, Finn, Latvian, Pole, Lithuanian, Karelian, Bulgarian, Georgian, Armenian, Ossetian, Mordvinian, Jew, Moldavian, etc.). Frequently the Russian designation forms the basis of the main entry because no other one was found. The additional advantage in using the Russian designation, in particular for numerically small and less known groups, is that most sources on these peoples are written in Russian and these are the most commonly used ethnonyms. In these cases the Russian ending is put in parentheses (TSY) and the root forms the main entry. Since the Russian ending IN or INTSY indicates that the ethnonym itself ends in an A, the main entry used in this book will be found with the A ending (for example, Abazintsy is referenced as Abaza). This was preferred to the more usual conversion of such Russian ethnonyms to English by adding IAN to the IN ending in Russian (for example, Abazinian from the Russian Abazintsy). Therefore, when doing research on such groups one should drop the A and add IN or INTSY in order to find the Russian form. In general, I avoided the cumbersome IAN or INIAN ending forms in main entries, and instead chose to use the root form with no endings from any language (for example, Kabard is used as the main entry rather than Kabartai or Kabardai based on the Circassian form, or Kabardin or Kabardinian based on the Russian form). Only when such endings have become a more or less "standard" form in English (for example, Ukrainian, Moldavian, Latvian, Estonian, Russian, Mordvinian, etc.) is the IAN used in the main entry.

A particular problem exists for those groups that traditionally have used the Latin alphabet in the writing of their languages. Often the English form will have been derived from the Russian transliteration, which means a double transliteration and great distortion. In such cases I chose to use the original Latin spellings. This is found, in particular, when dealing with the various Finnish, Karelian, Estonian, Latvian, Lithuanian, and Latgalian groups.

Many ethnonyms are of Turkic origin. To form the main entry for many of these groups the Turkic grammatical endings CHI, LI, or CHILI (or variants thereof) or the plural ending LAR/LER were dropped. These endings are, however, indicated in parentheses and in the self designations when appropriate. Most often the umlauted Ü or Ö, so common in Uralo-Altaic languages, is converted to YU or E, respectively, in Russian. When it was known that the original form had these umlauted sounds, the umlauted form was used to form the main entry.

Some sounds are particularly problematic as they do not exist in English (and frequently not in Russian either). The voiced velar fricative sound (the equivalent of the French or German R, or the modern Greek *gamma*) does not exist in either Russian or English. In addition there is no standard way of writing this letter in either of the languages. Some have used the consonant cluster GH for it (for example, Noghai or Kirghiz). This is somewhat problematic inasmuch as this consonant cluster does exist in English (for example, plough, light, enough, or spaghetti) but never for a voiced velar fricative sound. It is sometimes employed to "harden" the G before an E or an I (as in spaghetti) so that it is not pronounced like the G in "mirage" or "digest." This is frequently done in loan words. Russian is not consistent in the way it renders this sound in borrowed words. It appears in medial positions generally as a G, as in Nogai or Kirgiz, and in final positions as a KH, as in Bzhedukh or Abadzhekh. Often Russian uses either the G or the KH, as for example in Budug or Budukh (both forms are common). I decided to use the G spelling as the main entry for the sake of consistency. Thus as main entries the reader will find Nogai, Kirgiz, Uigur, Budug, Abadzeg, and Khinalug; but in all these cases the G is representative of the voiced velar fricative in the native languages. I felt this would not be a problem since, because English lacks this sound, it would be pronounced as a G no matter what the spelling. For self designations, on the other hand, the GH is employed throughout this book to indicate that the represented sound is a voiced velar fricative.

Although English lacks the voiceless velar fricative (i.e., the Russian KH), KH is commonly used when transliterating Russian. In this case, there is no confusion as to what the original sound was. Therefore, KH is used consistently here to represent that sound. Both English and Russian lack the voiceless velar plosive represented in Arabic by the letter *Qaf*. This sound is common in many of the languages of the USSR and is found in many self designations. Russian tends to turn this into the letter K in an initial or medial position (for example, Kirgiz, Kazakh, or Karakalpak). In final positions it is rendered either as a K, as in Karakalpak, or as a KH, as in Kazakh. Since English lacks this sound I chose to simply follow the Russian spelling. This was also done as it was frequently impossible to ascertain the original sound. Although a Q is used by some scholars, this spelling looks odd to most Westerners and can be confusing. Qazaq, Qirgiz, and Qaraqalpaq, although better renditions of the original ethnonyms of these peoples in their own languages, are less acceptable than Kazakh, Kirgiz, and Karakalpak to most Westerners. When indicating the self designation, however, the Q is employed for the voiceless velar plosive.

Palatalization (i.e., when Russian employs the soft sign, or *myagkiy znak*) is indicated in the self and Russian designations when appropriate by an apostrophe ('). This is not, however, indicated in the main entries or English designations. Throughout this work the English letter I rather than Y is used in diphthongs. This was preferred for two reasons: (1) the I is less confusing for pronounciation in English, and (2) the I can stand for either I *kratkoe*, or short i, which is the singular form, or I, the plural ending in Russian, thus eliminating the problem of choosing between the singular and plural forms. In general the main entry is based on the singular rather than the plural form of an ethnonym.

Throughout this book the term "former" (abbreviated for.)

indicates that a term is no longer commonly used. Most often it refers to the pre-Soviet designation; however, sometimes it refers to the ethnonym employed prior to the wholesale reclassification of ethnic groups carried out in the late 1920s and the early and middle 1930s.

For the convenience of the reader major entries are divided into 5 sections: (1) designations (self designation, other and alternative designations, and Russian designations); (2) ethnic data (prefaced by ETHN:) (including ethnogenesis, ethnic divisions, ethnic status, ethnic trends, and reclassification); (3) linguistic data (prefaced by LANG:) (including linguistic affiliation, dialect divisions, literary status, and alphabet); (4) population data (prefaced by POP:) (including population statistics, religious affiliations, and location); and (5) cross-references (prefaced by SEE).

A Note on Sources

Although hundreds of sources were used in the preparation of this book, by and large these had only a few sentences on a given people, or merely mentioned the ethnonym. In addition, the vast majority of sources give little information that could not be found in a few important basic sources. By far the single most important reference on the various peoples of the USSR (although far from exhaustive and somewhat outdated) are the volumes in the *Narody Mira* series put out by the Institut Etnografii imeni Miklukho-Maklaya (Akademiya Nauk SSSR). These include: *Narody Evropeiskoi Chasti SSSR*, vols. I and II; *Narody Sibiri* (available in English: *The Peoples of Siberia*, translation by Stephen P. Dunn, published by University of Chicago Press, 1964); *Narody Srednei Azii i Kazakhstana*, vols. I and II; and *Narody Kavkaza*, vols. I and II. These are not only excellent sources, but are also readily available in the libraries of many American universities. Another important source, and a simpler one to use for obtaining basic information, is S. A. Tokarev, *Etnografiya Narodov SSSR* (Moscow: Izdatel'stvo Moskovskogo Universiteta, 1958). The journal *Sovetskaya Etnografiya* is an excellent source for detailed information on various peoples and topics. Many articles from this journal appear in translation in the quarterly *Soviet Anthropology and Archeology*.

A number of valuable and important sources are also available in English. Among these are the following: Bernard Comrie, *The Languages of the Soviet Union* (Cambridge and New York: Cambridge University Press, 1981); Roman Jakobson, *et al.*, *Paleosiberian Peoples and Languages* (New Haven: HRAF Press, 1957); Karl Menges, *The Turkic Languages and Peoples* (Wiesbaden:

Otto Harrassowitz, 1968); William Matthews, *Languages of the USSR* (Cambridge: Cambridge University Press, 1951); Edward Allworth, *Nationalities of the Soviet East: Publications and Writing Systems* (New York: Columbia University Press, 1971); Bernard Geiger, *et al.*, *Peoples and Languages of the Caucasus* (The Hague: Mouton and Co., 1959); and Lawrence Krader, *Peoples of Central Asia* (Bloomington: Indiana University Press, 1963).

List of Abbreviations

alt.	alternative
AO	Autonomous Oblast (or Okrug)
ASSR	Autonomous Soviet Socialist Republic
col.	collective
des.	designation
Eng.	English
for.	former
eth.	ethnic
lang.	language
oth.	other
pl.	plural
pop.	population
Rus.	Russian
sing.	singular
spel.	spelling
SSR	Soviet Socialist Republic
Turk.	Turkish or Turkic

The Peoples of the USSR

A

ABA   Self des. Aba or Aba Kizhi; Rus. des. Aban(tsy); oth. des. Aban, Abin(tsy). A clan of Shors living along the Tom River in the vicinity of Kuznetsk in southwestern Siberia. Formerly considered a distinct people, they are now classified as Shors. SEE Shor.

ABA KIJI   Alt. spel. Aba Kizhi. SEE Aba Kizhi, Aba, Shor.

ABA KIZHI   Alt. des. Aba. SEE Aba, Shor.

ABAN (TSY)   Alt. des. Aba. SEE Aba, Shor.

ABADZEG   Self des. Abadzegh; Rus. des. Abadzekh. One of the ten major tribal divisions of the Adygei people. Each of these groups was formerly considered a distinct people. They are now classified as Adygei. The majority of Abadzeg, along with the other Abazgo-Circassian peoples, emigrated to Turkey in the mid-1860s. The Abadzeg lived in the area along the upper Psekups, Laba, and Belaya Rivers in the western North Caucasus. SEE Adygei, Circassian.

ABADZEGH (ABADZEKH)   Alt. des. Abadzeg. SEE Abadzeg, Adygei, Circassian.

ABAKAN (TSY)   For. des. of Khakass; alt. des. Abakan Tatar. SEE Khakass.

ABAKAN TATAR   For. des. of Khakass; oth. des.: Abakan(tsy), Minusa, Minusinsk Tatar. SEE Khakass.

1

ABAQAN   Alt. spel. Abakan. SEE Abakan, Khakass.

ABAQAN TATAR   Alt. spel. Abakan Tatar. SEE Abakan
                Tatar, Khakass.

ABAZA   Self des. Apswa; Rus. des. Abazin(tsy); for.
        alt. des. Beskesek Abaza, Kuban Abkhaz; oth.
des.: Abazian, Abazin, Abazinian. ETHN: In the pre-
Soviet period the Abaza were considered to be a group
of Abkhaz living in the Kuban region. The Abaza and
Abkhaz do not consider themselves separate peoples.
They each use the term "Apswa" to refer both to
themselves and each other. Up until the time of the
revolution the Abaza were being assimilated by the
Circassians (Cherkess). LANG: The Abaza language
belongs to the Abazgi division of the northwest branch
(Abazgo-Circassian) of the Caucasic language family.
The status of Abaza as a distinct language from Abkhaz
is still debated. The Abaza language is comprised of
two closely related dialects: Tapanta and Ashkharawa
(Shkharawa), the latter of which is similiar to and
mutually intelligible with Abkhaz. The Tapanta dialect
forms the basis of the Abaza literary language, which
was established in 1932 using the Latin script. It was
changed into the Cyrillic in 1938. POP: 29,497 (1979);
25,448 (1970); 19,591 (1959); 13,825 (1926). In the
1926 census they were listed as Beskesek Abaza, and in
1897 as Abkhaz. The majority of Abaza, along with the
other Abazgo-Circassian peoples, emigrated to Turkey in
the mid-1860s. The Abaza are Sunni Moslem in religion.
They live, primarily, in a few villages in the northern
part of the Karachai-Cherkess AO. SEE MAP 12.

ABAZGHI (AN)   Alt. spel. and des. Abazgi. SEE Abazgi,
                Abaza, Abkhaz, Ubykh.

ABAZGI For. col. des. of the Abaza and Abkhaz; oth.
        des. Apsua or Apswa. Prior to their
emigration to Turkey (1860s) the term Abazgi also
included the closely related Ubykh. SEE Abaza, Abkhaz,
Ubykh.

ABAZGIAN (ABAZGIN, ABAZGINIAN)   Alt. des. Abazgi. SEE
                                 Abazgi.

ABAZGO-CIRCASSIAN   Col. des. of the northwest
                     Caucasian language family and
peoples; oth. des. Abazgo-Kerketian. This term includes
the Abazgi (Abaza, Abkhaz, and Ubykh) and Circassians
(Adygei, Cherkess, and Kabard). Oth. des. Abazgo-
Kerketian.

ABAZGO-KERKETIAN   Alt. des. Abazgo-Circassian. SEE
                     Abazgo-Circassian.

ABAZIN (IAN)   Alt. des. Abaza. SEE Abaza.

ABHAZ (IAN)   Alt. spel. Abkhaz. SEE Abkhaz.

ABIN (TSY)   Alt. des. Aba. SEE Aba, Shor.

ABJUI (ABJUY)   Alt. spel. Abzhui. SEE Abzhui, Abkhaz.

ABKAZ (IAN)   Alt. spel. and des. Abkhaz. SEE Abkhaz.

ABKHAZ   Self des. Apswa; oth. des. Abkaz, Abkhazian.
          ETHN: The Abkhaz are closely related
ethnically and linguistically to the Abaza. Prior to
the revolution both were considered one people (self
des. Apswa; Rus. des. Abkhaz). The Abkhaz and Abaza
peoples still consider themselves to be one Apswa
people and apply the name Apswa to both themselves and
each other. In the pre-Soviet period the Abkhaz were
being ethnically and linguistically assimilated by the
Mingrelians (especially the Samurzakan Abkhaz) and to a
lesser extent by the Georgians. LANG: The Abkhaz
language belongs to the Abazgi division of the
northwest branch (Abazgo-Circassian) of the Caucasic
language family. The Abkhaz language is comrpised of
three closely related dialects that correspond to the
three major territorial divisions of this people:
Abzhui (the central dialect) spoken in the basin of the
Kodor River; Bzyb [(Bzyb-Guduat) the northern dialect]
spoken in the basin of the Bzyb River; and Samurzakan
(the southern dialect) spoken in the basin of the
Inguri River. The Abzhui dialect forms the basis of the
Abkhaz literary language. The Abkhaz literary language
was established in the mid-19th cent. using the
Cyrillic script. It was changed to the Latin script in
1928, to the Georgian script in 1938, and back to the
Cyrillic script in 1954. POP: 90,915 (1979); 83,240
(1970); 65,430 (1959); 56,957 (1926); 72,130 (1897).
The 1897 figures for the Abkhaz also include the Abaza
who in that year were listed as Abkhaz living in the
Kuban region. The majority of Abkhaz, along with the
other Abazgo-Circassians, emigrated to Turkey in the
mid- 1860s. Until that time the dominant religion among
the Abkhaz was Sunni Moslem. With the emigration of the
Moslem majority, the former Eastern Orthodox minority
became the majority. The Abkhaz live, primarily, in the
Abkhaz ASSR. SEE MAP 12.

ABKHAZIAN   Alt. des. of Abkhaz. SEE Abkhaz.

ABUGACH   Self des. Abugach; Rus. des.
          Abugachaev(tsy). A group of Tatarized
Samoyed that went into the formation of the Koibal
group of the Khakass. In 1859 their population was
estimated at 100. SEE Koibal, Khakass.

ABUGACHAEV (ABUGACHAIEV,   Alt. des. Abugach. SEE
          ABUGACHAYEV)   Abugach, Koibal, Khakass.

ABZHUI   One of the three major territorial divisions
           of the Abkhaz. The Abzhui dialect forms the
basis of the Abkhaz literary language and is considered
the least influenced by Mingrelian and Georgian. The
Abzhui live, primarily, in the basin of the Kodor River
in the Abkhaz ASSR. SEE Abkhaz.

ABZHUY   Alt. spel. Abzhui. SEE Abzhui, Abkhaz.

ACHA   Rus. des. Achin(tsy). A Turkic speaking people
        that went into the formation of the Kyzyl group
of the Khakass. The Acha should not be confused with
the Achan. SEE Kyzyl, Khakass.

ACHAN   For. Rus. des. of the Nanai; oth. des. Natki.
          The Achan should not be confused with the Acha
          or Achin(tsy). SEE Nanai.

ACHAR   Alt. des. Adzhar (derived from the Adzhar self
          des. Ach'areli). SEE Adzhar, Georgian.

ACHIKULAK (TSY)   Alt. des. Achikulak Nogai. SEE
                    Achikulak Nogai, Nogai.

ACHIKULAK NOGAI   Self des. Achikulak Nogai. One of
                    the three territorial (not tribal)
divisions of the Nogai (Achikulak Nogai, Ak Nogai, Kara
Nogai). The Achikulak Nogai speak a distinct dialect of
the Nogai language (Achikulak Nogai), which is the only
one of the three that has never been established as a
written language. They live, primarily, in the
Achikulak rayon in Stavropol Krai in the central North
Caucasus. SEE Nogai.

ACHIKULAK NOGAY (NOGHAI,   Alt. spel. Achikulak Nogai.
          NOGHAY)   SEE Achikulak Nogai. Nogai.

ACHIN   Alt. des. Acha. The Achin should not be
          confused with the Achan. SEE Acha, Kyzyl,
          Khakass.

ACHIQULAQ (NOGAI, NOGAY,   Alt. spel. and des. Achikulak
          NOGHAI, NOGHAY)   Nogai. SEE Achikulak Nogai,
                             Nogai.

ADJAR   Alt. spel. Adzhar. SEE Adzhar, Georgian.

ADIGE   Alt. spel. Adyge. SEE Adyge, Circassian.

ADIGEI (ADIGEY)   Alt. spel. Adygei. SEE Adygei,
                    Circassian.

ADIGHI (ADIGI)   Alt.   des.   Adyge.   SEE   Adyge,
                     Circassian,   Adygei,   Cherkess,
                     Kabard.

ADYGE   Col. self des. of the Circassians; oth. des.
           Adygi; Rus. des. Cherkess. SEE Circassian,
           Adygei, Cherkess, Kabard.

ADYGEI   Self des. Adyge; Rus. des. Adygei(tsy); for.
           Rus. and Turk. des. Cherkess. ETHN: In the
pre-Soviet period the Adygei were considered, along
with the Cherkess and Kabard peoples, one Circassian
people (self des. Adyge; Rus. and Turk. des. Cherkess)
speaking one Circassian language, by the Circassians
themselves. In the 1920s the Circassians were
officially divided by the Soviets into two groups:
western (Cherkess) and eastern (Kabard). For a short
time between the late 1920s and 30s another group
(Shapsug) was formed out of one of the western
(Shapsug) Adygei tribes. In the late 1930s the
Circassians were redivided into western (Adygei),
central (Cherkess), and eastern (Kabard) groups, each
having the status of a distinct ethnic group. The
Adygei people was formed by the unification of the
following Circassian tribes: Abadzeg, Beslenei,
Bzhedug, Egerukai, Khatukai, Makhosh, Mamkheg,
Natukhai, Shapsug, and Temirgoi (Kemirgoi). LANG:
Adygei belongs to the Circassian division of the
northwest branch (Abazgo-Circassian) of the Caucasic
language family. In the mid-19th cent. a Circassian
literary language was established. It was based on one
of the eastern dialects (Baksan) and used the Arabic
script. In 1923-24 it was changed to the Latin script.
In 1927 another Circassian literary language was
created on the basis of the Temirgoi dialect (one of
the western Adygei dialects) using the Latin script.
This became the literary language of the Adygei. In
1938 both were changed to the Cyrillic script. The
other Circassian language is used by the Kabards and
Cherkess. POP: 108,711 (1979); 99,855 (1970); 79,631
(1959). The majority of the Adygei, along with the
other Abazgo-Circassians emigrated to Turkey in the mid
1860s. The Adygei are Sunni Moslem in religion. They
live, primarily, in the Adygei AO, and in scattered
villages in Lazarevskiy, Tuapse, and Uspenskiy Rayons
in Krasnodar Kray in the western North Caucasus. SEE
Circassian. MAP 5.

ADYGEY   Alt. spel. Adygei. SEE Adygei, Circassian.

ADYGHE   Alt. spel. Adyge. SEE Adyge, Circassian,
           Adygei, Cherkess, Kabard.

ADYGHEI (ADYGHEY)   Alt. spel. Adygei. SEE Adygei,
                     Circassian.

ADYGHI   (ADYGI)   Alt.   des.   Adyge.   SEE Adyge,
                       Circassian,   Adygei,   Cherkess,
                       Kabard.

ADZHAR   Self des. Ach'areli; Rus. des. Adzhar(tsy);
          oth. des. Achar. ETHN: The Adzhars are a
distinct ethnographic group of Georgians. They are
distinct from the majority of Georgians in that they
are Sunni Moslem in religion and have been strongly
influenced by the Turks. Since the mid-1930s the
Adzhars have been officially classified as   an
ethnographic division of the Georgians. LANG: They
speak a somewhat Turkified form of the Gurian dialect
of Georgian. They use the standard Georgian literary
language. POP: 71,426 (1926). They live, primarily, in
the Adzhar ASSR. SEE Georgian.

AFGAN   The   Afgans of the USSR represent   the
          descendants of immigrants from Afghanistan
(probably Pushtun) who came primarily in the 19th
cent. POP: 4,184 (1970); 1,855 (1959); 5,348 (1926).
The Afgans are Sunni Moslem in religion. They live,
primarily, in the Tadzhik SSR.

AFGHAN   Alt. spel. Afgan. SEE Afgan.

AGRJAN   Alt. spel. Agrzhan. SEE Agrzhan, Astrakhan
          Tatar.

AGRZHAN   Rus. des. Agrzhan(tsy). A group of Moslem
          merchants from India (presumably from Agra)
that lived in Astrakhan. Their estimated population in
1857 was 107. They have been assimilated by the Tatars
of Astrakhan. SEE Astrakhan Tatar.

AGUL   No general self des.; identified by village;
          Rus. des. Aguly. ETHN: The Agul are one of the
numerically small ethnic groups of southern Dagestan.
The Agul were formerly being assimilated by the
Lezgins. LANG: The Agul language belongs to the
Samurian group of the northeast branch of the Caucasic
language family. There are two dialects of Agul: Agul
proper and Koshan (neither of which is written).
Between 1929 and the 1950s Lezgin served as their
literary language. Since that time only Russian serves
this purpose. POP: 12,078 (1979); 8,831 (1970); 6,709
(1959); 7,653 (1926). The Agul are Sunni Moslem. They
live, primarily, in four isolated gorges in southern
Dagestan, in the basin of the upper Kurakh and
Gyulgeri Rivers. SEE MAP 6.

AHTA (AHTIN)   Alt. spel. and des. Akhta. SEE Akhta,
                   Lezgin.

AHVAH (AHWAH)   Alt. spel. Akhwakh. SEE Akhwakh, Andi-
Dido Peoples, Avar.

AINO   Alt. des. Ainu. SEE Ainu.

AINU   Self des. Ainu; Rus. des. Kuril(tsy); oth. des.
Kurilian. ETHN: The Ainu are classified as a
Paleoasiatic people. Their origin is, however, still
debated. The Ainu today represent a remnant population
of a once more widespread people. Many were assimilated
by, and went into the formation of, the Itelmen,
Kamchadals, Nanai, and Nivkhi. POP: 32 (1926). The Ainu
are shamanist-animist in religion. They live,
primarily, on Sakhalin Island and in the Kurile
Islands. SEE Paleoasiatic Peoples.

AIRUM   Self des. Airum. A semi-nomadic group of
Azerbaidzhans living in the western part of
the Azerbaidzhan SSR. They speak a western dialect of
Azeri. The Airum, Padar, and Shahseven are semi-nomadic
groups of Azerbaidzhans that maintained (and to some
extent still maintain) distinct identities. SEE
Azerbaidzhan.

AISOR   Alt. des. Assyrian. SEE Assyrian.

AJAR   Alt. spel. Adzhar. SEE Adzhar, Georgian.

AK NOGAI   Self des. Ak Noghai; Rus. des. Ak or Belyy
Nogai(tsy); oth. des. Kuban Nogai; White
Nogai. One of the three territorial divisions of the
Nogai (Ak Nogai, Achikulak Nogai, and Kara Nogai).
LANG: They speak a distinct dialect of the Nogai
language (Ak Nogai) which forms the basis of the Nogai
literary language. The Ak Nogai literary language was
established in 1928 using the Latin script, and change
in 1938 to the Cyrillic. Kara Nogai (the dialect of the
Nogai of Dagestan) was established as a literary
language in the same year, but abolished in 1938. Since
that time Ak Nogai has been the literary language of
all of the Nogai. POP: They live, primarily, in the
northern part of the Karachai-Cherkess AO. SEE Nogai.

AK NOGAY (NOGHAI, NOGHAY)   Alt. spel. Ak Nogai. SEE
Ak Nogai, Nogai.

AKHTA   Alt. des. of the Lezgins of Akhta; Rus. des.
Akhtin(tsy). The term Akhta, like Kyurin, was
formerly used at times by Russians to designate all
Lezgins (Akhtintsy, Kyurintsy). SEE Lezgin.

AKHTIN (TSY)   Alt. des. Akhta. SEE Akhta, Lezgin.

AKHVAKH   Alt. des. Akhwakh. SEE Akhwakh, Andi-Dido
Peoples, Avar.

AKHWAKH   Self des. Atluatii; oth. des. Akhvakh. ETHN:
           Up until the early 1930s the Akhwakh, as
well as the other Andi-Dido peoples, were considered
distinct ethnic groups. Since that time they have been
classified as Avars. LANG: The Akhwakh language belongs
to the Andi group of the Avaro-Andi-Dido division of
the northeast branch of the Caucasic language family.
Up until the 1930s the Akhwakh language was considered
a distinct language. Since that time it has been
classified as a dialect of Avar. The Akhwakh language
is not generally written (although, periodically
publications have been printed in this language) and
Avar serves as the literary language of the Akhwakh.
POP: 3,683 (1926). The Akhwakh are Sunni Moslem in
religion. They, like the other Andi-Dido peoples, are
being assimilated by the Avars. They live in
southwestern Dagestan between the Avar and Andi
Rivers. SEE Andi-Dido Peoples, Avar.

AKNOGAI (AKNOGAY, AKNOGHAI   Alt. des. Ak Nogai. SEE Ak
           AKNOGHAY)   Nogai, Nogai.

AKSULAK   For. des. of the Uigurs who lived in the
           region around the town of Aksu. SEE Uigur.

AKSULUK   Alt. des. Aksulak. SEE Aksulak, Uigur.

ALAR   A geographic division of the Buryats. SEE
        Buryat.

ALATAULAK (ALATAULUK)   Alt. des. of Alatau Kirgiz.
                         SEE Alatau Kirgiz, Kirgiz.

ALATAU KIRGHIZ   Alt. spel. Alatau Kirgiz. SEE Alatau
                  Kirgiz, Kirgiz.

ALATAU KIRGIZ   Self des. Alatooluk Qyrgyz; for.
                 des. of the present Kirgiz people.
This name is still found among the Kirgiz as a self
designation. SEE Kirgiz.

ALATAU QIRGHIZ (QIRGIZ,   Alt. spel. Alatau Kirgiz.
           QYRGHYZ, QYRGYZ)   SEE Alatau Kirgiz, Kirgiz.

ALBANIAN   Self des. Shqipetar; Rus. des. Alban(tsy);
            oth. des. Arnaut. ETHN: The Albanians of
the USSR are the descendants of a relatively small
group of immigrants from the Ottoman Empire in the 18th
and 19th cents. POP: 4,402 (1970); 5,258 (1959). The
Albanians of the USSR are Eastern Orthodox in religion.
They live, primarily, in Zaporozhe Oblast, in the
Ukrainian SSR.

ALEUT   Self des. Unangan; alt. Rus. des. Unangun(y).
          ETHN: The Aleuts of the USSR are of mixed
origin. In 1825-26 Aleuts were moved from the Aleutian
Islands to the Komandirovskiy Islands to hunt furs.
There they mixed with other hunting communities
(Russian, Komi, Eskimo, and others). Of all of the
Peoples of the North they are among the most Russified.
LANG: The Aleut language is a Paleoasiatic language,
closely related to Eskimo. Their language is not
written, and Russian serves as their literary language.
POP: 546 (1979); 441 (1970); 421 (1959); 353 (1926).
The Aleuts are mixed Eastern Orthodox and shamanist-
animist in religion. They live on Bering and Mednyy
Islands (Komandirovskiy Islands). SEE Paleoasiatic
Peoples.

ALI ILI   Self des. Ali Ili; oth. des. Alili. One of
          the ten major tribal-territorial divisions
of the Turkmen. In the pre-Soviet period they were each
considered a distinct people. The Ali Ili speak a
distinct dialect (Ali Ili) of Turkmen. They live,
primarily, in the foothills of the eastern Kopet Dag
mountains in the Turkmen SSR. SEE Turkmen.

ALILI   Alt. des. of Ali Ili. SEE Ali Ili, Turkmen.

ALTAI   1- Self des. Altai; pre-Soviet period no
          general self des.; between 1922 and 1940 Rus.
des. Oirot.; present Rus. des. Altai(tsy). ETHN: The
Altai people are divided into two distinct groups who
each speak a distinct language. The northern Altai
(alt. Rus. des. Chenevyy Tatar; alt. Eng. des. Back
Country Tatar) group was formed by the unification of
the Tubalar, Chelkan, and Kumanda (Kumandin) tribal
groups. The southern Altai (alt. Rus. des. Belyy,
Altai, Gornyy, Porubezhnyy, or Biy Kalmyk; alt. Eng.
des. White, Altay, Mountain, Frontier, or Biy Kalmyk)
group was formed by the unification of the Altai,
Telengit, Telesy, and Teleut tribal groups. The Altai
people takes its name from the Altai tribe (Altai
Kizhi) around which some of the other tribes are
merging. Among some of these groups the processess of
consolidation is taking place at a slow pace, and the
Teleuts have formally requested recognition as a
distinct Soviet ethnic group. In the pre-Soviet period
each of these tribal-territorial groups was considered
a distinct people with its own dialect. LANG: The Altai
language has two distinct dialect groups belonging to
different divisions of the Turkic branch of the Uralo-
Altaic language family. The northern group belongs to
the Eastern division, while the southern group belongs
to the Kypchak division. Each of the tribes speaks its
own dialect. The southern group is closely related to
the Kirgiz language. In 1868 the Altai Church Mission

attempted to establish an Altai literary language
based on the southern (Teleut) dialect using the
Cyrillic script. This failed to achieve widespread
usage as a result of the great divergence in dialects.
In 1922 the Soviets created an Altai literary language
based on the Altai dialect using the Cyrillic script.
POP: 60,015 (1979); 55,812 (1970); 45,270 (1959);
39,062 (1926). The religion of the Altai is a mixture
of shamanist-animist and Eastern Orthodox beliefs. They
live, primarily, in the Gorno-Altai AO in western
Siberia.

2- In the pre-Soviet period the term Altai
referred exclusively to the Altai tribe (Altai Kizhi)
of what is today the Altai people. The dialect of the
Altai tribe forms the basis of the modern Altai
literary language, and it is around this group that the
some of the other Altai tribes are merging to form the
present Altai people. SEE MAP 9.

ALTAIAN   Alt. des. Altai. SEE Altai.

ALTAI KIJI   Alt. spel. Altai Kizhi. SEE Altai Kizhi,
                Altai.

ALTAI KIZHI   Alt. des. of the Altai tribe of the
                 present Altai people. The various
tribes of the Altai people are being unified around the
Altai Kizhi. The modern Altai literary language is
based on the dialect of the Altai Kizhi. It was
established in 1922 using the Cyrillic script. SEE
Altai.

ALTAY (AN)   Alt. spel. and des. of Altai. SEE Altai.

ALTAY KIJI (KIZHI)   Alt. spel. Altai Kizhi. SEE
                        Altai Kizhi, Altai.

ALIUTOR   Alt. spel. Alyutor. SEE Alyutor, Koryak.

ALYUTOR   The Alyutor are one of the nine major
             territorial divisions of the Koryaks. The
Alyutor, like each of the other eight groups, has its
own dialect, and in the pre-Soviet period was
considered a distict people. They were known for
combining reindeer breeding and sea mammal hunting in a
particularly rich locale. The Alyutor live, primarily,
on the Kamchatka Isthmus in the Koryak AO, in far
eastern Siberia. SEE Koryak.

ANATRI   Oth. des. Lower Chuvash. One of the two major
            divisions of the Chuvash (Anatri and Viryal).
The Anatri dialect forms the basis of the Chuvash
literary language. They live, primarily, in the
southeastern part of the Chuvash ASSR. SEE Chuvash.

ANAUL   A now extinct group of Yukagirs (as a result
           of epidemics in the 19th century). SEE
           Yukagir.

ANDI   Self des. Qwannal; oth. des. Kwanaly. ETHN:
           Until the early 1930s the Andi, like the other
Andi-Dido peoples, were considered a distinct ethnic
group. Since that time they have been classified as
Avars. LANG: The Andi language belongs to the Andi
group of the Avaro-Andi-Dido division of the northeast
branch of the Caucasic language family. Until the
1930s the Andi language was considered a distinct
language, but since that time it has been classified
as a dialect of Avar. The Andi language is not written
and Avar serves as the literary language of the Andi.
POP: 7,840 (1926). The Andi are being assimilated by
the Avars. The Andi are Sunni Moslem in religion. They
live, primarily, in the basin of the Upper Andi River
in southwestern Dagestan. SEE Andi-Dido Peoples, Avar.

ANDI PEOPLES   Col. des. of the Andi, Botlig,
                 Godoberi, Karata, Bagulal, Tindi,
Chamalal, and Akhwakh. ETHN: Each of these peoples was
considered a distinct ethnic group until the 1930s when
they were classified as Avars. At the same time their
languages were classified as dialects of the Avar
language. LANG: The Andi languages belong to the Andi
group of the Avaro-Andi-Dido division of the northeast
branch of the Caucasic language family. None of these
languages has a written form. Avar serves as the
literary language of the Andi peoples. POP: The Andi
peoples are Sunni Moslem in religion. They live,
primarily, in highland southwestern Dagestan. SEE
Andi-Dido Peoples, Avar.

ANDI-DIDO PEOPLES   Col. des. of the thirteen
                      numerically small ethnic groups
of highland southwestern Dagestan; oth. des. Ando-Tsez
peoples. ETHN: They are divided into two groups: Andi
(including the Andi, Akhwakh, Botlig, Godoberi,
Bagulal, Karata, Tindi, and Chamalal peoples) and the
Dido or Tsez (including the Bezheta, Dido, Ginug,
Khunzal, and Khwarshi peoples). To this group are often
added the Archi people who are closely related
culturally and who follow similar ethnic processes. All
of these peoples were considered distinct ethnic groups
until the 1930s when they were classified as Avars.
LANG: The Andi-Dido languages belong to the Avaro-Andi-
Dido division of the northeast branch of the Caucasian
language family. Until the 1930s these languages of the
various Andi-Dido peoples were considered distinct
languages. Since that time they have been classified as
dialects of Avar. None of these languages is written
and Avar serves as the literary language of these
peoples. POP: The Andi-Dido peoples are being

assimilated by the closely related Avars. They are
Sunni Moslem in religion. They live, primarily, in
highland southwestern Dagestan. SEE Avar.

ANDO-DIDO PEOPLES   Alt. des. Andi-Dido Peoples. SEE
                            Andi-Dido Peoples, Avar.

ANDO-TSEZ PEOPLES   Alt. des. Andi-Dido Peoples. SEE
                            Andi-Dido Peoples, Avar.

APSUA (APSWA)   Alt. des. of the Abazgi. SEE Abazgi,
                   Abaza, Abkhaz.

APUKA   Oth. des. Apukin(tsy). One the nine
        territorial divisions of the Koryaks. In the
pre-Soviet period each of these groups was considered a
distinct people. Each group has its own dialect. The
Apuka live, primarily, at the mouth of the Apuka River
and north along the Bering Sea in the Koryak AO in far
eastern Siberia. SEE Koryak.

APUKIN (TSY)   Alt. des. Apuka. SEE Apuka, Koryak.

AQ NOGAI (NOGAY,   Alt. spel. Ak Nogai. SEE Ak Nogai,
NOGHAI, NOGHAY)   Nogai.

AQNOGAI (AQNOGAY,   Alt. des. and spel. Ak Nogai.
AQNOGHAI, AQNOGHAY)   SEE Ak Nogai, Nogai.

AQSULAQ (AQSULUQ)   Alt. spel. Aksulak. SEE Aksulak,
                   Uigur.

ARA   Oth. des. Arin(tsy). A Kettic speaking group
      that went into the formation of the Kacha
      (Kachin) division of the Khakass. SEE Kacha,
      Khakass.

ARAB   Self des. Arab; oth. des. Arab of Central Asia.
        ETHN: The Arabs of the USSR are the descendants
of Arab conquerors and nomads who came to Central Asia
in the 8th cent. from Arabia and between the 16th and
19th cents. from northern Afghanistan. Most are
descended of the nomadic Arabs of northern Afghanistan.
LANG: The Arabic spoken by these people is
significantly different from that spoken in the Middle
East. The Arabs are being assimilated by the Uzbeks and
Tadzhiks. Few have retained either the Arabic language
or Arab customs. Pop: 28,978 (1926). The Arabs are
Sunni Moslem in religion. They live, primarily, in
scattered settlements in Uzbekistan and Tadzhikistan
(mainly along the Zeravshan River between Samarkand and
the Karakul oasis).

ARAB OF CENTRAL ASIA   Alt. des. Arab. SEE Arab.

ARCHI   Self des.   Arishishuw;   oth. des. Archin(tsy).
ETHN: The   Archi   are one of the   numerically
small peoples of highland   southwestern   Dagestan   that
are being assimilated by the Avars. They are culturally
closely   related   to   the   Andi-Dido   peoples,   albeit
linguistically distinct.   Up until the 1930s the Archi,
like   the   other   Andi-Dido   peoples,   were   considered
distinct ethnic groups.   Since that time they have been
classified   as Avars.   LANG: The position of the Archi
language   is debated.   It is usually grouped   with   the
Andi-Dido   languages,   but is sometimes classified with
Lak   in   the   Dargino-Lak   group.   It   is   transitional
between   the Avaro-Andi-Dido and Dargino-Lak   divisions
of   the   northeast   branch of   the   Caucasic   language
family.   The   Archi   language is not written   and   Avar
serves as the literary language of the Archi.   POP: 863
(1926).   The   Archi,   like the Andi-Dido   peoples,   are
being assimilated by the Avar. They are Sunni Moslem in
religion.   They   live in the single village (aul)   Ruch
Archi in west central Dagestan.   SEE Andi-Dido Peoples,
Avar.

ARIN (TSY)   Alt. des. Ara. SEE Ara, Kacha, Khakass.

ARMENIAN   Self des.   Haik;   Rus. des. Armyan(e);   Turk.
des.   Ermen.   ETHN: Although Armenians have
populated parts of the Caucasus for over two millennia,
the   majority   of Soviet Armenians are   descended   from
immigrants   from   Turkey   and Persia who   came   to   the
region of the Transcaucasus in the 19th cent. LANG: The
Armenian   language forms an independent branch   of   the
Indo-European   language family.   Armenian is the oldest
of the literary languages in use in the USSR today. The
Armenian   literary   language and alphabet date back   to
406 AD. The modern Soviet Armenian literary language is
based   on   the   Ararat dialect and is   written   in   the
Armenian   script.   POP: 4,151,241   (1979);   3,559,151
(1970);   2,786,912   (1959);   1,567,568   (1926).   Prior to
1944,   a   small   group   of   Islamicized   and   Turkified
Armenians   (Khemshil)   lived on the Black Sea   coast   in
southwestern Georgia (pop: 629 in 1926). In 1944 they
were   deported   to   Central Asia along with   the   other
Turkified   people   of   the   region   (Meskhetians).   The
Armenians   are   predominantly   Armeno-Gregorian   in
religion. The majority of Armenians are concentrated in
the Armenian SSR and adjacent areas of the Georgian and
Azerbaidzhan   SSRs (especially in the   Nagorno-Karabakh
AO   in   the   Azerbaidzhan   SSR).   Armenians   are   found
scattered throughout the USSR. SEE MAP 7.

ARMIAN (ARMYAN)   Alt. des. Armenian. SEE Armenian.

ARNAUT   Alt. des. Albanian. SEE Albanian.

AS   Alt. des. Asi. SEE Asi, Ossetian.

ASAN   A Kettic group that was assimilated by the Evenks in the 18th and 19th cents. The Asan should not to be confused with the As(i). SEE Evenk.

ASHKENAZIC JEWS (ASHKENAZIM)   Alt. des. East European (Yiddish speaking) Jews. SEE Jews.

ASHKARAWA   Alt. des. Ashkharawa. SEE Ashkharawa, Abaza.

ASHKHARAWA   Until the mid-19th cent. one of the two divisions of the Abaza (Ashkharawa and Tapanta). The Ashkharawa were comprised of the Mysylbai, Kyzylbek, Chagrei, Bag, Barakai, and Tam tribes. The Ashkharawa speak a distinct dialect of Abaza which is mutually intelligible with Abkhaz. SEE Abaza.

ASHQARAWA   Alt. spel. Ashkharawa. SEE Ashkharawa, Abaza.

ASI   For. des. Ossetian. The Ossetians do not call themselves Asi. This designation was applied to them by the Russians and the Georgians. The Ossetians, however, refer to the Balkars as Asi, and there is much evidence to show that there is a great admixture of Ossetian in the Balkars. The Asi should not be confused with the Asan. SEE Ossetian.

ASSIRIAN   Alt. des. Assyrian. SEE Assyrian.

ASSYRIAN   Self des. Sura'i or Aturai; Rus. des. Aisor(y) or Assiriy(tsy); oth. des. Aisor. ETHN: The majority of Assyrians came to the Russian Empire and the USSR in two waves of migration, both from around Lake Urmiye in Persia. The first came in the 19th century (the migrants going primarily to Transcaucasia; especially Georgia); the second after World War II (the majority of these settling in Tbilisi, Moscow, and Leningrad). LANG: The Assyrian language (Syriac) belongs to the Aramaic division of the western branch of the Semitic language family. The Assyrians of the USSR speak the Urmiye dialect of Assyrian. The Assyrian literary language was established in 1840 on the basis of the Urmiye dialect. It has two scripts (Estrangelo and Nestorian—both of which are script styles of the Syriac alphabet). Although both were formally recognized, Assyrian is no longer a recognized literary language in the USSR. POP: 25,170 (1979); 24,294 (1970); 21,803 (1959); 9,808 (1926). The Assyrians are Nestorian and Jacobite Christian in religion. The Assyrians live, primarily, in and around the cities of Tbilisi (in the Georgian SSR), Moscow, and Leningrad.

ASTRAHAN (ASTRAKAN) TATAR   Alt. spel. Astrakhan Tatar.
                            SEE Astrakhan Tatar, Tatar.

ASTRAKHAN TATAR   The Astrakhan Tatars are the
                   descendants of the Nogai Horde
(the Golden Horde) living between the Volga and the
Ural Rivers. They are divided into two distinct groups
[Kundrov Tatar and Karagash(Karashi)]. The Astrakhan
Tatars have also assimilated a group of Moslem Indian
merchants (Agrzhan) who had come to Astrakhan in the
18th cent. The Astrakhan Tatars are Sunni Moslem in
religion . SEE Tatar.

ASY   Alt. spel. Asi. SEE Asi, Ossetian.

ATAGAN   A group of Mongols from Mongolia assimilated
          by the Buryats. SEE Buryat.

AUKSHTAI (AUKSHTAITI,   Alt.   spel.   and   des.   of
AUKSHTAY, AUKSHTAYTY)   Aukštaičiai. SEE Aukštaičiai,
                          Lithuanian.

AUKŠTAI (AUKŠTAITI)   Alt. des. Aukštaičiai. SEE
                       Aukštaičiai, Lithuanian.

AUKŠTAIČIAI   Self des. sing. Aukštaitis, pl.
               Aukštaičiai; oth. des. Aukštaiti. One
of the five major former tribal-territorial divisions
of the Lithuanians. Each of these tribal-territorial
groups was formerly considered a distinct people. The
term Aukštaičiai now refers to the present inhabitants
of eastern and southern Lithuania. The term Aukštaičiai
in Lithuanian means "highlanders." The Aukštai dialect
forms the basis of the Lithuanian literary language
which was established in the 16th cent. SEE
Lithuanian.

AUKŠTAITI   Alt. des. Aukštaičiai. SEE Aukštaičiai,
             Lithuanian.

AVAR   Self des. Maarulal or Magarulal; formerly no
        general self des., but rather identified by
village or clan federation; in the north the Maarulal
and in the south Bagaulal; Rus. des. Avar(tsy); oth.
des. Awar. ETHN: The contemporary Avar people is
comprised of the Avars proper and the various Andi-Dido
and Archi peoples [Andi peoples (Andi, Botlig,
Godoberi, Karata, Bagulal, Tindi, Chamalal, and
Akhwakh); Dido peoples (Bezheta, Dido, Ginug,
Khwarshi, and Khunzal); and Archi]. Up until the 1930s
each of these peoples was considered a distinct ethnic
group, each having its own distinct language. Since
that time they have been classified as Avars and their
languages as dialects of Avar. All of these groups are
merging into one Avar nation. LANG: The Avar language

belongs to the Avaro-Andi-Dido group of the northeast division of the Caucasic language family. Avar is comprised of four major, non-mutually intelligible dialect groups (Khunzakh, Gidatl-Andalaly-Karakh, Antsukh, and Charoda), each having a number of dialects and sub-dialects. From the 16th cent. the Avar town of Khunzakh was a major political, military, economic, and religious-cultural center for all of western Dagestan. As such the Khunzakh dialect [also known as Bol Mats ("military language")] has been used since that time as a lingua franca among all highland western Dagestanis (Avars, Andi-Dido peoples, Archi, Lak, Dargin, northwestern Tsakhurs, and others). Khunzakh forms the basis of the modern Avar literary language. The Avar language has been literary since the 17th cent., however it was not widely used until the late 19th-early 20th cents. It was originally written in the Arabic script, changed in 1928 to the Latin, and in 1938 to the Cyrillic. POP: 482,844 (1979); 396,297 (1970); 270,394 (1959); 158,769 (1926), excluding the various Andi-Dido and Archi peoples, 197,392 including these peoples. The Avars are Sunni Moslem in religion. They live, primarily, in the mountainous western part of Dagestan and in adjacent areas in northern Azerbaidzhan. SEE MAP 6.

AVARO-ANDI-DIDO PEOPLES   Oth. des. Avaro-Andi-Tsez peoples. A col. des. of the peoples comprising the Avar, Andi, Dido, and Archi groups of peoples (virtually identical with what is today considered the Avar people). The Avaro-Andi-Dido people are comprised of four groups: the Avar proper; the Andi group (Andi, Akhwakh, Botlig, Godoberi, Bagulal, Karata, Tindi, and Chamalal peoples); the Dido (Tsez) group (Dido, Khwarshi, Bezheta, Khunzal, and Ginug peoples); and Archi (an independent group whose language is transitional between the Avaro-Andi-Dido languages and the Dargino-Lak languages). All these peoples share a common culture, history, religion (Sunni Moslem), literary language (Khunzakh Avar, formerly Arabic), and are merging into one Avar people. SEE Avar.

AVARO-ANDI-TSEZ PEOPLES   Alt. des. Avaro-Andi-Dido Peoples. SEE Avaro-Andi-Dido Peoples, Avar.

AVARO-ANDO-DIDO PEOPLES   Alt. des. Avaro-Andi-Dido Peoples. SEE Avaro-Andi-Dido Peoples, Avar.

AVARO-ANDO-TSEZ PEOPLES   Alt. des. Avaro-Andi-Dido Peoples. SEE Avaro-Andi-Dido Peoples, Avar.

AWAR   Alt. des. Avar. SEE Avar.

AWARO-ANDI-DIDO PEOPLES   Alt. spel. Avaro-Andi-Dido
                               Peoples. SEE Avaro-Andi-Dido
                               Peoples, Avar.

AWARO-ANDI-TSEZ PEOPLES   Alt. spel. and des. Avaro-
                               Andi-Dido Peoples. SEE Avaro-
                               Andi-Dido Peoples, Avar.

AWARO-ANDO-DIDO PEOPLES   Alt. spel. and des. Avaro-
                               Andi-Dido Peoples. SEE Avaro-
                               Andi-Dido Peoples, Avar.

AWARO-ANDO-TSEZ PEOPLES   Alt. spel. and des. Avaro-
                               Andi-Dido Peoples. SEE Avaro-
                               Andi-Dido Peoples, Avar.

ÄYRÄMÖINEN   Alt. des. and sing. of Äyrämöiset. SEE
Äyrämöiset, Finns of Leningrad Oblast.

ÄYRÄMÖISET   Self des.   Äyrämöiset;   Rus.   des.
                Evrimeiset. The Äyrämöiset come from
Äyräpää in western Karelia (Rus. Evriapiya). They
migrated to the area of what is now Leningrad Oblast in
the 17th cent. The Äyrämöiset and the Savakot comprise
the Finns of Leningrad Oblast. They speak Finnish, are
Lutheran in religion, and live, primarily, on the
Karelian Isthmus and along the southern shores of the
Finnish Gulf from the Neva to the Kovsha Rivers. SEE
Finns of Leningrad Oblast.

AYRUM   Alt. spel. Airum. SEE Airum, Azerbaidzhan.

AYSOR   Alt. spel. Aisor; alt. des Assyrian. SEE
Aisor, Assyrian.

AZERBAIDJAN (IAN)   Alt. spel. Azerbaidzhan. SEE
                       Azerbaidzhan.

AZERBAIDZHAN   Self des. Azerbaidzhan; for.   self
                  des. (pre-1930s) Türk; oth.   des.
Azeri, Azeri Turk, Tyurk; oth. for. des. Azeri Tatar,
Tatar of Transcaucasia, Caucasian Tatar. ETHN: Although
the Azerbaidzhans speak a Turkic language they are of
mixed Turkic, Iranian, and Caucasian ethnic background.
The   Azerbaidzhans   are still in the process   of
assimilating the Moslem Tati, Talysh, Kurds, Shahdag
peoples, Udi, and southern Dagestani (Lezgins, Avars,
and Tsakhurs) residing in the Azerbaidzhan SSR, and the
Ingiloi (Shiite Moslem Georgians) in adjacent areas of
the Georgian SSR.   Among the Azerbaidzhans there are
three   numerically small semi-nomadic (or formerly
semi-nomadic) groups that maintain distinct identities:
Airum, Padar, and Shahseven. LANG: The Azeri language

belongs to the southwest (Oguz) group of the Turkic division of the Uralo-Altaic language family. The Azeri language is similar to Turkish, and up until the 1930s they were considered to be the same language. The Azeri language has four closely related dialect groups, each with a number of sub-dialects: eastern (including Kuba, Baku, and Shemakha dialects), western (including Kazak, Gandzha, Karabag, and Airum dialects), northern (including Nukha and Zakatalo-Kazak dialects), and southern (including Nakhichevan and Erevan, and the dialects spoken in Iran). The Baku dialect (eastern) forms the basis of the modern Azeri literary language. Until 1929 Azeri was written in the Arabic script (being virtually the same written language as Ottoman Turkish), at which time it was changed to the Latin. In 1939 it was changed to the Cyrillic. In addition to being the literary language of all of the Moslem peoples living in the Azerbaidzhan SSR, between 1923 and 29 it was the official language of the Dagestan ASSR. Until that time the Azerbaidzhans exerted a strong cultural and linguistic influence on all of the peoples living in southern Dagestan. POP: 5,477,330 (1979); 4,379,937 (1970); 2,939,728 (1959); 1,706,605 (1926). In the 1926 census the Azerbaidzhans appear as Tyurki. The Azerbaidzhans are predominantly Shiite Moslem in religion, with a significant Sunni Moslem minority. They live, primarily, in the Azerbaidzhan SSR, the adjacent areas of the Georgian and Armenian SSRs, and the Dagestan ASSR. In the 1950s the Meskhetians were classified as Azerbaidzhans (formerly Turks), and appear as Azerbaidzhans in various regions of Soviet Central Asia (the area to which they had been deported from southwestern Georgia in 1944). SEE MAP 4.

AZERBAIJAN (AZERBAYDJAN,   Alt. spel. Azerbaidzhan.
AZERBAYDZHAN, AZERBAYJAN)   SEE Azerbaidzhan.
             (IAN)

AZERI   Alt. des. Azerbaidzhan. SEE Azerbaidzhan.

AZERI TATAR   For. alt. des. Azerbaidzhan. SEE Azerbaidzhan.

AZERI TURK   Alt. des. Azerbaidzhan. SEE Azerbaidzhan.

B

BACK COUNTRY TATAR   Eng. alt. des. Chernevyy Tatar.
                          SEE Chernevyy Tatar, Altai.

BADJUI (BADJUY)   Alt. spel. Badzhui. SEE Badzhui,
                    Shugnan, Pamir Peoples, Tadzhik.

BADZHUI   Self des. Badzhuvedzh. A group of Shugnan
            who speak a distinct dialect of the Shugnan
language. They are sometimes considered a distinct
ethnographic group. Like the Shugnan, the Badzhui are
Ismaili Moslem in religion and are being assimilated by
the Tadzhiks. SEE Shugnan, Pamir Peoples, Tadzhik.

BADZHUY   Alt. spel. Badzhui. SEE Badzhui, Shugnan,
            Pamir Peoples, Tadzhik.

BAGAOLAL   Alt. des. Bagaulal. SEE Bagaulal, Avar.

BAGAULAL   The southern clan federation of the Avars.
             The Bagaulal should not be confused with
             the Bagulal. SEE Avar.

BAGOLAL   Alt. des. Bagulal. SEE Bagulal, Avar.

BAGULAL   Self des. Kwantl Hekwa or Bagolal; oth.
            des. Kwanadi; Rus. des. Bagulal(tsy) or
Kvanadin(tsy). ETHN: Until the early 1930s the Bagulal,
as well as the other Andi-Dido peoples, were considered
distinct peoples. Since that time they have been
classified as Avars. LANG: The Bagulal language belongs
to the Andi group of the Avaro-Andi-Dido division of
the northeast branch of the Caucasic language family.
Until the 1930s the Bagulal language was considered a
distinct language.   Since that time it has been
classified as a dialect of Avar. The Bagulal language
is divided into two dialects: Bagulal proper and Tlisi.
Neither of these dialects is written and Avar serves as
the literary language of the Bagulal. POP: 3,054
(1926). The Bagulal are Sunni Moslem in religion. They,
like the other Andi-Dido peoples, are being assimilated
by the Avars. They live, primarily, in southwestern
Dagestan along the Andi River. SEE Andi-Dido Peoples,
Avar.

BAIHA OSTIAK (OSTYAK)   Alt. spel. Baikha Ostyak. SEE
                         Baikha   Ostyak,   Turukhan
                         Selkup, Selkup.

BAIKAL BURIAT   Alt. spel. Baikal Buryat. SEE Baikal
                 Buryat, Buryat.

BAIKAL BURYAT   Des. of the Buryats living west of
                 Lake Baikal; oth. des. Cis-Baikal
Buryat. The principal distinguishing difference between
the western (Baikal) and eastern (Transbaikal) Buryats
was religion. Whereas the eastern Buryats were,
primarily, Buddhist in religion, the western Buryats
were, basically, traditional Buryat shamanist with
Buddhist influences. SEE Buryat.

BAIKAT   Alt. spel. Baikot. SEE Baikot, Koibal,
          Khakass.

BAIKHA OSTIAK   Alt. spel. Baikha Ostyak. SEE Baikha
                 Ostyak, Turukhan Selkup, Selkup.

BAIKHA OSTYAK   Alt. des. Turukhan Selkup; oth. des.
                 Baisha Ostyak. SEE Turukhan Selkup,
                 Selkup.

BAIKOT   A Kettic group that was Turkified in the
          18th-19th cents. and which became part of
          the Koibal division of the Khakass. SEE
          Koibal, Khakass.

BAIQAT (BAIQOT)   Alt. spel. Baikot. SEE Baikot,
                   Koibal, Khakass.

BAISHA OSTIAK (OSTYAK)   Alt. des. Baikha Ostyak. SEE
                          Baikha Ostyak, Turukhan
                          Selkup, Selkup.

BAJUI (BAJUY)   Alt. spel. Badzhui. SEE Badzhui,
                 Shugnan, Tadzhik.

BAKHSAN (CHI)(CHILI)(LI)   Alt. des. Baksan. SEE
        (CHY)(CHYLY)(LY)   Baksan, Balkar.

BAKSAN   Self des. Bakhsanchi. One of the five
          tribes (societies) that went into the
formation of the Balkars. They live, primarily, in the
valley of the Baksan River in the Kabardino-Balkar ASSR
in the North Caucasus. SEE Balkar.

BAKSAN (CHI)(CHILI)(LI)   Alt. des. Baksan. SEE
       (CHY)(CHYLY)(LY)   Baksan, Balkar.

BALKAR   Self des. Malkarli; in the pre-Soviet period
            no self des. for Balkars as a whole; Rus.
des. Balkar(tsy);   oth. pre-Soviet des. Taulu
("Mountaineer") which was also applied to other North
Caucasian Mountaineer peoples; Five Mountain Societies
of Kabarda (Rus. Pyatigorskie Obshchestva Kabardy);
Five Mountain Tatars (Rus. Pyatigorskie Tatary). ETHN:
In the pre-Soviet period the five Balkar tribes
(Malkar, Baksan, Byzyngy, Chegem, and Kholam did not
consider themselves to be one Balkar people. The
Balkars are ethnically, culturally, and linguistically
closely related to the Karachai, with whom they share a
common literary language (Karachai-Balkar). The Balkars
are of very mixed origin (Kypchak Turks, Khazar,
Bolgar, Alan, Caucasic, and Hunnic elements). LANG: The
Karachai- Balkar language belongs to the Kypchak
division of the Turkic branch of the Uralo-Altaic
language family. The Karachai-Balkar language was first
written in 1924 in the Latin script, and was changed in
1939 into the Cyrillic. The Karachai-Balkar literary
language is based on the Baksan-Chegem dialect of
Balkar. POP: 66,334 (1979); 59,501 (1970); 42,408
(1959); 33,307 (1926). The Balkars were deported to
Central Asia in 1944, where they remained until 1958-
59. During that period the Balkars suffered a severe
loss of population. The Balkars are Sunni Moslem in
religion. They formerly lived in the mountainous
southern region of the Kabardino-Balkar ASSR, but since
their return to the region in 1958-59 they have been
resettled in the foothills of that territory. SEE MAP
14.

BALQAR   Alt. spel. Balkar. SEE Balkar.

BALTIC GERMAN   Self des. Baltdeutsche; Rus. des.
                 Baltiskie Nemtsy. The Baltic Germans
came to the Baltic coastal region of Latvia and Estonia
originally in the 13th cent. as religious crusaders.
During the Reformation they became Lutherans and
introduced the Lutheran religion among the Latvians and
Estonians. Many Baltic Germans emigrated to East
Prussia after land reform programs were carried out in
independent Latvia and Estonia. During and after World
War II the remaining Baltic Germans either were killed,
evacuated east (to Kazakhstan or southern Siberia), or
retreated with the German armies to Germany. At present
there are few Germans living in this region. SEE
German.

BALTIC PEOPLES   Col. des. for the speakers of Baltic
  *   languages (Latvians and Lithuanians).
This group is sometimes referred to as Letto-
Lithuanian. It is sometimes used in a geographic-ethnic
sense in which case it also includes the Estonians who

speak a Finnic tongue. SEE Latvian, Lithuanian, Estonian.

BALTO-FINNIC PEOPLES   Oth.   des.   Western Finns. The
                        Balto-Finns are divided into two
groups: northern (including the Finns, Izhora,
Karelians, and Veps) and southern (including the
Estonians, Vod, and Liv).

BALTORUS (BALTORUSIN, BALTORUSSIAN   For.   des.   of
          BALTORUTHENIAN)   Belorussian.
                                         SEE Belorussian.

BALUCH (BALUCHI, BALUDJ, BALUDJI,   Alt. des. Beluchi.
    BALUDZH, BALUDZHI, BALUJ,   SEE Beluchi.
               BALUJI)

BAQSAN (CHI)(CHILI)(LI)   Alt. spel. and des. Baksan.
       (CHY)(CHYLY)(LY)   SEE Baksan, Balkar.

BARABA TATAR   Oth. des. Barabinsk Tatar; alt. Rus.
                des. Baraban(tsy). The Baraba Tatars
live, primarily, in the Baraba steppe in southwestern
Siberia. They form one of the West Siberian Tatar
territorial groups. The Baraba Tatars maintain kinship
divisions (Tara, Terena, Barama, Keleke, Longa, Lovei,
and Kargan). Although Baraba Tatar is a distinct
dialect of Tatar, the Baraba Tatars use the Kazan Tatar
literary language. They were formerly considered (up
until the 1930s) a distinct ethnic group, after which
time they were classified as Tatars. POP: 7,528 (1926).
The Baraba Tatars are Sunni Moslem in religion. SEE
Tatar.

BARABIN(SK) TATAR   Alt. des. Baraba Tatar. SEE Baraba
                     Tatar, Tatar.

BARGU BURIAT (BURYAT)   Alt. des. Bargut. SEE Bargut,
                         Buryat.

BARGUT   Oth. des. Bargu Buryat or Bargut Buryat. A
          geographical division of the Buryats. SEE
          Buryat.

BARGUT BURIAT (BURYAT)   Alt. des. Bargut. SEE Bargut,
                          Buryat.

BARTANG   Self des. Bartangidzh. ETHN: The Bartang are
           a distinct people in the Shugnan-Rushan
group of the Pamir peoples. LANG: Bartang belongs to
the Shugnan-Rushan division of the East Iranian
language division of the Iranian branch of the Indo-
European language family. Virtually all Bartang are
bilingual and are being assimilated by the Tadzhiks.
The Bartang are Ismaili Moslem in religion. They live,
primarily, in villages along the Bartang River in the

Gorno-Badakhshan AO in the Tadzhik SSR. SEE Pamir
Peoples, Tadzhik.

BASHKIR   Self des. Bashkort; oth.   des.   Bashkord,
            Bashkurd, Bashkurt. ETHN: The origin of the
Bashkirs is still disputed. It is known that the
Kypchak Turks, especially among the western Bashkirs,
were a major element in the formation of the Bashkirs,
in particular linguistically. Some ethnographers feel
that   Turkic   tribes   from   the Altai, southwestern
Siberia, and Central Asia form a major part of the
Bashkirs, while others feel that there is a strong
Ugrian (especially Hunnic or Magyar) sub-stratum. There
may also be Iranian and Mongolian strata as well. It
is clear that there were also Oguz, Pecheneg, and
Volga Bulgar elements as well. Most influential in
modern times have been the Tatars, and until very
recently the Bashkirs were being linguistically and
culturally assimilated by them. LANG: The Bashkir
language belongs to the Kypchak division of the Turkic
branch of the Uralo-Altaic language family. It is very
close and mutually intelligible with Tatar. Bashkir is
comprised of two closely related dialects: southern
(Yurmatyn) and eastern (Kuvakan). Bashkir was first
written in 1923, using the Arabic script. It was
changed to Latin in 1928-29, and to the Cyrillic in
1940. POP: 1,371,452 (1979); 1,239,681 (1970); 989,040
(1959);   713,693 (1926).   The Bashkir   suffered
particularlly high loses in population during the Civil
War and collectivization periods. Until the 1930s there
was also a loss of population through assimilation by
the Tatars. As late as 1979 almost a third of the
Bashkirs declared Tatar their native language. The
Bashkirs are Sunni Moslem in religion. Among the
Bashkirs there is a small minority of Eastern Orthodox
Christians, the Nagaibak. Their population in 1926 was
11,219. Since the 1930s they have been classified as
Bashkirs. The Bashkirs live, primarily, in the Bashkir
ASSR and also in the Tatar ASSR, Orenburg, Kurgan, and
Chelyabinsk Oblasts. SEE MAP 4.

BATS   Alt. des. Batsbi. SEE Batsbi.

BATSBI   Self des. Batsaw; oth. des. Tsova
           Tush(in)(intsy). ETHN: The Batsbi are the
descendants of Veinakh tribes that resettled from
mountainous Ingushetia into the Tushetia region of
Georgia.   The Batsbi have been under strong
assimilation pressure by the Georgians. LANG: The
Batsbi language belongs to the Veinakh branch of the
northeast division of the Caucasic language family.
Although ethnically and linguistically related to the
Ingush and the Chechens, Batsbi and those languages are
not mutually intellibigle. The Batsbi language is not
written and Georgian serves as the literary language of

the Batsbi. POP: In 1926 only 7 individuals declared Batsbi as their nationality; however, 2,459 declared Batsbi their native language. For the most part, these were Batsbi who were listed as Georgians, but who spoke Batsbi as their native language. SEE Georgian.

BAYHA OSTIAK (OSTYAK)   Alt. spel. Baikha Ostyak. SEE Baikha Ostyak, Turukhan Selkup, Selkup.

BAYKAL BURIAT (BURYAT)   Alt. spel. Baikal Buryat. SEE Baikal Buryat, Buryat.

BAYKAT   Alt. des. and spel. Baikot. SEE Baikot, Koibal, Khakass.

BAYKHA OSTIAK (OSTYAK)   Alt. spel. Baikha Ostyak. SEE Baikha Ostyak, Turukhan Selkup, Selkup.

BAYKOT   Alt. spel. Baikot. SEE Baikot, Koibal, Khakass.

BAYQAT (BAYQOT)   Alt. des. and spel. Baikot. SEE Baikot, Koibal, Khakass.

BAYSHA OSTIAK (OSTYAK)   Alt. des. Baikha Ostyak. SEE Baikha Ostyak, Turukhan Selkup, Selkup.

BEJETA (BEJETIN)   Alt. des. and spel. Bezheta. SEE Bezheta, Andi-Dido Peoples, Avar.

BELIY KALMUK (KALMYK)   Alt. des. Teleut. SEE Teleut, Altai.

BELIY NOGAI (NOGAY, NOGHAI, NOGHAY)   Alt. des. Ak Nogai. SEE Ak Nogai, Nogai.

BELIY QALMUQ (QALMYQ)   Alt. des. Teleut. SEE Teleut, Altai.

BELORUS (BELORUSIN)   Alt. des. Belorussian. SEE Belorussian.

BELORUSSIAN   Self des.   Belarus(y);   oth.   des. Baltorusin, Baltorussian, Baltoruthenian, Belorus, Belorusin, Beloruthenian, White Russian, White Ruthenian; for. alt. des. Krivichi. ETHN: Although the Belorussian language is basically unified, the Belorussians are divided culturally into two heavily outside-influenced cultural groups. The eastern Belorussians are Eastern Orthodox in religion, have been under strong Russian influence, and in the past used the Russian literary language. The western

Belorussians are predominantly Uniate or Catholic in
religion (although there is a sizable Eastern Orthodox
population in the region), were under a strong Polish
influence, and used the Polish literary language. One
other small ethnographic group stands out. The
Poleshchuk (the inhabitants of the swampy Polesie
region of southwestern Belorussia and northwestern
Ukraine) speak a distinct dialect, and maintain a
number of cultural distinctions. Until the post-World
War II period the eastern Belorussians were being
assimilated by the Russians, the western Belorussians
by the Poles, and the southern Belorussians (those in
the Ukraine) by the Ukrainians. LANG: Belorussian
belongs to the East Slavic division of the Slavic
branch of the Indo-European language family.
Belorussian is comprised of three closely related
dialects: southwestern, northeastern, and central. The
differences are slight and the central dialect is
transitional between the other two. The Belorussian
literary language is based on the central (Minsk)
dialect. The modern Belorussian literary language was
created in the late 19th century, but was not used
widely until the Soviet period when it became the
official language of the Belorussian SSR. POP:
9,462,715 (1979); 9,051,755 (1970); 7,913,488 (1959);
4,738,923 (1926). The 1926 figures do not reflect the
Belorussian population living in the western part of
Belorussia at that time, as it was part of the
independent Polish state. The Belorussians are
primarily Eastern Orthodox in religion, with
substantial Uniate and Catholic minorities. The
Belorussians live primarily in the Belorussian SSR and
adjacent areas in the Lithuanian and Ukrainian SSRs,
and the RSFSR. Belorussians are also found in
relatively small numbers scattered throughout the USSR.
SEE MAP 2.

BELORUTHENIAN   Alt. for. des. of Belorussian. SEE
                  Belorussian.

BELTIR   One of the five territorial and kinship
           divisions of the Khakass. The Beltirs are of
Tuvinian origin, and still consider themselves related
to the Tuvinians. The Beltirs are shamanist-animist in
religion and live, primarily, along the left bank of
the middle course of the Abakan River and on both banks
of its upper course. SEE Khakass.

BELUCH   Alt. des. Beluchi. SEE Beluchi.

BELUCHI   Self des. Baluch; oth. des. Baluch(i),
            Baludzh(i), Beludzh(i). The Beluchi of the
USSR are the descendants of Beluchi immigrants who came
to Central Asia (primarily, Turkmenistan) in the end of
the 19th-early 20th cents. from Afghanistan and Iran.

The majority came between 1923 and 1928. The Beluchi in
Turkmenistan, as well as in Pakistan, have also
assimilated the Dravidian speaking Brahui. In
Turkmenistan the Brahui call themselves Beluchi of the
Brahui clan, although some still maintain the Brahui
language. The Beluchi, in turn, are under strong
assimilation pressure by the Turkmen in Turkmenistan
and by the Tadzhiks in Tadzhikistan. Despite their
small numbers and these assimilation pressures, many
Beluchi are still semi-nomadic in Turkmenistan. LANG:
The Beluchi language belongs to the northwest division
of the Iranian branch of the Indo-European language
family. Beluchi is not a written language. Turkmen (in
Turkmenistan) and Tadzhik (in Tadzhikistan) serve as
the literary languages of the Beluchi of the USSR. The
Beluchi of the USSR speak the western dialect of
Beluchi (that of Khorasan). POP: 18,997 (1979); 12,582
(1970); 7,842 (1959); 9,974 (1926). The Beluchi are
Moslem (mixed; Shiite and Sunni) in religion. They
live, primarily, in Mariy Oblast in the Turkmen SSR; a
small number also live in Tadzhikistan where they have
all but lost the Beluchi language and have been
assimilated by the Tadzhiks.

BELUDJ   (BELUDJI, BELUDZH,   Alt. spel. Beluchi. SEE
    BELUDZHI, BELUJ, BELUJI)   Beluchi.

BELY(Y) KALMUK (KALMYK)   Alt. des. Teleut. SEE
                             Teleut, Altai.

BELY(Y) (NOGAI, NOGAY)   Rus. alt. des. Ak Nogai. SEE
    NOGHAI, NOGHAY)   Ak Nogai, Nogai.

BELY(Y) QALMUK (QALMYK)   Rus. alt. des. Teleut. SEE
                             Teleut, Altai.

BERBER   Alt. des. Khazara. SEE Khazara.

BEREZOV (TSY)   A regional (town) division of the
                   Khant(y). SEE Khant.

BESARAB (IAN)   Alt. spel. Bessarabian; alt. des.
                   Moldavian. SEE Bessarabian, Moldavian.

BESARABIAN GERMAN   Alt. spel. Bessarabian German. SEE
                       Bessarabian German, German.

BESERABIAN   Alt. spel. Bessarabian. SEE Bessarabian,
                Moldavian.

BESERABIAN GERMAN   Alt. spel. Bessarabian German. SEE
                       Bessarabian German, German.

BESERMEN (BESERMIAN)   Alt. des. and spel. Besermyan.
                          SEE Besermyan, Udmurt.

BESERMYAN   Self des. Besermen. ETHN: The Besermyan
             are a group of Middle Volga Turks that
were Finnicized by the Udmurts. Their culture is quite
distinct from the majority of Udmurts in that they have
many Turkic (Tatar and Chuvash) elements. They speak a
dialect of Udmurt that has many Tatar words. They have
almost completely merged with the Udmurts. POP: 10,035
(1926). In the 1926 census the Besermyan were listed as
a distinct people; since the 1930s they have been
classified as Udmurts. Although officially Eastern
Orthodox in religion, the Besermyan maintained many
pre-Christian, animist, and Islamic elements. They live,
primarily, in Glazovskiy and Balezinskiy Rayons in the
Udmurt ASSR. SEE Udmurt.

BESHITL   Alt. des. Bezheta. SEE Bezheta, Andi-Dido
             Peoples, Avar.

BESKESEK ABAZA   For. alt. des. Abaza. The Abaza
                    appeared as Beskesek Abaza in the
                    1926 census. SEE Abaza.

BESKESEK ABAZIN (TSY)   Alt. des. Beskesek Abaza; for.
                         alt. des. Abaza. SEE Beskesek
                         Abaza, Abaza.

BESLENEI   Self des. Beslenei. One of the ten major
             tribal divisions of the Adygei. Each of
these was formerly considered a distinct people. They
are now classified as Adygei. The majority of Beslenei,
along with the other Abazgo-Circassian peoples
emigrated to Turkey in the mid-1860s. They lived in a
large area between the upper Urup and Khozdya, and
middle Laba Rivers in the western North Caucasus. SEE
Adygei, Circassian.

BESLENEY   Alt. spel. Beslenei. SEE Beslenei, Adygei,
             Circassian.

BESSARAB   Alt. des. Bessarabian, Moldavian. SEE
             Bessarabian, Moldavian.

BESSARABIAN   For. des. Moldavian; Romanian des. of
                Moldavian. The Romanians refer to the
Moldavian population of Romanian Moldavia as Romanians
and to the Moldavians of the USSR as Bessarabians
(named for the former territorial designation of Soviet
Moldavia which was Bessarabia). SEE Moldavian.

BESSARABIAN GERMAN   The Germans of Bessarabia
                       migrated to Moldavia during
the reign of Catherine the Great. During and after
World War II they were either killed, evacuated
eastward (or deported) to northern Kazakhstan or
southwestern Siberia, or retreated with the German

armies. There are few Germans in Moldavia at the present time. SEE Germans.

BESSARABIN (TSY)   Alt. Rus. des. Bessarabian. SEE Bessarabian, Moldavian.

BESSERABIAN   Alt. spel. Bessarabian. SEE Bessabian, Moldavian.

BESSARABIAN GERMAN   Alt. spel. Bessarabian German. SEE Bessarabian German, German.

BEZENGI (CHI)(CHILI)(LI)   Alt. des. Bizingi. SEE Bizingi, Balkar.

BEZHETA   Self des. Kapuchias Suko or Bezhtlas Suko; oth. des. Bezhetin(tsy), Bezhta, Kapucha, Kapuchin(tsy). ETHN: Until the early 1930s the Bezheta, as well as the other Andi-Dido peoples, were considered distinct ethnic groups. Since that time they have been classified as Avars. LANG: The Bezheta language belongs to the Dido group of the Avaro-Andi-Dido division of the northeast branch of the Caucasic language family. Until the 1930s the Bezheta language was considered a distinct language. Since that time it has been classified as a dialect of Avar. The Bezheta language is mutually intelligible with Ginug and Khunzal. The Bezheta language is not written and Avar serves as the literary language of the Bezheta. POP: 1,448 (1926). The Bezheta are Sunni Moslem in religion. They live in the highest and most inaccessible part of southwestern Dagestan near the Georgian border in the upper basin of the Avar River. SEE Andi-Dido Peoples, Avar.

BEZHETIN (BEZHTA,   Alt. des. Bezheta. SEE Bezheta
BEZHTIN)   Andi-Dido Peoples, Avar.

BIELIY KALMUK (KALMYK)   Rus. alt. des. Teleut. SEE Teleut, Altai.

BIELIY NOGAI (NOGAY,   Alt. Rus. des. Ak Nogai. SEE
NOGHAI, NOGHAY)   Ak Nogai, Nogai.

BIELIY QALMUQ (QALMYQ)   Rus. alt. des. Teleut. SEE Teleut, Altai.

BIELORUS (BIELORUSIN, BIELORUSSIAN,   Alt. des. and
BIELORUTHENIAN)   spel. Belorussian. SEE Belorussian.

BIELY(Y) KALMUK (KALMYK)   Rus. alt. des. Teleut. SEE Teleut, Altai.

BIELY(Y) NOGAI (NOGAY,   Rus. alt. des. Ak Nogai. SEE
          NOGHAI, NOGHAY)   Ak Nogai, Nogai.

BIELY(Y) QALMUQ (QALMYK)   Rus. alt. des. Teleut. SEE
                              Teleut, Altai.

BIRAR (BIRARI,   For. tribal division of the Evenk. In
       BIRARY)   the past they were sometimes
                    considered a distinct ethnic group.
                    SEE Evenk.

BII KALMUK (KALMYK,   Alt. spel. Biy Kalmyk. SEE Biy
    QALMUQ, QALMYQ)   Kalmyk, Altai.

BIY KALMUK   Alt. spel. Biy Kalmyk. SEE Biy Kalmyk,
                 Altai.

BIY KALMYK   For. col. des. (17th-19th cents.) for the
                 southern Altai tribal division (including
the Altai Kizhi, Telengit, Teleut, and Telesi) of the
present day Altai; oth. des. Mountain Kalmyk. The term
Kalmyk used here was a misnomer as the Biy Kalmyks were
Turkic and not Mongolic. SEE Altai.

BIY QALMUQ (QALMYQ)   Alt. spel. Biy Kalmyk. SEE Biy
                          Kalmyk, Altai.

BIZINGI   Self des. Bezengili, Byzyngyly; oth. des.
             Bezengi. One of the five tribes (societies)
that went into the formation of the Balkars. They live,
primarily, in the valley of the Cherek River and its
tributary the Cherek-Bezenchi. SEE Balkar.

BIZINGI (CHI)(CHILI)(LI)   Alt. des. Bizingi. SEE
                               Bizingi, Balkar.

BJEDUG (BJEDUGH, BJEDUKH)   Alt. spel. Bzhedug. SEE
                               Bzhedug, Adygei,
                               Circassian.

BLACK KIRGIZ (KIRGIZ,   Alt. des. Kara Kirgiz. SEE
      KYRGHYZ, KYRGYZ)   Kara Kirgiz, Kirgiz.

BLACK (NOGAI, NOGAY,   Alt. des. Kara Nogai. SEE Kara
       NOGHAI, NOGHAY)   Nogai, Nogai.

BLACK (QIRGHIZ, QIRGIZ,   Alt. des. Kara Kirgiz. SEE
       QYRGHYZ, QYRGYZ)   Kara Kirgiz, Kirgiz.

BOHARAN   Alt. des. Bukharan. SEE Bukharan, Sart,
             Uzbek.

BOHARAN JEW   Alt. des. Central Asian Jew. SEE Central
                 Asian Jew, Jew.

BOHARLIK (BOHARLUK, BOHARLYK)   Alt. des. Bukharan. SEE
                                 Bukharan, Sart, Uzbek.

BOIKI   Self des. Boiki. The Boiki are one of the
          three ethnographic groups of the western
Ukraine collectively called Carpatho-Rusin (Boiki,
Hutsul, Lemky). They share numerous cultural
similarities with Poles and Slovaks. Formerly they were
primarily Uniate in religion. Since the incorporation
of their territory into the USSR (Lvov and Ivano-
Frankovsk Oblasts) after World War II, the Uniate
Church was abolished and incorporated into the Eastern
Orthodox one. All Boiki of the USSR are now officially
Eastern Orthodox in religion. They live, primarily, in
the mountainous parts of Lvov and Ivano-Frankovksk
Oblasts between the San and Lomnitsa Rivers, and also
in Zakarpatskaya Oblast between the Uzh and Torets
Rivers. SEE Carpatho-Rusin, Ukrainian.

BOIKO (BOIKY)   Alt. des. and spel. Boiki. SEE Boiki,
                 Ukrainian.

BOKHARAN   Alt. des. Bukharan. SEE Bukharan, Sart,
            Uzbek.

BOKHARAN JEW   Alt. des. Central Asian Jew. SEE
                Central Asian Jew, Jew.

BOKHARLIK (BOKHARLUK,   Alt. des. Bukharan. SEE
           BOKHARLYK)   Bukharan, Sart, Uzbek.

BOLGAR   1-Alt. des. Bulgarian. SEE Bulgarian.
          2-For. alt. des. Chuvash. The Volga Bolgars
went into the formation of the Chuvash, Tatars,
Bashkirs, and other peoples of the Middle Volga. Only
the Chuvash and Tatars of the Middle Volga maintain the
ethnonym Bolgar to any extent today. SEE Chuvash,
Tatar.

BOLGARIAN   Alt. spel. Bulgarian. SEE Bulgarian.

BOLGHAR   Alt. spel. Bolgar. SEE Bolgar, Chuvash,
           Tatar.

BORDERLAND KALMUK (KALMYK,   Alt. des. Teleut. SEE
          QALMUQ, QALMYQ)   Teleut, Altai.

BOSHA   A group of Gypsies living in Armenia that have
         given up the Romany (Gypsy) language and are
being assimilated by the Armenians. Pop. 31 (1926).
They lived in the border area between the Azerbaidzhan
and Armenian SSRs. SEE Gypsy.

BOSHIN (TSY)   Alt. des. Bosha. SEE Bosha, Gypsy.

BOTLIG   Self des. Buikhatli; oth. des. Botligh,
            Botlikh. ETHN: Until the early 1930s the
Botlig, as well as the other Andi-Dido peoples, were
considered distinct ethnic groups. Since that time
they have been classified as Avars. LANG: The Botlig
language belongs to the Andi group of the Avaro-Andi-
Dido division of the northeast branch of the Caucasian
language family. Until the 1930s the Botlig language
was considered a distinct language. Since that time it
has been classified as a dialect of the Avar language.
The Botlig language is not written and Avar serves as
the literary language of the Botlig. POP: 3,354
(1926). The Botlig are Sunni Moslem in religion. They,
like the other Andi-Dido peoples, are being assimilated
by the Avars. They live in highland southwestern
Dagestan along the Andi River. SEE Andi-Dido Peoples,
Avar.

BOTLIGH (BOTLIKH)   Alt. des. Botlig. SEE Botlig,
            Andi-Dido Peoples, Avar.

BOYKI (BOYKO, BOYKY)   Alt. des. Boiki, SEE Boiki,
            Ukrainian.

BRAGUI (BRAGUY)   Alt. des. Brahui. SEE Brahui.

BRAHUI   Self des. Brahui; Rus. des. Bragui. The
            Brahui migrated to the Soviet Union in the
early 20th cent. along with the majority of the
Beluchi. They were first registered in 1927. The Brahui
are a Dravidian people. The Brahui of the USSR have
been all but completely assimilated by the Beluchi.
They call themselves Beluchi of the Brahui clan,
although some still maintain the Brahui language. They
live in Mariy Oblast in the Turkmen SSR. SEE Beluchi.

BRAHUY   Alt. spel. Brahui. SEE Brahui, Beluchi.

BRAGUI (BRAGUY)   Rus. des. Brahui. SEE Brahui,
            Beluchi.

BUDUG   No self des. as an ethnic group; Rus. des.
            Budukh. ETHN: The Budug are one of the
numerically small Shahdag peoples who have been all
but assimilated by the Azerbaidzhans. LANG: The Budug
language belongs to the Samurian group of the
northeast branch of the Caucasic language family.
Budug is not written and Azeri serves as the literary
language of the Budug. POP: Only 1 person declared
himself a Budug in the 1926 census, however, 1,995
listed Budug as their native language. These were,
probably, Budugs who declared Azerbaidzhan their
ethnic identification but Budug their native language.
In 1886 their population was estimated at 3,400. The
Budug are Shiite Moslem in religion. They live in the

region of Mt. Shahdag in Konakhkend Rayon in the
Azerbaidzhan SSR. SEE Shahdag Peoples, Azerbaidzhan.

BUDUGH (BUDUKH)   Rus. des.   Budug.   SEE   Budug,
            Shahdag Peoples, Azerbaidzhan.

BUGIAN   Alt. des. Buzhan. SEE Buzhan, Belorussian,
      Ukrainian.

BUHTARMAN   Alt. spel. Bukhtarman. SEE Bukhtarman,
      Russian.

BUJAN   Alt. spel. Buzhan. SEE Buzhan, Belorussian,
      Ukrainian.

BUKHARAN   Self des. Bukharlyk; Rus. des. Bukhar(tsy).
      ETHN: The Bukharans are the descendants of
Uzbek merchants from Bukhara who set up trading
colonies in Siberia and other areas in the 17th
century. They maintained the identity of Bukharan,
although they were also known as Sarts and mistakenly
at times as Tatars. POP: 12,012 (1926) In addition to
these .there were 11,659 Bukharans who were mistakenly
listed as Tatars (total 1926 pop. 23,671). The
Bukharans are Sunni Moslem in religion. They live,
primarily, in Tobolsk, Tara, Tyumen, and Astrakhan.

BUKHARAN JEWS   Alt. des. Central Asian Jew. SEE
            Central Asian Jew, Jew.

BUKHARLIK (BUKHARLUK, BUKHARLYK)   Alt. des. Bukharan.
            SEE Bukharan.

BUKHTARMAN   Oth. des. Kamenshchik. The Bukhtarman are
            one of the early settler groups of
Siberia who are collectively known as Starozhily. They
are a group of Russian Old Believers who originated in
Nizhegorodskaya Gubernaya, where they lived along the
Kerzhenets River. They settled in the Gornyy Altai
region of southern Siberia. Being stonemasons they
became known as Kamenshchiki (stonemasons). Living
along the Bukhtarma River they became known as
Bukhtarman. SEE Starozhily, Russian.

BULAGAT   Self des. Bulagat. One of the largest of the
            five major tribal divisions of the Buryats.
The Bulagat live along the Angara River and its
tributaries. SEE Buryat.

BULGAR   1- Alt. des. Bolgar. SEE Bolgar, Chuvash,
      Tatar.
      2- Alt. des. Bulgarian. SEE Bulgarian.

BULGARIAN   Self des. Bulgar(i); Rus. des. Bolgar(y).
             The   Bulgarians of   the   USSR are   the
descendants of migrants from the Balkans during Ottoman
rule (late 18th-19th cents.). POP: 361,926 (1979);
351,168 (1970); 324,251 (1959); 111,296 (1926). The
Bulgarians are Eastern Orthodox in religion. They live,
primarily,   in southern Moldavia and the southwestern
Ukraine. SEE MAP 14.

BULGHAR   Alt. spel. Bulgar; alt. des. Bolgar. SEE
             Bolgar, Bulgar, Bulgarian, Chuvash, Tatar.

BURGUT   For. des. of the Buryats. SEE Buryat.

BURIAT (MONGOL)   Alt. spel. and des. Buryat. SEE
             Buryat.

BURYAT   Self des. Buryat; oth. des . Buryat Mongol,
             for. des. Burgut. ETHN: The Buryats were
formerly divided into five major tribes or divisions:
Bulagat, Khora, Ekhirit, Khongodor and Tabunut. In
addition, a number of Mongols from Mongolia were
assimilated by the Buryats and are now found among them
(Sartol, Atagan, and Daur). There is also a group of
Buryats who have been assimilated by the Russians.   The
Russified Buryats (who now form an ethnographic group
of Russians) are called Karym(y). Besides having tribal
divisions, the Buryats also have major territorial
divisions which in the past were significant. Among
the more important of these territorial divisions are
the Bargu(t), Baikal, Alar, Soyot, and Solon. The
Buryats are also divided into two major geographical-
cultural groups: western (Baikal Buryat) and eastern
(Trans-Baikal Buryat). LANG: Buryat is one of the
Mongolic languages and is closely related to Mongol
(Khalkha) itself. The Buryat dialects are concomitant
with the tribal divisions. Formerly the Buryats used
both the Tibetan and Mongol literary languages. In the
1920s a Buryat literary language was created based on
the Khora dialect using the Latin script. This was
changed in 1939 to the Cyrillic. POP: 352,646 (1979);
314,671 (1970); 252,959 (1959); 237,501 (1926). The
religious adherance of the Buryats is a complex one.
The eastern Buryats were primarily Buddhists. The
religion of the western Buryats combined Buddhist and
shamanist beliefs. Even a "nativist" Buryat religion
(called Burkhanism) developed. Eastern Orthodoxy was
also adopted by some Buryats as their religion. They
live, primarily, in the Buryat Mongol ASSR, the Aga
Buryat AO, the Ust Orda Buryat AO, and adjacent areas
in southern Siberia. SEE MAP 1.

BURYAT MONGOL   Alt. des. Buryat. SEE Buryat.

BUZAVA   A group of Kalmyks who did not go along with
          the rest of the Kalmyks on the Great
Migration back to Mongolia in 1771, but rather remained
on the Don as part of the Don Cossacks. SEE Kalmyk,
Cossack (Don Cossack).

BUZAVIN (BUZAWA)   Alt. des. Buzava. SEE Buzava,
                     Kalmyk.

BUZHAN   A group of Eastern Orthodox Ukrainians who
          lived along the Bug river in the Hrodno
(Grodno) region of Belorussia (pop. 1861: 5,463) and
the Volynia region of the Ukraine (pop. 1861: 74,845).
They have subsequently been totally assimilated by the
Ukrainians. SEE Ukrainian.

BYELIY KALMUK (KALMYK)   Rus. alt. des. Teleut. SEE
                          Teleut, Altai.

BYELIY NOGAI (NOGAY,   Rus. alt. des. Ak Nogai. SEE Ak
   NOGHAI, NOGHAY)   Nogai, Nogai.

BYELIY QALMUQ (QALMYQ)   Rus. alt. des. Teleut. SEE
                          Teleut, Altai.

BYELORUS (BYELORUSIN, BYELORUSSIAN, Alt. des. and spel.
     BYELORUSSIAN, BYELORUTHENIAN) Belorussian. SEE
                                   Belorussian.

BYELY(Y) KALMUK (KALMYK)   Rus. alt. des. Teleut. SEE
                           Teleut, Altai.

BYELY(Y) NOGAI (NOGAY,   Rus. alt. des. Ak Nogai. SEE
     NOGHAI, NOGHAY)   Ak Nogai, Nogai.

BYELY(Y) QALMUQ (QALMYQ)   Rus. alt. des. Teleut. SEE
                           Teleut, Altai.

BYZYNGY   (CHY)(CHYLY)(LY)   Alt. spel. and des.
                             Bizingi. SEE Bizingi,
                             Balkar.

BZHEDUG   Self des. Bzhedugh; Rus. des. Bzhedukh. One
          of the ten major tribal divisions of the
Adygei. Each of these was formerly considered a
distinct people. They are now classified as Adygei. The
majority of the Bzhedug, along with the other Abazgo-
Circassians, emigrated to Turkey in the mid 1860s. They
live in a small area on the left bank of the Kuban
River near Krasnodar (Ekaterinodar) in the western
North Caucasus. SEE Adygei, Circassian.

BZHEDUGH (BZHEDUKH)   Rus. des. Bzhedug. SEE Bzhedug,
                       Adygei, Circassian.

BZIB   Alt. spel. Bzyb. SEE Bzyb, Abkhaz.

BZIB GUDAUT   Alt. des. Gudaut; alt. spel. and des.
               Bzyb Gudaut. SEE Gudaut, Bzyb, Abkhaz.

BZYB   One of the three divisions of the Abkhaz. They
        live, primarily, in the valley of the Bzyb
river in northern Abkhazia in northwestern Georgia.
They form, with the Gudaut (who are often considered a
subgroup of Bzyb), the northern group of Abkhaz. They
speak a distinct (Bzyb) dialect of Abkhaz. SEE Abkhaz.

BZYB GUDAUT   Alt. des. Gudaut; col. des. of the
               northern Abkhaz. SEE Gudaut, Bzyb,
               Abkhaz.

C

CABARD (CABARDIN, CABARDINIAN)   Alt. des. and spel.
                                  Kabard. SEE Kabard,
                                  Circassian.

CABARTAI (CABARTAY)   Alt. spel. Kabartai; alt. des.
                       Kabard. SEE Kabard, Circassian.

CACHA (CACHIN)   Alt. spel. and des. Kacha. SEE Kacha,
                  Khakass.

CADJAR (CADZHAR)   Alt. spel. Kadzhar. SEE Kadzhar.

CAHELI   Alt. spel. Kakheli; alt. des. Kakhetian. SEE
          Kakheli, Kakhetian, Georgian.

CAHETIAN   Alt. spel. Kakhetian. SEE Kakhetian,
            Georgian.

CAHUR   Alt. spel. Tsakhur. SEE Tsakhur.

CAIBAL   Alt. des. and spel. Koibal. SEE Koibal,
          Khakass.

CAIDAK (CAITAK)   Alt. des. and spel. Kaitak. SEE
                   Kaitak, Dargin.

CAIVAN   Alt. spel. Kaivan; for. alt. des. Veps. SEE
          Kaivan, Veps.

CAJAR   Alt. spel. Kadzhar. SEE Kadzhar.

CAKHELI   Alt. spel. Kakheli; alt. des. Kakhetian. SEE Kakheli, Kakhetian, Georgian.

CAKHETIAN   Alt. spel. Kakhetian. SEE Kakhetian, Georgian.

CAKHUR   Alt. spel. Tsakhur. SEE Tsakhur.

CALCHA (CALCHIN)   Alt. spel. and des. Kalcha. SEE Kalcha, Kirgiz.

CALMAK (CALMUK, CALMYK)   Alt. spel. Kalmyk. SEE Kalmyk.

CAMASIN   Alt. spel. Kamasin; alt. des. Kamasa Samoyed. SEE Kamasa Samoyed, Khakass.

CAMASIN SAMODI (SAMOED, SAMOIED, SAMOYED)   Alt. des. Kamasa Samoyed. SEE Kamasa Samoyed, Khakass.

CAMASSIAN SAMODI (SAMOED, SAMOIED, SAMOYED)   Alt. des. Kamasa Samoyed. SEE Kamasa Samoyed, Khakass.

CAMCHADAL   Alt. spel. Kamchadal. SEE Kamchadal, Russian.

CAMENSHCHIK   Alt. spel. Kamenshchik; alt. des. Bukhtarman. SEE Kamenshchik, Bukhtarman, Russian.

CAMEN (TSY)   Alt. spel. Kamen(tsy). SEE Kamen, Koryak.

CAPSAI (CAPSAY)   Alt. spel. Kapsai. SEE Kapsai, Suvalkiečiai, Lithuanian.

CAPUCHA (KAPUCHIN)   Alt. spel. Kapucha; alt. des. Bezheta. SEE Bezheta, Andi-Dido Peoples, Avar.

CARA CYRGHYZ (CYRGYZ)   Alt. spel. Kara Kirgiz. SEE Kara Kirgiz, Kirgiz.

CARA NOGAI (NOGAY, NOGHAI, NOGHAY)   Alt. spel. Kara Nogai. SEE Kara Nogai, Nogai.

CARA TATAR   Alt. spel. Kara Tatar. SEE Kara Tatar, Tatar.

CARACAIDAK (CARACAITAK)   Alt. spel. Karakaitak. SEE Karakaitak, Kaitak, Dargin.

CARACALPAK   Alt. spel. Karakalpak. SEE Karakalpak.

CARACAYDAK (CARACAYTAK)   Alt. spel. Karakaitak. SEE
                           Karakaitak, Kaitak, Dargin.

CARACHAEV (CARACHAI, CARACHAIEV,   Alt. des. and spel.
        CARACHAILI, CARACHAY,   Karachai. SEE
        CARACHAYEV, CARACHAYLY)   Karachai.

CARADASH (CARADASHLI,   Alt. spel. Karadash. SEE
        CARADASHLY)   Karadash, Turkmen.

CARAGA   Alt. spel. Karaga. SEE Karaga, Koryak.

CARAGASH   Alt.   spel.   Karagash.   SEE   Karagash,
        Astrakhan Tatar, Tatar.

CARAGASS   Alt. spel. Karagass. SEE Karagass, Tofalar.

CARAGIN (TSY)   Alt. spel. Karaga. SEE Karaga, Koryak.

CARAIM (CARAIT, CARAITE)   Alt. spel. and des. Karaim.
                            SEE Karaim.

CARALPAK   Alt. spel. Karalpak; alt. des. Karakalpak.
        SEE Karakalpak.

CARANOGAI   (CARANOGAY,   Alt. spel. Kara Nogai. SEE
    CARANOGHAI, CARANOGHAY)   Kara Nogai, Nogai.

CARAPAPAH (CARAPAPAK,   Alt. spel. Karapapakh. SEE
        CARAPAPAKH)   Karapapakh, Meskhetian.

CARASA SAMODI (SAMOED,   Alt. spel. and des. Karasa
    SAMOIED, SAMOYED)   Samoyed. SEE Karasa Samoyed,
                           Ent.

CARASHI   Alt. spel. Karashi; alt. des. Karagash. SEE
        Karagash, Astrakhan Tatar, Tatar.

CARASIN SAMODI (SAMOED,   Alt. spel. and des. Karasa
    SAMOIED, SAMOYED)   Samoyed. SEE Karasa Samoyed,
                           Ent.

CARATA   Alt. spel. Karata. SEE Karata, Andi-Dido
        Peoples, Avar.

CARATAI (CARATAY)   Alt. spel. Karatai. SEE Karatai,
                     Mordvinian.

CARELIAN   Alt. spel. Karelian. SEE Karelian.

CARIM   Alt. spel. Karym. SEE Karym, Buryat, Russian.

CARIN (SKIY) TATAR   Alt. spel. Karinskiy Tatar; alt.
                       des. Kara Tatar. SEE Kara Tatar,
                       Tatar.

CARPATHO-RUS   Alt.   des.   Carpatho-Rusin.   SEE Carpatho-Rusin, Ukrainian.

CARPATHO-RUSIN   No standard self des. The term Carpatho-Rusin was not used by these people themselves until recently, rather, it was applied to them by others. Oth. des.: Karpatsko Rusyn, Carpatho-(Carpato, Carpatsko, Ugro, Uhro) -Rus, -Rusin, -Russian, -Ruthenian, -Ukrainian; Rusnak. A Russian and Ukrainian des. for those Ukrainians inhabiting the present Zakarpatskaya Oblast. Formerly they lived under Hungarian, and later Czechoslovak, rule. Their population was incorporated into formally Russian or Soviet ruled territory only after World War II. They form a distinct cultural group of Ukrainians. The Carpatho-Rusins are comprised of three Ukranian ethnographic groups: Hutsuls, Boiki, and Lemky. The term Carpatho-Rusin was never used by these people themselves; rather, it was applied to them by the Russians. They identified themselves by any of the three above names, or referred to themselves as either highlanders (Verkhovinitsy) or lowlanders (Dolyshany). They speak a distinct dialect of Ukrainian, with local subdialects, and they formerly wrote in the Cyrillic script (and also in the Latin script with Slovak, Polish or Hungarian orthography depending on local influence). The Carpatho-Rusins were, primarily, Uniate in religion (with an Eastern Orthodox minority). With the incorporation of the western Ukraine following World War II the Uniate Church was abolished and formally incorporated into the Eastern Orthodox Church. The Carpatho-Rusins of the USSR are now officially Eastern Orthodox in religion. They live, primarily, in the far western mountainous areas of the Ukraine (Zakarpatskaya, Ivano-Frankovsk, and Lvov Oblasts). SEE Ukrainian.

CARPATHO-RUSSIAN (RUSYN,   Alt. des. Carpatho-Rusin.
RUTHENIAN, UKRAINIAN)   SEE Carpatho-Rusin. Ukrainian.

CARPATO-RUS (RUSIN, RUSSIAN,   Alt. des. Carpatho-
RUSYN, RUTHENIAN, UKRAINIAN)   Rusin. SEE Carpatho-Rusin, Ukrainian.

CAPARTSKO-RUS (RUSIN, RUSSIAN,   Alt. des. Carpatho-
RUSYN, RUTHENIAN, UKRAINIAN)   Rusin. SEE Carpatho-Rusin, Ukrainian.

CARTLI (CARTLIAN, CARTLIN)   Alt. spel. and des. Kartli. SEE Kartli, Georgian.

CARTVELI (CARTVELIAN,   Alt. spel. Kartveli; alt. des.
         CARTVELIN)   Kartvelian. SEE Kartvelian,
                           Georgian.

CARYM   Alt. spel. Karym. SEE Karym, Buryat, Russian.

CASHGAR (LIK)(LUK)(LYK)   Alt. spel. and des. Kashgar.
                           SEE Kashgar, Uigur.

CASIMOV TATAR   Alt. spel. Kasimov Tatar. SEE Kasimov
                  Tatar, Tatar.

CASOG   Alt. spel. Kasog, Azerbaidzhan.

CAUCASIAN   Col. des. of all the indigenous peoples of
              the   North   Caucasus   region   and
              Transcaucasia.

CAUCASIAN JEW   A term generally used to denote the
                  Mountain Jews (oth. des. Tat or
Dagestani Jew). At times it is used to include also
the Georgian Jews. SEE Mountain Jews, Georgian Jews.

CAUCASIAN MOUNTAINEERS   Col. des. of all the
                           indigenous peoples of the
mountainous region of the North Caucasus (Karachai,
Balkar,   Ossetian,   Ingush,   Chechen,   Dagestani
Mountaineers, and sometimes the Circassians). In
general, the Transcaucasian mountaineer peoples
(Abkhaz, Svanetian, Mingrelian, Georgian, Azerbaidzhan,
and other peoples) are not included in this
designation. At times the Circassians, Abaza, Nogai,
and Kumyk are included in this designation, albeit they
are   inhabitants   of   the steppe area and not
mountaineers.

CAUCASIAN TATAR (TURK)   For. des. of Azerbaidzhan.
                           SEE Azerbaidzhan.

CAYBAL   Alt. spel. and des. Koibal. SEE Koibal,
           Khakass.

CAYDAK (CAYTAK)   Alt. spel. Kaitak. SEE Kaitak,
                    Dargin.

CAZAH   Alt. spel. Kazakh. SEE Kazakh.

CAZAK   1-Alt. spel. Kazakh. SEE Kazakh.
          2-Alt. des. Kasog. SEE Kasog, Azerbaidzhan.

CAZAN TATAR   Alt. spel. Kazan Tatar. SEE Kazan Tatar,
                Tatar.

CAZANLIK (CAZANLYK)   Alt. des. Kazan Tatar. SEE Kazan Tatar, Tatar.

CAZICUMUH (CAZICUMUK, CAZICUMUKH)   Alt. spel. Kazikumukh; alt. des. Lak. SEE Kazikumukh, Lak.

CENTRAL ASIAN   Col. des. of the peoples of Central Asia. In general, it includes the major indigenous peoples of the region (Uzbek, Tadzhik, Turkmen, Kirgiz). It can however, include also the neighboring Kazakhs, and the numerically smaller Karakalpaks. It rarely includes other Central Asian groups such as: Uigurs, Beluchi, Dungans, Koreans, etc.

CENTRAL ASIAN ARAB   Alt. des. Arab. SEE Arab.

CENTRAL ASIAN GYPSY   Self des. Mugat;oth.des. Luli, Dzhugi, and Mazang, Multani. ETHN: Unlike other Gypsies, the Central Asian Gypsies officially neither call themselves Rom nor speak Romany (Gypsy). They do, however, have clear Indian (Dravidian) racial characteristics. There is also much evidence to show that many Central Asian Gypsies in fact do speak Romany (the Indic Gypsy language). The Central Asian Gypsies came to Central Asia long before the Timurid period, and may have come as far back as the 5th cent. LANG: Although officially Tadzhik is the native language of the Central Asian Gypsies, many, if not most, speak a form of Romany as their native language. In addition to speaking Tadzhik, the Central Asian Gypsies are also fluent in Uzbek. Many also speak Russian or other languages of Central Asia. POP: They profess the Sunni Moslem religion, but have many pre-Islamic holdovers .(beliefs in spirits, etc.). They live in and around the main cities of Uzbekistan and Tadzhikistan. SEE Gypsy.

CENTRAL ASIAN JEW   Self des. Yahudi, Isroel, or Bane Isroel ("sons of Israel"); oth. self des. Yahudikhoi Makhalli ("local Jews"); oth. des. Bukharan (Bokharan) Jew. ETHN: The exact origin of the Central Asian Jews is still debated. They appear to be of mixed origin. They have lived in Central Asia since at least the 10th cent. Since that time various individuals and groups of Jews have settled in Central Asia from various parts of Iran, Afghanistan, and Arabia. A group of Central Asian Jews in Bukhara officially converted to Islam under pressure. They continued, however, to practice their Jewish religion secretly. Their religion is a blend of Judaic and Islamic beliefs. These crypto Jews are called Chala. LANG: Most Central Asian Jews consider Tadzhik their native language, and Tadzhik is officially considered the native language of the Central Asian Jews

(including in the census). They speak the Samarkand-
Bukharan dialect of Tadzhik with Hebrew intrusions.
Most, and particularly those of the major cities of
Uzbekistan, also speak Uzbek. Until 1928 the Central
Asian Jews wrote their language (Tadzhik) in the Hebrew
script. It was abolished in 1928, at which time they
began to use standard Tadzhik (at that time written in
the Latin script; changed in 1940 to the Cyrillic).
Until the 1930s the Central Asian Jews were considered
a distinct ethnic group; after that time they were
reclassified as Jews, and appear as such in all
statistical publications. POP: 18,698 (1926). Since the
early 1970s there has been a substantial emigration of
Central Asian Jews to Israel. The religion of the
Central Asian Jews, although basically Jewish, differs
significantly in practice from its European-American
form (having many Central Asian Islamic and other
influences). The Central Asian Jews live, primarily,
in the cities of Samarkand, Tashkent, Kokand, and
Bukhara. SEE Jew.

CENTRAL ASIAN TURK   1-The Central Asian Turks are
                        divided linguistically into
three main groups: Oguzic (southwest Turkic),
including the Turkmen; Kypchak (including the Kazakh,
Kirgiz, and Karakalpak); and Chagatai or Turki
(including the Uzbek and Uigur). All are Sunni Moslem
in religion.
                        2-A term sometimes used as an
alt. des. of the Turki of Fergana and Samarkand. SEE
Turki of Fergana and Samarkand, Uzbek.

CHAAS   Alt. spel. Khaas. SEE Khaas, Khakass.

CHACASS   Alt. spel. Khakass. SEE Khakass.

CHAGATAI   Self des. Chaghatai; Oth. des. Chagatai
             Tadzhik, or Tadzhik Chagatai. Little is
known of the origin of the this ethnographic group but
it is clear that the name is of Mongol origin.
Chagatai was a grandson of Chingis (Ghengis) Khan.
There is also an Uzbek clan Chagatai of known Mongol
origin. The Chagatai (Turkic) literary language was
also important throughout Central Asia from the 15th-
early 20th cents. The ethnonmym Chagatai, however, is
used to designate a group of Tadzhiks living in Surkhan
Darya Oblast in Uzbekistan and in southern
Tadzhikistan. They refer to themselves, and are
referred to by the neighboring peoples, as Chagatai.
Their population was estimated in 1924-25 as
approximately 63,500. SEE Tadzhik.

CHAGATAY (CHAGHATAI,   Alt. spel. Chagatai. SEE
         CHAGHATAY)   Chagatai, Tadzhik.

CHAIDAK (CHAIDAQ,   CHAITAK,   Alt. spel. Khaidak; alt.
               CHAITAQ)   des. Kaitak. SEE Kaitak,
Dargin.

CHALA   The Chala are a group of Central Asian Jews
from Bukhara who, under pressure, officially
converted to Islam. They, however, secretly practiced
Judaism and usually married within their own group.
Chala literally means incomplete (referring to their
religious conversion). Their religion is basically
Judaic, but with many Moslem adoptions. SEE Central
Asian Jews.

CHALA CAZAH (CAZAK,   Alt. des. and spel. Chala Kazak.
            CAZACH)   SEE Chala Kazak, Kirgiz.

CHALA KAZAH   Alt. des. Chala Kazak. SEE Chala Kazak,
Kirgiz.

CHALA KAZAK   A tribe of Kirgiz comprised of
Kirgizified Kazakhs living near Frunze
(in the village of Kyzyl Asker) and in the Talass
valley in Kirgizia. Although they consider themselves
Kirgiz, they do not belong to any of the three major
tribal groupings of the Kirgiz. SEE Kirgiz.

CHALA KAZAKH   Alt. des. Chala Kazak. SEE Chala Kazak,
Kirgiz.

CHALCHA (MONGOL)   Alt. spel. Khalkha. SEE Khalkha,
Mongol.

CHALCHIN (MONGOL)   Alt. des. Khalkha. SEE Khalkha,
Mongol.

CHAMALAL   Self des. Chamalali, or by village. ETHN:
Up until the early 1930s the Chamalal, as
well as the other Andi-Dido peoples, were considered
distinct ethnic groups. Since that time they have been
classified as Avars. LANG: The Chamalal language
belongs to the Andi group of the Avaro-Andi-Dido
division of the northeast division of the Caucasic
language family. Chamalal has two dialect groups:
Gidatl and Gakwari-Gaidari. Gakwar, in turn, has five
sub-dialects and Gaidari two. Up until the 1930s the
Chamalal language was considered a distinct language.
Since that time it has been classified as a dialect
of Avar. The Chamalal language is not written and Avar
serves as the literary language of the Chamalal. POP:
3,438 (1926). The Chamalal are Sunni Moslem in
religion. They, like the other Andi-Dido peoples, are
being assimilated by the Avars. They live, primarily,
in highland southwestern Dagestan along the Andi River.

SEE Andi-Dido Peoples, Avar.

CHAN   Alt. des. Laz. SEE Laz, Georgian.

CHANDEIAR (CHANDEYAR)   Alt. spel. Khandeyar. SEE
                          Khandeyar, Nenets.

CHANT   Alt. spel. Khant. SEE Khant.

CHANTAIKA   Alt. spel. Khantaika. SEE Khantaika, Ent.

CHANTAIKA SAMODI (SAMOED,   Alt. des. Khantaika. SEE
     SAMOIED, SAMOYED)   Khantaika, Ent.

CHANTAYKA SAMODI (SAMOED,   Alt. des. Khantaika. SEE
     SAMOIED, SAMOYED)   Khantaika, Ent.

CHAPUT   Alt. des. Gaput. SEE Gaput, Dzhek, Shahdag
           Peoples.

CHAQASS   Alt. spel. Khakass. SEE Khakass.

CHARDURI   Alt. spel. Kharduri. SEE Kharduri, Tadzhik.

CHATUCAI (CHATUCAY, CHATUKAI,   Alt. spel. Khatukai.
    CHATUKAY, CHATUQAI,CHATUQAY)   SEE Khatukai, Adygei,
                                    Circassian.

CHAVCHU   Alt. des. Chavchuven. SEE Chavchuven,
            Chukchi, Koryak.

CHAVCHUVEN   Self des. Chavchyvav or Chavchyo.
          1-Des. of the Chukchi and Koryak reindeer
herders (as opposed to the settled coastal
inhabitants).
          2-The largest (approximately 1/2 the total
Koryak population) of the nine territorial groups of
Koryaks. They live scattered throughout the Koryak AO
in far eastern Siberia. SEE Chukchi, Koryak.

CHAYDAK (CHAYDAQ, CHAYTAK,   Alt. des. Kaitak. SEE
          CHAYTAQ)   Kaitak, Dargin.

CHAZARA   Alt. spel. Khazara. SEE Khazara.

CHECHEN   Self des. Nakhchuo or Nokhcho; for. des.
          Michik(iz) or Minkiz. ETHN: The status of
Chechen and Ingush as distinct peoples and languages is
still debated. Both refer to themselves and each
other as Nakhchuo and consider themselves one Nakh
people who speak dialects of one Nakh language. The
Ingush are considered by many to be western Chechens.
The division between the Chechen and Ingush resulted
from the Caucasian Wars of the mid-18th cent. Whereas
the eastern Nakh tribes fought bitterly against the

Russians, the western tribes did not take part in any
fighting. The Russians, therefore, considered them to
be two distinct groups and named them for the largest
villages in their respective areas (Chechen and
Ongusht). LANG: Chechen forms with Ingush the Veinakh
group of the Northeast Caucasian branch of the Caucasic
language family. The Chechen and Ingush languages are
mutually intelligible and are considered by many
linguists to be closely related dialects of one
language. Chechen itself is divided into two dialects
(Highland and Lowland). The highland dialect has
numerous sub-dialects, but all are relatively closely
related. The dialect of Chechen spoken by the Chechens
living in or near the border of Dagestan is quite
distinct. It is considered by some a separate language,
having many Dagestani and Turkic words. The lowland
dialect forms the basis of the Chechen literary
language. The first attempts to create a Chechen
literary language were made in Tiflis (Tbilisi) in the
mid-19th cent. using the Cyrillic script. This did not
catch on as the Chechens used Arabic as their literary
language and were suspicious of a foreign script as
well. Even when Chechen was later written on the basis
of the Arabic script in the late 19th and early 20th
cents., few Chechens used it (preferring the Arabic
language). In 1923-24 Chechen was put into the Latin
script, and in 1938 into the Cyrillic. POP: 755,782
(1979); 612,674 (1970); 418,756 (1959); 318,522 (1926).
The Chechens were deported to northern Kazakhstan in
1944 where they remained until the late 1950s when the
survivors were permitted to return to the North
Caucasus region. During that period the Chechens
suffered great losses of population. The Chechens are
Sunni Moslem in religion, and are reported to be among
the most conservative Moslems in the USSR. They live
primarily in the Chechen-Ingush ASSR and adjacent areas
in Dagestan. Prior to their deportation they lived,
primarily, in the mountainous regions of Chechnya, but
since their return they have been resettled in the
foothills and plains areas. SEE MAP 11.

CHEGEM   Self des. Chegemli. One of the five tribes
          (societies) that went into the formation of
the Balkars. The Chegem live mainly in the valley of
the Chegem River and its tributaries in the Kabardino-
Balkar ASSR. SEE Balkar.

CHEGEM   (CHI)(CHILI)(LI)   Alt. des. Chegem. SEE
          Chegem, Balkar.

CHELKAN   The Chelkan are one of the seven
          territorial-tribal groups that went into
the formation of the Altai people. They were formerly
called Chernevyy Tatars, as were the Tubalars and
Kumanda. The Chelkan are part of the northern Altai

tribal group. SEE Chernevyy Tatar, Altai.

CHEMGUI (CHEMGUY)   Alt. des. Temirgoi. SEE Temirgoi,
Adygei, Circassian.

CHEMSHIL (CHEMSHIN)   Alt. spel. and des. Khemshil.
SEE Khemshil, Armenian,
Meskhetian, Azerbaidzhan.

CHEREMIS(S)   For. des. (pre-1930s) of Mari. SEE Mari.

CHERKAS   1-For. alt. des. Cossack.
2-A term used by Belorussians and Ukrainians
in the 19th cent. for Russians in Belorussia
and the Ukraine.

CHERKESS   1-Self des. Adyge; Rus. and Turk. des.
Cherkess. ETHN: In the pre-Soviet period
the Cherkess were considered, along with the Adygei and
Kabard peoples, as one Circassian people (self des.
Adyge; Rus. and Turk. des. Cherkess) speaking one
Circassian language. In the 1920s the Circassians were
officially divided into two groups: western (Cherkess)
and eastern (Kabard). This western group included what
are today the Adygei and most of the Cherkess. Some of
the present day Cherkess were called Kabard at that
time. In the late 1930s the Circassians were redivided
into the groups still in use today: western (Adygei),
central (Cherkess), and eastern (Kabard) groups, each
having the status of a distinct ethnic group. The
Cherkess were formed out of those Circassian tribes
inhabiting what is today the Karachai-Cherkess AO.
Prior to the revolution the Cherkess were in the
process of assimilating the Abaza. SEE Abaza. LANG: The
Cherkess speak the same language as the Kabards
(Kabardino-Cherkess) which is similar to, and mutually
intelligible with Adygei. Adygei and Kabardino-Cherkess
are closely related dialects of one Circassian
language. Kabardino-Cherkess belongs to the Circassian
division of the northwest branch (Abazgo-Circassian) of
the Caucasic language family. A Circassian literary
language arose in the early 19th cent., based on the
Baksan dialect. It was originally written in the Arabic
script, changed in 1923 to the Latin, and in 1936 to
the Cyrillic. The Adygei were given a separate literary
language in the 1920s, based on the Temirgoi dialect.
POP: 46,470 (1979); 39,785 (1970); 30,453 (1959). The
vast majority of Cherkess, like the other Abazgo-
Circassians, emigrated to Turkey in the 1860s. The
Cherkess are Sunni Moslem in religion. They live,
primarily, in scattered villages in the northern part
of the Karachai-Cherkess AO. SEE Circassian, MAP 5.
2-For. alt. des. Circassian. SEE Circassian.

CHERNEVIY TATAR   Alt. spel. Chernevyy Tatar. SEE
Chernevyy Tatar, Altai.

CHERNEVYY TATAR   Col. des. of the northern Altai
tribes (including, the Chelkan,
Kumanda, and Tubalar); oth. des. Back Country Tatar.
The language of the Chernevyy Tatars belongs to the Old
Uigur group of the eastern division of the Turkic
language branch of the Uralo-Altaic language family,
unlike the southern group of Altai, who speak Kypchak
dialects. SEE Altai.

CHERNYY KIRGIZ   For. Rus. sing. des. of Kara Kirgiz;
for. des. Kirgiz. SEE Kara Kirgiz,
Kirgiz.

CHERNYY KLOBUK   For. Rus. sing. des. of Karakalpak.
SEE Karakalpak.

CHERNYY NOGAI   For. Rus. sing. des. of Kara Nogai.
SEE Kara Nogai, Nogai.

CHERNYE KIRGIZI   For. Rus. pl. des. of Kara Kirgiz;
for. des. Kirgiz. SEE Kara Kirgiz,
Kirgiz.

CHERNYE KLOBUKI   For. Rus. pl. des. of Karakalpak.
SEE Karalpak.

CHERNYE NOGAI (TSY)   For. Rus. pl. des. of Kara
Nogai. SEE Kara Nogai, Nogai.

CHEVSUR (IAN)   Alt. spel. and des. of Khevsur. SEE
Khevsur, Georgian.

CHINALUG   Alt. spel. Khinalug. SEE Khinalug, Shahdag
Peoples, Azerbaidzhan.

CHINALUGH (CHINALUCH)   Alt. des. Khinalug. SEE
Khinalug, Shahdag Peoples,
Azerbaidzhan.

CHINESE MOSLEM (MUSLIM)   Alt. des. Dungan. SEE Dungan.

CHITRI   Alt. spel. Khitri. SEE Khitri, Chuvash.

CHIURKILI   Alt. spel. Khürkili. SEE Khürkili, Dargin.

CHOLAM (CHY)(CHYLY(LY)   Alt. spel. and des. Kholam.
SEE Kholam, Balkar.

CHONGODOR   Alt. spel. Khongodor. SEE Khongodor,
Buryat.

CHORA (CHORIN)   Alt. spel. and des. Khora. SEE Khora,
                      Buryat.

CHORNIY KIRGIZ   Alt. spel. Chernyy Kirgiz; for. Rus.
                      sing. des. Kara Kirgiz.; for. des.
                      Kirgiz. SEE Kara Kirgiz, Kirgiz.

CHORNIY KLOBUK   Alt. spel. Chernyy Klobuk; for. Rus.
                      sing. des. Karakalpak. SEE Karakalpak.

CHORNYY NOGAI   Alt. spel. Chernyy Nogai; for. Rus.
                      des. Kara Nogai. SEE Kara Nogai,
                      Nogai.

CHORNIE KIRGIZI   Alt. spel. Chernye Kirgizi; for. Rus.
                      pl. des. Kara Kirgiz; for. des.
                      Kirgiz, SEE Kara Kirgiz, Kirgiz.

CHORNIE KLOBUKI   Alt. spel. Chernye Klobuki; for.
                      Rus. pl. des. Karakalpak. SEE
                      Karakalpak.

CHORNYE NOGAI (TSY)   Alt. spel. Chernye Nogai(tsy);
                      for. Rus. des. Kara Nogai. SEE
                      Kara Nogai, Nogai.

CHORVAT   Alt. spel. Khorvat. SEE Khorvat, Ukrainian.

CHOSHEUT   Alt. spel. Khosheut. SEE Khosheut, Kalmyk.

CHOUDOR   Oth. des. Choudur, Chovdor, or Chovdur. One
            of the ten major tribal-territorial
divisions of the Turkmen. In the pre-Soviet period they
were each considered distinct peoples. The Choudor
speak a distinct dialect (Choudor) of Turkmen. POP:
They live, primarily, in the Khorezm Oasis. SEE
Turkmen.

CHOUDUR (CHOVDOR, CHOVDUR)   Alt. des. Choudor. SEE
                                Choudor, Turkmen.

CHUD (CHUDIN)   For. alt. des. Veps. SEE Veps.

CHUF (CHUFIDJ, CHUFIDZH,   Alt. spel. and des. Khuf.
           CHUFIJ)   SEE Khuf, Rushan, Tadzhik.

CHUHAR (CHUHON)   Alt. spel. and des. of Chukhar
                      (Chukhon); for. alt. des. Veps. SEE
                      Veps.

CHUKCHA   Alt. des. Chukchi. SEE Chukchi.

CHUKCHI   Self des. Lyg Oravetlyan ("real man"); for.
Rus. des. Luoravetlan(tsy); Oth. des.
Chukcha, Chukot(ian). ETHN: Culturally the Chukchi,
like the closely related Koryak, are divided into two
groups: nomadic or semi-nomadic reindeer herders
(Chavchu or Chavchuven), and settled coastal dwellers
(An' Kalyn). In 1926 70% of the Chukchi were nomads and
30% settled. Today some Chukchi continue to be semi-
nomadic reindeer breeders. The Chukchi and Koryak are
closely related peoples, and their languages are
mutually intelligible. The Chukchi have assimilated
most of the Asiatic Eskimoes, and have adopted many
Eskimo linguistic and cultural elements. They have also
assimilated the Chuvan (a group of Yukagirs) LANG:
Chukchi forms with Koryak and Itelmen the Chukotic
(Chukchan) group of languages, which have been
classified as Paleoasiatic. Chukchi itself has no
dialect divisions. The Chukchi literary language was
created in 1931 using the Cyrillic script. POP: 14,000
(1979); 13,597 (1970); 11,727 (1959); 12,332 (1926).
The Chukchi are shamanist-animist in religion. They
live primarily, in scattered settlements in the Chukchi
AO, and adjacent areas in the Koryak AO and Yakut ASSR.
SEE Paleoasiatic Peoples, MAP 1.

CHUKHAR (CHUKHON)   For. alt. des. Veps. SEE Veps.

CHUKOT (IAN)   Alt. des. Chukchi. SEE Chukchi.

CHULAM (CHI)(CHILI)(LI)   Alt. spel. and des. Kholam.
SEE Kholam, Balkar.

CHULIM (TATAR)   Alt. spel. Chulym Tatar. SEE Chulym
Tatar, Kyzyl, Khakass.

CHULYM TATAR   The Chulym Tatars were formed when a
group of West Siberian Tatars were
forced out of their territory by Ermak Timofeevich's
Cossacks and their native allies (1582). They resettled
on the Chulym River in south central Siberia. There
they mixed with other local Turkic peoples forming the
Chulym Tatars. The Chulym Tatars were later
incorporated into the Kyzyl tribal-territorial division
of the Khakass. The Chulym Tatars speak a distinct
dialect of Tatar. SEE Kyzyl, Khakass.

CHUNZAL   Alt. spel. Khunzal. SEE Khunzal, Andi-Dido
Peoples, Avar.

CHURKILI   Alt. spel. Khürkili. SEE Khürkili, Dargin.

CHUVAN   Alt. des. Shelga. A group of Yukagirs (one
of the major Yukagir tribes) that were assimilated by
the Chukchi. They maintain, however, a distinct Chuvan
identity. A group of Yukagir Chuvans living on the

Kolyma River have been assimilated by the Russians.
POP: 705 (1926). SEE Yukagir.

CHUVASH   Self des. Chavash or Tavas; for. des.
               Bolgar. The Chuvash are of mixed origin.
They are descended from Volga Bolgars who assimilated
local Finnic and Turkic (Kypchak) peoples. ETHN: The
Chuvash are divided into two ethnographic groups, which
correspond to the major dialect divisions of the
Chuvash: Viryal (upper) and Anatri (lower) Chuvash.
LANG: The exact place occupied by Chuvash in the Uralo-
Altaic language family is still debated. The Chuvash
language forms a distinct group in the Turkic branch of
the Uralo-Altaic language family. Some linguists
consider it a Hunnic language. The Chuvash literary
language is based on the Anatri dialect and was first
established in the 1870s using the Cyrillic script.
POP: 1,751,366 (1979); 1,694,351 (1970); 1,469,766
(1959); 1,117,419 (1926). The Chuvash are Eastern
Orthodox in religion. They live, primarily, in the
Chuvash ASSR. Many Chuvash, however, live in
settlements in the Tatar and Bashkir ASSRs and in
Kuibyshev, Ulyanovsk and Saratov Oblasts. SEE MAP 12.

CHVARSHI   (CHVARSHIN,   Alt. des. and spel. Khwarshi.
   CHWARSHI, CHWARSHIN)   SEE Khwarshi, Andi-Dido
                           Peoples, Avar.

CHYURKILI (N)   Alt. spel. and des. Khürkili. SEE
            Khürkili, Dargin.

CIGAN   Alt. spel. Tsygan; alt. des. Gypsy. SEE Gypsy.

CIRCASSIAN   Self des. Adyge; oth. for. des. Cherkess;
              oth. des. Kerketian. ETHN: Circassian is
a collective ethnonym for the peoples of the Circassian
group of the Abazgo-Circassian peoples. In the pre-
Soviet period they were considered one people speaking
one language. In the 1920s the Circassians were
officially divided into two groups: western (Cherkess)
and eastern (Kabard). For a short time, between the
late 1920s and 1930s, another group (Shapsug) was
formed out of one of the western (Shapsug) Circassian
tribes. In the late 1930s the Circassians were
redivided into three groups: western (Adygei), central
(Cherkess), and eastern (Kabard) groups, each having
the status of a distinct ethnic group. LANG: The
Circassian language belongs to the northwest (Abazgo-
Circassian) branch of the Caucasic language family.
Circassian is divided into numerous closely related
dialects, which correspond roughly to tribal divisions.
A Circassian literary language arose in the mid-19th
cent. on the basis of the Baksan dialect (the dialect
of Greater Kabarda) using the Arabic script. In the
early 1920s a distinct Adygei literary language was

created on the basis of the dialect of the Temirgoi
(Kemirgoi) tribe. In 1923-24 both literary Circassian
languages (Kabardino-Cherkess and Adygei) were changed
into the Latin script, and in 1936 into the Cyrillic.
.Today the Kabards and Cherkess use the eastern
(Kabardino-Cherkess form) and the Adygei the western
(Adygei) form of the literary language. These languages
are closely related and mutually intelligible.
Sometimes the Abaza are included in the col. term
Circassian. The Circassians live in the foothills and
lowland steppe areas in the western North Caucasus. SEE
Adygei, Cherkess, Kabard. SEE MAP 5.

COIBAL   Alt. spel. Koibal. SEE Koibal, Khakass.

COJLA CHEREMISS (MARI)   Alt. des. and spel. Kozhla
                            Mari. SEE Kozhla Mari, Mari.

COLVA IURAK (NENETS, SAMODI,   Alt. des. and spel. Kolva
    SAMOED, SAMOIED, SAMOYED,   Nenets. SEE Kolva Nenets,
                    YURAK)   Nenets.

COLVIN IURAK (NENETS, SAMODI,   Alt. des. and spel.
    SAMOED, SAMOIED, SAMOYED,   Kolva Nenets. SEE Kolva
                    YURAK)   Nenets.

COLIMCHAN (COLYMCHAN)   Alt. spel. Kolymchan.   SEE
                          Kolymchan, Russian.

COMI   Alt. spel. Komi. SEE Komi.

COMI IJEM (IJMI, IZHEM,   Alt. des. and spel. Izhmi.
          IZHMI)   SEE Izhmi, Komi.

COMI PERMIAK (PERMYAK)   Alt. spel. Komi Permyak. SEE
                          Komi Permyak.

CONDOMA   Alt. spel. Kondoma Tatar. SEE Kondoma Tatar,
           Shor.

COREL (CORELIAN)   Alt. des. and spel. Karelian. SEE
                     Karelian.

CORIAK (CORYAK)   Alt. spel. Koryak. SEE Koryak.

COSSACK   The Cossacks were a social group, with some
           developing ethnic characteristics. They were
formed during the 16th-18th cents. by runaway serfs who
settled in the frontiers of the Russian Empire and
formed independent social units. Although they
maintained the Eastern Orthodox religion, they often
mixed with local ethnic groups and adopted many social
and economic customs of neighboring peoples. The
Cossacks identified less as Russians or Ukrainians,
but rather maintained a strong Cossack identity. They

were, however, divided into Russian and Ukrainian
speaking groups. There is a linguistic link between the
word Cossack and Kazakh. Both derive from the Turkic
Kazak (Qazaq) meaning "free man." The following are the
main Cossack divisions:

RUSSIAN SPEAKING COSSACKS

DON COSSACK   The Don Cossacks were one of the
                 first Cossack groups to be formed
(16th–17th cents.). They are   of mixed Russian
and "Eastern" (probably Kalmyk) origin. The Buzava
(Don Kalmyks) formed part of the Don Cossacks. The
Don Cossacks were divided into upper and lower
groups which differed in cultural and physical
type. The Don Cossacks were the largest of the
Cossack divisions. They lived in areas between the
Don and lower Volga Rivers.

URAL COSSACK   For. des. Yaik. The Ural Cossacks
                 were an offshoot group of the Don
Cossacks (formed in the late 16th cent.). The Ural
Cossacks were also of mixed origin (with Kazakh
and Tatar elements). They lived between the Volga
and Ural Rivers.

TRANSBAIKAL (ZABAIKAL) COSSACK   The Transbaikal
                                    Cossacks were
an offshoot of the Ural Cossacks (formed in the
later half of the 18th cent.). Besides Russians,
many Buryats and Evenks went into the formation of
the Transbaikal Cossacks. They live in the
Transbaikal region of southern Siberia.

AMUR-USSURI COSSACK   The Amur-Ussuri Cossacks
                         were an offshoot of the
Transbaikal Cossacks (formed in the 19th cent.).
Besides Russians, many of the peoples of the Amur-
Ussuri region (Tungusic and Manchu peoples) went
into the formation of the Amur-Ussuri Cossacks.
They lived along the Amur and Ussuri Rivers in
southeastern Siberia.

GREBEN (SKOI) COSSACK   The Greben Cossacks were
                         formed in the 16th cent.
as a southern offshoot of the Don Cossacks. The
culture of the Greben Cossacks has many North
Caucasian elements (most notably Chechen and
Nogai). Most Greben Cossacks were bilingual
(Russian and Nogai). They lived in the steppe
region of the eastern North Caucasus.

TEREK COSSACK   The Terek Cossacks were formed in
                 the 16th cent. as an offshoot of
the Don Cossacks. The culture of the Terek

Cossacks has many North Caucasian elements (most notably Circassian, Ossetian, and Nogai). Many Ossetians were part of the Terek Cossack group. Most Terek Cossacks were bilingual (Russian and Nogai). They lived in the steppes of the central North Caucasus.

UKRAINIAN SPEAKING COSSACKS

ZAPOROZHE (ZAPOROGIAN) COSSACK   The Zaporozhe Cossacks were formed in the 16th-17th cents. The Zaporozhe Cossacks are of mixed origin (basically Ukrainian with a Crimean Tatar admixture). The Zaporozhe Cossacks were strongly influenced culturally by the Tatars living in the steppes of the central Ukraine. In 1775 the Zaporozhe Cossack were officially disbanded. Part of the Zaporozhe Cossacks fled beyond the Danube into Turkish held territory. From those remaining on territories now controlled by the Russian Empire the Black Sea (Chernomorskiy) Cossacks were formed. The Zaporozhe Cossacks lived in the steppe region of the central Ukraine.

BLACK SEA (CHERNOMORSKIY) COSSACK   After the Zaporozhe Cossacks were officially disbanded in 1775 part of their group fled beyond the Danube into Turkish held territory. From those remaining on territories now controlled by the Russian Empire the Black Sea Cossaacks were formed. After the Russo-Turkish War (1787-1791) the Black Sea Cossacks were resettled in the Kuban region where they formed the Kuban Cossacks.

KUBAN COSSACK   After the Russo- Turkish War (1787-1791) the Black Sea Cossacks were resettled in the Kuban region of the western North Caucasus. In 1828-29 the bulk of the Transdanubian Cossacks (former Zaporozhe Cossacks who fled into Turkish held territory in 1775) joined the Black Sea Cossacks and officially became part of the Kuban Cossacks. The Kuban Cossacks were strongly influenced culturally by the Circassians among whom they lived. The official reclassification of the Kuban Cossacks from Ukrainian to Russian at the end of the 1920s resulted in a dramatic decline in the Ukrainian population (by between 2 to 3 million). The Kuban Cossacks lived in the steppe region of the eastern North Caucasus in the vicinity of the Kuban River.

COTT   Alt. spel. Kott. SEE Kott.

COURISH KINGS   Alt. des. Kuršu Ķoniņi. SEE Kuršu
Ķoniņi, Latvian, Lithuanian.

COURLANDERS   Alt. des. Kurzemnieki. SEE Kurzemnieki,
Latvian, Lithuanian.

COURONIAN   Alt. des. Kurši. SEE Kurši, Latvian.

COVA TUSH (IN)   Alt. spel. Tsova Tush(in); alt. des.
Batsbi. SEE Batsbi, Nakh, Georgian.

COYBAL   Alt. spel Koibal. SEE Koibal, Khakass.

COZHLA CHEREMISS (MARI)   Alt. spel. and des. Kozhla
Mari. SEE Kozhla Mari, Mari.

CRESHEN   Alt. spel. Kryashen. SEE Kryashen, Tatar.

CREVIN (GI)   Alt. des. and spel. Krieviņi. SEE
Krieviņi, Vod, Latvian.

CRIASHEN   Alt. spel. Kryashen. SEE Kryashen, Tatar.

CRIEVIN (GI)   Alt. des. and spel. Krevingi. SEE
Krevingi, Vod.

CRIM TATAR   Alt. spel. Krym Tatar; alt. des. Crimean
Tatar. SEE Crimean Tatar.

CRIMCHAK   Alt. spel. Krymchak. SEE Krymchak, Jew.

CRIMEAN JEW   Alt. des. Krymchak. SEE Krymchak, Jew.

CRIMEAN TATAR   Self des. Kyrym Tatar; oth. des. Krym
Tatar. The Crimean Tatars are the
descendants of Tatars that settled in the Black Sea
coast region around the Crimean Peninsula (the Golden
Horde). For centuries the Crimean Khanate prevented the
southern expansion of the Slavs into this region. Many
Slavs, however, were assimilated by them and went into
the formation of the Crimean Tatars. LANG: The Crimean
Tatar language belongs to the Kypchak division of the
Turkic branch of the Uralo-Altaic language family.
Crimean Tatar is one of the oldest of the literary
languages of Russia's Moslem peoples dating back to
the 18th cent. Crimean Tatar was originally written in
the Arabic script, but was changed in 1928 to the
Latin, and in 1938-39 to the Cyrillic. In 1944 with the
deportation of the Crimean Tatars to Central Asia, the
Crimean Tatar literary language was abolished. Only in
the 1970s has publication again begun in this language
(in Tashkent). At the turn of the century Crimean Tatar
was one of the most important literary languages among
the Moslems of the USSR, and served as a model for the
creation of secular literary languages based on spoken

Turkic languages. POP: The population of the Crimean Tatars is estimated at 200-300,000. Since 1944 the Crimean Tatars have been officially reclassified as Tatars and do not appear separately in statistical literature. These former inhabitants of the Crimean Peninsula now reside in and around Tashkent, and other areas in Uzbekistan. The Crimean Tatars have made numerous attempts to be permitted to move back to the Crimea, including petitioning Moscow and the United Nations, however, none of these have been fruitful. SEE Tatar.

CRIMEAN TATAR JEW   Alt. des. Krymchak. SEE Krymchak, Jew.

CRIVICHI   Alt. spel. Krivichi. SEE Krivichi, Belorussian.

CRYASHEN   Alt. spel. Kryashen. SEE Kryashen, Tatar.

CRYM TATAR   Alt. des. and spel. Crimean Tatar. SEE Crimean Tatar, Tatar.

CRYMCHAK   Alt. spel. Krymchak. SEE Krymchak, Jew

CRYZ   Alt. spel. Kryz. SEE Kryz, Dzhek, Shahdag Peoples.

CUANADI (CUANADY)   Alt. spel. Kwanadi; alt. des. Bagulal. SEE Bagulal, Andi-Dido Peoples, Avar.

CUBACHI   Alt. spel. Kubachi. SEE Kubachi.

CUBAN ABHAZ (ABKAZ,   Alt. spel. Kuban Abkhaz; for.
ABKHAZ)   alt. des. Abaza. SEE Abaza.

CUBAN NOGAI (NOGAY,   Alt. spel. Kuban Nogai; alt. des.
NOGHAI, NOGHAY)   Ak Nogai. SEE Ak Nogai, Nogai.

CUMANDA (CUMANDIN)   Alt. spel. and des. Kumanda. SEE Kumanda, Altai.

CUMARCHEN   Alt. spel. Kumarchen; alt. des. Manegir. SEE Manegir, Evenk.

CUMIK (CUMUK, CUMYK)   Alt. spel. Kumyk. SEE Kumyk.

CUNDROV (SKIY) TATAR   Alt. spel. Kundrov Tatar. SEE Kundrov Tatar, Astrakhan Tatar, Tatar.

CURAMA   Alt. spel. Kurama. SEE Kurama, Uzbek.

CURD   Alt. spel. Kurd. SEE Kurd.

CURIAN   Alt. spel. Kurian; alt. des. Kurši. SEE
            Kurši, Latvian.

CURIK CHEREMISS (MARI)   Alt. des. and spel. Kuryk
                            Mari. SEE Kuryk Mari, Mari.

CURIL (IAN)   Alt. spel. Kurilian; alt. des. Ainu.
                 SEE Ainu.

CURISH KINGS   Alt. des. Kuršu Ķoniņi. SEE Kuršu
                   Ķoniņi, Latvian, Lithuanian.

CURISHE KENIGE   Rus. alt. des. Kurische Könige; alt.
                    des. Kuršu Ķoniņi. SEE Kuršu Ķoniņi,
                    Kurši, Latvian, Lithuanian.

CURMANDJ (CURMANDZH,   Alt. spel. Kurmandzh; alt. des.
         CURMANJ)   Kurd. SEE Kurd.

CURONIAN   Alt. des. Kurši. SEE Kurši, Latvian.

CURYK CHEREMISS (MARI)   Alt. des. and spel. Kuryk
                            Mari. SEE Kuryk Mari, Mari.

CURZEME (CURZEMIAN)   Alt. spel. Kurzeme; alt. des.
                        Kurzemnieki. SEE Kurzemnieki,
                        Latvian, Lithuanian.

CUZNETS TATAR   Alt. spel. Kuznets Tatar; for. alt.
                   des. Shor. SEE Shor.

CVANADI (CVANADY)   Alt. des. and spel. Kwanadi; alt.
                       des. Bagulal. SEE Bagulal, Andi-
                       Dido Peoples, Avar.

CVANALI (CVANALY)   Alt. des. and spel. Kwanaly; alt.
                       des. Andi. SEE Andi, Andi-Dido
                       Peoples, Avar.

CWANADI (CWANADY)   Alt. spel. Kwandi; alt. des.
                        Bagulal. SEE Bagulal, Andi-Dido
                        Peoples, Avar.

CWANALI (CWANALY)   Alt. spel. Kwanaly; alt. des.
                       Andi. SEE Andi, Andi-Dido Peoples,
                       Avar.

CYPCHAK (CYPSHAK)   Alt. spel. and des. Kypchak. SEE
                       Kypchak, Uzbek.

CYRGHYZ (CYRGYZ)   Alt. spel. Kirgiz. SEE Kirgiz.

CYZYL (CYZL)   Alt. spel. and des. Kyzyl. SEE Kyzyl,
                  Khakass.

D

DAG CHUFUT Alt. des. Mountain Jew. A somewhat
pejorative term, albeit commonly used,
for the Mountain Jews. SEE Mountain Jew,
Jew.

DAGESTANI PEOPLES Col. des. of the indigenous
peoples of Dagestan. This term
usually includes the: Avar (including the Andi-Dido and
Archi peoples), Dargin (including the Kaitak and
Kubachi), Lezgin, Kumyk, Lak, Tabasaran, Nogai, Rutul,
Tsakhur, and Agul peoples. POP: 1,656,676 (1979);
1,264,649 (1970); 944,213 (1959); 698,104 (1926). All
of the Dagestani are Sunni Moslem in religion. They
live, primarily, in the Dagestan ASSR and adjacent
areas in the eastern Caucasus region. SEE MAP 6.

DAGESTANI JEW Alt. des. Mountain Jew. SEE Mountain
Jew, Jew.

DAGH CHUFUT Alt. spel. Dag Chufut; alt. des.
Mountain Jew. SEE Dag Chufut, Mountain
Jew, Jew.

DAGHESTANI PEOPLES Alt. spel. Dagestani Peoples.
SEE Dagestani Peoples.

DAGHESTANI JEW Alt. spel. Dagestani Jew; alt. des.
Mountain Jew. SEE Mountain Jew, Jew.

DAGHUR (DAGUR) Alt. des. Daur. SEE Daur, Buryat.

DARGHIN Alt. spel. Dargin. SEE Dargin.

DARGIN Formerly no self des. for people as an ethnic
group; contemporary self des. Dargwa; for.
alt. des. Khürkili; oth. des. Dargva, Dargin. ETHN: The
contemporary Dargin people is comprised of the Dargin
proper and the two numerically small Kaitak and Kubachi
peoples. Until the 1930s the Dargins, Kaitaks, and
Kubachi were considered distinct ethnic groups, each
having its own distinct language. Since that time they
have been classified as Dargins and their languages as
dialects of Dargin. These three peoples are merging

into one Dargin nation. In the pre-Soviet period the
Dargins were being assimilated by the Avars in the
highlands and the Kumyks in the lowlands. The majority
of Dargins are still bilingual, knowing either Avar or
Kumyk as well as Dargin. LANG: The Dargin language
belongs to the Dargino-Lak group of the northeast
division of the Caucasic language family. Dargin is
comprised of three major, non-mutually intelligible,
dialect groups: Khürkili (Urakhi), spoken on the high
plateau area in the Dargin territory; Akusha (spoken by
the majority of Dargins), spoken in the central plateau
area; and Tsudakhar, spoken in the eastern plains area.
Tsudakhar and Khürkili both have numerous sub-dialects.
Kaitak and Kubachi are distinct languages (the former
having two dialects of its own). The Dargin town of
Akusha was a major political, economic, and religious-
cultural center of the Dargins. As such, the Akusha
dialect was chosen as the basis of the Dargin literary
language. The Dargin language has been literary since
the late 19th cent. It was originally written in the
Arabic script, changed in 1928 to the Latin, and in
1938 to the Cyrillic. POP: 287,282 (1979); 230,932
(1970); 158,149 (1959); 108,963 (1926), excluding the
Kaitak and Kubachi, 125,764 including these peoples.
The Dargins are Sunni Moslem in religion, with a small
Shiite minority. The Dargins live, primarily, in south-
central Dagestan.

DARGVA (DARGWA)   Alt. des. Dargin. SEE Dargin.

DAUR   Oth. des. Daghur or Dagur. The Daur are a
        Mongol tribe that was assimilated by the
Buryats. They lived along the upper Amur River. SEE
Buryat.

DERBET   One of the three major tribal divisions
          [based on the former military ("ulus")
structure of the Kalmyks. The Derbet dialect became
the basis of the Kalmyk literary language. The Kalmyk
literary language was established in the 17th cent.
using the Mongol script. It was changed in 1924 to the
Cyrillic, in 1930 to the Latin, and in 1938 back to the
Cyrillic. The Derbet live in the northern and western
parts of the Kalmyk ASSR. SEE Kalmyk.

DIDO   Self des. Qwanal; oth. des. Didur, Didoi, Tsez.
        ETHN: Until the early 1930s the Dido, as well
as the other Andi-Dido peoples, were considered
distinct ethnic groups. Since that time they have been
classified as Avars. LANG: The Dido language belongs
to the Dido group of the Avaro-Andi-Dido division of
the northeast branch of the Caucasic language family.
Until the 1930s the Dido language was considered a
distinct language. Since that time it has been
classified as a dialect of Avar. The Dido language is

not written and Avar serves as the literary language of
the Dido. POP: 3,276 (1926). The Dido are Sunni Moslem
in religion. They, like the other Andi-Dido peoples,
are being assimilated by the Avars. They live in the
highest and most isolated region of southwestern
Dagestan near the Georgian border. SEE Andi-Dido
Peoples, Avar.

DIDO PEOPLES   Col. des. of Dido, Bezheta, Ginug,
                 Khwarshi, and Khunzal. Each of these
peoples was considered a distinct ethnic group until
the 1930s when they were reclassified as Avars. At the
same time their languages were reclassified as dialects
of the Avar language. LANG: The Dido languages belong
to the Dido group of the Avaro-Andi-Dido division of
the northeast branch of the Caucasic language family.
None of these languages has a written form. Avar serves
as the literary language of the Dido peoples. POP: The
Dido peoples are Sunni Moslem in religion. They live
primarily in highland southwestern Dagestan. SEE Andi-
Dido Peoples, Avar.

DIDOI (DIDOY)   Alt. des. Dido. SEE Dido, Andi-Dido
                 Peoples, Avar.

DIDOI (DIDOY) PEOPLES   Alt. des. Dido Peoples. SEE
                         Dido Peoples, Andi-Dido
                         Peoples, Avar.

DIDUR   Alt. des. Dido. SEE Dido, Andi-Dido Peoples,
         Avar.

DIGOR   Self des. Digoron; oth. des. Digori. ETHN: The
         Digor are Sunni Moslem Ossetians who had been
strongly influenced culturally and linguistically by
the Circassians (Kabards). LANG: The Digor speak an
archaic form of Ossetian that was also influenced by
Circassian. The Digor dialect had its own literary form
written in the Arabic script (established in the late
19th cent.). It was changed to the Latin in 1923, and
abolished in 1939, at which time standard Iron Ossetian
became their literary language. POP: The Digor are
Sunni Moslem in religion. They were deported in 1944
along with other Moslem North Caucasian peoples to
Central Asia. Some have been permitted to return to the
Caucasus region (as Ossetians). Prior to their
deportation, the Digor lived, primarily, in the Digor
valley in the western part of the North Ossetian ASSR.,
near the border of the Kabardino-Balkar ASSR, in the
central North Caucasus. SEE Ossetian.

DJAVAHI (DJAVAKHI)   Alt. spel. Dzhavakhi. SEE
                      Dzhavakhi, Georgian.

DJEK   Alt. spel. Dzhek. SEE Dzhek, Shahdag Peoples,
           Azerbaidzhan.

DJEMSHID   Alt.   spel.   Dzhemshid.   SEE   Dzhemshid,
               Tadzhik.

DJUNGAR (IAN)   Alt.   spel.   Dzhungar.   SEE Dzhungar,
                   Oirot.

DOLGAN   Self des. Dulgaan. ETHN: The Dolgan are a
           Yakut speaking people of Tungusic origin.
They are being assimilated by the Yakuts, but still
maintain a separate identity. LANG: The Dolgans speak a
dialect of Yakut with Evenk additions. They use the
Yakut literary language. POP: 5053 (1979); 4,877
(1970); 3,932 (1959); 656 (1926). The Dolgans are
basically shamanist-animist in religion, with some
Christian (Eastern Orthodox) adoptions. They live,
primarily, in the Dolgano-Nenets (Taimyr) AO in north
central Siberia. SEE Yakut, MAP 4.

DON KALMUK (KALMYK,   Alt. des. Buzava. SEE Buzava,
    QALMUQ, QALMYQ)   Kalmyk.

DREVLIAN (E) (IAN)   Alt. spel. and des. Drevlyan. SEE
                       Drevlyan, Ukrainian.

DREVLYAN (E)   A group of Eastern Orthodox Ukrainians
                 who still retained an old Slavic tribal
designation as late as the mid-19th cent. In 1861 their
population was 196,900. They lived primarily in the
Volynia region of the Ukraine (especially around
Ovruch, Kovel, Novhorod, Volynsky, and Rivne). They
have since been totally assimilated by the Ukrainians.
SEE Ukrainian.

DULEB (IAN) (Y)   A group of Eastern Orthodox
                      Ukrainians who still retained an
old Slavic tribal designation as late as the mid-19th
cent. In 1861 their population was 12,904. They lived
around Volodymir and Starokonstantyniv in the Volynia
region of the Ukraine. They have since been totally
assimilated by the Ukrainians. SEE Ukrainian.

DUNGAN   Self des. Lao Khuei Khuei or Chzhun Yuan'
           Zhyn; oth. des. Chinese Moslems, Tung-an.
ETHN: The Dungans are Chinese Moslems who migrated from
China to Central Asia in the late 19th cent. Most
Dungans live today in northwestern China. The term
Dungan appeared in Sinkiang province in the later half
of the 18th cent. and referred to the immigrant Chinese
from Central China who settled in that area. In China
they are called Khuei Tzu (Khuei Khuei) which also
refers to the Uigurs. Their origin is still debated.

Some hold that they are Islamicized Chinese converted through contact with Islamic Turkic, Arabic and Iranian peoples. Others, that they were Islamic Turks, Persians, and Arabs who settled in China and became Sinified except for their religion. Others, yet, that it is a combination of both factors. The Dungans of the USSR are divided into two major and one minor groups. The two major ones are the Hansu (Rus. des. Khansuitsy) and Shensi (Rus. des. Shensiytsy) based on the province of origin and dialect of Chinese spoken by them. The Dungan of Kirgizia are primarily Hansu, whereas those of the Chu valley region of Kazakhstan are primarily Shensi. There is a small group called Yage or Dungan-Yage, who were Dungans from Lanchzhou and Inchzhou who settled in Russia in the villages of Aleksandrovka, Sokuluk, and Chilik. The Yage speak the Ninsya-Lanchzhou dialect of Chinese, which occupies a transitional position between Hansu and Shensi. The Yage are culturally distinct and share many cultural ties with the Uigurs. Yage also carries a pejorative meaning (refugee). LANG: The Dungan dialects belong to the Sinitic branch of the Sino-Tibetan language family. The linguistic situation of the Dungans is complicated. They are divided into three linguistic communities: Hansu, Shensi, and Yage. In addition the Dungans in Osh Oblast in Kirgizia have given up Chinese and speak only Uzbek. Most Dungan are bi or multi-lingual, knowing besides Chinese and Russian, Kazakh, Uigur, Kirgiz, and/or Uzbek. Prior to 1929 Russian, Tatar, and Uzbek served as the literary languages of the Dungans (depending on place of residence). Dungan became an officially recognized language of the USSR in 1929. The Hansu dialect forms the basis of the Dungan literary language. It was originally written in both standard Chinese characters and in the Arabic script. This was changed to the Cyrillic in 1954. POP: 51,694 (1979); 38,644 (1970); 21,928 (1959); 14,600 (1926). The Dungans are Sunni Moslem in religion. They live, primarily, in the Chu valley in Kazakhstan, and in various cities in Kirgizia and Uzbekistan (Tashkent, and cities in the Fergana valley). SEE MAP 13.

DUNGAN IAGE (YAGE)   Alt. des. Yage. SEE Yage, Dungan.

DZHAVAHI   Alt. spel. Dzhavakhi. SEE Dzhavakhi, Georgian.

DZHAVAKHI   One of the numerous Kartvelian ethnographic groups that went into the formation of the Georgians. The Dzhavakhi are primarily Eastern Orthodox in religion. SEE Georgian.

DZHEK   No general self des.; identified by village (Dzhek, Kryz, and Gaput); oth. des. Kryz, Gek. The Dzhek are one of the numerically small Shahdag

peoples. They are being assimilated by the
Azerbaidzhans. LANG: Dzhek belongs to the Samurian
division of the northwest branch of the Caucasic
language family. Dzhek is divided into three closely
related dialects: Dzhek, Kryz, and Gaput. Dzhek is not
a written language and Azeri serves as the literary
language of the Dzhek, as well as all Shahdag peoples.
POP: 607 (1926). Although only 607 individuals claimed
Dzhek ethnicity, 4,348 listed Dzhek as their native
language. These were probably Dzheks who listed
themselves as Azerbaidzhans speaking Dzhek as their
native language. In 1886 their population was estimated
at 7,767. The Dzhek are Sunni Moslem in religion. They
live, primarily, in the region around Mount Shahdag in
Konakhkend Rayon in northeastern Azerbaidzhan. SEE
Shahdag Peoples, Azerbaidzhan.

DZHEMSHID   The Dzhemshid of the USSR are the
              descendants of immigrants who came to
Central Asia from Afghanistan and Iran. Their origin is
not clear. They are either Tadzhikified Mongols or
Turks. They are Shiite Moslem in religion. Their
population in 1926 was 932. They are being assimilated
by the Tadzhiks. SEE Tadzhik.

DZHUNGAR (IANS)   Alt. des. Oirot. SEE Oirot.

DZŪKAI   A group of Lithuanians inhabiting the
           southeastern part of Lithuania. They are
deliniated on the basis of their distinct dialect
which shows strong Polish influence. They are a sub-
group of the Aukštaičiai. SEE Aukštaičiai, Lithuanian.

DZUNGAR (IAN)   Alt. des. Oirot. SEE Oirot.

E

EAST SLAV   Col. des. of the peoples forming the
              Eastern group of the Slavic language
branch of the Indo-European language family. This term
includes the Russians, Ukrainians, and Belorussians.
Together they comprise roughly three fourths of the
population of the USSR. SEE Russian, Ukrainian,
Belorussian.

EESTI   Estonian des. of Estonian; Alt. des.
          Estonian. SEE Estonian.

EGERUKAI   Self des. Egerukai. One of the ten major
             tribal divisions of the Adygei people.
Each of these was formerly considered a distinct
people. They are now classified as Adygei. The majority
of Egerukai, along with the other Abazgo-Circassians,
emigrated to Turkey in the mid-1860s. They live between
the middle Laba and Belaya Rivers in the western North
Caucasus. SEE Adygei, Circassian.

EGERUKAY (EGERUQAI,   Alt. spel. Egerukai. SEE
         EGERYQAY)   Egerukai, Adygei, Circassian.

EHERIT (EHRIT)   Alt. spel. and des. Ekhirit. SEE
                   Ekhirit, Buryat.

EHSTI   Alt. spel. Eesti; alt. des. Estonian. SEE
          Estonian.

EKHERIT (EKHRIT)   Alt. spel. and des. Ekhirit. SEE
                     Ekhirit, Buryat.

EKHIRIT   One of the five main tribal divisions of the
            Buryats. They live, primarily, along the
upper reaches of the Lena River in south central
Siberia. SEE Buryat.

EMRELI   One of the tribal-territorial divisions of
           the Turkmen. In the pre-Soviet period they
were each considered distinct peoples. The Emreli speak
a distinct dialect of Turkmen. They live, primarily, in
the western part of the Khorezm Oasis in the Turkmen
SSR. SEE Turkmen.

ENETS   Alt. des. Ent. SEE Ent.

ENISEI (ENISEY)   Alt. spel. Yenisei; for. des. Ket.
                    SEE Ket.

ENT   In the pre-Soviet period no self des.;
        contemporary self. des. Enete; alt. des. Enets,
pl. Entsy; oth. des. Yenisei Samoyed; form des.
Khantaika, Karasa Samoyed. ETHN: The Ent are closely
related ethnically, culturally, and linguistically to
the Nenets and Nganasan. In the early 17th cent. their
population was roughly 3,000, but due to epidemics,
clashes with the Selkups, and assimilation by the
Nenets, Selkups, and Dolgans, their numbers have been
severely reduced. Although small in number, they
were once territorially widespread. Formerly they were
divided into two distinct cultural groups: Khantaika
[alt. des. Tundra Yenisei Samoyed (nomads of the
Tundra)], comprised of the Somatu clan; and the Karasa
[alt. des. Forest Yenisei Samoyed (nomads of the
forest and tundra)], comprised of the Muggadi, Bai, and
Yuchi clans. The Khantaika are the more numerous of the

two. LANG: The Ent language is closely related to
Nenets and Nganasan. These three form the Samoyedic
division of the Uralian branch of the Uralo-Altaic
language family. The Ent language is not written. POP:
378 (1926). The Ents are shamanist-animist in religion.
They live, primarily, in the Taz and Turukhan basins
and the lower reaches of the Yenisei River in north
central Siberia.

ENTSY   Rus. pl. des. Ent. SEE Ent.

ENZEBI   Alt. des. Khunzal. SEE Khunzal, Andi-Dido
          Peoples, Avar.

ERMEN (I)   Turk. and alt. des. Armenian. SEE
             Armenian.

ERSARI   Self des. Ersary. The second largest of the
          major tribal-territorial divisions of the
Turkmen. In the pre-Soviet period each of these groups
was considered a distinct people. The Ersari speak a
distinct dialect (Ersari) of Turkmen. They live,
primarily, along the left (and partly right) bank of
the Amu Darya River between Kelif and Chardzhou in
Turkmenistan. SEE Turkmen.

ERSARY   Alt. spel. Ersari. SEE Ersari, Turkmen.

ERZIA (MORDOVIAN, MORDVA,   Alt. spel. and des. Erzya.
    MORDVIN, MORDVINIAN)   SEE Erzya, Mordvinian.

ERZYA   Oth. des. Erzya Mordvinian (Mordovian,
         Mordva), Mordva-Erzya. The Erzya are one of
the two main divisions of the Mordvinians (Erzya and
Moksha). There are approximately twice as many Erzya as
Moksha Mordvinians. Erzya and Moksha are distinct, non-
mutually intelligible languages, and both have their
own literary forms. The Erzya literary language was
created in 1922 using the Cyrillic script. The Erzya
live scattered throughout the Middle Volga region. They
live in the northeastern parts of the Mordvinian ASSR,
Gorkiy, Kuybyshev, Saratov, and Orenburg Oblasts, and
in the Tatar and Bashkir ASSR. A group of Erzya
(Tengushev Mordvinian) resettled in the southern part
of the Mordvinian ASSR where they now form a
transitional group between the Erzya and Moksha. Within
the Mordvinian ASSR itself there are no mixed Erzya and
Moksha villages. SEE Mordvinian.

ERZYA MORDOVIAN (MORDVA,   Alt. des. Erzya. SEE Erzya,
    MORDVIN, MORDVINIAN)   Mordvinian.

ESKIMO (E)   Self des. Yugyt or Yupigut; oth. for.
              des. Onkilon, Namol, Yuity (1931-1938);
Rus. des. Eskimosy. ETHN: The Eskimoes of the USSR are

culturally related to the Chukchi, with whom they were
formerly confused. In the early 19th cent. the Eskimoes
were alternatively called Onkilon (a distortion of the
Eskimo word Ankalyn, meaning coastal dweller) or
Namol(ly) (a distortion of the Koryak word Numylgyn,
meaning settled). Between 1931-1938 the term Yuit(y)
(from the Eskimo self des. Yugut) was officially used.
It was changed in 1938 to Eskimo. The Asiatic Eskimoes
are being assimilated by the Chukchi. LANG: Eskimo has
been classified as a Paleoasiatic language. At times
publications appear in Eskimo (in the Cyrillic
script), but it is not a regularly used language in the
USSR. Chukchi and Russian serve as their literary
languages. Most Eskimoes are bilingual (Eskimo and
Chukchi). POP: 1,510 (1979); 1,308 (1970); 1,118
(1959); 1,293 (1926). The Eskimoes are shamanist-
animist in religion (basically the same religious
beliefs as the Chukchi but with whale and walrus
festivals particularly significant). In the USSR the
Eskimoes live along the coast of the Chukchi Peninsula,
from the Bering Strait in the north to Kresta Bay in
the west, and on Wrangel (Vrangel) Island, in
northeastern Siberia. SEE Paleoasiatic Peoples.

ESTI   Alt. spel. Eesti; alt. des. Estonian. SEE
        Estonian.

ESTONIAN   Self des. Eesti (Eestlased); Rus. des.
            Eston(tsy); Finnish des. Virolaiset;
Latvian des. Igauni; oth. des. Ehsti, Esti. ETHN: The
Estonians are closely related culturally, religiously,
and linguistically to the Finns. Among the Estonians
are a small group of Eastern Orthodox Estonians who
live around Lake Peipus and who maintain a separate
identity, the Setu. SEE Setu. LANG: Estonian belongs to
the southern sub-group of the western (Balto-Finnic)
group of the Finnic divison, of the Uralian branch of
the Uralo-Altaic language family. There are three
dialects of Estonian, which are quite distinct from one
another: northern (the one spoken by the majority of
Estonians), also called Tallinn, as the city of Tallinn
is in this region; southern, also called Tartu, as the
city of Tartu is in this region; and coastal (spoken in
the northeast), which is closest to Finnish. The Setu
have their own dialect as well. The earliest attempts
at creating an Estonian literary language date back to
the 13th cent. Until the mid-19th cent. both the
northern and southern dialects had literary forms, but
since that time only the northern dialect has been
used. Estonian has always been written in the Latin
script. POP: 1,019,851 (1979); 1,007,356 (1970);
988,616 (1959). During World Wars I and II, and during
the incorporation period of Estonia into the USSR, the
Estonian population declined markedly due to loss of
life and emigration to the West. Between World Wars I

and II Estonia was an independent state. In 1926,
however, there were still 154,666 Estonians living in
the USSR, mainly in adjacent areas in the RSFSR,
Leningrad, and Moscow. The Estonians are Lutheran in
religion (the Eastern Orthodox Setu being the only
major exception). They live, primarily, in the Estonian
SSR, and adjacent areas in the RSFSR and Latvia. SEE
MAP 5.

EVEN   For. no self des., names dependent on location
        and tribe; contemporary self des. Even; for.
des. Lamut (pre-1931); oth. des. Orochen (reindeer
keepers). ETHN: The Even are similar in origin,
language, and culture to the Evenks, and formerly were
considered a sub-group of them. The Even have been
strongly influenced by the peoples among whom they live
(Koryaks, Yukagirs, and especially Yakuts). The Even of
the Yakut ASSR are bilingual, with strong cultural and
linguistic influences from the Yakuts. The northern
Evens have, in turn, assimilated a large number of
Yukagirs. LANG: Even belongs to the Tungusic division
of the Tungus-Manuchu branch of the Uralo-Altaic
language family. There are two dialect groups of Even:
Eastern (including the Kolyma-Omolon, Ola, Kamchatka,
Okhotsk, and several other sub-dialects) and western
(including Indigirka, Tompon, Allaikha and other sub-
dialects spoken in the Yakut ASSR). The Ola dialect
forms the basis of the Even literary language, which is
written in the Cyrillic script. Few publications,
however, exist in Even; Yakut and Russian serve as the
literary languages of the Even. POP: 12,286 (1979);
12,029 (1970); 9,121 (1959); 2,044 (1926). In 1926 many
Even of Yakutia and the Sea of Okhotsk area were listed
as Evenks (about 5,000). The Even population in that
year should have been around 7,000 rather than 2,000.
The Even religion is a mixture of shamanist-animist and
Eastern Orthodox beliefs. They live over a vast area in
scattered settlements throughout eastern Siberia, east
of the Lena River, including the Kamchatka Peninsula.
Their widespread distribution and relatively small
population have given rise to the many dialect
divisions found among this people. SEE Evenk. SEE MAP
14.

EVENK   Formerly no self des.; contemporary self des.
        Evenk; for. des. Tungus (Tongus), Orochen,
Birar, Manegir (Manegry). ETHN: The Evenk are closely
related to the Even. Formerly the Even were considered
a group of Evenks. The Evenk were formerly divided into
a number of territorial and tribal groups that covered
a vast territory (e.g. Orochen, Birar, and Manegir).
Until the 1930s each of these tribal-territorial groups
was considered a distinct ethnic group. The Evenk are
divided into two non-contiguous groups. The northern
Evenk are hunters and reindeer breeders; the southern

Evenk are horse and cattle breeders. Many Evenk have
been assimilated by the Russians, Buryats, Yakuts, and
Mongols (in Mongolia). LANG: Evenk belongs to the
Tungusic division of the Tungus-Manchu branch of the
Uralo-Altaic language family. The Evenk language is
divided into three dialect groups: northern, southern,
and eastern. The Evenk literary language was created in
1928-29 using the Cyrillic script. This language,
however, is not widely used and Russian serves as the
literary language of the Evenks. POP: 27,531 (1979);
25,149 (1970); 24,151 (1959); 38,805 (1926). The 1970
census publication corrected the 1959 statistics from
the 24,710 published in the 1959 census itself. In
1926, the census listed Evenks (Tungus) (pop. 37,546),
Manegir (pop. 59), and Orochon (pop. 1,200) separately.
In addition, about 5,000 Even of Yakutia and the Sea of
Okhotsk area were mistakenly listed as Evenk. The
Evenk population in 1926, then, was closer to 34,000.
The Evenk religion is a mixture of shamanist-animist
and Eastern Orthodox beliefs. The Evenk live over a
vast area, which includes roughly one fourth of the
entire area of Siberia. The boundaries of their
territory are: the Ob-Irtysh watershed in the west; the
Sea of Okhotsk and Sakhalin Island in the East; the
Upper Tunguska (Angara) River, Lake Baikal, and the
Amur River in the south; and the territories of the
Even, Dolgan, Yakut, and Nenets in the north. The Evenk
population movement and distribution was associated
with the historical spread of reindeer breeding. Their
widespread distribution and relatively small population
has given rise to the dialect divisions of this people.
SEE Even, MAP 2.

EVREI (EVREY)   Rus. des. of Jews. SEE Jews.

EVRIMEISET (EVRIEMYSET)   Rus. des. of Ayramoiset. SEE
                           Ayramoiset, Finns of
                           Leningrad Oblast.

EWEN   Alt. spel. Even. SEE Even, Evenk.

EWENK   Alt. spel. Evenk. SEE Evenk, Even.

F

FEAPP   Alt. des. Feappi. SEE Feappi, Ingush.

FEAPPI   One of the two clan federations that went
          into the formation of the Ingush (Feappi and
Galgai). The Feappi are the westernmost of the Veinakh
clan federations. The Feappi and Galgai free societies
(federations) did not take part in the wars in the mid-
19th cent. against the Russians. They were thus united
by the Russians and called Ingush (after the village
Ongusht). SEE Ingush.

FEPI   1-Alt. des. Kist. SEE Kist, Ingush.
          2-Alt. des. Feappi. SEE Feappi, Ingush.

FERGANA (FERGHANA) TURK   Alt. des. Turk of Fergana.
                           SEE Turk of Fergana and
                           Samarkand, Uzbek.

FINN   Self des. Suomi, Suomalaiset. ETHN: In 1801
          Finland officially became part of the Russian
Empire, and it remained part of Russia until the end of
World War I. In the Russian Empire the Finns enjoyed a
great deal of autonomy (albeit not independence). The
Finns were divided into two religious-cultural
communities. The western Finns (the vast majority) are
Lutheran in religion; the eastern Finns (Karelian) are
Eastern Orthodox. The boundary of independent Finland
was roughly concomitant with the religious border. The
Western Finns, due to their religious-cultural ties
with the Swedes, were strongly influenced by the Swedes
and were being assimilated by them. The Karelians, on
the other hand, due to their religious-cultural ties
with the Russians, were strongly influenced by them and
were being Russified. After World War I, Karelia
remained (albeit against the will of many Karelians)
part of the USSR. LANG: Finnish belongs to the northern
sub-group of the Balto-Finnic division of the Uralian
branch of the Uralo-Altaic language family. The Finnish
literary language was established in the 16th cent.,
and is based on the Häme (central region of southern
Finland) dialect. Finnish is still the literary
language of the few Finns of the USSR, as well as that
of the Karelians. It is sometimes referred to as
Karelo-Finnish. POP: 77,079 (1979); 84,750 (1970);

92,717 (1959); 19,467 (1926)- excluding Finns of
Leningrad Oblast (134,791 including them). The Finns
are Lutheran in religion. In the pre-Soviet period they
lived primarily in Finland, Karelia, and the area
around the city of Leningrad. After World War II there
was a substantial migration of Finns out of the Soviet
occupied areas of Finland (especially from the Baltic
coastal area near Viipuri). Approximately a quarter
million migrated. The Finns in the USSR today live,
primarily, in and around the city of Leningrad.
SEE MAP 8.

FINN OF LENINGRAD OBLAST   General self. des. Suomi.
                            The Finns of Leningrad
Oblast are the descendants of Finns who came to the
area around what is today Leningrad Oblast, starting in
the 17th cent. They came from two regions of Finland:
Savo and Äyräpää (Rus. Euriapia). Most refer to
themselves as Savakot or Äyrämöiset (Rus. des.
Evrimeiset) depending on the places of origin of their
ancestors. During the period of Swedish rule the Finns
of this region assimilated many Vod and Izhora. LANG:
The Finns of Leningrad Oblast speak a dialect of
Finnish and use the Finnish (and Russian) literary
language. POP: 115,234 (1926); 122,500 (1897). The
Finns of Leningrad Oblast no longer appear as a
distinct ethnic group in Soviet statistical
publications, but rather as Finns. Their population has
been declining due to emigration to Finland after
World War II, emigration to Karelia, and assimilation
by the Russians. The Finns of Leningrad Oblast are
Lutheran in religion. They live, primarily, along the
coast of the Finnish Gulf. SEE Finn.

FINNIC PEOPLES   Col. des. for the peoples of the USSR
                  that speak languages belonging to the
Finnic division of the Uralian branch of the Uralo-
Altaic language family. The Finnic peoples of the USSR
are divided linguistically into five groups: western
(Balto-Finnic), northern (Lapp), Mordvinian, eastern
(Mari), and Permian. The Balto-Finnic languages are
subdivided into two groups: northern (Finnish, Izhora,
Karelian, Veps) and southern (Estonian, Vod, Liv). The
northern group is comprised of the Lapps (Saami). The
Mordvinian group is comprised of the Erzya and Moksh
Mordvinians. The eastern (Mari) group is comprised of
the Mari (for. des. Cheremiss). The Permian group is
comprised of Udmurt, Komi, and Komi Permyak (Permyak).
All of the Finnic peoples are represented in the USSR.

FINNO-UGORIAN PEOPLES   Alt. col. des. Finno-Ugrian
                         peoples. SEE Finno-Ugrian
                         Peoples.

FINNO-UGRIAN PEOPLES   Col. des. for the peoples of the
                        USSR   that   speak   languages
belonging to the Finno-Ugrian division of the Uralian
branch of the Uralo-Altaic language family. The Finno-
Ugrians are divided into two major groups (Finnic and
Ugrian). The Finnic languages are divided into five
groups: western (Balto-Finnic), northern (Lapp or
Saami), Mordvinian, eastern (Mari), and Permian. The
western group is subdivided into northern (Finnish,
Izhora, Karelian, and Veps) and southern (Estonian,
Vod, and Liv) groups. The northern group is comprised
of the Lapps (Saami).   The Mordvinian group is
comprised of the Erzya and Moksha Mordvinians. The
eastern group is comprised of the Mari (for. des.
Cheremiss). The southern group is comprised of the
Udmurts, Komi, and Komi Permyaks (Permyaks). The Ugrian
division   is divided into two groups: Ob-Ugrian
[comprised of the Khant(y) and Mansi] and the Magyar
(Hungarian). All Finno-Ugrian peoples are represented
in the USSR.

FIVE MOUNTAIN SOCIETIES OF   For. des. Balkars. SEE
         KABARDA   Balkar.

FIVE MOUNTAIN TATARS   For. des. Balkars. SEE Balkar.

FOREST CHEREMISS   Alt. des. Kozhla Mari. SEE Kozhla
                    Mari, Mari.

FOREST ENISEI SAMODI (SAMOED,   Alt.   des.   Karasa
        SAMOIED, SAMOYED)   Samoyed. SEE Karasa
                                   Samoyed, Ent.

FOREST ENISEY SAMODI (SAMOED,   Alt.   des.   Karasa
        SAMOIED, SAMOYED)   Samoyed. SEE Karasa
                                   Samoyed, Ent.

FOREST ENT (SY)   Alt. des. Karasa Samoyed. SEE Karasa
                   Samoyed, Ent.

FOREST IENISEI SAMODI (SAMOED,   Alt.   des.   Karasa
          SAMOIED, SAMOYED)   Samoyed. SEE Karasa
                                   Samoed, Ent.

FOREST IURAK   Alt. des. and spel. Forest Yurak; alt.
                des. Khandeyar. See Khandeyar, Nenets.

FOREST MARI   Alt. des. Kozhla Mari. SEE Kozhla Mari,
                Mari.

FOREST NENETS   Alt. des. Khandeyar. SEE Khandeyar,
                 Nenets.

FOREST YENISEI SAMODI (SAMOED,   Alt. des. Karasa
        SAMOIED, SAMOYED)   Samoyed. See Karasa
                                      Samoyed, Ent.

FOREST YENISEY SAMODI (SAMOED,   Alt. des. Karasa
        SAMOIED, SAMOYED)   Samoyed. SEE Karasa
                                      Samoyed. Ent.

FOREST YURAK   Alt. des. Khandeyar. SEE Khandeyar,
        Nenets.

FRONTIER KALMUK (KALMYK,   Alt. des. Teleut, SEE
        QALMUQ, QALMYQ)   Teleut, Altai.

G

GAGAUZ   Self des. Gagauz. ETHN: The origin of the
        Gagauz is still debated. Some ethnographers
maintain that they are Christianized (Eastern Orthodox)
and Bulgarianized Turks. Others maintain that they are
linguistically Turkicized Christian Bulgarians. Others,
that   the Gagauz were formed as a result of   a
combination of these two processes. The Gagauz migrated
to Bessarabia (Moldavia) in the late 18th-early 19th
cents. from Bulgaria. LANG: The Gagauz speak a dialect
of   Turkish that has many Slavic (in   particular
Bulgarian) additions. Turkish belongs to the Oguz
division of the Turkic branch of the Uralo-Altaic
language family. POP: 173,179 (1979); 156,606 (1970);
123,821 (1959; 844 (1926). In the inter-war period
Moldavia was   part of Romania, therefore, the 1926
population figures reflect only those living outside
Moldavia (primarily, in adjacent areas in the Ukraine).
The Gagauz are Eastern Orthodox in religion. They live,
primarily, in the southern part of the Moldavian SSR
and adjacent areas in the southwestern Ukrainian SSR.
SEE MAP 11.

GALCHA   The Galcha are a group of Mountain Tadzhiks
        of non-Iranian origin. They are the Tadzhiks
of the Darvaz and Karategin Mountains. Among them one
finds continuation of the ancient Iranian belief in the
worship of fire (from Zoroastrianism). SEE Tadzhik.

GALGAI   The Galgai are one of the two Veinakh clan
        federations that went into the formation of
the Ingush (the other- Feappi). The Galgai were a free

society (federation) of three western Chechen (Veinakh)
tribes living in the gorge of the Assa River. They and
the Feappi did not take part in the wars of the mid-
19th cent. against the Russians. They were thus united
by the Russians and called Ingush (after the village
Ongusht). SEE Ingush.

GALGAY   Alt. spel. Galgai. SEE Galgai, Ingush.

GAPUT   Oth. des. Gaputlin, Ghaput(lin), Khaput(lin).
           The Gaput are a sub-division of the Dzhek
people. They are the Dzhek who inhabit the village of
Gaput. They speak a variant of the Dzhek language. They
have been almost totally assimilated by the
Azerbaidzhans.   SEE   Dzhek,   Shahdag   Peoples,
Azerbaidzhan.

GAPUTLIN   Alt. des. Gaput. SEE Gaput, Dzhek, Shahdag
              Peoples, Azerbaidzhan.

GAZI KUMUK (KUMUKH,   Alt. des. Kazi Kumukh; for. alt.
   QUMUKH, QUMUQ)   des. Lak. SEE Kazi Kumukh, Lak.

GEK   Alt. spel. Dzhek. SEE Dzhek, Shahdag Peoples,
         Azerbaidzhan.

GEORGIAN   Self des. Kartveli; Rus. des. Gruzin;
              Turk. des. Gurcu; oth. des. Gruzian. ETHN:
The Georgians are descended from some of the earliest
inhabitants of the Caucasus Mountain region. The
Georgian nation was formed by the consolidation of a
large number of Kartvelian territorial groups. Each of
these was formerly considered a distinct ethnographic
group, speaking its own dialect of Georgian (all of
which are mutually intelligible). They were divided
into two groups: eastern (Kartli, Kakhetian, Meskhi,
Dzhavakhi, Ingilo, Tusha, Khevsur, Pshav, Mokhev, and
Mtuili) and western (Imereli, Racha, Lechkhum, Guri,
and Adzhar). The Georgian nation was formed by the
unification of these groups around the Kartli. In
addition to these, the Georgians are still in the
process of assimilating the culturally related
Mingrelians, Svanetians, and Laz, as well as many of
the Abkhaz, Ossetians, Kurds, Armenians, and Assyrians
living in Georgia. One group of Georgians (the Ingiloi,
who are Shiite Moslem in religion, and who inhabit
eastern Georgia on the border with Azerbaidzhan) is
also being assimilated by the Azerbaidzhans. LANG:
Georgian belongs to the southwestern branch of the
Caucasic language family. The Georgians had a written
language in pre-Christian times. Upon their conversion
to Christianity (Eastern Orthodoxy) they created a new
writing system (5-6th cents.). The modern Georgian
literary language is based on the Kartli dialect and
is written in the Georgian script. Georgian is the

literary language of the Georgians, Mingrelians,
Svanetians, Laz, and Adzhars. It is also used by many
of the South Ossetians, Abkhaz, Armenians, Assyrians,
Kurds, and others living in the Georgian SSR. POP:
3,570,504 (1979); 3,245,300 (1970); 2,691,950 (1959);
1,564,333 (1926). The population figures presented here
for the Georgians for 1926 do not include the Adzhars,
Laz, Svanetians, and Mingrelians. All of these peoples
were considered distinct ethnic groups at that time,
and were listed separately. Their population together
with the Georgians in 1926 was 1,821,184. The Georgians
are diverse in their religious adherence. The majority
of Georgians are Eastern Orthodox in religion. There is
also a Shiite Moslem group (Ingiloi), a Sunni Moslem
group (Adzhar), Animists (Khevsur and Pshav), and some
Uniates. Although the Georgian Jews are basically
Georgians of the Judaic faith, they are officially
designated as Jews rather than as Georgians. Most
Georgian Jews consider themselves Georgians and their
native language Georgian. A group of Turkified
Georgians from the province of Meskhetia, near the
Turkish border (the Meskhetians), were deported to
Central Asia in 1944. They have subsequently been
reclassified as Turks and Azerbaidzhans and have not
been permitted to return to Georgia, or to classify
themselves as Georgians. The Georgians live primarily
in the Georgian SSR. Of all the major nationalities of
the USSR, the Georgians have the lowest rate for
members of an ethnic group leaving their home
territory. SEE MAP 2.

GEORGIAN JEW The origin of the Georgian Jews is
still debated. Some claim they are
immigrants to Georgia from other areas of the Caucasus
and Iran, while others that they are Georgians who
adopted the Jewish faith under the influence of the
Khazars sometime between the 8th and 12th cents. In
either case, the Georgian Jews consider themselves to
be Georgians, and Georgian is their native language.
Unlike most other Judaic groups the Georgian Jews do
not use the Hebrew alphabet to write their native
Georgian language; however, Hebrew continues to serve
as the language of their sacred texts. Until the 1930s
the Georgian Jews were classified as a distinct ethnic
group. Since that time they have been reclassified as
Jews. Their population in 1926 was 21,471. There has
been a substantial emigration of Georgian Jews to
Israel since the 1970s. SEE Georgian, Jew.

GERMAN Self des. Deutsch; Rus. des. Nemets (pl.
Nemtsy). ETHN: The Germans of the USSR are
the descendants of Germans who migrated to various
parts of what is today the USSR. The first migration
was in the 13th cent. under the influence of the
Teutonic Knights (Crusaders). They established

themselves along the Baltic coast from Germany to the
Gulf of Finland in Estonia. The second major migration
was in the 18th century under the influence of
Catherine the Great who invited Germans to come to
Russia. These Germans settled, primarily, in the
Ukraine and Volga regions, and some in Bessarabia.
During World War II the vast majority of Baltic Germans
opted to leave and retreat with the German armies (i.e.
the survivors of the War itself). The Volga Germans
were deported en masse to southwestern Siberia and
northern Kazakhstan at the onset of the war. During and
after the war the Ukrainian and Bessarabian Germans
were either killed, evacuated (or deported) eastward to
southwestern Siberia and northern Kazakhstan, or
retreated with the German armies to Germany. LANG: The
Germans of the USSR speak dialects of German with many
Slavic intrusions, and used the German literary
language. German was the official language of the
German ASSR in the Volga region until it was
disestablished in 1939. All German schools in the USSR
were closed during the war and none have as yet been
reopened. Although some publication in German has now
been resumed by the Soviet Germans it is limited.
Russian serves as the literary language of the Soviet
Germans. POP: 1,936,214 (1979); 1,846,317 (1970);
1,619,655 (1959); 1,238,549 (1926). The Germans of the
USSR are predominantly Lutheran or Mennonite in
religion. They now live, primarily, in the cities of
northern Kazakhstan and southwestern Siberia. Since the
mid 1970s there has been a steady emigration of Germans
to West Germany. SEE MAP 13.

GERMAN OF THE BALTICS   Alt. des. Baltic German. SEE
                          Baltic German, German.

GERMAN OF BESSARABIA   Alt. des. Bessarabian German.
                          SEE Bessarabian German, German.

GERMAN OF THE UKRAINE   Alt. des. Ukrainian German.
                          SEE Ukrainian German, German.

GERMAN OF THE VOLGA   Alt. des. Volga German. SEE
                          Volga German, German.

GHAPUT (GHAPTULIN)   Alt. des. Gaput. SEE Gaput,
                          Dzhek, Shahdag Peoples,
                          Azerbaidzhan.

GHAZI KUMUK (KUMUKH,   Alt. des. Kazi Kumukh; for.
     QUMUKH, QUMUQ)   alt. des. Lak. SEE Kazi
                          Kumukh, Lak.

GILIAK   Alt. spel. Gilyak; for. des. of Nivkhi. SEE
           Nivkhi.

GILYAK   For. des. of Nivkhi. SEE Nivkhi.

GINUG   No self des.;   Rus. des. Ginukh, oth. des.
         Ginugh. ETHN: Until the early 1930s the
Ginug, as well as the other Andi-Dido peoples, were
considered distinct ethnic groups. Since that time they
have been classified as Avars. LANG: The Ginug language
belongs to the Dido group of the Avaro-Andi-Dido
division of the northeast branch of the Caucasic
language family. Until the 1930s the Ginug language
was considered a distinct language. Since that time
it has been classified as a dialect of Avar. The Ginug
language is not written and Avar serves as the literary
language of the Ginug. POP: The Ginug have never
appeared in any census of the USSR. The Ginug are Sunni
Moslem in religion. They, like the other Andi-Dido
peoples are being assimilated by the Avars. They live,
primarily, in the highest and most inaccessible part of
southwestern Dagestan near the Georgian border. In 1944
the majority of Ginug moved to the village Kidero in
Vedeno Rayon, in Dagestan. SEE Andi-Dido Peoples, Avar.

GINUGH (GINUKH)   Alt. des. Ginug. SEE Ginug, Andi-
                   Dido Peoples, Avar.

GLAZOV (SKIY) TATAR   Like the Kara Tatars the Glazov
                       Tatars are an isolated group
of Tatars of   Volga Bulgar descent living on the
Cheptsa River (a tributary of the Vyatka), in the
Middle Volga region. SEE Tatar.

GODOBERI   Self des.   Ghibditli;   Rus.   des.
            Godoberin(tsy). ETHN: Until the early
1930s, the Godoberi, as well as the other Andi-Dido
peoples, were considered distinct ethnic groups. Since
that time they have been classified as Avars. LANG:
The Godoberi language belongs to the Andi group of the
Avaro-Andi-Dido division of the northeast branch of the
Caucasic language family. Until the 1930s the Godoberi
language was considered a distinct language. Since that
time it has been classified as a dialect of Avar. The
Godoberi language is not written and Avar serves as the
literary language of the Godoberi. POP: 1,425 (1926).
The Godoberi are Sunni Moslem in religion. They, like
the other Andi-Dido peoples, are being assimilated by
the Avars. They live, primarily, in highland west
central Dagestan. SEE Andi-Dido Peoples, Avar.

GÖKLEN   Self des. Göklen. One of the ten major
          tribal-territorial divisions of the Turkmen.
In the pre-Soviet period they were each considered
distinct peoples. The Göklen speak a distinct dialect
(Göklen) of Turkmen. They live, primarily, in far
western Turkmenistan along the Caspian coast. SEE
Turkmen.

GOLD (I)   Alt. des. Nanai. SEE Nanai.

GOLEND   (RY)   Alt.   des.   Golyad.   SEE   Golyad,
Belorussian.

GOLIAD (GOLJAD) (Y)   Alt. spel. Golyad. SEE Golyad,
Belorussian.

GOLYAD   (Y)   The Golyad are the descendants of a
Baltic   tribe   (Galinds)   who   were
assimilated by the Belorussians (in Brest and Grodno
Guberniyas) and Ukrainians (in Volynia). They lived
along the Ugra and Protva rivers. There were still
individuals who referred to themselves as Golyad in the
19th cent. SEE Belorussian, Ukrainian.

GORNO-BADAGHSHANI   Alt.   spel. Gorno-Badagshani; alt.
des.   Pamir Peoples. SEE Pamir
Peoples, Tadzhik.

GORNO-BADAGSHANI   Alt. des. Pamir Peoples. SEE Pamir
Peoples, Tadzhik.

GORNO-BADAHSHANI   Alt. spel. Gorno-Badagshani; alt.
(BADAKHSHANI)   des.   Pamir Peoples. SEE Pamir
Peoples, Tadzhik.

GORETS (GORTSY)   Rus. des. Caucasian Mountaineers.
SEE Caucasian Mountaineers.

GORNY(Y) KALMUK   Alt. des. Gornyy Kalmyk; alt. des.
Biy Kalmyk. SEE Biy Kalmyk, Altai.

GORNY(Y) KALMYK   Eng. des. Mountain Kalmyk; for. Rus.
alt. des. Biy Kalmyk. SEE Kalmyk,
Altai.

GORNY(Y) SHOR   Eng. des. Mountain Shor; alt. Rus.
des. Shor. SEE Shor.

GORNY(Y) TADJIK   Alt. spel. Gornyy Tadzhik; alt. des.
Mountain   Tadzhik.   SEE   Mountain
Tadzhik, Tadzhik.

GORNY(Y) TADZHIK   Eng. des. Mountain Tadzhik; Rus.
des. Mountain Tadzhik. SEE Mountain
Tadzhik, Tadzhik.

GORNY(Y) TAJIK   Alt. spel. Gornyy Tadzhik; alt des.
Mountain   Tadzhik.   SEE   Mountain
Tadzhik, Tadzhik.

GORNY(Y) TATAR   Eng. des. Mountain Tatar; for. Rus.
des. of Balkar. SEE Balkar.

GORSKIY EVREI Rus. des. Mountain Jew. SEE Mountain Jew, Jew.

GORSKIY EVREY (IEVREI, Alt. spel. Gorskiy Evrei; Rus. YEVREI, YEVREY) des. Mountain Jew. SEE Mountain Jew, Jew.

GREAT RUSSIAN Alt. des. Russian. SEE Russian.

GREEK Self des. Romeos (less frequently Grekos or Ellinos), or Urum (for Turkish, rather than Greek speakers). The Greeks migrated to Georgia and the Black Sea littoral in the North Caucasus and the Ukraine, in the 19th cent. They are divided into two groups: those who retained the Greek language (Romeos) and those that did not (Urum). The Greeks of the USSR use local languages (Georgian, Ukrainian, and/or Russian) as their literary language. POP: 343,809 (1979); 336,869 (1970); 309,308 (1959); 213,765 (1926). The Greeks of the USSR are Eastern Orthodox in religion. They live, primarily, in scattered settlements on the Black Sea littoral concentrated primarily in Georgia, Krasnodar Krai (in the North Caucasus), and the Crimea. SEE MAP 10.

GRUZIN (GRUZIAN) Rus. and oth. des. Georgian. SEE Georgian.

GRUZINSKIY EVREI Rus. des. Georgian Jew. SEE Georgian Jew, Jew.

GRUZINSKIY EVREY (IEVREI, Alt. spel. Gruzinskiy Evrei; YEVREI, YEVREY) Rus. des. Georgian Jew. SEE Georgian Jew, Jew.

GUDAUT A sub-group of the Bzyb (Abkhaz). They live in the northern part of Abkhazia. They form with the Bzyb the northern group of the Abkhaz. They speak the Bzyb dialect of Abkhaz. SEE Bzyb, Abkhaz.

GUDAUTI (GUDAUTY) Alt. des. Gudaut. SEE Gudaut, Bzyb, Abkhaz.

GUNZEB (GUNZIB) Alt. des. Khunzal. SEE Khunzal, Andi-Dido Peoples, Avar.

GURI (AN) Self des. Guruli. One of the numerous Kartvelian ethnographic groups that went into the formation of the Georgian nationality. The Gurians speak a distinct dialect of Georgian. The majority of Gurians are Eastern Orthodox in religion. They live, primarily, south of the lower Rioni River, as far west as the Black Sea between Poti and Kobuleti. SEE Georgian.

GUTSUL   Rus. des. Hutsul. SEE Hutsul, Carpatho-Rusin,
             Ukrainian.

GYPSY   Self des. Rom (Lom); Rus. and oth. des.
             Tsygan. ETHN: The Gypsies of the USSR
are the descendants of nomads who came originally
from northern India. Although officially all Gypsies
are now settled, many groups are semi-nomadic. Among
the Gypsies the relevant divisions were (and to a great
extent are) clan or tribal-territorial or cultural-
historical occupational groupings. In addition to the
Gypsies proper, two distinct Gypsy groups live in the
USSR: the Bosha (Armenian speaking Gypsies of Armenia)
and the Central Asian Gypsies (Tadzhik speaking Gypsies
of Central Asia). Although officially the Central Asian
Gypsies no longer speak Romany (the Hindic Gypsy
language) and have adopted Tadzhik as their native
language, there is much evidence to show that Romany is
still widely used by many of these Gypsies. LANG: The
Romany (Gypsy) language is distantly related to Hindi
and other Indic languages. In the USSR many dialects of
Romany are spoken. The Gypsies usually speak Romany
plus the language of the territory in which they
reside. An attempt was made to create a literary Romany
language in 1926. This language was based on the Moscow
dialect of the Russian Gypsies using the Cyrillic
script. Although some individual works have
subsequently been published the Romany literary
language was officially dropped in the late 1930s. POP:
209,159 (1979); 175,335 (1970); 132,014 (1959); 61,234
(1926). The official Gypsy population has continuously
fluctuated as Gypsies will frequently espouse the
"local" nationality as their own to non-Gypsies. In
addition, the Gypsy population was sharply decreased by
the Nazis as a result of their extermination policy
aimed at the Gypsies during World War II. Gypsies
customarily claim the religion of the people among whom
they reside, but in general the Gypsies have their own
beliefs to which they add elements of the religions of
the local people. They live scattered thoughout the
USSR, with concentrations in the major cities.

GYPSY OF CENTRAL ASIA   Alt. des. Central Asian Gypsy.
                           SEE Central Asian Gypsy, Gypsy.

H

HAIDAK (HAIDAQ, HAITAK,   Alt. spel. Khaitak; alt. des.
        HAITAQ)   Kaitak. SEE Katiak, Dargin.

HAKASS   Alt. spel. Khakass. SEE Khakass.

HALHA (MONGOL)   Alt. spel. and des. Khalkha-Mongol.
        SEE Khalkha Mongol.

HANSU   Alt. des. Hansu Dungan. SEE Hansu Dungan,
        Dungan.

HANSU DUNGAN   Rus. des. Khansui(tsy). One of the two
        divisions of the Dungans of the USSR.
These   divisions are based on the province of origin
and the dialect of Chinese spoken by them. The Hansu
Dungans came originally from Hansu province in China
and speak the Hansu dialect of Chinese. The other group
are   the Shensi-Dungans who originated in   Shensi
province and speak the Shensi dialect. The Dungans are
Sunni Moslem in religion. The Hansu-Dungans live,
primarily, in Osh Oblast in the Kirgiz SSR. SEE Dungan.

HANSUI (HANSUY)   Alt. des. Hansu Dungan. SEE Hansu
        Dungan, Dungan.

HANT(E)   Alt. des. Khant(y). SEE Khant.

HANTAIKA (SAMODI,   SAMOED,   Alt. spel. Khantaika
      SAMOIED, SAMOYED)   Samoyed. SEE Khantaika
                         Samoyed, Ent.

HANTAYKA (SAMODI,   SAMOED,   Alt. spel. Khantaika
      SAMOIED, SAMOYED)   Samoyed. SEE Khantaika
                         Samoyed, Ent.

HAPUT (LIN)   Alt. spel. and des. Gaput. SEE Gaput,
        Shahdag Peoples, Azerbaidzhan.

HAQASS   Alt. spel. Khakass. SEE Khakass.

HARDURI   Alt. spel. Kharduri. SEE Kharduri, Tadzhik.

HATUKAI (HATUKAY,   HATUQAI,   Alt. spel. Khatukai. SEE
                    HATUQAY)   Khatukai, Adygei,
                                 Circassian.

HAYDAK (HAYDAQ, HAYTAK,   Alt. spel. Khaitak; alt. des.
        HAYTAQ)   Kaitak. SEE Kaitak, Dargin.

HAZARA   Alt. spel. Khazara. SEE Khazara, Tadzhik.

HEMSHIL (HEMSHIN)   Alt. spel. and des. Khemshil. SEE
                      Khemshil, Armenian,   Meskhetian,
                      Azerbaidzhan.

HEMŞIL (I)   Turk. spel. Khemshil. SEE Khemshil,
                 Armenian, Meskhetian, Azerbaidzhan.

HEVSUR   Alt. spel. Khevsur. SEE Khevsur, Georgian.

HINALUG (HINALUGH,   Alt. spel. and des. Khinalug. SEE
         HINALUKH)   Khinalug, Shahdag Peoples,
                       Azerbaidzhan.

HITRI   Alt. spel. Khitri. SEE Khitri, Chuvash.

HIURKILI   Alt. spel. Khürkili. SEE Khürkili, Dargin.

HOLAM (CHI)(CHILI)(LI)   Alt. spel. and des. Kholam.
      (CHY)(CHYLY)(LY)   SEE Kholam, Balkar.

HONGODOR   Alt.   spel.   Khongodor. SEE Khongodor,
             Buryat.

HORA (HORIN)   Alt. spel. and des. Khorin. SEE Khorin,
                 Buryat.

HORVAT   Alt. spel. Khorvat. SEE Khorvat, Ukrainian.

HOSHEUT   Alt. spel. Khosheut. SEE Khosheut, Kalmyk.

HUF (HUFIDJ, HUFIDZH,   Alt. spel. Khuf. SEE   Khuf,
     HUFIJ)   Rushan, Pamir Peoples, Tadzhik.

HULAM (CHI)(CHILI)(LI)   Alt. spel. and des. Kholam.
      (CHY)(CHYLY)(LY)   SEE Kholam, Balkar.

HUNGARIAN   Self des. Magyar; Rus. des. Vengry
              (Vengertsy). ETHN: A relatively small
group of Hungarians became part of the USSR after World
War II with the incorporation of territories (Ruthenia)
taken from Czechoslovakia [now called Zakarpatskaya
(Transcarpathian) Oblast]. A significant part of the
Hungarian population of this territory, however, are
actually Magyarized Ukrainians and Slovaks in origin.
LANG: Hungarian belongs to the Magyar group of the
Ugrian division of the Uralian branch of the Uralo-

Altaic language family. The Hungarians use the
Hungarian literary language which is written in the
Latin script. POP: 170,553 (1979); 166,451 (1970);
154,738 (1959); 5,476 (1926). Most Hungarians of the
USSR are, or were, primarily Uniate or Catholic in
religion. They live, primarily, in Zakarpatskaya Oblast
and adjacent areas in the western Ukraine.

HUNZAL   Alt. spel. Khunzal. SEE Khunzal, Andi-Dido
          Peoples, Avar.

HURKILI (HURKILI)   Alt. spel. Khürkili. SEE Khürkili,
                     Dargin.

HUTSUL   Self des. Hutsuly; Rus. des. Gutsul. The
          Hutsuls form a distinct ethnographic group of
Ukrainians. They are one of the three ethnographic
groups of western Ukrainians collectively called
Carpatho-Rusin (Hutsul, Boiki, Lemky). They share
numerous cultural similarities with Moldavians,
Rumanians, and Slovaks. Formerly they were mixed Uniate
and Eastern Orthodox in religion. Since the
incorporation of their territory into the USSR
(Transcarpathia and Bukovina) after World War II, the
Uniate Church was abolished and incorporated into the
Orthodox one. All Hutsuls of the USSR are now
officially Eastern Orthodox in religion. They live,
primarily, in the mountainous parts of Ivano-Frankovsk,
Chernovits, and Zakarpatskaya Oblasts in the western
Ukraine. SEE Carpatho-Rusin, Ukrainian.

HVARSHI (N)   Alt. des. Khwarshi. SEE Khwarshi, Andi-
               Dido Peoples, Avar.

HWARSHI (N)   Alt. spel. and des. Khwarshi. SEE
               Khwarshi, Andi-Dido Peoples, Avar.

HYURKILI   Alt. spel. Khürkili. SEE Khürkili, Dargin.

I

IAGE (DUNGAN)   Alt. des. and spel. Yage-Dungan. SEE
                 Yage-Dungan, Dungan.

IAGNOB   Alt. spel. Yagnob. SEE Yagnob, Tadzhik.

IAKUT   Alt. spel. Yakut. SEE Yakut.

IAKUTIANE   Alt.   spel.   Yakutyane.   SEE   Yakutyane,
Russian.

IARA (IARIN)   Alt. spel. and des.   Yara.   SEE Yara,
Kacha, Khakass.

IARKENLIK   (IARKENDLIK)   Alt.   des.   and   spel.
Yarkendlik. SEE Yarkendlik,
Uigur.

IASTA (IASTIN)   Alt. spel. and des. Yasta. SEE Yasta,
Kacha, Khakass.

IATVIAG (IATVIG,   IATVIGIAN,   Alt. des. and spel.
IATVING,   IATVINGIAN)   Yatvig. SEE Yatvig,
Belorussian.

IAZGUL (IAZGULEM, IAZGULIAM)   Alt. spel. Yazgul. SEE
Yazgul, Pamir Peoples,
Tadzhik.

IAZVA (KOMI PERMIAK, ZIRIAN,   Alt. spel. and des.
ZYRIAN, ZYRYAN)   Yazva. SEE Yazva, Komi
Permyak.

IAZVIN (SKY) (KOMI PERMIAK,   Alt. des. Yazva. SEE
ZIRIAN, ZYRIAN, ZYRYAN)   Yazva, Komi Permyak.

ICHKILIK   Self des.   Ichkilik;   oth. des.   Pamir-Alai
Kirgiz. The exact origin of the Ichkilik is
not known other than that they are not of direct Kirgiz
origin. The members of this group of tribes call
themselves collectively Ichkilik. They also maintain
their tribal names and divisions [Kypchak, Naiman,
Teüt, Kesek, Zhoo Kesek, Kangdy, Boston, Noigut, Avagat
(Avgat), and Töölös (Döölös)]. They are mainly Yak
breeders. The Ichkilik, live, primarily, in the Pamir-
Alai Mountains of southwestern Kirgizia. SEE Kirgiz.

IDERA (IDERIN)   Alt. des. Tindi. SEE Tindi, Andi-
Dido Peoples, Avar.

IENISEI (OSTIAK)   Alt. des. and spel. Yenisei Ostyak;
for. des. Ket. SEE Ket.

IENISEI SAMODI (SAMOED,   Alt. des. and spel. Yenisei
SAMOIED, SAMOYED)   Samoyed; for. des. Ent. SEE
Ent.

IENISEI TATAR   Alt. spel. Yenisei Tatar; for. des.
Khakass. SEE Khakass.

IEZID   Alt. spel. Yezid. SEE Yezid, Kurd.

IMERELI (AN)   Self des. Imereli; oth. des. Imeretian.
One of the numerous Kartvelian
ethnographic groups that went into the formation of the
Georgian nationality. They speak a distinct (Imereli)
dialect of Georgian. They are Eastern Orthodox in
religion. They live, primarily, between the main
Caucasian chain, the Suram and Adzharo-Akhaltsikh
ranges, and the Tskhenis-Tskali River in the Georgian
SSR. SEE Georgian.

IMERETIAN   Alt. des. Imereli. SEE Imereli, Georgian.

INBAK   For. des. of the Kets who lived on the
Yelogui River. SEE Ket.

INGERMANLAND (IAN)   1-Alt. des. Finns of Leningrad
Oblast. SEE Finns of Leningrad
Oblast, Finns.
2-Alt. des. Izhora. SEE Izhora.

INGILOI   Self des. Ingiloi; oth. des. Inkiloi. One
of the numerous ethnographic groups that
went into the formation of the Georgians. They speak a
distinct dialect of Georgian that also contains many
Azeri words. The Ingiloi are also culturally distinct
from the majority of Georgians in that they are Shiite
Moslem in religion and have been under strong
Azerbaidzhan influence. The Ingiloi are being
assimilated by the Azerbaidzhans. They live, primarily,
between the Alazani River and the main Caucasian chain
in eastern Georgia near the border of Azerbaidzhan. SEE
Georgian, Azerbaidzhan.

INGILOY   Alt. spel. Ingiloi. SEE Ingiloi, Georgian,
Azerbaidzhan.

INGRIAN   Alt. des. Izhora. SEE Izhora.

INGUSH   Self des. Nakhchuo, Galgai, Lamur
(Mountaineer); for. des. Kist. ETHN: The
Ingush are the western Nakh (Veinakh) tribes. The
status of Ingush and Chechen as distinct peoples and
languages is still debated. Both refer to themselves
and each other as Nakhchuo and consider themselves one
Nakh people who speak dialects of one Nakh language.
The Ingush are considered by many to be western
Chechens. The division of the Ingush and Chechens dates
back only to the 1860s when the two western clan
federations of the Chechens (Galgai and Feappi) did not
take part in the wars against the Russians. At that
time the Russians began to distinguish between the
eastern (i.e., hostile) and western (non-hostile)
Chechens. The eastern tribes were designated Chechen
(after the village Chechen) and the western tribes
either Ingush (after the village Ongusht) or Kist

[after the Kist (Galgai) federation]. LANG: Ingush forms with Chechen the Veinakh division of the northeast branch of the Caucasic language family. The Ingush and Chechen languages are mutually intelligible and are considered by many linguists to be closely related dialects of one language. The Ingush language is comprised of two closely related dialects: lowland and Galanchozh. The lowland dialect is spoken by the Feappi and the Galanchozh dialect by the Galgai (each of the three tribes having its own sub-dialect). The Ingush literary language was established in 1923 on the basis of the lowland dialect. It was originally written in the Latin script and was changed in 1938 to the Cyrillic. POP: 186,198 (1979); 157,605 (1970); 105,980 (1959); 74,097 (1926). The Ingush were deported to northern Kazakhstan in 1944 where they remained until the late 1950s when the survivors were permitted to return to the North Caucasus region. During that period the Ingush suffered great population losses. The Ingush are Sunni Moslem in religion. They lived, primarily, in the mountainous regions of Ingushetia (the western part of the Chechen-Ingush ASSR), but since their return they have been resettled in the foothills and plains areas. Many also live in the adjacent area in the North Ossetian ASSR as part of the Ingush territory was transferred to North Ossetia in 1944 and was not subsequently returned to the jurisdiction of the Chechen-Ingush ASSR. SEE Chechen. SEE MAP 11.

INKAROISET (INKERI,   INKERIKOT,   Alt. des. Izhora. SEE
           INKEROISET)   Izhora.

INKILOI (INKILOY)   Alt. spel. Ingiloi. SEE Ingiloi,
                      Georgian, Azerbaidzhan.

IOMUD (IOMUT)   Alt. des. and spel. Yomud. SEE Yomud,
                  Turkmen.

IR   Alt. des. Iron. SEE Iron, Ossetian.

IRON (TSY)   1-Self des. Iron. The Iron are the
               Ossetians who live on the northern slopes of the Caucasus Mountains (in what is now the North Ossetian ASSR) and who are Eastern Orthodox in religion. The Moslem North Ossetians are called Digor. SEE Digor. The Iron speak one of the three dialects of Ossetian, and the Iron dialect forms the basis of the Ossetian literary language. Until 1939 both Iron and Digor had separate literary languages (in that year Digor was abolished). The Iron live, primarily, in the central and eastern thirds of the North Ossetian ASSR in the cental North Caucasus. SEE Ossetian.
               2-For. alt. des. Ossetian. SEE Ossetian.

IRTISH (IRTYSH) TATAR   Alt. des. Tara Tatar. SEE Tara
                         Tatar, West Siberian Tatar,
                         Tatar.

ISHKASHIM   Self des. Shikoshumi. The Ishkashim are
             one of the six distinct Pamir peoples.
They are Ismaili Moslem in religion and live in the
village of Ryn in Ishkashim Rayon in southeastern
Tadzhikistan (Gorno-Badakhshan AO). SEE Pamir Peoples,
Tadzhik.

ITELMEN   Self des. Itel'men; oth. des. Kamchadal.
           ETHN: The Itelmen were a predominantly
settled fishing, hunting, and gathering people who are
ethnically and linguistically closely related to the
Chukchi and Koryak. In the 18th cent. the Itelmen were
found throughout Kamchatka, the Kurile Islands and on
Cape Lopatka. Those of the Kurile Islands and Cape
Lopatka were assimilated with the Ainu and are called
Near Kurilians. The Itelmen were historically divided
by language and culture into northern, southern and
western groups. Two sub-dialects of western Itelmen
survive to the present (Sedanka and Khairyuzovo), both
of which have been strongly influenced by Koryak and
Russian. Epidemics in the 18th-19th cents. severely
decreased the Itelmen population. The survivors mixed
with local Russian settlers (many Russians taking
Itelmen wives). The term Itelmen has come to refer
exclusively to the few relatively pure Itelmen
survivors. Those who have a strong Russian admixture,
or who are predominantly Russian, are called Kamchadal.
The terms Itelmen and Kamchadal have been frequently
confused. LANG: The Itelmen language is closely related
to, and mutually intelligible with both Chukchi and
Koryak. These three languages form the Chukotic
(Chukotan) languages, which have been classified as
Paleoasiatic. Itelmen is not a written language, and
Russian serves as the literary language of the Itelmen.
Most Itelmen are at least bilingual (Itelmen and
Russian) or speak only Russian. In 1979 roughly three
fourths of the Itelmen were listed as Russian
speakers, and only one fourth Itelmen. POP: 1,307
(1979); 1,301 (1970); 1,109 (1959); 4,217 (1926). The
Itelmen are shamanist-animist (the same as the Chukchi
and Koryak) in religion. All but a few villages of
Itelmen have completely merged with the Russians. They
live, primarily, on the Kamchatka Peninsula in the
Koryak AO in far eastern Siberia. SEE Kamchadal,
Paleoasiatic Peoples, MAP 8.

ITKAN (TSY)   One of the nine territorial groups of
               Koryaks. They live, primarily, on the
east coast of the Taigonos Peninsula in the Koryak AO
in far eastern Siberia. SEE Koryak.

IUGO OSET (IN)   Rus. des. of Tual (South Ossetian).
                  SEE Tual, Ossetian.

IUGRI (AN)   Alt. spel. Yugri; Rus. des. Ugrian
                  peoples. SEE Ugrian Peoples, Finno-
                  Ugrian Peoples.

IUIT (IUITI, IUITY)   Alt. spel. Yuit(y); alt. des.
                       Eskimo. SEE Eskimo.

IUKAGHIR (IUKAGIR)   Alt. spel. Yukagir. SEE Yukagir.

IURAK (SAMODI, SAMOED,   Alt. spel. and des. Yurak;
     SAMOIED, SAMOYED)   for. des. Nenets. SEE Nenets.

IZHEM (TSY)   Alt. des. Izhmi. SEE Izhmi, Komi.

IZHMI   Self des. Izva Tas (people of Izhma); oth.
         des. Izhem(tsy), Izhmy. The Izhmi are a group
of Komi who live between the Pechora and Izhma Rivers,
and who form a distinct ethnic group of Komi. About
10,000 Izhmi live in the Yamalo-Nenets AO and Tyumen
Oblast. They speak a distinct dialect of Komi, albeit
they use the Komi literary language. SEE Komi.

IZHMY   Alt. spel. Izhmi. SEE Izhmi, Komi.

IZHOR   Alt. des. Izhora. SEE Izhora.

IZHORA   Self des. Karjala or Karjalainen (Karyala or
          Karyalainen); oth. self des. Inkaroiset,
Inkeroiset, or Inkerikot; oth. des. Ingrian, Inkeri,
Ingermanlandian. ETHN: The Izhora are the descendants of
a group of Karelians who moved south into the lands
along the Izhora River in the 11th-12th cents. By the
20th cent. the majority of Izhora no longer referred to
themselves as Karelians. The term Izhora has come into
use only recently. They, like the Vod live among
Russians and are being assimilated by them. The lands
inhabited by the Izhora are also called Ingermanland,
hence the ethnonym Ingermanlandian. LANG: The Izhora
language belongs, along with Finnish, Karelian, and
Veps, to the northern sub-group of the Balto-Finnic
group of the Finnic division of the Uralian branch of
the Uralo-Altaic language family. An attempt was made
shortly after the revolution to create an Izhora
literary language. It was, however, discontinued within
a few years and Russian serves as the literary language
of the Izhora. POP: 748 (1979); 781 (1970); 1,062
(1959); 16,137 (1926); 21,700 (1897). The rapid decline
in the Izhora population is due, primarily, to
assimilation by the Russians, and to a much lesser
extent to a minor emigration to Finland and Karelia in
the inter- and post-War period. The Izhora are Eastern
Orthodox in religion, and should not be confused with

the later Finnish immigrants (Finns of Leningrad
Oblast) to this region, who came in the 17th cent. and
who are Lutheran in religion. The Izhora were the
numerically smallest group listed in the 1979 census.
They live, primarily, near the Izhora River.

J

JATVIG (IAN)   Alt. spel. and des. Yatvig. SEE Yatvig,
                  Belorussian.

JATVING (IAN)   Alt. spel. Yatving; alt. des. Yatvig.
                  SEE Yatvig, Belorussian.

JATVJAG   Alt. spel. Yatvyag; alt. des. Yatvig. SEE
             Yatvig, Belorussian.

JEK   Alt. spel. Dzhek. SEE Dzhek, Shahdag Peoples,
         Azerbaidzhan.

JEMSHID   Alt. spel. Dzhemshid. SEE Dzhemshid, Tadzhik.

JEW   1-Col. des. of all of the peoples of the USSR
         who are of the Jewish religion [Ashkenazic
(Yiddish speaking or Eastern European Jews); Krymchak
(Crimean Tatar speaking Jews); Mountain (Dagestani,
Tati) (Tat speaking Jews); Georgian (Georgian speaking
Jews); and Central Asian (Bukharan)(Tadzhik speaking
Jews)]. Rus. des. Evrei. These peoples are of varied
backgrounds, are ethnically distinct, and were
considered distinct ethnic groups in the USSR until
around World War II. Each was listed separately in the
1926 census. The Karaim (Karaite) Jews have always been
listed separately and are still considered a distinct
ethnic group. Hebrew was the written religious language
of all Jews of the Russian Empire, regardless of ethnic
or linguistic background. SEE Central Asian Jew,
Georgian Jew, Krymchak, Mountain Jew.
         2-Self des. Yid (pl. Yidden); Rus. des. Yevrei;
         for. Rus. des. Zhid (now pejorative); oth. des.
Ashkenazic Jew (pl. Ashkenazim), East European Jew.
ETHN: Jews first came to the Russian territories in
about the 10th cent. (to Kievan Rus), settling in and
around Kiev, in the Khazar controlled areas, and on the
Crimea. The vast majority of Jews, however, became part
of Russia in the 18th cent. when the territories in
which they lived (Poland-Lithuania) were incorporated

into the Russian Empire. LANG: Yiddish belongs to the
German group of the Germanic languages. It is close in
vocabulary and structure to German. In the USSR itself,
Yiddish is divided into three closely related dialects:
Litvak (spoken in the Baltic region and Belorussia),
Ukrainian (spoken in most of the Ukraine), and Galician
(spoken in the Galician provinces of the western
Ukraine and northern Moldavia). The Yiddish literary
language is based on the Litvak dialect and uses the
Hebrew script. Yiddish became a literary language in
the mid-late 19th cent. reached its literary zenith
between the two World Wars, and has been declining ever
since (both in the USSR and elsewhere). POP: 1,810,876
(1979); 2,150,707 (1970); 2,267,814 (1959); 2,599,973
(only Ashkenazim) (1926). The Jewish population of the
USSR has been steadily declining since the turn of the
century, when a great exodus of Jews began to the
United States and other Western countries. The
population under Soviet rule was sharply decreased as a
result of the creation of independent Polish,
Lithuanian, and Latvian states, and the incorporation
of the western parts of the Ukraine and Belorussia into
Poland and of Bessarabia (Moldavia) into Romania. The
Jewish population was decimated during World War II,
and this was followed by another exodus (this time
primarily to Israel, and to a lesser extent to western
countries). In the 1970s the Soviets began to allow yet
another wave of emigration. The bulk of these Jews have
gone to the United States, and to a lesser extent to
Israel and other Western states. In addition to these
processes, the Jews have been declining in population
as a result of an extremely low birth rate (below zero
population growth), and through intermarriage and
assimilation (mainly with Russians, and to a lesser
extent Ukrainians, Belorussians, and others). The Jews
are Jewish in religion. They live primarily in the main
cities of the western part of the USSR. The largest
concentrations are in Moscow (roughly one fourth of all
Soviet Jews), Leningrad, Kiev, and Minsk. SEE MAP 15.

JEW OF BUKHARA   Alt. des. Central Asian Jew. SEE
                    Central Asian Jew, Jew.

JEW OF THE CAUCASUS   Alt. des. Mountain Jew. SEE
                    Mountain Jew, Jew.

JEW OF CENTRAL ASIA   Alt. des. Central Asian Jew. SEE
                    Central Asian Jew, Jew.

JEW OF THE CRIMEA   Alt. des. Krymchak. SEE Krymchak,
                    Jew.

JEW OF DAGESTAN (DAGHESTAN)   Alt. des. Mountain Jew.
                    SEE Mountain Jew. Jew.

JEW OF GEORGIA   Alt. des. Georgian Jew. SEE Georgian
Jew, Jew.

JUNGAR (IAN)   Alt. spel. and des. Dzhungar (ian); alt.
des. Oirot. SEE Oirot, Mongol.

K

KABARD   Self des.   Adyge, K'eberdei; oth. des.
Kabardin, Kabardinian, Kabartai. ETHN: In
the pre-Soviet period the Kabard were considered, along
with the Adygei and Cherkess peoples, as one Circassian
people (self des. Adyge; Rus. and Turk. des. Cherkess)
speaking one Circassian language. The Kabard-
Circassians had already developed into a unified group
of tribes before the 19th cent. and were often
considered a distinct people by the Russians. The other
Circassian tribes were still divided into distinct
tribal groups. In the 1920s the Circassians were
officially divided into two groups: western (Cherkess)
and eastern (Kabard). For a short time, during the late
1920s and early 30s, anther group (Shapsug) was formed
out of one of the western (Shapsug) Circassian tribes.
In the late 1930s the Circassians were redivided into
western (Adygei),   central (Cherkess),   and eastern
(Kabard) groups,   each having the status of a distinct
ethnic group. LANG: The Kabards share a common language
with the Cherkess (Kabardino-Cherkess). This language
belongs to the Circassian division of the northwest
branch (Abazgo-Circassian) of the Caucasic language
family. A Circassian literary language arose in the mid
19th cent. (using the Arabic script) based on the
dialect of Greater Kabarda. It was changed to the Latin
in 1924, and to the Cyrillic in 1936. Kabardino-
Cherkess is divided into a number of closely related,
and mutually intelligible dialects: Baksan, Beslenei,
Kuban, Malka, Mozdok, and others. The Baksan dialect
still forms the basis of the Kabardino-Cherkess
literary language. POP: 321,719 (1979); 279,928 (1970);
203,620 (1959);   139,925 (1926). The classification
"Kabard" in 1926 also included the majority of the
people now called Cherkess. The Kabards are Sunni
Moslem in religion. Relative to the other Abazgo-
Circassians few Kabards emigrated to Turkey in the mid-
19th cent. This was due to the fact that they were
among the last of the Circassians to be Islamicized
(formerly being Eastern Orthodox) and had gotten along

better with the Russians. The Kabards live, primarily, in the northern foothill and steppe region of the Kabardino-Balkar ASSR and adjacent areas in the North Caucasus. SEE Circassian, MAP 5.

KABARDIAN (KABARDIN, KABARDINIAN,   Alt. des. Kabard.
         KABARTAI, KABARTAY)   SEE Kabard,
                                           Circassian.

KACHA   The Kacha are one of the five territorial (not tribal) divisions of the Khakass. The Kacha are of mixed origin. Of the eleven ulus that went into the formation of the Kacha, six were Turkic (the two wings of the Shalosa, Mungat, Tatar, Kuba, and Tuba) and five were Kettic (Tatysh, Yara-Yasta, Abalak, Tin, and Aboltai). The nucleus around which the Kacha were formed was a group of Yenisei Kirgiz and Siberian Tatars. The Kacha form the core around which the other four territorial groups were consolidated to form the Khakass. Although officially Eastern Orthodox in religion, they maintain many pre-Christian samanist-animist traditions. The Kacha inhabit, primarily, the steppe land of the left bank of the Yenisei River and its upper tributaries in the Khakass AO. SEE Khakass.

KACHIN (TSY)   Alt. des. Kacha. SEE Kacha, Khakass.

KADJAR   Alt.   spel.   Kadzhar.   SEE   Kadzhar,
           Azerbaidzhan.

KADZHAR   A Turkic tribe that inhabited Armenia. They were Moslem in religion. Their population was estimated at 5,000 in 1873. It is presumed that they have been officially classified as Azerbaidzhans.

KAHELI (KAHETIAN)   Alt. des. and spel. Kakhetian. SEE
                      Kakhetian, Georgian.

KAIBAL   Alt. des. Koibal. SEE Koibal, Khakass.

KAIDAK   Alt. des. Kaitak. SEE Kaitak, Dargin.

KAITAK   Self des. Qaidaqlan; oth. des. Kaidak, Karakaitak, Karakaidak. ETHN: Up until the early 1930s the Kaitak were considered a distinct ethnic group. Since that time they have been reclassified as Dargin. LANG: The Kaitak language belongs to the Dargin subgroup of the Dargino-Lak group of the northeast division of the Caucasic language family. Up until the 1930s the Kaitak language was considered a distinct language. Since that time it has been reclassified as a dialect of Dargin. Kaitak is divided into two dialects: northern (Magalis-Kaitak) and southern (Karakaitak). The Kaitak language is not written and Dargin serves as the literary language of

the Kaitak. POP: 14,430 (1926). The Kaitak are Sunni
Moslem in religion. They live, primarily, in south
central mountainous Dagestan among the Dargins. SEE
Dargin.

KAIVAN   For. Rus. alt. des. Veps. SEE Veps.

KAJAR   Alt. spel. Kadzhar. SEE Kadzhar.

KAKHELI   Alt. des. Kakhetian. SEE Kakhetian,
Georgian.

KAKHETIAN   Self des. K'akheli. One of the numerous
Kartvelian ethnographic groups that went
into the formation of the Georgian nationality. They
speak a distinct (Kakheli) dialect of Georgian. They
are Eastern Orthodox in religion and live in the
easternmost part of Georgia (east of the Kura and
Aragvi Rivers). SEE Georgian.

KALAMIED   Des. of the more easterly Livonians of the
Latvian coast. Kalamied means "fishermen."

KALCHA   A numerically small tribe of Kirgiz, of non-
Kirgiz origin, that belongs to none of the
three major Kirgiz tribal groupings (right and left
wings, and Ichkilik). SEE Kirgiz.

KALCHIN (TSY)   Alt. des. Kalcha. SEE Kalcha, Kirgiz.

KALMAK   A relatively small tribe of Kirgiz (some 100
families) of Kalmyk origin. They should not
be confused with the Sart Kalmyks who are also being
assimilated by the Kirgiz. They belong to none of the
three major Kirgiz tribal groupings (right and left
wings, and Ichkilik). They live in the Chu valley in
Tyen Shan Oblast, in the Kirgiz SSR. SEE Kirgiz.

KALMUK   Alt. spel. Kalmyk. SEE Kalmyk.

KALMYK   Self des. Khal'mg; oth. des. Kalmuk; for. des
Oirat. ETHN: The Kalmyks are the descendants
of Mongols who settled in the lower reaches of the
Volga basin. In 1771 the majority of Kalmyks attempted
to return to Mongolia, having heard that the Chinese
were attempting to destroy the Oirot (Eastern relatives
of the Kalmyks). The majority of Kalmyks were killed
either en route (by the Bashkirs and Kazakhs, who were
their enemies), in Dzhungaria (by the Chinese), or on
their return trip. One group of Kalmyks did not go on
this trek, and remained in Kalmykia. This group had
settled in the Don River region and had become part of
the Don Cossacks (Buzava). Their settlement pattern
follows former tribal-military group lines ("ulus").
The descendants of the Derbet Ulus inhabit the northern

and western parts of Kalmykia; the Torgout Ulus, the
south and east; and the Khosheut Ulus, the left bank of
the Volga. The Kalmyks have maintained both this
tribal-military division and are further divided into
clan and descendant groups. LANG: Kalmyk belongs to the
western division of the Mongolic languages of the
Uralo-Altaic language family. The dialects of Kalmyk
are concomitant with their ulus divisions. Until 1648
the Kalmyks used the Old Mongol language and script
(and to a lesser extent Tibetan). In 1648 the Kalmyk
(Oirot) language was put into a distinct form using the
Old Mongol script. The dialect of the Derbet Ulus forms
the basis of the Kalmyk literary language. In 1924 it
was changed into the Cyrillic script, in 1930 into the
Latin, and in 1938 back to Cyrillic. POP: 146,631
(1979); 137,194 (1970); 106,066 (1959); 129,321 (1926).
The Kalmyk today represent a small remnant of a once
fairly numerous people. Not only was their population
decimated during the period of the Great Migration
(18th cent.), but their population losses in the Civil
War and collectivization period were also very high,
and a fairly large group of Kalmyks left the USSR
during World War II. The Kalmyks were deported to
Siberia in 1943 and allowed to return to Kalmykia only
between 1956-60. During the period of deportation they
again suffered heavy loses in life. Most Kalmyks are
Buddhist in religion. They live, primarily, in the
Kalmyk ASSR, with settlements also in Astrakhan,
Rostov, and Volgograd Oblasts, and Stavropol Krai. SEE
MAP 8.

KAMASA SAMODI (SAMOED,   Alt. spel. Kamasa Samoyed.
            SAMOIED)   SEE Kamasa Samoyed, Koibal,
                             Khakass.

KAMASA SAMOYED   Oth. des. Kamasin (Kamassian)
                   Samoyed; Rus. des. Kamasin(tsy). A
Samoyedic speaking group that went into the formation
of the Koibal division of the Khakass. Although
culturally Turkified, the Kamasa Samoyeds (at least as
late as 1925) retained their Samoyedic language (it
is now almost extinct). All other Samoyedic groups of
the Sayan region (Koibal and Karagas) have also been
linguistically Turkified. They live, primarily, in the
Sayan uplands in the Khakass AO in south central
Siberia. SEE Koibal, Khakass.

KAMASIN SAMODI (SAMOED,   Alt. des. Kamasa Samoyed.
      SAMOIED, SAMOYED)   SEE Kamasa Samoyed, Koibal,
                              Khakass.

KAMASSIAN SAMODI (SAMOED,   Alt. des. Kamasa Samoyed.
      SAMOIED, SAMOYED)   SEE Kamasa Samoyed, Koibal,
                              Khakass.

KAMCHADAL   Current self des. Kamchadal, from an early
             Russian term for a native of Kamchatka. An
ethnographic group of Russians of mixed Russian and
Itelmen origin. Few relatively pure Itelmen survive
today. Although the Kamchadals speak Russian and
consider themselves part Russian they maintain many
Itelmen cultural elements. They live on the Kamchatka
Peninsula. SEE Itelmen, Russian.

KAMENSHCHIK   Alt. des. Bukhtarman. SEE Bukhtarman,
               Russian.

KAMEN (TSY)   One of the nine territorial groups of
               Koryaks. They live along the coast of
Penzhina Bay in the Koryak AO in far eastern Siberia.
SEE Koryak.

KAPSAI   Des. of the eastern most group of the
          Suvalkiečiai. SEE Suvalkiečiai, Lithuanian.

KAPSAY   Alt. spel. Kapsai. SEE Kapsai, Suvalkiečiai,
          Lithuanian.

KAPUCHA (KAPUCHIN)   Alt. des. and spel. Bezheta. SEE
                      Bezheta, Andi-Dido People, Avar.

KARA KIRGHIZ   Alt. spel. Kara Kirgiz; for. des.
                of Kirgiz. SEE Kara Kirgiz, Kirgiz.

KARA KIRGIZ   Pre-1930s des. of Kirgiz. Until that
               time the term Kirgiz referred to the
people known today as the Kazakhs, and Kara Kirgiz to
the people known today as the Kirgiz. SEE Kirgiz.

KARA KYRGHYZ (KYRGYZ)   Alt. spel. Kara Kirgiz; for.
                         des. Kirgiz. SEE Kara Kirgiz,
                         Kirgiz.

KARA NOGAI   Self des. Qara Noghai; Rus. des. Kara or
              Chernyy Nogai(tsy); oth. des. Black
Nogai. One of the three territorial divisions of the
Nogai (Ak Nogai, Achikulak Nogai, and Kara Nogai). They
speak a distinct dialect of the Nogai language (Kara
Nogai). In 1928 two literary Nogai languages were
created based on both Ak and Kara Nogai, using the
Latin script. In 1938, however, the Kara Nogai literary
language was abolished. Ak Nogai now serves as the
literary language of all Nogai. They live, primarily,
in the northern part of the Dagestan ASSR. SEE Nogai.

KARA NOGAY (NOGHAI, NOGHAY)   Alt. spel. Kara Nogai.
                               SEE Kara Nogai, Nogai.

KARACHAEV   Alt. des. Karachai. SEE Karachai.

KARACHAI   Self   des.   Qarachaili;   oth.   des.
Karachaev(tsy). ETHN: The exact origin of
the Karachai is still debated. They are descended from
a mixture of peoples: Kypchak Turks (Polovtsy), Alans
(Iranian), Khazars, Bolgars, Hunns, and Caucasians.
They are ethnically and linguistically related to the
Balkars with whom they share a common literary language
(Karachai-Balkar). LANG: The Karachai-Balkar language
belongs to the Kypchak division of the Turkic branch of
the Uralo-Altaic language family. The Karachai-Balkar
language was first written in 1924 in the Latin script
and changed in 1939 to the Cyrillic. The Karachai-
Balkar literary language is based on the Baksan-Chegem
dialect of Balkar. POP: 131,074 (1979); 112,741 (1970);
81,403 (1959); 55,123 (1926). The Karachai were
deported to Central Asia in 1944 where they remained
until 1958-59. During that period the Karachai suffered
a severe loss of population. The Karachai are Sunni
Moslem in religion. They formerly lived in the
mountainous southern region of the Karachai-Cherkess
AO, but since their return to the region they have been
resettled in the foothills of that territory. The
Karachai are Sunni Moslem in religion. SEE MAP 14.

KARACHAIEV (KARACHAILI, KARACHAY,   Alt. des. and spel.
KARACHAYEV, KARACHAYLY)   Karachai.   SEE
Karachai.

KARADASH   Self des. Qaradashly. One of the ten major
tribal-territorial   divisions   of   the
Turkmen. In the pre-Soviet period they were each
considered distinct peoples. The Karadash speak a
distinct dialect (Karadash) of Turkmen. They live,
primarily, in the western part of the Khorezm Oasis in
Turkmenistan. SEE Turkmen.

KARADASHLI (KARADASHLY)   Alt. des. Karadash. SEE
Karadash, Turkmen.

KARAGA   Oth. des.   Karagin(tsy). One of the nine
territorial groups of the Koryaks. They
live on the southeastern coast of the Kamchatka
Peninsula in the Koryak AO. SEE Koryak.

KARAGASH   Self des. Qaragashly. A group of Tatars
living around Astrakhan. They, like the
Kundrov Tatars, are descended from the Nogai Tatars
(Golden Horde), and together they make up the Astrakhan
Tatars. They are Sunni Moslem in religion. SEE
Astrakhan Tatar, Tatar.

KARAGASHLI (KARAGASHLY)   Alt. des. Karagash. SEE
Karagash, Astrakhan Tatar,
Tatar.

KARAGASS   For. des. of Tofalar. SEE Tofalar.

KARAGIN (TSY)   Alt. des. Karaga. SEE Karaga, Koryak.

KARAIM   Self des. Karaim; oth. des. Karait(e); ETHN:
The origin of the Karaim is still debated.
Some say they are descended from the Turkic Khazars who
resettled on the Crimea. Others maintain that they are
descended from Judaicized and Turkified Crimean Goths.
Others claim that they are a combination of both. In
the 14th cent. many were resettled by Vitovt of
Lithuania in Lithuania and the western Ukraine. They
are distinct from other Jews of the USSR in that they
reject the Talmud. They have never been classified as
Jews and are still considered a distinct ethnic group
in the USSR. LANG: Although Crimean Tatar is the
official native language of the Karaim, those of
Lithuania adopted the Lithuanian language and gave up
Crimean Tatar centuries ago. Most Karaim have abandoned
Crimean Tatar and now speak Russian as their native
language (roughly 80% of the Karaim in the 1979 census
declared Russian their native language). POP: 3,341,
(1979); 4,571 (1970); 5727 (1959); 8,324 (1926). The
Karaim population was not considered as Jews by the
Nazis during World War II, and were therefore not
exterminated. The Nazis accepted the theory that they
were Germanic Goths who had adopted a distinct form of
Judaism as a religion, and the Crimean Tatar tongue as
a language. The decline in the Karaim population is the
result of assimilation by Jews and Russians with whom
they commonly intermarry. They live, primarily, in the
Crimea, and in Lithuania and the Ukraine. SEE Jew.

KARAIT (KARAITE)   Alt. des. Karaim. SEE Karaim, Jew.

KARAKAIDAK (KARAKAITAK)   Alt. des. Kaitak. SEE
Kaitak, Dargin.

KARAKALPAK   Self des. Qaraqalpak; for. Rus. des.
Chernye Klobuki; oth. des. Karalpak.
ETHN: The Karakalpaks are closely related,
linguistically and culturally, to the Kazakhs and
Kirgiz. Their status as a distinct ethnic group, as
opposed to a sub-group of Kazakhs, is still debated.
The Karakalpak were formerly divided into tribal-
territorial groups. LANG: Karakalpak belongs to the
Nogai group of the Kypchak division of the Turkic
branch of the Uralo-Altaic language family. The
Karakalpak literary language was established in 1924-25
using the Arabic script. It was changed in 1928 to the
Latin, and in 1940 to the Cyrillic. Virtually all
Karakalpaks are bilingual (Karakalpak and Uzbek). POP:
303,324 (1979); 236,009 (1970); 172,556 (1959); 146,317
(1926). The Karakalpaks are under strong Uzbek
influence, and many are being assimilated by them. The

Karakalpaks of Samarkand and Fergana have been almost totally assimilated by the Uzbeks, and have become predominantly agricultural. The Karakalpaks are Sunni Moslem in religion. They live, primarily, in the Karakalpak ASSR, with settlements in Bukhara and Samarkand Oblasts, and in the Fergana valley, in the Uzbek SSR. SEE MAP 11.

KARAKAYDAK (KARAKAYTAK)   Alt.   spel.   and   des. Karakaitak;   alt.   des. Kaitak. SEE Kaitak, Dargin.

KARAKIRGHIZ   (KARAKIRGIZ,   Alt. des. Kara Kirgiz; KARAKYRGHYZ, KARAKYRGYZ)   for. des. Kirgiz.   SEE Kirgiz.

KARALPAK   Alt. des. Karakalpak. SEE Karakalpak.

KARANOGAI   (KARANOGAY,   Alt. des. Kara Nogai. SEE KARANOGHAI, KARANOGHAY)   Kara Nogai, Nogai.

KARAPAPAH (KARAPAPAK)   Alt.   spel.   and   des. Karapapakh. SEE Karapapakh, Meskhetian,   Azerbaidzhan.

KARAPAPAKH   No self des. as an ethnic group. The Karapapakh were formerly a semi-nomadic group of Turks who lived in southwestern Georgia, near the border of Turkey. In 1944 the Karapapakhs were deported to Central Asia along with the other Turkified residents [Georgians (Meskhi), Kurds, and Armenians (Khemshil)] of Meskhetia. They, like the other Meskhetians, were reclassified as Turks in 1944, and in the 1950s as Azerbaidzhans. They have as yet, not been permitted to return to Georgia, and still reside in Central Asia (primarily, around Tashkent in the Uzbek SSR). POP: 6,316 (1926). The Karapapakh are mixed Shiite, Sunni, and Ali-Ilahi Moslem in religion. SEE Meskhetian, Azerbaidzhan.

KARASA SAMODI (SAMOED,   Alt. des. and spel. Karasa SAMOIED)   Samoyed. SEE Karasa Samoyed. Ent.

KARASA SAMOYED   Oth. des. Forest Yenisei Samoyed, Forest Ent(sy). One of the two groups of the Ents (Karasa and Khantaika Samoyed). The Karasa Samoyed were nomads of the forest and tundra. The Karasa Samoyed were made up of the Muggadi, Bai, and Yuchi groups. SEE Ent.

KARASHI   Alt. des. Karagash. SEE Karagash, Astrakhan Tatar, Tatar.

KARASIN SAMODI (SAMOED,   Alt.   des.   Karasa Samoyed.
SAMOIED, SAMOYED)   SEE Karasa Samoyed, Ent.

KARATA   Self des. Kirtle; oth. des. Karatin(tsy).
ETHN: Until the early 1930s the Karata, as
well as the other Andi-Dido peoples, were considered
distinct ethnic gorups. Since that time they have been
reclassified as Avars. LANG: The Karata language
belongs to the Andi group of the Avaro-Andi-Dido
division of the northeast branch of the Caucasic
language family. Until the 1930s the Karata language
was considered a distinct language. Since that time it
has been reclassified as a dialect of Avar. The Karata
language is not written and Avar serves as their
literary language. POP: 5,305 (1926). The Karata are
Sunni Moslem in religion. They, like the other Andi-
Dido peoples, are being assimilated by the Avars. They
live, primarily, in highland southwestern Dagestan
along the Andi River. SEE Andi-Dido Peoples, Avar.

KARATAI   A small ethnic sub-group of Mordvinians
who live in three villages in Tetyushkiy
Rayon in the Tatar ASSR. The Karatai have given up the
Mordvinian language in favor of Tatar, and their
culture has been stongly influenced by both Tatar and
Russian. SEE Mordvinian.

KARA TATAR   Self des. Qara Tatar; oth. des. Nukrat
Tatar. The Kara Tatars, like the Glazov
Tatars, are an isolated group of Tatars descended from
the Volga Bolgars. They live on the Cheptsa River (a
tributary of the Vyatka). SEE Tatar.

KARATAY   Alt. spel. Karatai. SEE Karatai, Mordvinian.

KARATIN (TSY)   Alt. des. Karata. SEE Karata, Andi-
Dido Peoples, Avar.

KARELIAN   Self des. Karjala or Karjalainen (Karyala,
Karyalainen); Rus. des. Karely; oth. des.
Korela. ETHN: The Karelians are Finns who in the past
adopted the Eastern Orthodox religion from the
(Novgorodian) Russians, and, as such fell, under strong
Russian influence. The western Finns were under Swedish
influence and adopted the Lutheran religion. In
essence, the Karelians are Eastern Orthodox Finns.
LANG: Karelian is basically a somewhat Russianized form
of Finnish. Karelian has three dialects: Livvi (spoken
in southwestern Karelia), the dialect of the people
called Livviki; Karjala (spoken in northern and central
Karelia; and Lyydi (spoken in Kondopozhskiy and part of
Olonets Rayons in southern Karelia), the dialect of the
people called Lyydiki. Lyydi and Livvi have many Veps
elements. The dialects of Karelian are quite divergent,
and the speakers of southern dialects can understand
the northern ones only with difficulty. Attempts at

establishing a distinct Karelian literary language
failed and the Karelians use Russian and/or Finnish as
their literary languages (mainly Finnish in the north,
and Russian in the south). POP: 138,429 (1979); 146,081
(1970); 167,278 (1959); 248,120 (1926). The Karelian
population has been steadily declining since the turn
of the century. This is due to two major factors:
intense assimilation by the Russians, and the
emigration of many Karelians to Finland during and
after the revolution, and again during and after World
War II. SEE MAP 8.

KARIM   Alt. spel. Karym. SEE Karym, Russian.

KARIN (SKIY) TATAR   Alt. des. Kara Tatar. SEE Kara
                        Tatar, Tatar.

KARJALAN (KARJALAINEN)   Finnish and Karelian des.
          KARJALAISET)   Karelian. SEE Karelian.

KARPATSKO-RUS (RUSIN, RUSSIAN,   Alt. des. Carpatho-
    RUSYN, RUTHENIAN, UKRAINIAN)   Rusin. SEE Carpatho-
                                     Rusin, Ukrainian.

KARPATO-RUS (RUSIN, RUSSIAN,   Alt. des. Carpatho-
    RUSYN, RUTHENIAN, UKRAINIAN)   Rusin. SEE Carpatho-
                                     Rusin, Ukrainian.

KARTLI   Self des. Kartleli. One of the numerous
            Kartvelian ethnographic groups that went
into the formation of the Georgian nationality. It was
around the Kartli that the other groups were
consolidated into this nation. The Kartli dialect forms
the basis of the modern Georgian literary language. The
Kartli are Eastern Orthodox in religion, and are found
throughout the Georgian SSR. SEE Georgian.

KARTLIAN (KARTLIN)   Alt. des. Kartli. SEE Kartli,
                        Georgian.

KARTVELIAN PEOPLE   Col. des. for the peoples that
                      speak Kartvelian languages
(South Caucasian). This group is made up of the
Mingrelians (Megreli or Megrelian), Laz, Svanetians,
and the numerous ethnographic groups that went into the
formation of the Georgians (Kartli, Kakhetian, Tusha,
Khevsur, Pshav, Mokhev, Mtiuli, Ingiloi, Meskhi,
Dzhavakhi, Imereli (Imeretian), Racha, Lechkhum, Guri,
and Adzhar. The Kartvelian language family is divided
into three groups: Georgian, Svanetian, and Megrelo-Laz
(Chan or Zan). Mingrelian (Megrelian) and Laz (Zan or
Chan) are closely related languages that make up the
Megrelo-Laz group. SEE Georgian, Mingrelian, Laz,
Svanetian, Adzhar.

KARYALAN   Alt. des. Karelian. SEE Karelian.

KARYM   An ethnographic group of Russians of Buryat
origin (Russified Buryats). They live in the
Transbaikal region. SEE Russian.

KASHGAR   Self des. Kashkarlik. A group of Uigurs who
came to Central Asia from Chinese Turkestan
(from around the town of Kashgar) in the 18th-19th
cents. Until the 1930s they were considered a distinct
ethnic group. Since that time they have been classified
as Uigurs. POP: 13,010 (1926). The Kashgars are Sunni
Moslem in religion. SEE Uigur.

KASHGARLIK (KASHGARLUK,   Alt. des. Kashgar. SEE
KASHGARLYK)   Kashgar, Uigur.

KASIMOV TATAR   The Kasimov Tatars are the descendants
of a group of Tatars headed in the
15th cent. by Prince Kasim, who established the Kasimov
Khanate. Some of their descendants, who today live in
scattered settlements in Ryazan Oblast, still maintain
a distinct identity as Kasimov Tatars. SEE Tatar.

KASOG   Self des. Qasoq or Qazaq; oth. des. Kasog,
Kazakh. An Azerbaidzhan tribe in western
Azerbaidzhan that formerly maintained a distinct
identity. They speak a western dialect of Azeri. In
1893 their population was estimated at 1,100. SEE
Azerbaidzhan.

KAVKAZ (SKIY) EVREI   Rus. des. Mountain Jew. SEE
Mountain Jew, Jew.

KAVKAZ (SKIY) EVREY, IEVREI,   Alt. spel. Kavkaz(skiy)
YEVREI, YEVREY)   Evrei; Rus. des.
Mountain Jew. SEE
Mountain Jew, Jew.

KAYBAL   Alt. des. Koibal. SEE Koibal, Khakass.

KAYDAK (KAYTAK)   Alt. des. and spel. Kaitak. SEE
Kaitak, Dargin.

KAYVAN   Alt. spel. Kaivan; for. alt. Rus. des. Veps.
SEE Veps.

KAZAK   1-Alt. des. Kazakh. SEE Kazakh.
2-Alt. des. Kasog, SEE Kasog, Azerbaidzhan.

KAZAKH   1-Self des. Qazaq; for. self des. Qyrghyz;
for. des. Kirgiz, Kirgiz-Kaisak, Kirgiz-
Kazak. ETHN: The Kazakhs are ethnically, culturally,
and linguistically closely related to the Kirgiz and
Karakalpaks. At various times they were considered

minor divisions of a single Kirgiz people. The status
of Karakalpak as distinct from Kazakh is still
debated. Formerly the pastoral Kazakhs were divided
into three territorial groups (zhüz or hordes): Greater
(also called Elder), Central, and Lesser (also called
Younger) Zhüz. The Greater Zhüz was comprised of the
Sary Uisin, Kangli, Dulat, Alban, Suan, Zhalayir, and
other tribes. They live, primarily, in southern
Kazakhstan. The Central Zhuz is made up of the Kypshak,
Argyn, Naiman, Kerei, Kongrat and other tribes. They
live, primarily, in northern and eastern Kazakhstan.
The Lesser Zhüz is made up of three tribal federations
(Zheti Ru, Alim Uly, and Bai Uly). In 1801, under
Tsarist auspices a group representing all the tribes in
the Lesser Zhuz (under the leadership of Sultan Bukei)
moved to a new teritory across the Ural River (between
the Ural and Volga Rivers). They became known as the
Bukei (or Internal) Zhüz. The Kazakhs were Islamicized
primarily under the influence of the Tatars. This was
supported by the Tsars who preferred the Kazakhs to be
under the Tatars rather than the more conservative and
anti-Russian Central Asians. As a result the Kazakh
language and culture were influenced heavily by the
Tatars. LANG: Kazakh belongs to the Nogai group of the
Kypchak division of the Turkic branch of the Uralo-
Altaic language family. Kazakh has three dialects which
correspond to the three hordes. The Kazakh literary
language was established at the end of the 19th
century, based on the dialect of the Central Zhüz,
using the Arabic script. Due to the strong influence of
the Tatars, however, Tatar remained the dominant
literary language among the Kazakhs until the
revolution. As part of the struggle against Pan-
Turkism, the Soviet strongly supported the development,
spread, and use of the Kazakh literary language among
the Kazakhs, in order to weaken the Tatar influence.
The Kazakh literary language was changed to the Latin
script in 1929, and to the Cyrillic in 1938. POP:
6,556,442 (1979); 5,298,818 (1970); 3,621,610 (1959);
3,968,289 (1926). The Kazakh population suffered severe
losses in population during the Civil War period, and
in particular during the period of collectivization and
settlement (late 1920s - early 30s). During
collectivization it is estimated that the Kazakhs lost
almost half their population (mostly through deaths,
but also through a migration of Kazakhs to Sinkiang
Province in China). The Kazakhs are Sunni Moslem in
religion, with many pre-Islamic shamanist traditions.
They live primarily in the Kazakh SSR, and adjacent
areas in Uzbekistan, and the RSFSR. SEE MAP 3.
                2-Alt. des. Kasog. SEE Kasog, Azerbaidzhan.

KAZAN TATAR   Self des. Qazanlyk, Tatar; oth. des.
               Kazanlik, Volga Tatar, Tatar. The Kazan
Tatars are the most numerous and important of the Tatar

territorial groups. They are of mixed origin (Volga
Bolgar, Volga Finns, and Kypchak Turks). The language
of the Kazan Tatars belongs to the Kypchak-Bolgar group
of the Kypchak division of the Turkic branch of the
Uralo-Altaic language family. The Tatar literary
language is based on the Kazan dialect. The term Tatar
has come to be almost synonomous with Kazan Tatar. SEE
Tatar.

KAZANLIK (KAZANLUK,   Alt. des. Kazan Tatar. SEE Kazan
         KAZANLYK)   Tatar, Tatar.

KAZI KUMUH (KUMUK)   Alt. spel. Kazi Kumukh; for. alt.
                      des. Lak. SEE Lak.

KAZI KUMUKH   For. alt. des. Lak. SEE LAk.

KAZIKUMUH (KAZIKUMUK,   Alt. spel. and des. Kazi
          KAZIKUMUKH)   Kumukh; alt. des. Lak. SEE
                         Lak.

KELDIKE   A Kirgiz tribe of non direct Kirgiz origin.
           They do not belong to any of the three
major tribal groupings of the Kirgiz (right and left
wings, or Ichkilik). SEE Kirgiz.

KEMIRGOI   Alt. des. Temirgoi. SEE Temirgoi, Adygei,
            Circassian.

KEMIRGOY   Alt. spel. Kemirgoi; alt. des. Temirgoi. SEE
            Temirgoi, Adygei, Circassian.

KEREK   One of the nine territorial groups of the
         Koryaks. They live along the Bering Sea
         coast. SEE Koryak.

KERJAK   Alt. spel. Kerzhak. SEE Kerzhak, Russian.

KERKETIAN   Alt. des. Circassian. SEE Circassian.

KERZHAK   A group of Russian Old Believers originating
           in Nizhegorodskaya Gubernya (along the river
Kerzhenets) who resettled in Siberia, where they were
known as Kerzhaks. They are one of the numerous early
settlers of Siberia (collectively known as Starozhily).
SEE Starozhily, Russian.

KET   Self des. Ket (meaning person or man); for.
       des. Yenisei or Yenisei Ostyak; oth. des. Kett.
ETHN: The Kettic peoples were formerly widespread
throughout the region of the Yenisei basin. In the 17th
cent., when Russians reached the Yenisei River, there
were five Kettic speaking peoples: Kott, Asan, Ara,
Yara, and Baikot. By the 18th-19th cents. most Kettic
tribes lost their languages and identities through

assimilation with other peoples. The Kotts assimilated
with the Russians; Asans with the Evenk; the Ara and
Yara with the Kacha (Khakass); and Baikot with the
Koibal (Khakass). Only the most northern Kettic tribe
was not assimilated. LANG: Ket is not related to any
known surviving languages, and is sometimes classified
as Paleoasiatic. Ket is not written and Russian serves
as their literary language. POP: 1,122 (1979), 1,182
(1970); 1,019 (1959); 1,428 (1926). The Ket are being
assimilated by the Russians. The Ket are shamanist-
animist in religion. They live in Turukhan and
Yartsevskiy Rayons in Krasnoyarsk Kray in the Yenisei
basin. SEE Paleosiberian Peoples, MAP 9.

KETT   Alt. spel. Ket. SEE Ket.

KHAAS   Alt. des. Khakass. SEE Khakass.

KHAIDAK (KHAIDAQ, KHAITAK,   Alt. des. Kaitak. SEE
             KHAITAQ)   Kaitak, Dargin.

KHAKASS   Self des. Khaas (none in pre-Soviet period);
          for. des. Minusa, Abakan, or Yenisei Tatar;
or by territorial tribe or clan. ETHN: The Khakass are
of extremely complex origin. The Khakass are divided
into five territorial groupings Kacha, Kyzyl, Sagai,
Beltir, and Koibal. The Kacha and Kyzyl are of mixed
Uigur Turkic and Kettic origin; the Beltir are of
Tuvinian origin; the Koibal are of Samoyedic and Kettic
origin; and the Sagai are of Shor and Yenisei Kirgiz
origin. Beyond doubt the numerically small Khakass are
among the most ethnically complex people of the USSR.
They were formed by the consolidation of these various
groups around the Kacha (Khaas). LANG: The dominant
language among the Khakass is Kacha (Khaas), which
belongs to the Uigur group of the eastern division of
the Turkic branch of the Uralo-Altaic language family.
The Khakass literary language was established on the
basis of the Kacha dialect using the Cyrillic script in
1924-25. It was changed to the Latin in 1929, and to
the Cyrillic in 1939. The establishment of a Khakass
literary language has sped up the process of
consolidation of the Khakass. POP: 70,776 (1979);
66,725 (1970); 56,584 (1959); 45,608 (1926). The
Khakass religion is a mixture of shamanist-animist and
Eastern Orthodox beliefs. The Khakass live, primarily,
in the Khakass AO, and adjacent areas in southern
central Siberia. SEE MAP 14.

KHALKHA   Alt. des. Khalkha Mongol. SEE Khalkha
          Mongol.

KHALKHA MONGOL (IAN)   Self des. Khalkha; oth. des.
                  Mongol(tsy)(y)   or Mongolian.
The term Khalkha Mongol refers to the Mongols (from

Mongolia) living in the USSR, as opposed to the
Buryats. POP: 3,228 (1979); 5,170 (1970); 1,774 (1959);
559 (1926). The Khalkha Mongols are being assimilated
by the ethnically, culturally, and linguistically
related Buryats. Like many Buryats, they are Buddhist
in religion. SEE Buryat.

KHANDEIAR   Alt. spel. Khandeyar. SEE Khandeyar,
              Nenets.

KHANDEYAR   Oth. des. Forest Nenets, Forest Yurak. One
              of the two divisions of the Nenets
(Khandeyar and Tundra Nenets). The dialect groups of
the Nenets follow this division as well. The Tundra
dialect forms the basis of the Nenets literary
language. SEE Nenets.

KHANT   Self des. Hant(e); for. des. Ostyak; oth. des.
          Obdor, Ob Ostyak, Surgut Ostyak, Beresov(tsy);
Rus. des. Khanty. ETHN: The Khant are closely related
culturally and linguistically to the Mansi. The Khant
are divided into several kinship groups, with dialect
divisions based on these divisions. LANG: Khant and
Mansi form the Ob Ugrian group of the Ugrian division
of the Uralian branch of the Uralo-Altaic language
family. These languages are distantly related to
Hungarian (Magyar). The Khant literary language was
established in 1930 using the Latin script, which was
changed in 1939-40 to the Cyrillic. Actually there are
five written forms of the Khant language: Surgut, Vakh-
Vasyugan, Sharyshkary, Kazym, and Central Ob. The last
is most widely used, and bilingualism (with Russian) is
encouraged. POP: 20,934 (1979); 21,138 (1970); 19,410
(1959); 17,800 (1926). The Khant religion is a mixture
of shamanist-animist (with a strong emphasis on
ancestor worship) and eastern Orthodox beliefs. They
live, primarily in the western and northern parts of
the Khanty-Mansi AO., with outlying settlements in the
southern Ob region of the Yamalo-Nenets AO (Obdor
Khant) and in the northern part of Tomsk Oblast. in
western Siberia. SEE MAP 2.

KHANTAIKA SAMODI (SAMOED,   Alt. des. and spel.
                 SAMOIED)   Khantaika Samoyed. SEE
                              Khantaika Samoyed, Ent.

KHANTAIKA SAMOYED   Oth. des. Tundra Yenisei Samoyed.
                      The Khantaika Samoyeds are the
more numerous of the two divisions of the Ents
(Khantaika and Karasa Samoyed). The Khantaika Samoyed
were nomads of the Tundra, as opposed to the Karasa
Samoyeds who were nomads of the forest. SEE Ent.

KHANTAYKA SAMODI (SAMOED,   Alt. des. and   spel.
    SAMOIED, SAMOYED)   Khantaika Samoyed. SEE
                               Khantaika Samoyed. Ent.

KHAPUT (LIN)   Alt. des. Gaput. SEE Gaput, Dzhek,
    Shahdag Peoples, Azerbaidzhan.

KHAQASS   Alt. spel. Khakass. SEE Khakass.

KHARDURI   The Kharduri are a group of formerly semi-
            nomadic Tadzhiks of unknown origin. Their
population was estimated at roughly 8,400 in 1924-25.
They live in Surkhan-Darya Oblast in Uzbekistan,
between Baisun and Guzar. SEE Tadzhik.

KHATUKAI   Self des. Khatukai.   One of the ten major
            tribal divisions of the Adygei people. The
Khatukai lived in a narrow region between the Pshish
and Belaya Rivers in the western North Caucasus. The
vast majority of Khatukai emigrated along with the
other Abazgo-Circassians to Turkey in the mid-1860s.
Formerly considered a distinct people they are now
classified as Adygei. SEE Adygei, Circassian.

KHATUKAY   Alt. spel. Khatukai. SEE Khatukai, Adygei,
            Circassian.

KHAYDAK (KHAYDAQ, KHAYTAK,   Alt. des. and spel. Kaitak.
    KHAYTAQ)   SEE Kaitak, Dargin.

KHAZARA   Self des. Khazara or Berber; oth. des.
           Berber. The Khazara are a group of
Tadzhikified Mongols from Afghanistan. In Afghanistan
they are mixed Shiite (eastern Khazara) and Sunni
(western Khazara) Moslem in religion. It is unclear to
which group the Soviet Khazara belong. POP: 146 (1926).
They live in Tadzhikistan and have been nearly
assimilated by the Tadzhiks. SEE Tadzhik.

KHEMSHIL   Self des. Hemshili; oth. des. Khemshin.
            ETHN: The Khemshil are a group of Armenians
who converted to Sunni Islam in the 18th cent. The
majority of the Khemshil live in Turkey. LANG: Although
Armenian in origin only few had not shifted to speaking
Turkish by the 19th cent. Of the 629 Khemshil
registered in the USSR in 1926 only 2 spoke Armenian as
their native language (the others mainly Turkish). POP:
Until 1944 the Khemshil lived on the Black Sea coast in
the Adzhar ASSR (in Georgia, near the border with
Turkey). In 1944 the Khemshil, like the other Turkified
peoples of this region (Meskhi Georgians, Kurds, and
Karapapakhs), were deported to Central Asia (mainly
around Tashkent) where they still reside. In 1956 their
special settlement restrictions were lifted.
Collectively these people are known as Meskhetians. At

the time of their deportation they were reclassified as
Turks and in the 1950s as Azerbaidzhans. SEE Armenian,
Meskhetian, Azerbaidzhan.

KHEMSHIN   Alt. des. Khemshil. SEE Khemshil, Armenian,
            Azerbaidzhan.

KHEVSUR   Self des. Khevsuri. One of the numerous
           Kartvelian ethnographic groups that went
into the formation of the Georgian nationality. They
speak a distinct (Khevsuri) dialect of Georgian. They
claim descent from European crusaders, and have some
north European racial and cultural traits. They are
also culturally distinct in that their religion is
basically animistic with some Eastern Orthodox
intrusions. The Khevsur live along the upper course of
the Eastern Aragvi and Argun Rivers in the Georgian
SSR. SEE Georgian.

KHEVSURIAN   Alt. des. Khevsur. SEE Khevsur, Georgian.

KHINALUG   Self des. Kattitturdur; oth. des.
           Khinalugh. ETHN: The Khinalug are one of
the numerically small Shahdag peoples who have been
nearly totally assimilated by the Azerbaidzhans. LANG:
The Khinalug language belongs to the Samurian group of
the northeast branch of the Caucasic language family.
Khinalug is not written and Azeri serves as their
literary language. POP: Although only 105 people
declared themselves Khinalug in the 1926 census, 1,540
listed Khinalug as their native language. These were
probably Khinalug who declared Azerbaidzhan their
ethnic identification but Khinalug their native
language. The Khinalug are Sunni Moslem in religion.
They live in the region of Mount Shahadag in
Konakhkend Rayon, in the Azerbaidzhan SSR. SEE Shahdag
Peoples, Azerbaidzhan.

KHINALUGH (KHINALUKH)   Alt. des. Khinalug. SEE
           Khinalug, Shahdag Peoples,
           Azerbaidzhan.

KHITRI   The Khitri are a sub-group of the Anatri
           (lowland) Chuvash. Their culture has been
strongly influenced by the Tatars, among whom they
live. They live in the extreme southeastern part of the
Chuvash ASSR. SEE Chuvash.

KHIURKILI (N)   Alt. spel. and des. Khürkili. SEE
           Khürkili, Dargin.

KHOLAM   Self des. Kholamly; oth. des. Khulam(ly). One
           of the five tribes (societies) that went into
the formation of the Balkars. The Kholam live,
primarily, in the valley of the Cherek River in the

Kabardino-Balkar ASSR in the central North Caucasus.
SEE Balkar.

KHOLAMCHI (KHOLAMCHILI, KHOLAMCHY,   Alt. des. Kholam.
  KHOLAMCHYLY, KHOLAMLI, KHOLAMLY)   SEE Kholam,
                                          Balkar.

KHONGODOR   One of the five main tribal divisions of
             the Buryat. They live, primarily, in the
upper reaches of the Angara River, south of the Bulagat
tribal group. SEE Buryat.

KHORA   Oth. des. Khorin(tsy). One of the largest of
          the five major tribal divisions of the Buryat.
The Khora live around lake Baikal and on Olkhon Island.
SEE Buryat.

KHORIN (TSY)   Alt. des. Khora. SEE Khora, Buryat.

KHORVAT   A group of Eastern Orthodox Ukrainians who
            still   retained   an   old   Slavic   tribal
designation as late as the mid-19th cent. In 1861 their
population was 17,228. They lived around Dubno in the
Volynia region of the Ukraine. They have since been
totally assimilated by the Ukrainians. Although their
self designation is the same as that of the Croats
(Hrvat) of Yugoslavia, and there may be a remote
historical connection between them, the Khorvat of the
Ukraine should not be confused with Croatians. SEE
Ukrainian.

KHORVATIAN (KHORVATY)   Alt. des. Khorvat. SEE
                         Khorvat, Ukrainian.

KHOSHEUT   One of the three major ulus (military-
            tribal) divisions of the Kalmyk. The
majority of the Khosheut were killed on the Great
Migration to Mongolia in the 18th cent. The Khoshuet
today are a relatively small remnant of a once
important group. They inhabit the regions on the left
bank of the Lower Volga. SEE Kalmyk.

KHUF   Self des. Khufidzh. The Khuf are a group of
         Rushan who speak a distinct dialect. They are
sometimes considered a distinct ethnographic group.
Besides speaking Rushan, virtually all speak Shugnan
and Tadzhik. The Khuf, like the other Pamir peoples,
are being assimilated by the Tadzhiks. SEE Rushan,
Pamir Peoples, Tadzhik.

KHUFIDJ   Alt. spel. Khufidzh; alt. des. Khuf. SEE
           Khuf, Rushan, Pamir Peoples, Tadzhik.

KHUFIDZH   Alt. des. Khuf. SEE Khuf, Rushan, Pamir
            Peoples, Tadzhik.

KHUFIJ   Alt. spel. Khufidzh; alt. des. Khuf. SEE Khuf, Rushan, Pamir Peoples, Tadzhik.

KHULAM (CHI)(CHILI)(CHY)   Alt. des. Kholam. SEE
(CHYLY)(LI)(LY)   Kholam, Balkar.

KHUNZAL   Self des. Khunami; oth. des. Enzebi, Gunzebi, Gunzibi, Nakhada. ETHN: Until the 1930s the Khunzal, as well as the other Andi-Dido peoples, were considered distinct ethnic groups. Since that time they have been reclassified as Avars. LANG: The Khunzal language belongs to the Dido group of the Avaro-Andi-Dido division of the northeast branch of the Caucasic language family. Until the 1930s the Khunzal language was considered a distinct language. Since that time it has been reclassified as a dialect of Avar. The Khunzal language is not written and Avar serves as the literary language of the Khunzal. POP: 106 (1926). The Khunzal are Sunni Moslem in religion. They, like the other Andi-Dido peoples, are being assimilated by the Avars. They live in the highest and most isolated part of southwestern Dagestan near the Georgian border, on the upper course of the Avar River. SEE Andi-Dido Peoples, Avar.

KHÜRKILI   Oth. des. Khyurkili(n); For. alt. des. Dargin. SEE Dargin.

KHVARSHI (N)   Alt. des. Khwarshi. SEE Khwarshi, Andi-Dido Peoples, Avar.

KHWARSHI   Self des. Kedaes Hikwa, or Khuani; Rus. des. Khvarshi(n). ETHN: Until the early 1930s the Khwarshi, as well as the other Andi-Dido peoples, were considered distinct ethnic groups. Since that time they have been classified as Avars. LANG: The Khwarshi language belongs to the Dido group of the Avaro-Andi-Dido division of the northeast branch of the Caucasic language family. Khwarshi has two major dialects: Khwarshi proper (Kadaes) and Inkhokari (Inkhies). Until the 1930s the Khwarshi language was considered a distinct language. Since that time it has been classified as a dialect of Avar. The Khwarshi language is not written and Avar serves as their literary language. POP: 1,019 (1926). The Khwarshi are Sunni Moslem in religion. They, like the other Andi-Dido peoples, are being assimilated by the Avars. They formerly (pre-1944) lived in the highest and most isolated region of southwestern Dagestan near the Georgian border on the Ori-Tskalis River (a tributary of the Andi River). Since that time they live in Vedeno Rayon in highland southwestern Dagestan. SEE Andi-Dido Peoples, Avar.

KHWARSHIN (TSY)   Alt. des. Khwarshi. SEE Khwarshi.
Andi-Dido Peoples, Avar.

KHYURKILI (N)   Alt. des. Khürkili. SEE Khürkili,
Dargin.

KILE   The Kile are a group of Nanai of Evenk origin.
They maintain a distinct identity. They live
along the Kur and Gorin Rivers. SEE Nanai.

KIPCHAK (KIPSHAK)   Alt. des. Kypchak. SEE Kypchak,
Uzbek, Turkic Peoples.

KIRGHIZ   Alt. spel. Kirgiz. SEE Kirgiz.

KIRGHIZ KAISAK (KAYSAK)   Alt.   spel.   Kirgiz Kaisak;
for. alt. des. Kazakh. SEE
Kirgiz Kaisak, Kazakh.

KIRGHIZ KAZAK (KAZAKH)   Alt. spel. Kirgiz Kazakh;
for. alt. des. Kazakh. SEE
Kirgiz Kazakh, Kazakh.

KIRGIZ   Self des. Kyrghyz; for. des. Kara Kirgiz,
Alatau Kirgiz; oth. des. Black Kirgiz. ETHN:
The origin of the Kirgiz is still debated. Most
ethnographers maintain that the Kirgiz are not direct
descendants of the Yenisei Kirgiz (although there may
be some minor relationship), but rather are probably
descendants of mixed Mongolic, Eastern Turkic, and
Kypchak Turkic origin. The Kirgiz are both
linguistically and culturally very closely related to
the Kazakhs, and to a lesser degree the Karakalpaks.
Some maintain that the Kirgiz are a sub-group of
Kazakhs. The Kirgiz differ in that they have more
Mongolic and Altai-Turkic elements in their background,
and that they were predominantly transhumant nomads, as
opposed to steppe nomads like the Kazakhs. The Kirgiz
are divided into a number of tribes, which are
organized into two major groups [right and left wings
(based on the former military-tribal organization of
the Kirgiz)]. In addition to these there are a number
of tribes of either mixed (Kirgiz and other) or non-
Kirgiz origin. The Ichkilik (Pamir-Alai Kirgiz) are a
group of Kirgiz tribes whose origins are not known,
other than they are non-Kirgiz. They live in the high
southwestern Kirgiz territory and are Yak breeders. SEE
Ichkilik. The others do not have a collective
designation as do the Ichkilik, and are made up of the
following tribes: Chala Kazakh (mixed Kazakh-Kirgiz);
Sart Kalmyk and Kalmak (of Kalmyk origin); and the
Kürküröö, Kürön, Kalcha, and Keldike. SEE each of
these. The Kirgiz have often been confused with the
Kazakhs, which in part stems from the problem of
nomenclature. Until 1925 the term Kirgiz referred

either to the Kirgiz and Kazakhs collectively, or only
to the Kazakhs. At that time the Kirgiz were called
Kara Kirgiz. LANG: Kirgiz belongs to the Nogai group of
the Kypchak division of the Turkic branch of the Uralo-
Altaic language family. Until 1926 Kirgiz and Kazakh
were considered one language. In northern Kirgizia the
Kirgiz used either the Tatar or Kazakh literary
languages, and in southern Kirgizia either Tatar or
Uzbek. In 1923 a Kirgiz literary language (Kara Kirgiz)
was established on the basis of the northern dialects,
with additions of other dialect elements, using the
Arabic alphabet. In 1928 it was changed to the Latin,
and in 1940 to the Cyrillic. POP: 1,906,271 (1979);
1,452,222 (1970); 968,659 (1959); 762,736 (1926). The
Kirgiz are Sunni Moslem in religion with many pre-
Islamic shamanist-animist traditions. The Kirgiz live,
primarily, in the Kirgiz SSR, and adjacent areas in the
Uzbek and Tadzhik SSRs. SEE MAP 7.

KIRGIZ KAISAK   For. alt. des. Kazakh. SEE Kazakh.

KIRGIZ KAYSAK   Alt. spel. Kirgiz Kaisak; for. alt.
                   des. Kazakh. SEE Kirgiz Kaisak,
                   Kazakh.

KIRGIZ KAZAK   Alt. spel. Kirgiz Kazakh; for. alt.
                   des. Kazakh. SEE Kirgiz Kazakh,
                   Kazakh.

KIRGIZ KAZAKH   For. alt. des. Kazakh. SEE Kazakh.

KIRIM TATAR   Alt. spel. Kyrym Tatar; alt. des.
                   Crimean Tatar. SEE Kyrym Tatar,
                   Crimean Tatar, Tatar.

KIRIMCHAK   Alt. des. Krymchak. SEE Krymchak, Jew.

KIST   1- A group of western Veinakh (Ingush) tribes
          (Maista, Malkha, Khildykharo and Erstkho) that
resettled in the 1840s and 50s in the Pankis gorge in
Tushetia (northern Georgia). The Kist are sometimes
called Ingush, although they maintain the name Kist for
themselves.
          2- Alt. des. Feappi. SEE Feappi, Ingush.
          3- A for. des. used at times for either or
          both the Chechens and Ingush.

KISTIN (TSY)   Alt. and Rus. des. Kist. SEE Kist,
                  Ingush.

KIURIN   Alt. spel. Kurin. SEE Kurin, Lezgin.

KIZIL   Alt. spel. Kyzyl. SEE Kyzyl, Khakass.

KOIBAL   Self des. Koibal; oth. des. Mator. One of the
          five territorial groups of the Khakass. The
Koibal are comprised of seven ulus (Tarazhak, Kol,
Abugach, Greater and Lesser Baikot, Kandyk, and Arsh),
based on former kinship-military organizations.
Although these ulus were of Samoyedic and Kettic
origin, they had been linguistically Turkified by the
first half of the 18th cent. They speak the Kacha
dialect of Khakass. Although officailly Eastern
Orthodox in religion, their religion is a mixture of
shamanist-animist and Eastern Orthodox beliefs. They
live, primarily, in the Abakan steppes, bounded in the
south by the Sayan foothills, in the northeast by the
Yenisei River, and in the northwest by the Abakan
River. SEE Khakass.

KOJLA CHEREMISS (MARI)   Alt. des. and spel. Kozhla
                          Mari. SEE Kozhla Mari, Mari.

KOLA LAPP   Alt. des. Lapp. SEE Lapp.

KOLIMCHAN   Alt. spel. Kolymchan. SEE Kolymchan,
             Russian.

KOLIN (TSY)   Rus. and oth. des. Lapp. SEE Lapp.

KOLVA (KOLVA IURAK)   Alt. des. Kolva Nenets. SEE
                       Kolva Nenets, Nenets.

KOLVA NENETS   Oth. des. Kolva, Kolva Samoyed, Kolva
                Yurak; Rus. des. Kolvin(tsy). The Kolva
Nenets are a group of Nenets of mixed Nenets and Komi
origin. This group was formed in the 19th cent. when a
group of Nenets men intermarried with Komi (Izhmi)
women. Their descendants call themselves Nenets while
they speak the Izhmi dialect of Komi. They live along
the Kolva River where it empties into the Usa. SEE
Nenets.

KOLVA SAMODI (SAMOED, SAMOIED,   Alt. des. Kolva
             SAMOYED, YURAK)   Nenets. SEE Nenets.

KOLVIN (TSY)   Rus. des. Kolva Nenets. SEE Kolva
                Nenets, Nenets.

KOLYMCHAN (E)   An ethnographic group of Russians of
                 mixed Russian and Yakut origin.
Although they call themselves Russians, many not only
have adopted Yakut culture, but also the Yakut
language. They live along the Kolyma River in far
eastern Siberia. SEE Russian, Yakut.

KOMI   Self des. Komi Mort or Komi Voityr; for. des.
        Zyryan, Komi Zyryan. ETHN: The Komi are closely
related ethnically, culturally, and linguistically to

the Komi Permyaks. Their status as two distinct ethnic
groups is still debated. The Komi and Komi Permyaks
consider themselves to be one ethnic group (Komi Mort)
speaking one language (Komi). A group of Komi, who were
heavily influenced by the Nenets form a distinct
ethnographic group of Komi called Izhmi. SEE Izhmi. The
Komi have historically been under considerable Russian
influence, and were well known as traders in Northern
Siberia. LANG: The Komi language belongs to the Permian
group of the Finnic division of the Uralian branch of
the Uralo-Altaic language family. Komi, Komi Permyak
and Udmurt are all closely related languages (and
basically mutually intelligible). The first attempts at
creating a Komi literary language go back to the 14th
cent. (by Novgorodian missionaries), however written
Komi was little used. In 1918 a Komi alphabet was
created using a mixture of Latin and Cyrillic letters,
but it was not used in printing until 1920. In 1938 it
was changed to the Cyrillic. Komi has three major
dialects: Pechora, Udor, and Verkhne-Vyshegod, and one
minor one (Izhmi). POP: 326,700 (1979); 321,894 (1970);
287,027 (1959); 226,383 (1926). In the 1926 census the
Komi were listed as Zyryan. The Komi religion is a
mixture of Eastern Orthodox and shamanist-animist
beliefs. They live, primarily, in the Komi ASSR and
adjacent areas in northern Russia. SEE MAP 6.

KOMI IJEM (IJMI, IZHEM,   Alt. des. Izhmi. SEE Izhmi,
   IZHMI, IZHMY)   Komi.

KOMI PERMYAK   Self des. Komi Mort or Komi Otir; oth.
                 des. Permyak; Rus. for. des. Permyane.
The Komi Permyaks are closely related ethnically,
culturally, and linguistically to the Komi. Their
status as distinct ethnic groups is still debated. They
both consider themselves to be one ethnic group (Komi
Mort) with one (Komi) language. Both are closely
related to the Udmurts. Two groups of Komi Permyaks
live outside the Komi Permyak AO and form distinct
ethnographic groups: the Zyuzda and Yazva Komi
Permyaks. The Zyuzda dialect forms a transitional group
between Komi and Komi Permyak. The Yazva speak a
dialect of Komi (not Komi Permyak). SEE Yazva and
Zyuzda. LANG: The Komi Permyak language belongs to the
Permian group of the Finnic division of the Uralian
branch of the Uralo-Altaic language family. The Komi
Permyak language forms a transitional language between
Komi and Udmurt and is mutually intelligible with both
of them. Komi Permyak has two dialects: northern
(Kosinsko-Kama) and southern (Inven). The Inven
dialect forms the basis of the Komi Permyak literary
language which was established in 1920 using the
Cyrillic script. Komi Permyak is one of the few
literary languages of the USSR that did not undergo
alphabet changes in the 1920s and 1930s. The Komi

Permyak religion is a mixture of Eastern Orthodox (some
being Old Believers) and shamanist-animist beliefs. The
Komi Permyaks live, primarily, in the Komi Permyak AO
and adjacent areas. SEE Komi, MAP 6.

KOMI ZIRIAN (ZYRIAN)   Alt. spel. Komi Zyryan; for.
                        des. Komi. SEE Komi Zyryan,
                        Komi.

KOMI ZYRYAN   For. des. Komi. SEE Komi.

KONDOMA TATAR   For. (17th-18th cent.) des. of the
                 Shors. They were also referred to as
                 Mrassa and Kuznets Tatars. SEE Shor.

KOREAN   Self des. Koryosaram; Rus. des. Korei(tsy);
          oth. des. Korean of Central Asia. The Koreans
of the USSR are the descendants of Koreans who were
deported to Central Asia in the mid-19th cent.
They formerly lived in the far eastern part of Siberia
near the border of present day Korea. Only a few Soviet
Koreans live in their original territory. Most of the
Koreans living in the Soviet Far East are immigrants
who came to this area during and after the Japanese
incorporation of Korea in the early part of the 20th
cent. LANG: The Koreans of the USSR speak the northern
dialect of Korean (with some Russian, Uzbek, and Kazakh
additions to the vocabulary). Korean is not an
officially recognized literary language of the USSR and
Russian serves as the main literary language of the
Soviet Koreans. POP: 388,926 (1979); 357,507 (1970);
313,735 (1959). Although officially Eastern Orthodox in
religion, the actual religion of the Koreans of the
USSR is complex. They individually combine Buddhist-
Confucionist with some Eastern Orthodox beliefs. The
Koreans live, primarily, in scattered settlements in
Uzbekistan (mainly in Tashkent Oblast), and in Kzyl-
Orda and Alma Ata Oblasts in the Kazakh SSR. SEE MAP 5.

KOREANS OF CENTRAL ASIA   Alt. des. Koreans, SEE
                           Koreans.

KOREL (KORELA, KORELIAN,   Alt. des. Karelian. SEE
       KORELY, KORELYAN)   Karelian.

KORIAK   Alt. spel. Koryak. SEE Koryak.

KORYAK   Formerly no general self des. as an ethnic
          group, but rather by mode of living
[Chavchyvav (settled coastal dwellers) or Nymylyn
(nomadic reindeer breeders); oth. des. Chavchuven (from
Chavchyvav), Nymylan (from Nymylyn)]. ETHN: Culturally
the Koryaks, like the closely related Chukchi, are
divided into two groups: semi-nomadic reindeer herders
and settled coastal dwellers. In 1926 55% of the

population were nomadic and 45% settled. With
increasing Russian influence, many Koryak have become
settled, although some remain semi-nomadic. The Koryaks
and Chukchi are closely related peoples, and their
languages are mutually intelligible. The Koryaks are
divided into nine territorial groups, each having its
own dialect (only minor phonetic differences):
Chavchuven, Kamen(tsy), Paren(tsy), Itkan(tsy), Apuka
(Apukintsy), Kerek, Alyutor(tsy), Karaga (Karagintsy),
and Palan(tsy). LANG: Koryak forms with Chukchi and
Itelmen the Chukotic (Chukotan) group of languages,
which are classified as Paleoasiatic. The nine dialects
of Koryak are similar to one another, and Chavchuven
forms the basis of the Koryak literary language. Koryak
was first established as a literary language in 1932
using the Latin script. It was changed in 1937 to the
Cyrillic. POP: 7,879 (1979); 7,487 (1970); 6,287
(1959); 7,439 (1926). The Koryaks are shamanist-animist
in religion, with a complex cosmology and calendar of
festivals. They live, primarily, in the Koryak AO in
northeastern Siberia. SEE Paleoasiatic Peoples, MAP 3.

KOTT   A former Kettic speaking group that was
            assimilated by the Russians in the 18th and
            19th centuries. SEE Ket, Russian.

KOYBAL   Alt. spel. Koibal. SEE Koibal, Khakass.

KOZHLA CHEREMISS   Alt. des. Kozhla Mari. SEE Kozhla
                        Mari, Mari.

KOZHLA MARI   Oth. des. Olyk Mari (Meadow Mari); for.
                   des. Kozhla (Olyk) Cheremiss; oth. des.
Forest Mari. The Kozhla Mari (Forest Mari) form with
the Olyk Mari (Meadow Mari) the eastern (lowland)
division of the Mari. They are distinct in that they
never accepted Christianity (holding strongly to their
shamanist-animist beliefs), and have a distinct
language of their own. Highland (Kuryk Mari) and
Lowland Mari are not mutually intelligible. The lowland
literary language is based on the Meadow (Olyk)
dialect, which is shared by the Kozhla Mari. The Kozhla
Mari live, primarily, in the forested areas on the
left bank of the Volga in the Mari ASSR. SEE Mari.

KRASNIY ESTONIAN   Alt. spel. Krasnyy Estonian. SEE
                        Krasnyy Estonian, Setu, Estonian.

KRASNYY ESTONIAN   Self des. Kraasna Maarahvas (sing.
                        Krasna Maamees). The Krasnyy
Estonians are a group of Setu Estonians who lived
around the market town Krasnyy in the former Pskov
Gubernia. They probably migrated to the Pskov region in
the 17th cent. Although officially Eastern Orthodox in
religion they preserve many shamanist-animist

traditions. At the end of the 19th cent. there were 32
villages of Krasnyy Estonians (approx. 2,000 people).
By 1900 they were on the verge of total linguistic
assimilation by the Russians, although many still
retained the Estonian ethnic identity. SEE Setu,
Estonian.

KRESHEN   Alt. spel. Kryashen. SEE Kryashen, Tatar.

KREVINI (KREVINGI)   Alt. des. Krieviņi. SEE Krieviņi.
                      Latvian, Vod.

KRIASHEN   Alt. spel. Kryashen. SEE Kryashen, Tatar.

KRIEVIŅI   Self des. Krieviņi (sing: Krieviņš); Rus.
            des. Krevini, Krevingi; oth. des. Krieviņi,
Krievingi, Rusaki. The Krieviņi are a group of Eastern
Orthodox Vod who were resettled in Zemgale (Latvia) in
the 15th cent. Since that time they have been merging
with the Latvians. Although almost totally assimilated
at the present time, the assimilation of the Krieviņi
by the Latvians was slowed dramatically by the fact
that the Latvians were, primarily, Lutheran in
religion, with a Catholic minority (Latgal) whereas the
Krieviņi were Eastern Orthodox in religion. The term
Krieviņi derives from the Latvian Krieviņš, which is a
diminutive of Krievs "Russian" (from the Krivichi). The
Krieviņi inhabit the Kurland area of Latvia. SEE
Latvian, Vod.

KRIEVINGI (KRIEVIŅŠ, KRIEVINSH)   Alt. des. Krieviņi,
                                   SEE Krieviņi, Vod,
                                   Latvian.

KRIM TATAR   Alt. des. Crimean Tatar. SEE Crimean
              Tatar.

KRIMCHAK   Alt. spel. Krymchak. SEE Krymchak, Jew.

KRIVICHI   For. alt. des. of Belorussian. The Krivichi
            were an old tribal group of East Slavs for
whom the entire Belorussian people were formerly named.
In 1861 in Lyda Uezd of Vilno Gubernia 23,016 people
still declared themselves Krivichi as their ethnic
group in the census of that year. SEE Belorussian.

KRIVICHIAN   Alt. des. Krivichi. SEE Krivichi,
              Belorussian.

KRIZ   Alt. spel. Kryz. SEE Kryz, Dzhek, Shahdag
        Peoples, Azerbaidzhan.

KRYASHEN   Self des. Kreshen; oth. des. Christian
            Tatar. ETHN: The Kryashen are a group of
Volga Tatars who converted to Eastern Orthodoxy

(Kryashen meaning convert to Christianity). Until the
1930s the Kryashen were considered a distinct ethnic
group. Since that time they have been officially
reclassified as Tatars. LANG: The Kryashen speak a
dialect of Volga Tatar. Since they were Christian the
dialect of Tatar spoken by the Kryashen lacked many of
the Persian and Arabic terms found in the standard
Tatar language, and in turn, had more Russianisms.
Prior to the 1930s the Kryashen had their own literary
language, using the Cyrillic script. Since that time
they have used the standard Tatar literary language.
POP: 101,447 (1926). The Kryashen are Eastern Orthodox
in religion. SEE Tatar.

KRYM TATAR   Alt. des. Crimean Tatar. SEE Crimean
             Tatar, Tatar.

KRYMCHAK   Self des. Kyrymchak; oth. des. Crimean Jew,
           Crimean Tatar Jew; Rus. des. Krymsko-
Tatarskiy Evrei. ETHN: The origin of the Krymchaks is
still debated. Some claim they are descendants of the
Khazars who moved to the Crimea after the fall of their
Empire; others, that they are a group of Crimean Tatars
converted to Judaism by Sephardic Jews who moved to the
Crimea and mixed with them; and yet others, that they
are a group of Jews who were Tatarized after moving to
the Crimea. The Krymchaks spoke Crimean Tatar (with a
few Hebrew borrowings for religious terminology). The
Krymchaks should not be confused with the Karaim. The
Krymchaks accepted the Talmud whereas the Karaim did
not. As such the Krymchaks were considered to be Jews
by other Jews (and by non-Jews as well), whereas the
Karaim were considered a different people. POP: 6,383
(1926). Until the 1930s the Krymchaks were considered a
distinct ethnic group. After that time they were
classified as Jews. During World War II the Krymchak
population was almost entirely exterminated by the
Nazis. Prior to that time the Krymchaks were being
assimilated by the Ashkenazic Jews, and to a lesser
extent by the Russians. The Krymchak formerly resided,
primarily, in the main cities on the Crimean peninsula.
SEE Jew, Crimean Tatar.

KRYZ   1-The Kryz are a subdivision of the Dzhek
       They are the Dzhek who inhabit the village
of Kryz. They speak a variant of the Dzhek language
(Kryz). They have been almost totally assimilated by
the Azerbaidzhans. SEE Dzhek, Shahdag Peoples,
Azerbaidzhan.
       2-Alt. des. Dzhek. SEE Dzhek, Shahdag Peoples,
       Azerbaidzhan.

KUBACHI   Self des. Ughbug; Rus. des. Kubachin(tsy);
          oth. Zirekhgeran (Zerekhgeran). ETHN: The
Kubachi are closely related ethnically, culturally, and

linguistically to the Kaitak and Dargin. Until the
1930s the Kubachi (and Kaitak) were considered distinct
ethnic groups. Since that time they have been
classified as Dargins. The Kubachi were famous
throughout the Caucasus, Middle East and Russian Empire
as gold and silversmiths, and the makers of fine
daggers and chainmail. They were called Zirekhgeran
(makers of chainmail) by the Persians and Arabs. LANG:
The Kubachi language belongs to the Dargin sub-group of
the Dargino-Lak group of the northeast division of the
Caucasic language family. Until the 1930s Kubachi was
considered a distinct language. Since that time it has
been classified as a dialect of Dargin. The Kubachi
language is not written and Dargin serves as the
literary language of the Kubachi. POP: 2,371 (1926).
The Kubachi are Sunni Moslem in religion. They, like
the Kaitak, are being assimilated by the Dargins. They
live in the single village Kubachi in central Dagestan.
SEE Kaitak, Dargin.

KUBAN ABHAZ (ABKAZ)   Alt. spel Kuban Abkhaz; alt.
                         des. Abaza. SEE Kuban Abkhaz,
                         Abaza.

KUBAN ABKHAZ   For. des. Abaza. SEE Abaza.

KUBAN NOGAI   Alt. des. Ak Nogai. SEE Ak Nogai, Nogai.

KUBAN NOGAY (NOGHAI, NOGHAY)   Alt. spel. Kuban Nogai;
                                  alt. des. Ak Nogai. SEE
                                  Ak Nogai, Nogai.

KUMANDA   Oth. des. Kumandin(tsy). The Kumanda are one
             of the seven territorial-tribal groups that
went into the formation of the Altai people. They were
formerly called Chernevyy Tatars, as were the Chelkan
and Tubalar. The Kumanda are of the northern Altai
tribal group. SEE Chernevyy Tatar, Altai.

KUMANDIN (TSY)   Alt. des. Kumanda. SEE Kumanda,
                    Chernevyy Tatar, Altai.

KUMARCHEN   Alt. des. Manegir. The ethnonym Kumarchen
               derived from the river Kumara, along
               which the Manegir lived. SEE Manegir,
               Evenk.

KUMIK (KUMUK)   Alt. spel. and des. Kumyk. SEE Kumyk.

KUMYK   Self des. Qumuq; oth. des. Kumuk. ETHN: The
           Kumyk are Turkified (Kypchak) Caucasic peoples
of northern Dagestan. They were formed by the
assimilation of these Caucasians by the Kypchaks. This
process of assimilation was strong well into the mid-
20th cent., and many Dagestani peoples (Dargins and

Avars in particular), Chechens, and Nogai have shifted
over to the Kumyk language. The Kumyk language and
culture became very influential among the eastern North
Caucasians (Chechen, Avar, Andi-Dido people, Dargin,
Kaitak, Kubachi, and Nogai) because the Kumyk
controlled the lowland winter pasture areas used by
these mountaineers and the main cities in which they
found winter employment [Khasavyurt, Buinaksk, and
Makhachkala (Temir Khan Shura)] were in Kumyk
territory. Even though numerically small their
cultural, linguistic, political, and economic influence
was great. Kumyk also served as a lingua franca for all
eastern North Caucasians. LANG: The Kumyk language
belongs to the Oghuz group of the Kypchak division of
the Turkic language branch of the Uralo-Altaic language
family. Kumyk has three closely related dialects:
northern (Khasavyurt), central (Buinaksk), and southern
(Kaitak). The Kumyk literary language was established
in the late 19th cent. on the basis of the Khasavyurt
dialect, using the Arabic script. It was changed in
1927 to the Latin and in 1938 to the Cyrillic. At the
time of the revolution, the majority of Dagestani
intellectuals recommended that Kumyk be the official
language of all Dagestan, as it was the most widespread
language used by these linguistically diverse people.
POP: 228,418 (1979); 188,792 (1970); 134,967 (1959);
94,549 (1926). The Kumyk are Sunni Moslem in religion,
with some Shiite Moslems in Derbent and Makhachkala.
They live, primarily, in the northern steppe region of
Dagestan, and adjacent areas in the Chechen-Ingush ASSR
in the eastern North Caucasus. SEE MAP 6.

KUNDROV TATAR   The Kundrov Tatars are descendants of
                 the Nogai Tatars (the Golden Horde)
that lived in the region around Astrakhan, between the
Volga and Ural Rivers. Having lived among the Kalmyks,
they adopted many Kalmyk cultural traits. They are
Sunni Moslem in religion. They and the Karagash
(Karashi) form the Astrakhan Tatars. SEE Astrakhan
Tatar, Tatar.

KURAMA   Self des. Qurama. The Kurama are a culturally
          distinct group of Uzbeks. They are of mixed
Kypchak Turkic, Mongolic and Iranian origin. They lead
a nomadic lifestyle and form a transitional group
between the Kazakhs and Uzbeks (both culturally and
linguistically). Until the 1930s they were considered a
distinct ethnic group. Since that time they have been
classified as an ethnographic group of Uzbeks. Their
population in 1926 was 50,079. SEE Uzbek.

KURD   Self des. Kurmandzh; oth. des. Kurt. ETHN: The
        Kurds of the USSR are the descendants of Kurds
who migrated to the Caucasus from Turkey and Iran at
various times [10th-12th cents., in the 1820s, during

1853-56, during 1877-78 (during the Russo-Turkish
War), and during World War I]. While the Kurds who are
Sunni Moslem came to this area from both Turkey
(primarily) and Iran, the Shiite Kurds came exclusively
from Iran and the Yezid Kurds from Turkey. SEE Yezid.
The Kurds of Azerbaidzhan and Turkmenistan are being
assimilated by the Azerbaidzhans and Turkmen
respectively. They are the descendants of early
immigrants to those areas. The Kurds of Armenia are the
only Kurds having ethnic institutions (radio, eduation,
press, etc.) in their language. The Kurds of Kirghizia
and Kazakhstan represent the former Turkified Kurdish
population of the Meskhetia region of Georgia, who were
deported to Central Asia in 1944 and never allowed to
return to Georgia. The deported Kurds were classified
as Turks in 1944 and reclassified as Azerbaidzhans in
the 1950s. They make up part of the group now known as
Meskhetians. SEE Meskhetian. LANG: Kurdish is made up
of two dialect groups Kurmandzh and Kurdi. All Soviet
Kurds speak dialects of Kurmandzh. Kurdish is divided
into many dialects. The Kurdish literary language was
established in 1921 on the basis of one of the
Kurmandzh dialects spoken in the area of Soviet
Armenia. It was first written in the Armenian script,
changed in 1929 to the Latin, and in 1945 to the
Cyrillic. It has literary status only in Soviet
Armenia. All other Kurds must use either local
languages or Russian as their literary language. Radio
Yerevan also broadcasts to the Kurds of the Middle
East, who live just across the border in neighboring
Turkey, Iran, and Iraq. POP: 115,858 (1979); 88,930
(1970); 58,799 (1959); 69,184 (1926). In the 1926
census the Kurds and Yezids were listed separately. In
that year there were 69,184 Kurds and 14,726 Yezids.
There are both Sunni Moslem and Yezid Kurds in Soviet
Armenia; the Kurds of Azerbaidzhan and Turkmenistan are
Shiite (with a small Sunni minority); and the
Meskhetian Kurds now living in Central Asia are Sunni
Moslem in religion. The Kurds of the USSR live,
primarily, around Yerevan in Soviet Armenia, and in
scattered settlements in Kazakhstan, Kirgizia,
Turkmenistan, Azerbaidzhan and Georgia. SEE Yezid,
Azerbaidzhan, Turkmen. SEE MAP 15.

KURIK CHEREMISS (MARI)   Alt. spel. Kuryk Mari. SEE
                            Kuryk Mari, Mari.

KURIL (IAN)   Alt. des. Ainu. SEE Ainu.

KÜRIN   For. alt. des. Lezgin. SEE Lezgin.

KURISCHE KÖNIGE   Alt. (German) des. Kuršu Ķoniņi.
                     SEE Kuršu Ķoniņi, Kurši, Latvian,
                     Lithuanian.

KURISH KENIGE   Rus. des. Kuršu Ķoniņi. SEE Kuršu Ķoniņi, Kurši, Latvian, Lithuanian.

KURISH KINGS   Alt. des. Kuršu Ķoniņi. SEE Kuršu Ķoniņi, Kurši, Latvian, Lithuanian.

KÜRKÜRÖÖ   Self des. Kürküröö. A tribe of Kirgiz of non-direct Kirgiz origin. They do not belong to either of the two major Kirgiz tribal groupings (right and left wings) or to the Ichkilik. SEE Kirgiz.

KURMANDJ   Alt. spel. Kurmandzh; alt. des. Kurd. SEE Kurmandzh, Kurd.

KURMANDZH   Alt. des. Kurd. SEE Kurd.

KURMANJ   Alt. spel. Kurmandzh; alt. des. Kurd. SEE Kurmandzh, Kurd.

KÜRÖN   Self des. Kürön. A tribe of Kirgiz of non-direct Kirgiz origin. They do not belong to either of the two major Kirgiz tribal groupings (right and left wings) or to the Ichkilik. They live in At Bashin and Naryn Rayons in Tyen Shan Oblast in the Kirgiz SSR. SEE Kirgiz.

KURONIAN   Alt. des. and spel. Kurši. SEE Kurši, Latvian, Lithuanian.

KURSENIEKI   Self des. Kursenieki (sing. Kursenieks); Lithuanian des. Kuršininkai (sing. Kuršininkas). A group of Latvians who in the 16th cent. migrated to the Courish (Kurish) Spit, where they subsequently formed the fishing population. They retained their Latvian dialect until the 20th cent. After World War I, those on the southern half of the Courish Spit (then part of East Prussia) were assimilated by the Germans. Those on the northern half (belonging to Lithuania) kept their identity until 1944, when they fled westwards. SEE Kurši, Latvian, Lithuanian.

KURSHI   Alt. spel. Kurši. SEE Kurši, Latvian, Lithuanian.

KURŠI   Lithuanian des. Kuršiai; Latvian des. Kurši (sing. Kursis). An ancient Baltic tribe who inhabited the area around the Courish Lagoon, the coast of Lithuania, and the southern coast of Latvia (west and south of Riga). With the Teutonic (German) conquest and the breakdown of the tribal system, they merged into the Latvian and Lithuanian populations. In East Prussia, some of their descendants were doubtless

assimilated by the Germans. The name Kurši has also
been applied to a number of ethnographic groups of the
Baltic region, most notably the: Kuršu Ķoniņi or Ķēniņi
(Kurish Kings or Kurische Könige), Kurzemnieki, and
Kursenieki. See Kuršu Ķoniņi, Kurzemnieki, Kursenieki,
Latvian, Lithuanian.

KURŠIAI   Alt. (Lithuanian) des. Kurši. SEE Kursi,
               Latvian, Lithuanian.

KURŠININKAI (KURŠININKAS)   alt. (Lithuanian) des.
                                 Kursenieki. SEE
                                 Kursenieki, Latvian,
                                 Lithuanian.

KURŠU ĶĒNIŅI   Alt. des. Kuršu Ķoniņi; SEE Kuršu
                    Ķoniņi, Kurši, Latvian, Lithuanian.

KURŠU ĶONIŅI   Self des. Kuršu Ķoniņi (Ķēniņi); oth.
                    des. Kuršu Ķēniņi, Kurische Könige,
Kurish King. A group of Latvians who claim descent from
the nobility of the Kurši, who under German rule
enjoyed feudal recognition of their titles to their own
lands, and were not reduced to serfdom. There were
several such small groups of minor landlords and free
peasants, both among the Latvians and among the
Livonians. SEE Kurši, Latvian, Lithuanian.

KURT   Alt. des. Kurd. SEE Kurd.

KURYK CHEREMISS   Alt. des. Kuryk Mari. SEE Kuryk
                       Mari, Mari.

KURYK MARI   Self des. Kuryk Mari; for. des. Kuryk
                  Cheremiss; oth. des. Highland Mari. The
Kuryk Mari are the most numerous of the Mari groups.
They are culturally and linguistically distinct from
the lowland Mari [Kozhla (Forest), Olyk (Meadow), and
Üpö (Eastern) Mari]. Although basically shamanist-
animist in religion they accepted many Eastern Orthodox
beliefs from the Russians. Among the lowland Mari most
Christian beliefs were rejected. The highland and
lowland forms of Mari are distinct, non-mutually
intelligible, languages (not dialects of one Mari
language). Both have literary forms. Kuryk Mari was
first written in 1821 using the Cyrillic script. It is
one of the few languages of the USSR that did not
undergo major alphabet changes in the 1920s and 1930s.
SEE Mari.

KURZEMIAN   Alt. des. Kurzemnieki. SEE Kurzemnieki,
                 Kurši, Latvian, Lithuanian.

KURZEMNIEKI   Self   des.   Kurzemnieki   (sing.
Kurzemnieks).   Latvians   from   the
province   of   Kurzeme,   a part of   whom   are   doubtless
descended   from   the   original   Kurši,   but   who   are
certainly not to be simply identified with the   ancient
tribe having that name. SEE Kurši, Latvian, Lithuanian.

KUZNETS TATAR   For.   (17th-18th cent.) des.   of Shor;
oth. des. Mrassa or Kondoma Tatar. SEE
Shor.

KVANADI (KVANADY)   Alt.   des.   Bagulal.   SEE Bagulal,
Andi-Dido Peoples, Avar.

KVANALI (KVANALY)   Alt.   des.   Andi.   SEE Andi, Andi-
Dido Peoples, Avar.

KWANADI (KWANADY)   Alt.   des.   Bagulal.   SEE Bagulal,
Andi-Dido Peoples, Avar.

KWANALI (KWANALY)   Alt.   des.   Andi.   SEE Andi, Andi-
Dido Peoples, Avar.

KYPCHAK   Self des.   Qypshak;   oth.   des.   Kypshak. The
Kypchak are a tribe of Uzbeks who maintain a
distinct   identity   and   form   a   transitional   group
(culturally and linguistically) between the Uzbeks   and
Kazakhs.   They are of mixed Kypchak Turkic and Mongolic
origin,   and maintained a nomadic way of life until the
1930s.   They   are   a Kypchak speaking group (closer   in
language   and   culture   to   the   Kazakhs)   of   pre-Uzbek
origin   that   is being assimilated by   the   Uzbeks.   Up
until the 1930s the Kypchak were considered a   distinct
ethnic group. Since that time they have been classified
as an ethnographic group of Uzbeks. POP: 33,502 (1926).
SEE Uzbek.

KYPCHAQ   Alt. spel. Kypchak. SEE Kypchak, Uzbek.

KYPSHAK   (KYPSHAQ)   Alt.   des.   Kypchak.   SEE Kypchak,
Uzbek.

KYRGHYZ   Alt. spel. Kirgiz. SEE Kirgiz.

KYRGHYZ KAISAK   (KAYSAK)   Alt.   spel.   Kirgiz Kaisak;
for. alt. des. Kazakh. SEE
Kazakh.

KYRGHYZ KAZAK   (KAZAKH)   Alt.   spel.   Kirgiz Kazakh;
for. alt. des. Kazakh, SEE
Kazakh.

KYRGYZ   Alt. spel. Kirgiz. SEE Kirgiz.

KYRGYZ KAISAK   (KAYSAK)   Alt. spel. Kirgiz Kaisak;
                            for. alt. des. Kazakh. SEE
                            Kazakh.

KYRGYZ KAZAK   (KAZAKH)   Alt. spel. Kirgiz Kazakh;
                            for. alt. des. Kazakh, SEE
                            Kazakh.

KYRYM TATAR   Alt. des. Crimean Tatar. SEE Crimean
         \   Tatar, Tatar.

KYURIN   Alt. des. Kürin; for. alt. des. Lezgin. SEE
           Lezgin.

KYZYL   Self des. Qyzyl; oth. des. Kizil. The Kyzyl
          are one of the five territorial divisions of
the Khakass. The Kyzyl are comprised of twelve ulus
[Kyzyl, Melet of the first and second halves, greater
and lesser Acha, lesser Argun, Kurchik, Basagar of the
first and second halves, Igin, Kamlar, and Shusty (the
former eleven are Turkic and the latter Kettic in
origin)]. They speak the Kyzyl dialect of Khakass.
Although officially Eastern Orthodox in religion, their
religion is a mixture of shamanist-animist and Eastern
Orthodox beliefs. In early literature on the Kyzyl,
those living along the upper Chulym were called Kyzyl,
those in its middle course Melet, and those in its
lower reaches Chulym Tatars. The Kyzyl settled the
basins of the White and Black Iyus, and along the
Serezh, Pechishcha and Uryup Rivers around Bozhe Lake
in the Khakass AO. SEE Khakass.

KZYL   Alt. des. Kyzyl. SEE Kyzyl, Khakass.

L

LAHAMUL (TSY)   Alt. spel. Lakhamul. SEE Lakhamul,
                 Svanetian.

LAK   Self des. Laq; for. des. Ghazi Kumuq (Kazi
        Kumukh). ETHN: The Lak are culturally and
linguistically related to the Dargins (albeit their
languages are distinct and non-mutually intelligible).
LANG: The Lak language belongs to the Dargino-Lak
division of the northeast branch of the Caucasic
language family. Lak is divided into five closely
related dialects: Kumukh, Vitskh, Vikhli, Ashtikuli,

and Balkhar. Since the village of Kumukh was an
important cultural, religious, political, and economic
center in the Lak territory, its dialect was chosen as
the basis for the Lak literary language. Lak was
established as a literary language in the mid-19th
cent. using the Arabic script. It, however, was not
widely used as Arabic remained the dominant literary
language throughout Dagestan up until the period of the
revolution. Lak was changed to the Latin script in
1928 and to the Cyrillic in 1938. The Lak are among the
most multi-lingual of all Dagestanis. They frequently
know Kumyk and Russian, as well as their native Lak
language. Many are also fluent in Azeri, Avar and/or
Dargin. The Lak live, primarily, in the mountainous
part of south-central Dagestan, along the Kazi Kumukh
River and its tributaries. Since 1944 many Lak have
resettled in the northern foothills of the Dagestan
ASSR near the border of the Chechen-Ingush ASSR in Novo
Lakskiy Rayon in the eastern North Caucasus. SEE MAP 6.

LAKHAMUL (TSY)   The origin of the Lakhamul is still
                 debated. They appear to be either
Svanetianized Jews (most likely Georgian Jews) or
Svanetians who converted to Judaism. By the late 19th
cent. the Lakhamul had been converted to Eastern
Orthodoxy and were considered Svanetians. Their
population was estimated in 1864 as 300. SEE Svanetian.

LAMUT   Pre 1931 des. of Even. SEE Even.

LAPP   Self des. Saami (Sameh, Sapme, Samek,
        Samelats); oth. des. Lopar, Kola Lapp. ETHN:
The Lapps of the USSR are similar in culture to the
Lapps of Finland and Norway. LANG: The Lapp language
forms the Lapp (Saami) group of the Finnic branch of
the Uralo-Altaic language family. Three distinct (non-
mutually intelligible) dialects of Lapp are spoken in
the USSR: Notozer (spoken in the western part of the
Kola Peninsula), Kilda (spoken in the northern and
central part of the Kola Peninsula), and Iokang (spoken
in the eastern part of the Kola Peninsula). Many other
Lapp dialects are spoken among the Lapps of Norway,
Sweden, and Finland. In Finland the Inari dialect is
the dominant one. An attempt was made to create a Lapp
literary language in 1933 based on the Kilda dialect.
Since this dialect is not comprehensible to speakers of
the other two, and that there are so few Lapps
altogether, this attempt was shortly abandoned. Russian
serves as the literary language of the Soviet Lapps.
POP: 1,888 (1979); 1884 (1970); 1,792 (1959); 1,720
(1926). After World War II some Russian speaking Lapps
moved from Soviet territory to Finland, apparently with
the cooperation of both governments. The religion of
the Lapps of the USSR is a mixture of shamanist-animist
and Eastern Orthodox beliefs. The religion of the

Scandinavian Lapps is a mixture of shamanist-animist
and Lutheran beliefs. The Soviet Lapps live, primarily,
in the northern part of the Kola Peninsula in northern
European Russia. SEE MAP 10.

LAQ   Alt. spel. Lak. SEE Lak.

LATGAL (LATGAĻI,   LATGALIS)   Alt. des. Latgalian. SEE
                                Latgalian, Latvian.

LATGAĻI   An old Baltic tribal designation, sometimes
           used as a synonym for Latgalian.   SEE
           Latgalian, Latvian.

LATGALIAN   Self   des.   Latgolīši;   Latvian   des.
             Latgalieši (sing. Latgalietis); oth. des.
Latgaļi, Latgalis, Letgal(ian), Lettgal(ian). ETHN: The
Latgalians are a culturally distinct group of Latvians.
They differ from the majority of Latvians in that they
lived under Lithuanian-Polish, rather than German,
rule, and are Catholic in religion (the Latvians are
Lutheran). LANG: Latgalian is transitional between
Latvian and neighboring Lithuanian dialects and can be
understood, albeit with some difficulty, by both.
Latgalian has its own literary language, which uses the
Latin alphabet. Although it is not used in education in
the USSR it is still used to some degree in
publication. The Latgalians use standard Latvian as
their main literary language. POP: 9,707 (1926). In the
inter-War period Latgalia was part of the independent
state of Latvia and only few Latgalians were found in
the USSR. The Latgalians live, primarily, in the
eastern part of Latvia (Latgalia) near the border of
Lithuania and the RSFSR. SEE Latvian.

LATGALIEŠI (LATGALIETIS)   Latvian des. Latgalian (pl.
                            and sing). SEE Latgalian,
                            Latvian.

LATVIAN   Self des. Latvieši (pl.) Latvietis (sing);
           Rus. des. Latyshi; oth. des. Lett. ETHN: The
Latvians are the descendants of four Baltic tribes:
Latgaļi, Seļi, Zemgaļi, and Kurši. Although ethnically
and linguistically related to the Lithuanians they are
culturally different. Whereas the Latvians were
conquered and ruled by Teutonic and Scandinavian
peoples (i.e. influenced heavily by Germanic-
Protestants), the Lithuanians were under Polish
(Slavic-Catholic) influence. Culturally the Latvians
are closer to the Finnic Estonians, who share a common
historical and religious tradition, than they are to
the linguistically related Lithuanians. The Latgalians
are a group of Latvians that were under Polish-
Lithuanian influence and are Catholic in religion. The
Latgalians form a transitional group between the

Latvians and Lithuanians, and their dialect is mutually intelligible to both Latvian and neighboring Lithuanian dialects. The Latvians are also assimilating the Finnic Liv (Livonians) who live on the coast of northwestern Latvia. LANG: Latvian belongs to the Baltic (Letto-Lithuanian) branch of the Indo-European language family. Latvian was first written in the 16th cent. in Latin script. Latvian is comprised of three closely related dialects: central (spoken by the majority of Latvians; it is the dialect spoken in Riga); upper (Augszemnieks, spoken in eastern Latvia); and Livonian (Tāmnieks, spoken in northwestern Latvia). Latgalian is also a literary language, albeit little used at the present. SEE Latgalian. POP: 1,439,037 (1979); 1,429,844 (1970); 1,399,539 (1959); 141,703 (1926). In the inter-War period Latvia was an independent state, and few Latvians lived at that time in the USSR. Those who did lived, primarily, in Moscow and Leningrad, and in areas adjacent to Latvia. During World War II Latvia lost a large part of its population as a result of War deaths and a large migration to the West by those who did not want to live under Soviet-Russian rule. The Latvians live, primarily, in the Latvian SSR, and in adjacent areas in Estonia, Lithuania, and the RSFSR. SEE MAP 3.

LATVIEŠI (LATVIETIS)   Latvian des. Latvian (pl. and sing.). SEE Latvian.

LATYSH (I)   Rus. des. Latvian. SEE Latvian.

LAZ   Self des. Lazi; oth. des. Chan, Zan, Megrelo-Chan. ETHN: The majority of Laz live on the Black Sea coast of northeastern Turkey, near the Soviet border. Only few reside in the USSR. Until 1938 the Laz were considered a distinct ethnic group. Since that time they have been classified as an ethnographic group of Georgians. LANG: The Laz language belongs to the Megrelo-Laz division of the southern (Kartvelian) branch of the Caucasic language family. Laz and Mingrelian (Megrelian) are closely related languages, and are considerd by some linguists as dialects of one (Megrelo-Laz) language. A Laz literary language was created in 1927 although there were only 643 Laz in the entire Soviet Union in 1926. In 1938 the Laz were classified as Georgians, and Georgian became their official literary language. The Laz are Sunni Moslem in religion. They live on the left tributary of the Chorokh River in the Adzhar ASSR in southwestern Georgia, near the border of Turkey. SEE Georgian.

LECHHUMI   Alt. spel Lechkhumi. SEE Lechkhumi, Georgian.

LECHKHUMI   Self des. Lechkhumeli. One of the numerous Kartvelian ethnographic groups that went into the formation of the Georgian nation. The Lechkhumi speak a sub-dialect (Lechkhumi) of one of the western Georgian dialects (Imereli or Imeretian). The Lechkhumi are Eastern Orthodox in religion, and live along the middle course of the Rioni River in the Georgian SSR. SEE Georgian.

LEMKI (LEMKO)   Alt. spel. Lemky. SEE Lemky, Carpatho-Rusin, Ukrainian.

LEMKY   One of the three ethnographic groups of western Ukrainians collectively called Carpatho-Rusin (Lemky, Boiki, Hutsul). Like the Hutsuls and Boiki their culture is distinct from that of the main body of Ukrainians. Formerly they were predominantly Uniate in religion, but since World War II and the abolition of the Uniate church in the USSR, they have become Eastern Orthodox in religion. They speak a distinct (Lemky) dialect of Ukrainian and have a distinct culture. The majority of Lemky live in Poland (on the slopes of the Beskid Mountains between the San and Poprad Rivers, and also to the west of the Uzh). After the formation of the Polish state after World War II, many Lemky were resettled into the western part of the Ukrainian SSR. SEE Carpatho-Rusin, Ukrainian.

LETGAL (IAN)   Alt. des. Latgalian. SEE Latgalian, Latvian.

LETT   Alt. des. Latvian. SEE Latvian.

LETTGAL (IAN)   Alt. spel. Letgal(ian); alt. des. Latgalian. SEE Latgalian, Latvian.

LETTO-LITHUANIAN   Alt. des. Baltic peoples; Col. des. Latvians and Lithuanians. SEE Baltic Peoples, Latvians, Lithuanians.

LEZG (LEZGH, LEZGHIAN,   Alt. des. Lezgin. SEE Lezgin.
LEZGHIN, LEZGHINIAN)

LEZGIN   Self des. Lezghi; for. alt. des. Kürin, Akhta; for. Rus. alt. des. Kurin(tsy), Akhtin(tsy). ETHN: Up until the time of the revolution the term Lezgin was often used to refer to all Dagestani Mountaineers in general, and even to include the Chechens and Ingush. Since the revolution it has been used in the stricter sense to refer only to the Lezgins themselves. Up until the time of the revolution the Lezgins were being assimilated by the Azerbaidzhans (especially those living in Azerbaidzhan itself). The

Lezgin language and culture have been strongly
influenced by the Azerbaidzhans, and virtually all
Lezgins are bilingual (Lezgin and Azeri). The Lezgins,
themselves, were in the process of assimilating the
culturally related Aguls and Rutuls of southern
Dagestan, and to a lesser extent the Tabasaran. LANG:
The Lezgin language belongs to the Samurian group of
the northeast branch of the Caucasic language family.
Lezgin is comprised of three closely related dialects:
Kurin (Gunei) (the most widespread), Akhty, and Kuba
(spoken by the Lezgins of Azerbaidzhan). The Lezgin
literary language was established in the late 19th
cent. on the basis of the Kürin dialect. It was not
used widely until the revolution as Arabic was
considered by the majority of Lezgins, as well as all
other mountaineer Dagestani and Chechens, to be their
literary language. It was changed in 1928 to the Latin
script and in 1938 to the Cyrillic. The Lezgins of
northern Azerbiadzhan were provided with ethnic
institutions (education, media, etc.) in the Lezgin
language until 1939 when Lezgin was abolished in the
Azerbaidzhan SSR as an official language. Thus, Lezgin
serves as the literary language of the Lezgins of
Dagestan, and Azeri for those of Azerbaidzhan. Until
the late 1950s Lezgin also served as the literary
language of the Agul and Rutul. After that time their
official literary language (and language of education)
was changed to Russian. POP: 382,611 (1979); 323,829
(1970); 223,129 (1959); 134,529 (1926). Although only
134,529 people declared themselves Lezgins in the 1926
census, 164,763 listed Lezgin as their native language.
In addition, there were approximately 32,000 Lezgins
who declared themselves Azerbaidzhans speaking Lezgin.
The Lezgins are Sunni Moslem in religion. They live,
primarily, in southern Dagestan and contiguous northern
Azerbaidzhan. There is also a fairly large population
of Lezgins in Baku, and other cities of the
Azerbaidzhan SSR. SEE MAP 6.

LĪBI   Alt. des. Livonian.   SEE Livonian, Latvian.

LIETUVIAI   Lithuanian   des.   Lithuanian.   SEE
                 Lithuanian.

LITHUANIAN Self des. Lietuviai; Rus. des. Litov(tsy).
            ETHN: The Lithuanians are closely related
ethnically and linguistically to the Latvians. They
are, however, culturally different. Whereas the
Latvians were conquered and ruled by Germans and
Scandinavians (Germanic-Protestants), the Lithuanians
were under strong Polish (Slavic-Catholic) influence.
As a result the Latvians are Lutheran in religion, and
their culture reflects a strong Germanic influence. The
Lithuanians are Catholic and their culture reflects a
strong Slavic (Polish, and to a lesser extent

Belorussian) influence. The Lithuanians are divided
into geographical groups based on former Baltic tribal
divisions: Aukštaičiai, Žemaičiai, Suvalkiečiai
(Užnemuniečiai) and Dzūki. Formerly there were others
[Yatvig (Sudavi), Kurši, Skali, and Zemgaļi], however,
they were assimilated by the Belorussians (Yatvig), and
other peoples (Latvians or other Lithuanians). LANG:
Lithuanian belongs to the Baltic (Letto-Lithuanian)
branch of the Indo-European language family. It is
closely related to (albeit only partly mutually
intelligible with) Latvian. Lithuanian has been written
since the 16th cent. It was originally established as a
literary language as a result of the Protestant
reformation. The Lithuanian literary language is based
on a sub-dialect of the (Aukštai) dialect of Lithuanian
using the Latin script. Attempts were made during the
19th cent. by the Tsarist regime to change Lithuanian
into the Cyrillic script and printing in Lithuanian was
forbidden in the Russian Empire between 1832-1904.
During that period a lively Lithuanian press existed in
the Prussian controlled area of Lithuania. For decades
Lithuanian works were smuggled into Russian Lithuania
from there. POP: 2,850,905 (1979); 2,664,944 (1970);
2,326,094 (1959); 41,463 (1926). In the inter-War
period Lithuania was an independent state. During that
time few Lithuanians lived in the USSR. During World
War II Lithuania lost a large part of its Lithuanian
population as a result of war deaths and a large
emigration of Lithuanians to the West by Lithuanians
that did not want to live under Soviet-Russian rule.
The Lithuanians are primarily Catholic in religion,
with a sizable Lutheran minority (those formerly living
in the Prussian ruled part of Lithuania). The
Lithuanians live, primarily, in the Lithuanian SSR, and
adjacent areas in Latvia and Belorussia. SEE MAP 4.

LITHUANIAN TATAR   The descendants of Crimean Tatars
                    who were sent to Lithuania. Over
the centuries the Lithuanian Tatars have lost the Tatar
language and switched to speaking Lithuanian. They,
have, however, retained their Sunni Moslem religion.
Those who converted to Catholicism have been
assimilated by the Lithuanians among whom they live.
SEE Crimean Tatar, Tatar.

LITOV (TSY)   Rus. des. Lithuanian. SEE Lithuanian.

LITOV (SKIY) TATAR   Rus. des. Lithuanian Tatar. SEE
                      Lithuanian Tatar, Crimean Tatar,
                      Tatar.

LITTLE RUSSIAN   Eng. des. Malo Rus.; for. des.
                  Ukrainian. SEE Malo Rus, Ukrainian.

LIV (IAN)   Alt. des. Livonian. SEE Livonian, Latvian.

LIVONIAN   Self des. Liivi or Raandali; oth. des. Lībi,
            Livi; Latvian des. Lībieši. Those Livonians
living on the western most part of the Latvian coast
were called Raandalist ("coast dwellers"); those to the
east were called Kalamied ("fishermen"). ETHN: The
Livonians are a Finnic people that are being
assimilated by the Latvians. Formerly, the Livonians
lived over a much larger territory in what is now
central Latvia. Historically, the term Livonian has
been used to designate any inhabitant (Livonian,
Latvian, Estonian, or German) of the old territory of
Livonia (German des. Livland), which included much of
modern Latvia and Estonia. There is thus some confusion
in historical works between ethnic Livonians and
residents of Livonia. LANG: Livonian belongs to the
southern sub-group of the Balto-Finnic group of the
Finnic division of the Uralian branch of the Uralo-
Altaic language family. Livonian was first written in
the mid-19th cent. using the Latin script. It was never
widely used and was abandoned in favor of Latvian. POP:
In 1959 there were approximately 3,000 Livonians, of
whom only about 500 spoke Livonian. The Livonians have
been all but assimilated by the Latvians. They live on
the Latvian coast between the Baltic Sea and the Gulf
of Riga. SEE Latvian.

LIVVIKI   Self des. Livgilaine or Livvikei, Karjala
            (Karyala). The Livviki are the Karelians
living in the southwestern part of the Karelian ASSR
who speak the Livviki dialect of Karelian. The Livviki
dialect has many Veps elements. SEE Karelians.

LOPAR   Alt. des. Lapp. SEE Lapp.

LUOROVETLAN   Alt. des. Chukchi. SEE Chukchi.

LYDDIKI   1-Self des. Lyydilaine or Lyydikoi; Oth.
            des. Lyudiki, Karyala. The Lyddiki are a
distinct group of Karelians who live in Kondopozhskiy
and part of Olonetskiy Rayons, and speak a distinct
dialect of Karelian. The Lyydiki dialect has many Veps
elements. They form a transitional group between the
Karelians and Veps. SEE Karelian.
            2-Same self des.; oth. des. Lyydinikad or
            Lyydinik (Lyudinikad or Lyudinik). The
Lyydiki are the northern and central Veps who have been
assimilated by the Karelians, among whom they live.
They now call themselves Karelians. SEE Karelian.

LYUDDIKI (LYUDIKI)   Alt. des. Lyddiki. SEE Lyddiki,
            Karelian, Veps.

M

MAARULAL   Oth. des. Magarulal. The term Maarulal in the Avar language means Mountaineer. The Maarulal is the northern clan federation of Avars, around which the Avar nation was formed. Maarulal is now the self des. of the Avars in general. SEE Avar.

MADIAR (MADJAR, MADYAR,   Alt. spel. Magyar; alt. MADZHAR)   des. Hungarian. SEE Magyar, Hungarian.

MAGARULAL   Alt. des. Maarulal. SEE Maarulal, Avar.

MAGYAR   Self des. and alt. des. of Hungarian; SEE Hungarian.

MAHOSH   Alt. spel. Makhosh. SEE Makhosh, Adygei, Circassian.

MAJAR   Alt. spel. Magyar; alt. des. Hungarian. SEE Magyar, Hungarian.

MAKHOSH   One of the ten major tribal divisions of the Adygei. Each of these was formerly considered a distinct people. They are now classified as Adygei. The majority of Makhosh, along with the other Abazgo-Circassian peoples emigrated to Turkey in the mid-1860s. They live between the middle Laba and Belaya Rivers in the western North Caucasus. SEE Adygei, Circassian.

MALKAR   Self des. Malkarly; oth. des. Balkar. One of the five tribes (societies) that went into the formation of the Balkars. The Balkar nation was formed by the consolidation of the other four tribes (Byzyngy, Kholam, Chegem and Baksan) around the Malkar. They live, primarily, in the valley of the Malka (Balka) River in the Kabardino-Balkar ASSR in the central North Caucasus. SEE Balkar.

MALKAR (CHI)(CHILI)(LI)   Alt. des. Malkar. SEE Malkar, (CHY)(CHYLY)(LY)   Balkar.

MALQAR (CHI)(CHILI)(LI)   Alt. spel. and des. Malkar. (CHY)(CHYLY)(LY)   SEE Malkar, Balkar.

MALO   RUS   (RUSIN, RUSSIAN)   For.   alt.   des.   of
                                   Ukrainian. The term Malo
(Little) Rus, as opposed to Veliko (Great) Rus, derives
from   the Byzantine   system   of   ethno-geographical
nomenclature. Those   areas   closer to Byzantium were
called Little   or Lesser,   as the exact extent of the
territory was known. The area beyond that (presumed to
be larger) was designated Great or Greater. The pair
Lesser and Greater are not related to value judgements,
importance, or relative power. SEE Ukrainian.

MALORUS (MALORUSIN,   Alt. des. Malo Rus. SEE Malo
   MALORUSSIAN)   Rus, Ukrainian.

MAMKHEG   Self des. Mamkhegh. One of the ten major
           tribal divisions of the Adygei people. Each
of these groups was formerly considered a distinct
people. They are now classified as Adygei. The majority
of the Mamkheg, along with the other Abazgo-Circassian
peoples, emigrated to Turkey in the mid-1860s. The
Mamkheg lived in a small area along both sides of the
middle Belaya River in the western North Caucasus. SEE
Adygei, Circassian.

MAMKHEGH   Alt. des. Mamkheg. SEE Mamkheg, Adygei,
           Circassian.

MANCHU   Self des. Mandzhu; oth. des. Manchurian. The
          majority of Manchu live in northeastern China
(Manchuria). They are ethnically, culturally, and
linguistically related to the Manchu peoples of the
USSR (Nanai, Ulchi, Orok, Orochi, and Udegei). In 1926
23 people were listed as Manchu in the USSR. It is not
clear whether these were members of one of the Manchu
peoples of the USSR, or one of the Manchu peoples of
China living in the USSR. SEE MAP 6.

MANCHU PEOPLES   Col. des. of the peoples of the USSR
                 who speak languages that belong to
the Manchu division of the Tunguso-Manchu language
branch of the Uralo-Altaic family. The Manchu are
divided into two closely related groups: Nani and
Udegei. The Nani group is comprised of the Nanai,
Ulchi, Orok and Orochi. These peoples are closely
related ethnically, culturally, and linguistically.
They all speak closely related dialects of one Nani
language, and are considered by some to be sub-
divisions of one Nani people. The Udegei language is
the closest of the Manchu languages to the Tungusic
division. The religions of the Manchu peoples are all
similar and are basically a mixture of shamanist-
animist, Eastern Orthodox, and Chinese beliefs. The
Manchu peoples live, primarily, in Primorskiy and
Khabarovsk Krai and on Sakhalin Island, in southeastern
Siberia. SEE MAP 6.

MANCHURIAN   Although the term Manchurian usually
              refers to the Manchu of northeastern
China, it has at times been used (Manchurian peoples)
as an alt. des. for the Manchu peoples of the USSR. SEE
Manchu peoples.

MANDJU (MANDJURI,   MANDJURIAN,   Alt. des. Manchu,
                      MANDJURY)   Manchu peoples. SEE
                                           Manchu, Manchu
                                           Peoples.

MANDURI (MANDURY)   Alt. des. Manchu, Manchu peoples.
                      SEE Manchu, Manchu Peoples.

MANDZHU (MANDZHURI,   MANDZHURIAN,   Alt. des. Manchu,
                      MANDZHURY)   Manchu peoples.
                                           SEE Manchu, Manchu
                                           Peoples.

MANEGIR   Oth. des. Manyagir, Manegri, Kumarchan. The
           Manegir are a former division of the Evenks.
Until the 1930s the Manegir were considered a distinct
ethnic group. Since that time they have been classified
as Evenk. The Manegir lived mainly along the Kumara
River (from whence the alt. des. Kumarchen derives). In
the 1926 census 59 people were listed as Manegir
(Manegry). SEE Evenk.

MANEGRI (MANEGRY)   Alt. des. Manegir. SEE Manegir,
                      Evenk.

MANGU (MANGUN)   For. alt. des. Ulchi. SEE Ulchi.

MANIAGIR   Alt. des. Manegir. SEE Manegir. Evenk.

MANSI   For. des. Vogul. ETHN: The Mansi are closely
         related ethnically, culturally, and
linguistically to the Khant(y). LANG: Mansi forms with
Khant(y) the Ob-Ugrian group of the Ugrian divison of
the Uralian branch of the Uralo-Altaic language family.
The Mansi literary language was established in 1932
using the Latin script. It was changed in 1939-1940 to
the Cyrillic. Although Mansi is officially a literary
language it is little used in publishing and Russian
serves as the main literary language of the Mansi. POP:
7,563 (1979); 7,710 (1970); 6,449 (1959); 5,754 (1926).
In the 1926 census the Mansi appear as Vogul. The Mansi
religion is a mixture of shamanist-animist and Eastern
Orthodox beliefs. They live, primarily, in the eastern
part of the Khanty-Mansi AO in northwestern Siberia,
with major settlements also in Sverdlovsk Ob. SEE MAP
13.

MANYAGIR   Alt. des. Manegir. SEE Manegir, Evenk.

MARI   Self des. Mari ("Man"); for. des. Cheremiss.
ETHN: The Mari are one of the Finnic peoples of
the Middle Volga region. The Mari are culturally
distinct from the other Finnic peoples of the region in
that they never fully accepted Christianity, and
strongly adhered to their shamanist-animist beliefs.
The Mari are divided into two major groups: highland
(Kuryk Mari, or Forest Mari), and lowland (Olyk Mari,
or Meadow Mari). Each of these groups has its own
language (the two are not mutually intelligible).
Closely related linguistically to the Olyk Mari are the
eastern Mari (Üpö Mari), who are usually considered a
sub-division of them. Most Mari are in the highland
group. They live, primarily, on the right bank of the
Volga. The Olyk Mari live, primarily, in the forested
areas on the left bank, and the Üpö Mari live,
primarily, in settlements in the Bashkir and Tatar
ASSR, and Sverdlovsk Oblast. The division between
highland and lowland Mari goes back to the 12th
century. The main difference is linguistic and not
cultural. Mari nationalism since the mid-19th cent.
has manifested itself in a religious-nationalistic
form— i.e. the struggle to preserve their shamanist-
animist religion. In the 1870s a sect called the Kugu
Sorta (Great Candle) lead a nationalist movement
against the Christianization of the Mari. This has been
especially strong among the Olyk and Üpö Mari. LANG:
The Mari language forms the Mari group of the Finnic
division of the Uralian branch of the Uralo-Altaic
language family. There are two distinct Mari languages,
each with a number of dialects, and each having its own
literary language. Highland Mari (Kuryk Mari) has been
written since 1821 in the Cyrillic script. The lowland
Mari literary language is based on the Olyk (Meadow)
Mari dialect. It has also been written since the mid-
19th century in the Cyrillic script. The Upo (Eastern)
Mari use the closely related Olyk Mari literary
language. These literary languages were created by the
Russian Orthodox church of Kazan, in its attempt to
convert the Mari to Christianity. POP: 621,961 (1979);
598,628 (1970); 504,205 (1959); 428,192 (1926). The
Mari religion is basically animist-shamanist with some
Eastern Orthodox and Islamic intrusions. The Christian
elements are most common among the Kuryk Mari, and the
Islamic among the Üpö (who adopted them from the
Tatars, among whom they live). The Mari live, primarily,
in the Mari ASSR, and scattered settlements throughout
the Middle Volga region. SEE MAP 7.

MARKOV (TSY)   The Markov(tsy) are a group of Russians
who settled in the village of Markovo
on the Anadyr River in the Polar region who mixed with
local Chuvans and Yukagirs. Although they maintained a
Russian identity and the Russian language, they are
culturally related to the local Siberian tribes. They

engage, primarily, in fishing, hunting, and breeding reindeer and dogs. SEE Russian.

MATOR   Alt. des. Koibal. SEE Koibal, Khakass.

MEADOW CHEREMISS (MARI)   Alt. des. Olyk Mari. SEE
                            Olyk Mari, Mari.

MEGRELI (MEGRELIAN)   Alt. des. Mingrelian. SEE
                        Mingrelian, Georgian.

MEGRELO-CHAN   Alt. des. Megrelo-Laz. SEE Megrelo-Laz,
                 Mingrelian, Laz, Georgian.

MEGRELO-LAZ   Col. des. for the Mingrelian and Laz
                people. Although linguistically similar (their languages are mutually intelligible) they are culturally distinct. The Mingrelians are Eastern Orthodox in religion and culturally related to the Christian Georgians; the Laz are Sunni Moslem and culturally closer to the Moslem Georgian Adzhars and Turks. SEE Mingrelian, Laz, Georgian.

MEGRELO-ZAN   Alt. des. Megrelo-Laz. SEE Megrelo-Laz,
                Mingrelian, Laz, Georgian.

MESHCHERA   The Meshchera were a group of Volga Finns
              (Mordvinian) that were assimilated by the Russians and the Tatars. Those that mixed with the Russians and adopted the Eastern Orthodox religion formed the Meshcheryak, who consider themselves Russians, speak Russian, and are Eastern Orthodox in religion. Those that mixed with the Tatars formed the Mishars, who considered themselves either Mishars or Tatars. The Mishars speak Tatar and are Sunni Moslem in religion. SEE Mishar, Meshcheryak.

MESHCHERIAK   Alt. spel. Meshcheryak. SEE Meshcheryak,
                Russian, Meshchera.

MESHCHERYAK   Self des. Meshcheryak, Russkiy. The
                Meshcheryak are a group of Russians of mixed Volga Finnic (Meshchera) and Russian origin. They speak a distinct dialect of Russian which contains many Mordvinian elements. They are related to the Mishars. The Mishar are Tatarized Meshchera, as opposed to the Meshcheryak who are Russified Meshchera. They are Eastern Orthodox in religion. The Meshcheryak live, primarily, in the basin of the Oka River in Ryazan and Tambov Oblasts, with other settlements in Penza and Saratov Oblasts, in the Volga region. SEE Russian, Meshchera.

MESHETIAN   Alt. spel. Meskhetian. SEE Meskhetian,
              Georgian.

MESHI   Alt. des. Meskhi. SEE Meskhi, Meskhetian,
Georgian.

MESKHETIAN   The term Meskhetian has arisen only since
the late 1950s and early 1960s as a col.
des. for the Turkified peoples [Meskhi (Georgians),
Khemshil (Armenians), Kurds, and Karapapakh] who
formerly lived in the Meskhi region in southwestern
Georgia near the Turkish border. They became known as
Meskhetians only after their deportation in 1944 to
Central Asia (primarily in the Tashkent area), and
their subsequent petition to the United Nations for
assistance to return to Meskhetia. In 1944 the Soviets
classified them collectively as Turks. After their
petition to emigrate to Turkey in the 1950s the Soviet
then reclassified them as Azerbaidzhans. It is unclear
under what designation the Meskhetians are listed in
the 1959 or 1970 censuses (i.e. either as Azerbaidzhans
or under the general title Other Nationalities). In
1979 a group appeared under the designation Turki (pop.
92,689). These were probably Meskhetians who declared
themselves Turks. SEE Georgian, Azerbaidzhan.

MESKHI   One of the numerous Kartvelian ethnographic
groups that went into the formation of the
Georgian nation. Many Meskhi were heavily influenced by
the Turks and accepted Sunni Islam as their religion.
Those who had become Moslems were deported along with
the other Turkified people of the region of Meskhetia
(Khemshil, Kurd, and Karapapakh) to Central Asia in
1944. Those who remained Eastern Orthodox are still
resident in the Meskhetia region of southwestern
Georgia and are classified as Georgians. These
Georgians use the Georgian literary language. SEE
Meskhetian, Georgian.

MICHIGIZ (MICHIK)   Alt. des. Michikiz. SEE Michikiz,
Chechen.

MICHIKIZ   One of the major tribes of the Chechens.
Between the 14th-19th cents. the term
Michikiz was used as a designation for the Chechens as
a whole (usually, including the Ingush as well, who at
that time were not considered a distinct people from
the Chechens). SEE Chechen.

MINGRELIAN   Self des. Margali; oth. des. Megreli,
Megrelian. ETHN: The Mingrelians are
culturally related to the Georgians, although they are
lingustically distinct. Until the 1930s the Mingrelians
were considered a distinct ethnic group. After that
time they were classified as an ethnographic group of
Georgians. They were in the process of being
assimilated by the Georgians at that time. Many Abkhaz,
on the other hand, were being assimilated by the

western Mingrelians. LANG: Mingrelian forms, with Laz, the Megrelo-Laz division of the southern (Kartvelian) branch of the Caucasic language family. The status of Mingrelian and Laz as distinct languages, as opposed to mere dialects of one language, is still debated. The Mingelian language is comprised of two closely related dialects: western (Samurzakan-Zugdidi) and eastern (Senaki). The Mingrelian language is not written and Georgian has traditionally served as the literary language of the Mingrelians. POP: 242,990 (1926). Although only 242,990 people were listed as Mingrelians in the 1926 census, 284,834 listed Mingrelian as their native language. Given that many Mingrelians declared Georgian their native language, it appears that roughly 40,000 Mingrelians called themselves Georgians, while considering Mingrelian their native language. The Mingrelians are being assimilated by the Georgians. The Mingrelians are Eastern Orthodox in religion. They live, primarily, in Mingrelia (the southern slopes of the Great Caucasian chain in west-central northern Georgia). SEE Georgian.

MINGRELO-CHAN (MINGRELO-LAZ,   Alt. des. Megrelo-Laz.
            MEGRELO-ZAN)   SEE   Megrelo-Laz,
                                 Mingrelian, Laz,
                                 Georgian.

MINKIZ   Alt. des. Michikiz. SEE Michikiz, Chechen.

MINUSA (MINUSIN)   Alt. des. Minusa Tatar; for. des. Khakass. SEE Minusa Tatar, Khakass.

MINUSA TATAR   For. des. Khakass. SEE Khakass.

MISHAR   Self des. Mishar, Tatar. ETHN: The Mishars are of mixed Volga Finnic (Meshchera, a group of Mordvinians) and Tatar origin. The Mishars speak Tatar and use the Tatar literary language. Until the 1930s they were considered a distinct ethnic group. Since that time they have been classified as Tatars. The Mishars are ethnically, albeit not linguistically or culturally, related to the Meshcheryak, who are of mixed Meshchera and Russian origin. The Meshcheryaks consider themselves Russians, speak Russian, and are Eastern Orthodox in religion. POP: 242,640 (1926). The Mishars are Sunni Moslem in religion. They live, primarily, in the Tatar ASSR, and in scattered settlements in the Middle Volga region. SEE Meshchera, Tatar.

MISHER   Alt. des. Mishar. SEE Mishar, Tatar.

MOHEV   Alt. des. Mokhev. SEE Mokhev, Georgian.

MOKHEV   Self des. Mokhevi. One of the numerous
           Kartvelian ethnographic groups that went
into the formation of the Georgian nation. They speak a
distinct dialect of Georgian (Mokhevi). The Mokhev are
Eastern Orthodox in religion. SEE Georgian.

MOKSHA   Oth. des. Moksha Mordvinian (Mordovian,
           Mordva). The Moksha are one of the two main
division of the Mordvinians (the other- Erzya). Moksha
and Erzya are distinct (non-mutually intelligible)
languages and both have their own literary forms. The
Moksha literary language was created in 1923 using the
Cyrillic script. The Moksha, like the Erzya, are being
assimilated by the Russians. The Moksha live scattered
throughout the Middle Volga region. They live in the
western part of the Mordvinian ASSR, in Penza and
Orenburg Oblasts, and the Tatar ASSR. Within the
Mordvinian ASSR itself there are no mixed Moksha and
Erzya villages. SEE Mordvinian.

MOKSHA MORDOVIAN (MORDVA,   Alt. des. Moksha. SEE
        MORDVIN, MORDVINIAN)   Moksha, Mordvinian.

MOLDAVIAN   Self des. Moldoven; for. des. Bessarabian.
            ETHN: The Moldavians are ethnic Romanians
whose ancestors became part of the Russian Empire in
the 17th and 18th cent. as a result of Russian
expansion into the Balkans. They lived under Russian
rule and came into close contact with their Ukrainian
neighbors. The culture and language of the Moldavians
have been strongly influenced by the Ukrainians.
Whereas the Romanians changed the script of their
literary language from the Cyrillic to the Latin in the
mid-19th cent., the Moldavians continued to use the
Cyrillic script (under Tsarist pressure). LANG:
Moldavian is an eastern, Ukrainian influenced, form of
Romanian. The Moldavian (Romanian) language belongs to
the eastern division of the Romance language branch of
the Indo-European language family. The Moldavian
language is fairly uniform (having only minor speech
differences from region to region). Moldavian is
written in the Cyrillic script. POP: 2,968,224 (1979);
2,697,994 (1970); 2,214,139 (1959), 278,905 (1926). In
the inter-War period Moldavia was part of the
independent Romanian state. During that time the
Moldavian population of the USSR was comprised of the
Moldavians living in the Ukrainian SSR (near the border
with Moldavia). In 1924 the Soviets created the
Moldavian ASSR on the east bank of the Dniestr River.
When Moldavia (Bessarabia) was reincorporated in the
USSR after World War II the Moldavian ASSR was
abolished. During the inter-war period, the Romanian
government changed the Moldavian writing system to
conform to modern Romanian. With the reincorporation of
Moldavia after the war, the Soviets insisted that the

Moldavians go back to writing the Moldavian language in
the Cyrillic script. The Moldavians are Eastern
Orthodox in religion, with a small Uniate minority.
They live, primarily, in the Moldavian SSR and adjacent
areas in the Ukrainian SSR. SEE MAP 6.

MOLDOVEN   Alt. des. Moldavian. SEE Moldavian.

MONGOL   Alt. des. Khalkha Mongol. SEE Khalkha Mongol.

MORDOVIAN (MORDVA)   Alt.   des.   Mordvinian.   SEE
Mordvinian.

MORDVA ERZIA (ERZYA)   Alt. des. Erzya. SEE Erzya,
Mordvinian.

MORDVA MOKSHA   Alt.   des.   Moksha.   SEE Moksha,
Mordvinian.

MORDVIN   Alt. des. Mordvinian. SEE Mordvinian.

MORDVINIAN   Self des. Mordva, Erzya, Moksha; oth.
des. Mordva, Mordovian, Mordvin. ETHN:
The Mordvinians are divided into two major groups:
Erzya and Moksha. Although ethnically and culturally
closely related, they speak two different languages
that are not mutually intelligible. In addition to
these two major groups there are two small ethnographic
groups of Mordvinians that are merging with the
Russians and the Tatars. The Teryukhan Mordvinians are
Russian speaking Mordvinians (living near Gorkiy) who,
since the middle of the 20th century, have begun to
call themselves Russians. The Karatai live in three
villages in the Tatar ASSR, and are Tatar speaking. All
of the Mordvinians are being assimilated (primarily by
the Russians) and their population has continually
declined since the beginning of this cent. as a result
of this process: LANG: The Erzya and Moksha languages
form the Mordvinian group of the Finnic division of the
Uralian branch of the Uralo-Altaic language family.
Erzya and Moksha are distinct languages and both have a
literary form. Erzya was established as a literary
language in 1922, and Moksha in 1923, using the
Cyrillic script. POP: 1,191,765 (1979); 1,262,670
(1970); 1,285,116 (1959); 1,340,415 (1926).   The
Mordvinians are Eastern Orthodox in religion. They live
scattered throughout the Middle Volga region, with
their largest concentration in the Mordvinian ASSR. SEE
Erzya, Moksha. SEE MAP 10.

MOTOR   Alt. des. Mator; for. des. Koibal. SEE Koibal,
Khakass.

MOUNTAINEER   Rus. des. Gortsy, Tavlintsy (from the Turkic Taulu, meaning Mountaineer); oth. des. North Caucasian Mountaineers. A col. des. of the peoples that inhabit the northern slopes of the Great Caucasian Mountain chain. In general it includes all of these peoples (Karachai, Balkar, Ossetian, Ingush, Chechen, Avar, Dargin, Lak, Tabasaran, Agul, Rutul, Tsakhur, and Lezgin). The first two are Turkic, the third is Iranian, and the latter ten are Caucasic in speech. All but the Ossetians are Sunni Moslem in religion (the Ossetians being Eastern Orthodox). Sometimes the term Mountaineer is used in a more expansive sense and includes the inhabitants of the North Caucasian foreland as well (Circassians, Abaza, Nogai, and Kumyk). When used by the Russians it does not include these lowland peoples, and sometimes (especially in the past) was used in a more restrictive sense to refer only to the Dagestani, Chechen, and Ingush. In the 1926 census 4,188 individuals were listed as Mountaineers (without any ethnic designation). These individuals were probably Chechen, Avar, or one of the Andi-Dido peoples (given their place of residence). The term Mountaineer does not refer to the peoples of the southern slopes of the Caucasus (Abkhaz, Mingrelian, Svanetian, Southern Ossetian, Georgian, Azerbaidzhan, or the Shahdag peoples).

MOUNTAIN JEW   Oth. des. Dagestani Jew, Dag Chufut, Tat(i) Jew; Rus. des. Gorskiy Evrei. ETHN: The exact origin of the Mountain Jews is not known. Their ancestors lived in Azerbaidzhan where they adopted the language of the local Iranian population (Tati). They are old inhabitants of the Caucasus region. It is believed they are the descendants of a Jewish military colony established south of Derbent by Sassanian kings of Persia. Over the centuries the majority of the Mountain Jews adopted Islam and were assimilated by the other peoples around them (Azerbaidzhan and Dagestani). The present Mountain Jewish population represents that part of the Mountain Jewish population that moved into the mountains of eastern Dagestan, where they lived in isolation. The Mountain Jews are not related ethnically, linguistically, or culturally to the Ashkenazic (Eastern European) Jews. They may have some connection, however, to the Georgian Jews and the former Khazar Jews. Until the 1930s the Mountain Jews were considered a distinct ethnic group. Since that time they have been classified as Jews, and are not differentiated in statistical publications. Although the Mountain Jews speak the Tati language and may be of common ancestry with the ethnic group called Tati, the two peoples should not be confused. The Tati are either Armeno-Gregorian or Shiite Moslem in religion and are being

assimilated   by   the   Armenians   and   Azerbaidzhans,
respectively. The Jewish Tati are listed as Jews in all
publications, and not as Tati. LANG: The Mountain Jews
speak Tati as their native language. This language
belongs to the southwest group of the Iranian branch of
the Indo-European language family. There is a literary
language based on the dialect of Tati spoken by the
Mountain Jews. It was formerly written in the Hebrew
script (since the 19th cent.), changed in 1928 to the
Latin, and to the Cyrillic in 1938. The dialect of Tati
spoken by the Mountain Jews differs from those of the
Moslem and Armeno-Gregorian Tats in that it has many
borrowed words from Hebrew (for religious terminology)
and Dagestani languages. The Christian and Moslem Tati
do not use the Tati literary language, but rather Azeri
if they are Moslem or Armenian if they are Armeno-
Gregorian. SEE Tat. POP: 25,225 (1926). The population
of the Mountain Jews has not been published separately
since 1926.   There is now a substantial emigration of
Mountain Jews to Israel and the United States (since
the 1970s). The Mountain Jews live, primarily, in
Derbent, Buinaksk, and other towns in Dagestan, Baku
and Kuba in Azerbaidzhan, Groznyy in the Chechen-Ingush
ASSR, and Nalchik in the Kabardino-Balkar ASSR. SEE
Tat, Jew.

MOUNTAIN KALMUK (KALMYK,   Alt des. Biy Kalmyk. SEE Biy
        QALMUQ, QALMYQ)   Kalmyk, Altai.

MOUNTAIN SHOR (IAN)   Alt. des. Shor. SEE Shor.

MOUNTAIN TADJIK   Alt. spel. Mountain Tadzhik. SEE
                   Mountain Tadzhik, Tadzhik.

MOUNTAIN TADZHIK   Rus. des. Gorniy Tadzhik. One of
                    the two cultural divisions of the
Tadzhiks (mountain and lowland). The Mountain Tadzhik
live in the highland areas of the Tadzhik SSR, and are
close to the Pamir peoples in culture, as opposed to
the lowland Tadzhiks whose culture is indistinguishable
from the settled Uzbeks. The Mountain Tadzhiks speak
the southeastern (Darwaz) and southern (including the
Badagshan, Rog, and Kulyab sub-dialects) dialects of
Tadzhik. They are Sunni Moslem in religion. SEE
Tadzhik.

MOUNTAIN TAJIK   Alt. spel. Mountain Tadzhik. SEE
                  Mountain Tadzhik, Tadzhik.

MOUNTAIN TATAR   Alt. des. Balkar. SEE Balkar.

MRASSA   Alt. des. Mrassa Tatar; for. des. Shor. SEE
          Mrassa Tatar, Shor.

MRASSA TATAR   For. des. (17th-early 19th cent.) Shor.
                 SEE Shor.

MRASSIN (Y)   For. Rus. alt. des. Shor. SEE Shor.

MRASSIN (SKIY) TATAR   For. Rus. des.   (17th-early
                         19th cent.) Shor. SEE Shor.

MTIULI   Self des.   Mtiuli. One of the numerous
           Kartvelian ethnographic groups that went
into the formation of the Georgians. They speak a
distinct (Mtiuli) dialect of Georgian. The Mtiuli are
Eastern   Orthodox   in   religion.   SEE   Georgian.

N

NAGAIBAK   Self des. Noghaibaq: oth. des. Nogaibak.
             The Nagaibak are a group of Bashkirs who,
like the Kryashen among the Tatars, converted to
Eastern Orthodoxy.   They differed from the Moslem
Bashkirs in that their language and culture had many
Russian borrowings, whereas the Moslem Bashkirs had
been influenced by the Tatars. Like the Kryashen
(Christian) Tatars, the Nagaibak had a literary
language that used the Cyrillic script. Until the 1930s
the Nagaibak were considered a distinct ethnic group.
Since that time they have been classified as Bashkirs
and their literary language was replaced by standard
literary Bashkir. POP: 11,219 (1926). SEE Bashkir.

NAGAIBAQ (NAGAYBAK,   NAGAYBAQ,   Alt. spel. and des.
          NAGHAIBAK, NAGHAIBAQ,   Nagaibak. SEE
          NAGHAYBAK, NAGHAYBAQ)   Nagaibak, Bashkir.

NAH PEOPLES   Alt. spel. Nakh peoples. SEE Nakh
                 Peoples.

NAHADA (NAHADIN)   Alt. spel. Nakhada; alt. des.
                      Khunzal. SEE Nakhada, Khunzal,
                      Andi-Dido Peoples, Avar.

NAKH PEOPLES   Oth. des. Veinakh peoples. Col. des.
                 for the peoples who speak languages
belonging to the Nakh (Veinakh) division of   the
northeast branch of the Caucasic language family. These
peoples fall into two linguistic groups: northern
(Chechen, Ingush, and Kist), and southern (Batsbi).

Chechen and Ingush are actually closely related
(mutually inteligible) dialects of one Nakh (Veinakh)
language. The Kist are a group of western Nakh (Ingush)
who migrated to the Georgian SSR where they were
heavily influenced by the Georgians (their language is
not mutually intelligible with Chechen-Ingush). The
Batsbi also migrated to Georgia, however, much earlier.
The Batsbi language is radically different from the
other Nakh languages and the Batsbi culture has been
thoroughly Georgianized. The Chechens and Ingush are
Sunni Moslem in religion, and live, primarily, in the
Chechen-Ingush ASSR, and adjacent areas in the North
Ossetian and Dagestan ASSRs, in the eastern North
Caucasus. The Kist and Batsbi are Eastern Orthodox in
religion and live in the northern part of the Georgian
SSR, just south of the Chechen-Ingush ASSR. SEE
Chechen, Ingush, Kist, Batsbi.

NAKHADA   Alt. des. Khunzal. SEE Khunzal, Andi-Dido
             Peoples, Avar.

NAKHADIN (TSY)   Alt. des. Khunzal. SEE Khunzal, Andi-
                    Dido Peoples, Avar.

NAMOL (NAMOLI, NAMOLY)   For. (early 19th cent.) des.
                            Eskimo. This des. derives
from a distortion of the Koryak word Nymylgyn, meaning
a settled person. SEE Eskimo.

NANAI   Self des. Nani; for. des. Gold, Natki, Achan,
           or by place of residence. ETHN: The Nanai are
closely related ethnically, culturally, and
linguistically to the Ulchi, Orok, and Orochi. These
four peoples considered themselves to be one (Nani)
people who speak mutually intelligible dialects of one
(Nani) language. Their status as distinct peoples is
still debated. It has been suggested that the Nanai be
called Lower Amur Nani, the Ulchi Downriver Nani, the
Orok Sakhalin Nani, and the Orochi Southeastern Nani.
The Nanai are also assimilating two groups of Evenk
origin: the Kile (who have been totally assimilated)
and the Samogir [who were listed as a distinct ethnic
group in the 1926 census (pop: 551)]. LANG: Nanai
belongs with Ulchi, Orok, and Orochon to the Nani group
of the Manchu division of the Tunguso-Manchu branch of
the Uralo-Altaic language family. Of these peoples only
Nanai has a literary form. The Nanai literary language
was established in the 1930s based on the Naikha
dialect and used the Cyrillic script. Little, however,
is published in this language and Russian serves as
their main literary language. POP: 10,516 (1979);
10,005 (1970); 8,026 (1959); 5,309 (1926). The Nanai
were listed as Gold in the 1926 census. The religion
of the Nanai is a mixture of shamanist-animist and
Eastern Orthodox beliefs, with Chinese influences. The

Nanai live in the lower basin of the Amur River.
Approximately 80% of the Nanai live in the USSR, the
remainder live across the border in China. SEE MAP 6.

NANAY   Alt. spel. Nanai. SEE Nanai.

NANI   1-Col. des. of the Nanai, Ulchi, Oroks, and
          Orochi. These peoples consider themselves to be
one (Nani) people and they speak closely related
(mutually intelligible) dialects of one (Nani)
language. They also share a common culture and
religion. Their religion is a mixture of shamanist-
animist and Eastern Orthodox beliefs with Chinese
influences. They are considered by many ethnographers
to be geographic divisions of one (Nani) ethnic group.
It has been suggested that the Nanai be called Lower
Amur Nani, the Ulchi Downriver Nani, the Oroks
Sakhalin Nani, and the Orochi southeatern Nani. They
live, primarily, along the lower Amur River and on
Sakhalin Island in southeastern Siberia. SEE Nanai,
Ulchi, Orok, Orochi.
          2-Alt. des. Nanai. SEE Nanai.

NARIMI (NARIMY)   Alt. des. Narym Selkup. SEE Narym
                    Selkup, Selkup.

NARIM SELKUP   Alt. spel. Narym Selkup. SEE Narym
                 Selkup, Selkup.

NARODI....   Alt. spel. Narody (Peoples). For the
               various territorial groupings of peoples
of the USSR (i.e., Peoples of Dagestan, the Middle
Volga, Central Asia, the Baltics, etc.). SEE Peoples
of....

NARODY....   Rus. des. People of....   SEE Peoples
of....

NARODY BALTIKI	...the Baltics.
NARODY DAGESTANA	...Dagestan.
NARODY IUZHNOI SIBIRI	...Southern Siberia.
NARODY KAVKAZA	...the Caucasus.
NARODY PAMIRA	...the Pamirs.
NARODY POVOLGI (POVOLZHE)	...the Volga.
NARODY PRIBALTIKI	...the Pri-Baltics.
NARODY PRIPAMIRA	...the Pri-Pamirs.
NARODY SEVERA	...the North.
NARODY SEVERNOGO KAVKAZA	...the North Caucasus.
NARODY SIBIRI	...Siberia.
NARODY SREDNEI AZII	...Central Asia.
NARODY SREDNEI VOLGI	...the Middle Volga.

```
NARODY SREDNEY AZII              ...Central Asia.
NARODY SREDNEY VOLGI            ...the Middle
                                   Volga.
NARODY VOLGI                    ...the Volga.
NARODY VOSTOKA                  ...the East.
NARODY YUZHNOI (YUZHNOY) SIBIRI  ...Southern
                                   Siberia.
NARODY ZAKAVKAZIA (ZAKAVKAZYA)  ...Transcaucasia.
```

NARYM (NARIMI, NARYMY)   Alt. des. Narym Selkup. SEE
                           Narym Selkup, Selkup.

NARYM SELKUP   Oth. des. Narym(y), Taiga or Forest
                Selkup, Narym Ostyak. The Narym Selkup
are one of the two divisions of the Selkup [southern
or Forest (Narym) and northern or Tundra (Taz Turukhan)
Selkup]. The Narym are culturally distinct from the
Taz Turukhan Selkup. The Narym live in the Taiga belt
in the Ob basin and are culturally similar to the Ket.
Among the Narym Selkup two dialects of Selkup are
spoken: Tym (in Kargasokskiy Rayon) and Ket (in Verkhne
Ketskiy Rayon). The Narym Selkup are being assimilated
by the Russians and few still speak Selkup. The Narym
Selkup are shamanist-animist in religion. They live in
the southern part of the Yamalo-Nenets AO and in
Tomsk Oblast in northwestern Siberia. SEE Selkup.

NATKI   Alt. des. Achan; for. des. Nanai. SEE Nanai.

NATUHAI (NATUHAY, NATUKAI,   Alt. spel. and des.
         NATUKAY)   Natukhai. SEE Natukhai,
                                Adygei, Circassian.

NATUKHAI   One of the ten major tribal divisions of
            the Adygei. Each of these was formerly
considered a distinct people. They are now classified
as Adygei. The majority of Natukhai, along with the
other Abazgo-Circassians, emigrated to Turkey in the
mid-1860s. They live along the Black Sea coast between
the lower Kuban and Dzhuba (Pshad) Rivers in the
western North Caucasus. SEE Adygei, Circassian.

NATUKAY (NATUQAI, NATUQAY)   Alt. des. Natukhai. SEE
                               Natukhai, Adygei,
                               Circassian.

NEAR KURILER (KURILIAN)   A group of Itelmen living on
                           Cape Lopatka and the Kurile
Islands who assimilated with the Ainu. In physical
type, language, and culture they form a transitional
group between the Itelmen and Ainu. They are, however,
distinct from these two other peoples. SEE Ainu,
Itelmen.

NEGDA (NEGEDEN)   For. des. Negidal. SEE Negidal.

NEGIDAL   Self   des.   El'kan,   Beyenin or Eleke Beye
("Local Person"); oth. des. Negda, Niyegda,
Neidal, Nizhdal, Negeden (all of which are derived from
Ngegida). ETHN: The term Negidal comes from a Russified
form of the Evenk word Ngegida, which the Russians
applied to the Negidal, Nanai, and Ulchi. The Negidals
are Evenks who mixed with the Nivkhi, Nanai, and Ulchi
on the lower reaches of the Amgun and Amur Rivers.   The
Negidal language and culture differ only slightly from
Evenk (having some Orochi and Udegei elements). Many
Negidal were assimilated by the Ulchi in the 18th-19th
cents. They are divided into two groups (up and
downriver) which are separated by about 250km.   LANG:
The Negidal language belongs to the Tungusic division
of the Tunguso-Manchu branch of the Uralo-Altaic
language family. Negidal is basically Evenk with many
Orochi and Udegei elements. Negidal is not written and
Russian serves as the literary language of the Negidal.
POP: 504 (1979); 537 (1970); n.a. (1959); 683 (1926).
The Negidal are shamanist-animist in religion. They
live, primarily, in two compact settlements along the
Amgun and Amur Rivers in Khabarovsk Krai in
southeastern Siberia.

NEIDA (NEIDAL, NEIDEN)   Alt. des. Negidal. SEE
Negidal.

NEMETS (NEMTSY)   Rus. des. German. SEE German.

NENETS   Self des. Nenets or Khasava (among Nenets in
the Yamalo-Nenets AO); for. des. Yurak,
Samoyed. ETHN: The Nenets are the most numerous of the
Samoyedic peoples [Nenets, Ent(sy), Nganasan, and
Selkup]. They are among the most numerous of the
Peoples of the North. The Nenets were formerly called
Samoyeds (in the northern part of European Russia and
the Ob basin) or Yuraks (in the Yenisei basin). They
inhabit a very widespread area. The Nenets are divided
into two distinct culture groups: Forest (Khandeyar
Nenets) and Tundra Nenets. The dialect groups of the
Nenets follow this cultural division. A group of Nenets
in the Nenets AO and in the northern part of the Komi
ASSR have mixed with the Izhmi (Komi) and form a
transitional group between the Nenets and Komi.
Although they maintain a Nenets identity, they speak
the Izhmi dialect of Komi. LANG: The Nenets language
belongs to the Samoyed division of the Uralian branch
of the Uralo-Altaic language family. It is divided into
two closely (mutually intelligible) dialect groups
which correspond to the cultural division found among
the Nenets [Forest (Khandeyar) and Tundra]. The various
dialects of Nenets reflect influences from the
surrounding peoples (Selkup, Khant, Ent, Nganasan, and
Komi). The Nenets literary language is based on the
Bolshaya Zemlya form of the Tundra dialect. It was

established in 1932 using the Cyrillic script. Little is published in this language and Russian serves as the main literary language of the Nenets. POP: 29,894 (1979); 28,705 (1970); 23,007 (1959); 15,462 (1926). In the 1926 census the Nenets were listed as Samoyed. The religion of the Nenets is a mixture of shamanist-animist and Eastern Orthodox beliefs. They live primarily in the Yamalo-Nenets AO, the Taimyr (Dolgano-Nenets) AO, and the Nenets AO in northwestern Siberia, and on Kolguev and Novaya Zemlaya Islands in the Artic Ocean. SEE MAP 3.

NEYDA (NEYDAL, NEYDEN) Alt. des. Negidal. SEE Negidal.

NGANASAN   Self des. Nya, Nganasan; for. des. Tavgi Samoyed (17th-18th cents.) ETHN: The Nganasan are of mixed origin. In the 18th and 19th cents. the Tavgi (Nganasan) assimilated a group of Evenks that migrated to the Taimyr region (Vadeev Nganasan) and a group of Dolgans (Oko Nganasan). The Nganasan are closely related culturally and linguistically to the Nenets. They are known for a tradition of hunting wild reindeer. LANG: The Nganasan language belongs to the Samoyedic division of the Uralian branch of the Uralo-Altaic language family. It is closely related to (and mutually intelligible with) Nenets. Nganasan is not written and Nenets and Russian serve as the literary languages of the Nganasan. POP: 867 (1979); 953 (1970); 748 (1959); 867 (1926). The Nganasan are shamanist-animist in religion. They live, primarily in the Taimyr AO in northwestern Siberia. SEE MAP 12.

NIMILAN   Alt. spel. Nymylan. SEE Nymylan, Koryak.

NIVKHI   Self des. Nivkh ("Man"); for. des. Gilyak. The Nivkhi are a Paleoasiatic people whose culture is closely related to the four Manchu peoples (Nanai, Orok, Orochi, and Ulchi) among whom they live. There has been much culture and language borrowing between the Nivkhi and Manchu peoples. Among the Nivkhi aspects of ancient fishing, bear raising and social traditions remain. LANG: The Nivkhi language is classified as a Paleoasiatic language. The Nivkhi language also has many borrowings from Manchu languages. The Nivkhi literary language was established in 1931 using the Cyrillic script. Little is, however, published, in the Nivkhi language, and Russian serves as the main literary language of the Nivkhi. POP: 4,397 (1979); 4,420 (1970); 3,717 (1959); 4,076 (1926). The Nivkhi were listed as Gilyaks in the 1926 census. The sharp decline in the Nivkhi population between 1926-1959 was primarily the result of the decimation of the Nivkhi of the southern part of Sakhalin Island upon its incorporation into the USSR after World War II.

Since the Nivkhi of southern Sakhalin had lived under Japanese rule between the Russo-Japanese War and World War II they were defined as collaborators and executed. The Nivkhi religion is a mixture of shamanist-animist and Eastern Orthodox beliefs. There is an emphasis on bear worship in their religion. They live, primarily, on the lower reaches of the Amur River near its estuary and on Sakhalin Island. SEE Paleoasiatic Peoples, MAP 7.

NIEGDA (NIJDA, NIJDAL, NIYEGDA, Alt. des. Negidal. SEE NIYEGDAL, NIZHDA, NIZHDAL) Negidal.

NOGAI   Self des. Noghai. ETHN: The Nogai are the descendants of the Turko-Mongolic nomads (the Golden Horde) that moved into the steppe areas of the North Caucasus. The Nogai today represent a relatively small remnant of a once more powerful and numerous people. In the pre-Soviet period the Nogai were being assimilated by the Circassians (in the west) and the Kumyks (in the east). The Nogai of the Crimea and Romania were assimilated by the Crimean Tatars and those of Astrakhan by the Astrakhan Tatars. The Nogai are divided into three territorial groups: Ak, Achikulak, and Kara Nogai. The Ak Nogai live in the northern part of the Karachai-Cherkess AO where they are under a strong Cherkess influence; the Achikulak Nogai live in the northern part of the Chechen-Ingush ASSR where they are under a strong Kumyk influence; and the Kara Nogai live in the northern part of the Dagestan ASSR where they are under a very strong Kumyk influence (many Nogai have adopted the Kumyk language). ETHN: The Nogai language belongs to the Kypchak-Nogai group of the Kypchak division of the Turkic branch of the Uralo-Altaic language family. Nogai is comprised of three closely related (mutually intelligible) dialects which correspond to the territorial divisions of the Nogai. Two Nogai literary languages were established in 1928 (Ak and Kara Nogai). Both used the Latin script. In 1938 the Kara Nogai literary language was abolished and all Nogai began to use the Ak Nogai form. In 1938 the Nogai literary language was changed to the Cyrillic script. POP: 59,546 (1979); 51,784 (1970); 36,274 (1926); 64,080 (1897). As a result of continuous pressure from Russian settlers in the North Caucasian steppe there was a steady migration of Nogai to Turkey, the Crimea, and Romania (Dobrogea). The majority emigrated to Turkey, as did the Circassians, in the mid-1860s. The Nogai are Sunni Moslem in religion. They live, primarily, in the Nogai Steppe in northern Dagestan (the majority), and in settlements in the steppe rgions of the Karachai-Cherkess AO and Chechen-Ingush ASSR. SEE MAP 6.

NOGAIBAK (NOGAIBAQ)   Alt. spel. and des. Nagaibak. SEE
                       Nagaibak, Bashkir.

NOGHAI   Alt. spel. Nogai. SEE Nogai.

NOGHAIBAK (NOGHAIBAQ)   Alt. spel. and des. Nagaibak.
                         SEE Nagaibak, Bashkir.

NOGHAY   Alt. spel. Nogai. SEE Nogai.

NOGHAYBAK (NOGHAYBAQ)   Alt. spel. and des. Nagaibak.
                         SEE Nagaibak. Bashkir.

NORTH CAUCASIANS   Col. des. for the indigenous
                    peoples of the North Caucasus
region. This includes the Circassians (Adygei,
Cherkess, and Kabards), Abaza, Karachai, Balkars, North
Ossetians (Iron and Digor), Ingush, Chechens, and
Dagestani peoples (Avars, Andi-Dido peoples, Dargins,
Kaitaks, Kubachi, Kumyks, Nogai, Laks, Lezgins,
Tabasarans, Aguls, Rutuls, and Tsakhurs). This term is
not synonymous with Caucasian Mountaineers. The latter
term usually does not include the peoples of the
lowlands (Circassians, Abaza, Nogai, and Kumyks). SEE
Mountaineer, Dagestani Peoples.

NORTH OSETIAN (OSETIN)   Alt. spel. and des. North
                          Ossetian. SEE North Ossetian,
                          Iron, Digor, Ossetian.

NORTH OSSETIAN   Col. des. of the Ossetians living
                  north of the Great Cuacasian chain.
This includes the Iron (Eastern Orthodox Ossetians) and
Digor (Sunni Moslem Ossetians). SEE Iron, Digor,
Ossetian.

NORTH OSSETIN   Alt. des. North Ossetian. SEE North
                 Ossetian, Iron, Digor, Ossetian.

NOVOSELETS   Self des. Novoselets (pl. Novoseltsy). A
              col. des. for the Russians, Ukrainians,
and Belorussians that have settled in Siberia in the
Soviet period. Those who had settled Siberia in the
pre-Soviet period were known collectively as Sibiryak
(pl. Sibiryaki). SEE Russian, Ukrainian, Belorussian.

NOVOSELTSY   Pl. des. Novoselets. SEE Novoselets,
              Russian, Ukrainian, Belorussian.

NUKRAT (SKIY) TATAR   Alt. des. Kara Tatar. SEE Kara
                       Tatar, Tatar.

NYMYLAN   Self des. Nymylun, Nymylyn. The term Nymylan
           derives from the Koryak word "Nym," meaning
village or place of residence and refers to the settled

coastal Koryaks (as opposed to the nomadic reindeer breeders, the Chavchuven). SEE Koryak.

O

OB OSTIAK   Alt. spel. Ob Ostyak; for. des. of Khant(y). SEE Khant.

OB OSTYAK   For. des. of Khant(y). SEE Khant.

OB UGOR (TSY)   Alt. and Rus. des. Ob Ugrian. SEE Ob Ugrian.

OB UGRIAN   Col. des. of the Khant(y) and Mansi. SEE Khant(y), Mansi.

OBDOR   For. des. of Khant(y). SEE Khant.

ODUL   1-For. des. of Yukagir. SEE Yukagir.
2-Des. of the Tundra dwelling Yukagirs. SEE Yukagir.

OIRAT   Alt. spel. Oirot. SEE Oirot.

OIROT   Self des. Oirot, Dzhungar, Mongol; oth. des. Dzhungarian, Western Mongol. A group of western Mongols, who are closely related ethnically, linguistically, and culturally to the Buryats and Kalmyks. POP: 1,538 (1926) The Oirots are Buddhist in religion.

OKO NGANASAN   The Oko Nganasan are a group of Dolgans (the Oko clan) who lived among the Nganasan in the 19th cent. and were completely assimilated by them. As late as the early 20th cent. they were considered Dolgans, but by the mid-late 20th cent. they were considered Nganasan. SEE Nganasan, Dolgan.

OLCHI   Alt. spel. Ulchi. In the 1926 census the Ulchi were listed as Olchi. SEE Ulchi.

ÖLET   A Mongol tribe that was assimilated by the Buryats. SEE Buryat.

OLIK CHEREMISS (MARI)   Alt. des. and spel. Olyk Mari;
                         alt. des. Kozhla Mari. SEE
                         Olyk Mari, Kozhla Mari, Mari.

OLYK CHEREMISS   For. des. Olyk Mari; alt. des. Kozhla
                  Mari. SEE Olyk Mari, Kozhla Mari,
                  Mari.

OLYK MARI   Self des. Olyk Mari; oth. des. Kozhla
             Mari. The terms Olyk (Meadow) and Kozhla
             (Forest) Mari are interchangeable. SEE
             Kozhla Mari, Mari.

OMOK   The Omok are a now extinct group of Yukagirs.
        SEE Yukagir.

ONKILON   For. alt. des. (early 19th cent.) of Eskimo.
           The term Onkilon is a distortion of the
Eskimo word Ankalyn ("coastal dweller"). SEE Eskimo.

OROCHEN   1-A tribal division of the Evenks. The term
           Orochen means "reindeer people" in Evenk.
The Orochens, like the Birars, Manegirs, and Tungus,
have gone into the formation of the Evenks. In the 1926
census the Orochens (pop. 1,200), appeared as a
distinct ethnic group (as did the Birars and Manegirs).
In 1926 the Evenks were called Tungus. SEE Evenk.
           2- For. des. Orok and Orochi. SEE Orok,
           Orochi.

OROCHI   Self des. Nani; for. des. Orochen. ETHN: The
          Orochi are closely related ethnically and
culturally to the Nanai, Oroks, Ulchi, Udegei, Negidal,
and Nivkhi. The status of the Orochi as a distinct
ethnic group is still debated. Many ethnographers
consider the Orochi, Oroks, Ulchi, and Nanai to be
territorial divisions of one Nani people that speak
closely related dialects of the same (Nani) language.
These four peoples share a common self des. (Nani) and
consider themselves to be one people. The Orochi are of
mixed origin. They are descended of Udegei, Nanai,
Ulchi, Negidal, Nivkhi, and Evenk clans. Until recently
there was much confusion in Russian literature between
the Orochi and Udegei. The Orochi of the Amur region
have been assimilated by the Ulchi. LANG: The Orochi
language belongs to the Manchu division of the Tunguso-
Manchu branch of the Uralo-Altaic language family. The
Orochi language is closely related to (and mutually
intelligible with) the three other Manchu languages of
the USSR (Nanai, Orok, and Ulchi). Many consider them
dialects of one (Nani) language. Orochi is not written
and Russian serves as the literary language of the
Orochi. POP: 1,198 (1979); 1,089 (1970); 782 (1959);
647 (1926). The religion of the Orochi, like that of
the other Manchu peoples is a mixture of shamanist-

animist, Eastern Orthodox, and Chinese beliefs. They
live in Khabarovsk Krai south of the Amur River. SEE
Nani, MAP 6.

OROCHON   Alt. des. Orochen. SEE Orochen, Evenk,
Orochi, Orok.

OROK   Self des. Nani, Ul'ta, Ul'cha (literally having
reindeer); for. des. Orochen (Reindeer People).
ETHN: The Oroks are closely related culturally to the
Nanai, Orochi, Ulchi, Udegei, and Nivkhi. The status of
the Oroks as a distinct ethnic group is still debated.
Some ethnographers consider the Oroks, Nanai, Orochi,
and Ulchi to be territorial divisions of one Nani
people, that speak closely related dialects of the same
(Nani) language. These four peoples share a common self
des. (Nani) and consider themselves to be one (Nani)
people. LANG: The Orok language belongs to the Manchu
division of the Tunguso-Manchu branch of the Uralo-
Altaic language family. The Orok language is closely
related to (and mutually intelligible with) the three
other Manchu languages of the USSR (Nanai, Orochi, and
Ulchi). Many consider them dialects of one (Nani)
language. Orok is not written and Russian serves as the
literary language of the Oroks. POP: The last time the
Oroks appeared in the census was in 1926 when their
population was listed as 162. The Oroks lived on the
northern part (Soviet controlled) of Sakhalin Island.
It is estimated there were another 300 in the southern
part (Japanese controlled). After World War II, those
Oroks who formerly lived under Japanese control were
executed by the Soviets, as were the Gilyaks. The
surviving Oroks live on northern Sakhalin Island. The
Oroks are basically shamanist-animist in religion with
some Eastern Orthodox influences. SEE Nani, MAP 6.

OROSHOR   A numerically small group of
Rushan who speak a distinct dialect of
Rushan. They are sometimes considered a distinct
ethnographic group, although they differ from the
Rushan only in dialect. Like the Rushan and other Pamir
peoples they are Ismaili Moslem in religion and are
being assimilated by the Tadzhiks. SEE Rushan, Pamir
Peoples, Tadzhik.

OS (OSI, OSY)   For. alt. des. Ossetian. SEE Ossetian.

OSET (OSETIAN, OSETIN)   Alt. des. Ossetian. SEE
Ossetian.

OSMAN (LY) TÜRK   Self des. Türk. The term Osman(skiy)
or Osmanly Türk was applied (until
the late 1920s) to the Turks (Anatolian Turks) living
in the Russian Empire or USSR. The term Türk (Tyurk)
was at that time applied to the people known today as

the Azerbaidzhans. The difference was to some extent
religious. Shiite Moslem Turks were called Turks (later
Azerbaidzhan) whereas Sunni Turks were called Osman
Turks. In 1926 the population of Osman Turks in the
USSR was 8,570. They lived, primarily, in the Georgian
SSR near the Turkish border. They were probably
deported to Central Asia in 1944 along with the
Turkified Georgians, Kurds, Khemshil, and Karapapakhs
from the same region. These peoples are known today
collectively as Meskhetians. SEE Meskhetian,
Azerbaidzhan.

OSSET   Alt. des. Ossetian. SEE Ossetian.

OSSETIAN   Formerly no general self des. as Ossetian;
              Self des. Iron, or by ethnographic group
(Iron, Digor, Tualläg); for. des. As(y), Os(y); oth.
des. Oset(in). ETHN: The Ossetians are the descendants
of the Iranian Alans who mixed with local Caucasians
when forced to move into the mountains of the Great
Caucasian chain by Turkic and Mongol invaders. There
are three culturally and linguistically distinct
divisions of the Ossetians. Until recently they both
considered themselves and were considered by others to
be distinct ethnographic groups. The largest of these
are the Iron. The Iron are Eastern Orthodox in religion
(having accepted Eastern Orthodoxy from the Georgians
in the 12th-13th cents.) and live, primarily, on the
northern slopes of the Great Caucasian Chain in what is
now the North Ossetian ASSR. The Tualläg are the
descendants of Ossetians who crossed the Caucasus
Mountains and settled on their southern slopes in
Georgia where they came under a strong Georgian
influence. They speak a dialect of Ossetian that is
basically Iron Ossetian with many Georgian borrowings.
The assimilation of the Tuallägs by the Georgians
continues to the present. The Digor are the descendants
of the Ossetians who lived in the Digor valley and who
were converted in the 17th-18th cents. to Sunni Islam
by the Circassians (Kabards). Their dialect is an
archaic form of Ossetian with many Circassian
borrowings. The Digor were deported in 1944 to Central
Asia along with other Islamic peoples of the Caucasus
(Karachai, Balkars, Chechens, Ingush, Meskhetians, and
some coastal Adygei). Some survivors were permitted to
return to the Caucasus region in the 1950s (as
Ossetians). LANG: Ossetian is comprised of three
dialects which correspond to the ethnographic divisions
of this people (Iron, Tualläg, and Digor). Iron and
Tualläg are fairly similar and the Iron Ossetian
literary language is used by both. This literary
language was established in the 18th cent. and used the
Georgian and Cyrillic scripts (the former by the
Tuallägs; the latter by the Iron). By the mid-19th
cent. it was being written almost exclusively in the

Cyrillic. In 1923 it was changed to the Latin, and in 1938 back to the Cyrillic. Until 1939 the Digor had their own literary language based on their dialect. This literary language was established in the late 19th cent. using the Arabic script. In 1928 it was changed to the Latin, and in 1939 it was abolished. In 1939 the Iron form of Ossetian was the only official literary language of the Ossetians. At present Ossetian and Russian are used as literary languages among the North Ossetians, and Ossetian and Georgian by those in the Georgian SSR. POP: 541,893 (1979); 488,039 (1970); 412,592 (1959); 272,272 (1926). The Tualläg, especially those living outside of the South Ossetian AO (and particularly those in the city of Tbilisi), are being assimilated by the Georgians. The Ossetians are divided into two religious communities. The Iron and Tuallags are Eastern Orthodox in religion; the Digor are Sunni Moslem. The vast majority are Eastern Orthodox in religion. The Ossetians live, primarily, in the North Ossetian ASSR, the South Ossetian AO, and in adjacent areas in Georgia and the North Caucasus. SEE MAP 13.

OSSETIN   Alt. des. Ossetian. SEE Ossetian.

OSTIAK   Alt. spel. Ostyak. SEE Ostyak.

OSTIAKO-SAMODI (SAMOED,   Alt. des. and spel. Ostyako-
    SAMOIED, SAMOYED)   Samoyed; for. des. of Selkup.
    SEE Ostyako-Samoyed, Selkup.

OSTYAK   1-For. des. of Khant(y). SEE Khant.
    2-In the pre-Soviet period the term Ostyak was applied to a wide variety of peoples who lived in the West Siberian Lowland (the Ob basin) and who shared a similar culture. In the 18th and 19th cents. this term was applied to the Khant, Baraba Tatars, Kama Bashkirs, Kets, and Selkup. A number of hyphenated forms of Ostyak were used: Ob-, Obdor-, and Berezov-Ostyak (for. alt. des. of Khant); Baikha (Baisha)-, Taz Turukhan-, and Tym Karakon Ostyak (for. des. of Narym Selkup); and Yenisei-Ostyak (for. des. of Ket). It is often not clear to which of these groups the term Ostyak is being applied when it is not in a hyphenated form.

OSTYAKO-SAMODI (SAMOED,   Alt. des. and spel. Ostyako-
    SAMOIED)   Samoyed; for. des. of Selkup.
    SEE Ostyako-Samoyed, Selkup.

OSTYAKO-SAMOYED   For. des. of Selkup. The Selkup appeared as Ostyako-Samoyeds in the 1926 census. SEE Selkup.

OYRAT (OYROT)   Alt. des. and spel. Oirot. SEE Oirot.

ÖZBEK (ÖZBEQ)   Self and alt. des. Uzbek. SEE Uzbek.

P

PADAR   Self des. Padar. A semi-nomadic group of
           Azerbaidzhans living in the eastern part of
the Azeraidzhan SSR. They speak an eastern dialect of
Azeri and maintain a separate identity. The Padar,
Airum, and Shahseven are semi-nomadic groups of
Azerbiadzhans that maintained (and to some extent still
maintain) distinct identities. SEE Azerbaidzhan.

PALAN (TSY)   One of the nine major territorial
                 divisions of the Koryaks. Each of these
groups has its own dialect and in the pre-Soviet
period was considered a distinct people. The Palan(tsy)
live, primarily, along the coast of the Sea of Okhotsk
in the Koryak AO in northeastern Siberia. SEE Koryak.

PALEOASIATIC PEOPLES   Oth. des. Paleosiberian peoples.
                       Paleoasiatic is an umbrella term
which covers a variety of unrelated peoples. There is
no Paleoasiatic language "family"; rather the term is
used to collectively designate all of the languages of
Siberia that are not part of the Uralo-Altaic language
family. It is fairly well established that the
Paleoasiatic languages have been spoken in Siberia long
before they were replaced by Uralo-Altaic languages.
The Chukchi, Koryak, and Itelmen languages are related
to each other and form the Chukotic (Chukotan) language
group. Eskimo and Aleut are also related to each other,
and distantly to the Chukotic languages. Nivkhi is not
related to any known surviving languages, nor is Ket,
Ainu, or Yukagir. Each of these is a remnant language
whose relatives died out in the distant, or not so
distant, past. In addition, none of them are related to
each other.

PALEOSIBERIAN PEOPLES   Alt. des.   Paleoasiatic
                           Peoples; SEE Paleoasiatic
                           Peoples.

PAMIRI   Alt. des. Pamir Peoples. SEE Pamir Peoples,
            Tadzhik.

PAMIR PEOPLES   Col. des. of the Iranian speaking
peoples who live in the Pamir
Mountain region in the Gorno-Badakhshan AO in
southeastern Tadzhikistan. There are six Pamir peoples:
Shugnan, Rushan, Bartang, Yazgul, (Yazgulem),
Ishkashim, and Wakhan (Vakhan). The cultures and
languages of these peoples are related to each other.
They are culturally similar to, albeit linguistically
distinct from, the Mountain Tadzhiks. It should be
noted that the Yagnob are not one of the Pamir Peoples.
Until the 1930s each of these peoples was considered a
distinct ethnic group. Since that time they have been
classified as Tadzhiks. The Pamir peoples are being
assimilated by the Tadzhiks. LANG: The Pamir peoples
are divided linguistically into four groups: 1)
Shugnano-Rushan [including Shugnan (including the
Badzhui and upper Shahdar dialects), Rushan (including
the Khuf dialect), Bartang, Oroshor, and Sarykol
(spoken only in Sinkiang Province of China)], 2) Yagul
(Yazgulem), 3) Ishkashim, and 4) Wakhan. Only the
languages within the Shugnano-Rushan group are (to
greater or lesser degrees) mutually intelligible. Until
the 1930s Shugnan (Shugni), Rushan, Bartang, Yazgul,
Ishkashim, and Wakhan were considered distinct
languages. Since that time these languages have been
classified as dialects of Tadzhik. Since the Shugnan
language was used as a lingua franca among virtually
all of the Pamir peoples an attempt was made to
establish a Shugnan literary language in the early
1920s-late 1930s, using the Latin script. This attempt
was soon abandoned and Tadzhik has served as their
literary language since that time. POP: In the 1939
census the population of the Pamir peoples was given as
37,960. In 1959 they were listed as Tadzhiks. In 1959,
however, 42,400 individuals were listed as Tadzhiks who
spoke Pamir languages as their native tongue. In
addition to the Pamir peoples in the USSR, many also
live in the Badaghshan region of Afghanistan and in
Sinkiang province in China (where they are classified
as Tadzhiks). In the USSR the Pamir peoples live,
primarily, in the Gorno-Badakhsan AO in southeastern
Tadzhikistan. SEE Mountain Tadzhik, Tadzhik.

PAMIR-ALAI KIRGHIZ   Alt. spel. Pamir-Alai Kirgiz;
                       alt. des. Ichkilik. SEE Ichkilik,
                       Kirgiz.

PAMIR-ALAI KIRGIZ   Alt. des. Ichkilik. SEE Ichkilik,
                       Kirgiz.

PAMIR-ALAI KYRGHYZ (KYRGYZ,   Alt. spel. Pamir-Alai
           QIRGHIZ, QIRGIZ,   Kirgiz;   alt. des.
           QYRGHYZ, QYRGYZ)   Ichkilik. SEE Ichkilik,
                                Kirgiz.

PAMIR TADJIK   Alt. spel. Pamir Tadzhik; alt. des.
                    Pamir peoples. SEE Pamir Peoples,
                    Tadzhik.

PAMIR TADZHIK   Alt. des. Pamir peoples. SEE Pamir
                    Peoples, Tadzhik.

PAMIR TAJIK   Alt. spel. Pamir Tadzhik; alt. des.
                    Pamir peoples. SEE Pamir Peoples,
                    Tadzhik.

PAREN (TSY)   One of the nine territorial divisions of
                    the Koryaks. Each of these groups has
its own dialect and in the pre-Soviet period was
considered a distinct ethnographic group. The Paren
live along the Paren River in the Koryak AO in
northeastern Siberia. SEE Koryak.

PEOPLES OF THE BALTICS   Alt. des. Baltic peoples. SEE
                              Baltic Peoples.

PEOPLES OF THE CAUCASUS   Alt. des. Caucasian peoples.
                              SEE Caucasian Peoples.

PEOPLES OF DAGESTAN   Alt. des. Dagestani Peoples.
        (DAGHESTAN)   SEE Dagestani Peoples.

PEOPLES OF THE EAST   Col. des. used by the Russians
                          for the peoples living in the
"Eastern" part of the Russian Empire and the Soviet
Union. This includes the Peoples of: Siberia, Central
Asia, the Caucasus, and the Middle Volga. SEE Peoples
of Siberia, Central Asians, Caucasian Peoples, and
Peoples of the Middle Volga.

PEOPLES OF GORNO-BADAGSHAN   Alt. des. Pamir Peoples.
        (BADAKHSHAN)   SEE Pamir Peoples,
                                 Tadzhiks.

PEOPLES OF THE MIDDLE VOLGA   Col. des. of the Finnic
                                  and Turkic peoples who
inhabit the region of the Middle Volga. This term
includes the Volga Finns (Mari, Udmurts, and
Mordvinians), Turks (Tatars and Bashkirs), and the
Chuvash. The Kalmyks are not, however, considered one
of the peoples of the Middle Volga; neither are the
Komi nor the Komi Permyaks.

PEOPLES OF THE NORTH   Col. des. for the numerically
                           small peoples of northern
Russia and Siberia. This includes the: Ugrian peoples
(Khant and Mansi), the Lapps, the Samoyedic peoples
(Nenets, Ent, Nganasan, and Selkup), the Tungusic
peoples (Even, Evenk, and Negidal), the Manchu peoples
(Nanai, Ulchi, Orok, Orochi, and Udegei), the

Paleoasiatic peoples (Eskimo, Aleut, Chukchi, Koryak, Itelmen, Nivkhi, and Yukagir), and the Turkic speaking Dolgans and Tofalars. Although the Yakuts are generally not included in this group, at times they have been included as they are ethnically, culturally, and linguistically related to others in this collective group.

PEOPLES OF THE PAMIRS   Alt. des. Pamir peoples. SEE
                          Pamir Peoples, Tadzhik.

PEOPLES OF THE PRI-BALTICS   Alt. des. Baltic peoples.
                               SEE Baltic Peoples.

PEOPLES OF THE PRI-PAMIRS   Alt. des. Pamir peoples.
                              SEE Pamir Peoples,
                              Tadzhiks

PEOPLES OF SIBERIA   1-Col. des. of all of the
                       indigeneous peoples of Siberia.
This includes all of the peoples of the North (with the exception of the Lapps), the peoples of Southern Siberia (Buryats, Altai, Khakass, Tuvinian, West Siberian Tatars, and Shors), and the Yakuts.
                       2-Alt. des. Peoples of Southern
                       Siberia. Often the term Peoples
of Siberia is used only to designate the peoples of Southern Siberia (Buryats, Altai, Khakass, Tuvinians, West Siberian Tatars, and Shors). To this group the Yakuts are sometimes added. The distinguishing factor between these two groups is economic. The peoples of the North are predominantly hunters, fishermen, and reindeer herders, whereas the southern Siberians and Yakuts are primarily pastoral nomads by tradition. SEE Peoples of Southern Siberia.

PEOPLES OF SIBERIA AND THE FAR EAST   Col. des. of all
                                      of the indigenous
peoples of Siberia. It is usually used synonymously with the term Peoples of Siberia when it includes both the peoples of the North (excluding the Lapps) and the southern Siberians.

PEOPLES OF MOUNT SHAHDAG(H)   Alt. des.   Shahdag
                SHAKHDAG(H)   Peoples. SEE Shahdag
                                Peoples, Azerbaidzhan.

PEOPLES OF SOUTHERN SIBERIA   Col. des. for the
                                peoples that inhabit
southern Siberia. This grouping includes the: Buryats, Altai, Khakass, Tuvinians, West Siberian Tatars, Shors, Tofalars, and sometimes the Yakuts. These peoples were all traditionally pastoral nomads (as opposed to the peoples of the North who were, primarily, hunters, fisherman, or reindeer herders). This term was

sometimes used interchangeably with Peoples of Siberia.

PEOPLES OF THE SOVIET EAST   Col. des. of the
                              indigenous   peoples
that traditionally lived in the eastern and southern
parts of the Russian Empire and the USSR. This term
usually includes the Moslem peoples of the Soviet Union
(Central Asians, North Caucasians, Azerbaidzhans,
Tatars, and Bashkirs), and the Southern Siberians. This
term is not of Soviet origin and is used almost
exclusively by Western scholars. Its exact extent
depends on the author.

PEOPLES OF THE SOVIET WEST   Col. des. of the
                              indigenous peoples
that traditionally lived in the western part of
European Russia. This includes the: Russians,
Ukrainians, Belorussians, Latvians, Lithuanians,
Estonians, Finns, Karelians, Moldavians, Poles, and
Jews. Sometimes the Armenians and Georgians are added
to this group. This term is not of Soviet origin, and
is used almost exclusively by Western scholars. Its
exact extent depends on the author.

PEOPLES OF TRANSCAUCASIA   Col. des. for the
                            indigenous peoples who
lived south of the Great Caucasian Chain
(Transcaucasia). This term usually includes the
Georgians, Armenians, Azerbaidzhans, Mingrelians,
Svanetians, Laz, Udi, Tati, Talysh, and Shahdag
peoples. It usually does not include the Kurds,
Assyrians, or southern Dagestanis living in the
Azerbaidzhan SSR (Lezgins, Avars, or Tsakhurs).

PEOPLES OF TURKESTAN   Col. des. for the indigenous
                        peoples of the former territory
called Turkestan. Turkestan was basically concometant
with the contemporary republics of Uzbekistan,
Tadzhikistan, Turkmenistan, and Kirgizia. The peoples
usually included in this group are the Uzbeks,
Tadzhiks, Kirgiz, Turkmen, and Karakalpaks. Sometimes
it has also included the Pamir peoples and Yagnobs (who
in the pre-Soviet period were considered Tadzhiks), and
other numerically small groups of this region (Beluchi,
Arabs, etc.). In general, the Kazakhs are not included
under this designation.

PEOPLES OF THE VOLGA   Col. des. for the indigenous
                        Finnic, Turkic, and Mongolic
peoples that lived in the region along the Volga River
and its tributaries. This includes the Finnic Mari,
Mordvinians, and Udmurts, the Turkic Tatars, and
Bashkirs, and the Chuvash and Kalmyks. This grouping is
basically synonymous with Peoples of the Middle Volga,
with the addition of the Kalmyks. Sometimes the Komi

and Komi Permyaks are also included under this designation.

PERMIAK (PERMIAN, PERMYAK, PERMYAN)   Alt. spel. Permyak; alt. des. Komi Permyak. SEE Permyak, Komi Permyak.

PIATIGORSKIE OBSHCHESTVA KABARDY   Alt. spel. Pyatigorskie Obshchestva Kabardy; for. des. Balkar. SEE Balkar.

POLE   Self des. Polak; Rus. des. Polyak. ETHN: The Poles of the USSR are of mixed origin. The majority are the descendants of Poles who migrated to the western parts of Belorussia and the Ukraine and into Lithuania during the period that these areas were under Polish rule. Many, however, are descended from Belorussians, Ukrainians, and Lithuanians who were Polonized during that same period. Prior to World War I Greater Poland was part of the Russian Empire. After World War I Poland was again constituted as a sovereign state, however, it included much of the western Ukraine and Belorussia, and southeastern Lithuania (including Vilnius, the capital of Lithuania). During the inter-War period many Poles, especially administrators, moved into the cities in these areas. In 1939 Poland was partitioned between Germany and the USSR, during which time many Poles were deported to Siberia, the Urals, the Russian north, and northern Kazakhstan. During World War II the Polish population was again decimated, however, this time by the Nazis. After the War the Soviet Union maintained the areas of Poland that were populated primarily by Ukrainians, Belorussians, and Lithuanians. Many Poles emigrated to Poland just after the War from the areas incorporated into the Soviet State. The Poles of the USSR are being assimilated by the Ukrainians, Belorussians, and Lithuanians. LANG: The Polish language belongs to the Western division of the Slavic branch of the Indo-European language family. Polish has been a literary language since the 17th cent. and is written in the Latin script. Many attempts were made during the 19th cent. by the Tsarist administration to suppress the Polish language. None of these however succeded. Polish publications were always smuggled into Russian-Poland from German and Austrian held parts of Poland, much as Lithuanian ones were smuggled into Lithuania from Prussian held parts of Lithuania. In the inter-War period Polish ceased to be a literary language of the USSR, as most of the Poles were no longer in the Soviet State. Polish has not been resumed as an officially recognized language of the USSR in the post-World War II period (although some publishing is done in Polish in Vilnius; however, this is primarily for export). The Poles of the USSR use local languages (Ukrainian, Belorussian, or Lithuanian)

or Russian as their literary language. POP: 1,150,991
(1979); 1,167,523 (1970); 1,380,282 (1959); 782,334
(1926). The decline in the Polish population between
1959-1979 is the result of assimilation of the Poles by
the Ukrainians, Belorussians, and Lithuanians. The
Poles are Catholic in religion. They live, primarily,
scattered throughout the western parts of the Ukraine
and Belorussia, and in Lithuania. SEE MAP 9.

POLEH (I)   Alt. spel. Polekh(i). SEE Polekh, Russian.

POLEKH (I)   The Polekh are an ethnographic sub-group
              of Russians who lived in the far western
part of the ethnically Russian territory (in the basins
of the Seim and Desna Rivers). They adopted numerous
culture traits from the Belorussians, and to a lesser
extent from the Lithuanians. A sub-group of the Polekh
are the Goryun(y) who lived in Kursk Gubernya. This
territory was formerly in the Ukraine; now it is in the
RSFSR. The Goryun(y) adopted many culture traits from
the Ukrainians. SEE Russian.

POLESHAN   Alt. des. Polyan, Polishchuk. SEE Polyan
            Polishchuk, Ukrainian.

POLESHCHUK   1-The Poleshchuk are an ethnographic
              group of Belorussians. Their distinction
stems from the fact that they live in an extremely
swampy environment (swamp and swampy forest lands) and
have established a culture that is significantly
different from the majority of Belorussians. In
addition to these cultural differences the dialect of
the Poleshchuk has been strongly influenced by
Ukrainian and has many Ukrainian elements. As a result
of their geographic isolation they have also retained
many archaic customs. The Poleshchuk, although closely
related to them, should not be confused with the
Polishchuk, who are an ethnographic group of Ukrainians
who live in the same area. The Poleshchuk live in the
Polesie region of southwestern Belorussia (in Pinsk and
southwestern Brest Oblasts). The Poleshchuk are further
divided into the Pinchuki (those from Pinsk) and
Breshyki (those from Brest). SEE Belorussian.
              2-Alt. des. Polyan. SEE Polyan,
              Polishchuk, Ukrainian.

POLESHUK   Alt. des. Poleshchuk. See Poleshchuk,
            Belorussian.

POLESIAN   (POLESYAN,   Alt. des. Poleshchuk,
  POLIESHAN, POLIESIAN)   Polishchuk. SEE Poleshchuk,
                           Polishchuk, Belorussian,
                           Ukrainian.

POLIAK   Alt. spel. Polyak; alt. des. Pole. SEE Pole.

POLIAN   Alt. spel. Polyan; alt. des. Polishchuk. SEE
          Polyan, Polishchuk, Ukrainian.

POLIESHCHUK (POLIESHUK)   Alt.   des.   Poleshchuk,
          Polishchuk. SEE Poleshchuk,
          Polishchuk, Ukrainian.

POLISHAN   Alt. des. Polyan, Polishcuk. SEE Polyan,
          Polishchuk, Ukrainian.

POLISHCHUK   For. alt. des. Polyan. The   Polishchuk
          are an ethnographic group of   Ukrainians.
Their distinction stems from the fact that they live in
an extremely swampy environment in the Polesie region
of the northwestern Ukraine. They have developed a
distinct culture and speak a distinct dialect of
Ukrainian. The Polesie dialects of Ukrainian and
Belorussian form transitional groups between Ukrainian
and Belorussian and are mutually intelligible with
both. The Polishchuk, although closely related to them,
should not be confused with the Poleshchuk who are an
ethnographic group of Belorussians. SEE Ukrainian.

POLISHUK   Alt. des. Polishchuk. SEE Polishchuk,
          Ukrainian.

POLISIAN (POLISYAN)   Alt. des. Polyan, Polishchuk.
          SEE Polyan, Polishchuk,
          Ukrainian.

POLUVERTSY   1-Alt. Rus. des. Setu. SEE Setu, Estonian.
          2-A group of Lutheran Russians originally
          from around Gdov and Pskov who lived to
the north of Lake Peipus (Chud) in Estonia. They have
been assimilated by the Estonians. SEE Russian,
Estonian.

POLYAK   1-Rus. and oth. des. Pole. SEE Pole.
          2-The Polyaks are a group of Russian Old-
          Believers who fled to Poland (whence the name
Polyak) in the 17th-18th cents. After the partition of
Poland in the second half of the 18th cent. they left
Poland (for religious reasons) and resettled in the
Altai and Transbaikal regions of Siberia (in Buryatia).
Those who settled in the Buryat regions were also known
as   Semeiki as they lived in large strongly cohesive
family groups (from the Rus. sem'ya, family). The
Semeiki also adopted amany culture traits from the
Buryats. SEE Russian.

POLYAN (E)   A group of Eastern Orthodox Ukrainians
          who still retained an old Slavic tribal
designation as late as the mid-19th cent. In 1861 their
population was 108,453. They lived, primarily, in the
Volynia region of the Ukraine. They have subsequently

become known as Polishchuk(i), Polishan(e), or
Polisian(e). SEE Polishchuk, Ukrainian.

POLYESHCHUK (POLYESHUK)   Alt. spel. and des.
                          Poleshchuk. SEE Poleshchuk,
                          Belorussian.

POMORY   The Pomory are an ethnographic group of
          Russians who lived along the coast of the
White Sea. They are the descendants of Russian migrants
from Novgorod who became hunters, seamen, and
fishermen. SEE Russian.

PONTIC (GREEK)   Des. of the Greeks who come from the
                  northern (Black Sea) coast of Turkey.
The Pontic Greek culture is significantly different
from that of the Greeks from Greece itself. Although
the majority of Pontic Greeks maintained the Eastern
Orthodox religion, their culture was profoundly
influenced by the Turks. In addition, they maintain
many archaic forms of Greek culture that had been lost
in Greece itself. The Pontic Greeks are divided into
two groups: those who maintain the Greek language
(Romeos) and those who shifted to Turkish (Urum). The
majority of Greeks of the USSR are Pontic in origin.
They migrated to the Russian Empire in two major waves.
The first was a result of the Russo-Turkish Wars in the
mid-19th cent., and the second was immediately after
World War I. The Pontic Greeks of the USSR live,
primarily, along the Black Sea coast in Georgia, the
North Caucasus, and the Ukraine (particularly Crimea
and Odessa Oblasts). Not all Greeks of the USSR are
Pontic in origin. Some came from Greece, Bulgaria, and
Romania during the period of Ottoman rule. These Greeks
settled, primarily, in Bessarabia and adjacent areas in
the Ukraine. SEE Greek.

PORUBEZHNIY KALMUK   Alt. spel. and des. Porubezhnyy
   (KALMYK, QALMUQ,   Kalmyk; for. des. of Teleut. SEE
   QALMYQ)   Porubezhnyy Kalmyk, Teleut,
                         Altai.

PORUBEZHNYY KALMUK   Alt. spel. Porubezhnyy Kalmyk;
                         for. des. of Teleut. SEE
                         Porubezhnyy Kalmyk, Teleut,
                         Altai.

PORUBEZHNYY KALMYK   Oth. des. Frontier, Borderland or
                         White Kalmyk; for. des. (17th-
19th cent.) of the Teleuts (a Turkic tribe that went
into the formation of the Altai). The des. Kalmyk is a
misnomer as the Teleut were Turkic and not Mongolic in
origin. SEE Teleut, Altai.

PORUBEZHNYY   QALMUQ   Alt. des. and spel. Porubezhnyy
            (QALMYQ)   Kalmyk; for. des. Teleut. SEE
                            Porubezhnyy Kalmyk, Teleut,
                            Altai.

PSHAV   Self des. Pshaveli. One of the numerous
          Kartvelian ethnographic groups that went into
the formation of the Georgians. They speak a distinct
(Pshav) dialect of Georgian. The Pshav are Eastern
Orthodox in religion. They live south of the Khevsurs
on the Aragvi and upper Iori Rivers in the Georgian
SSR. SEE Georgian.

PYATIGORSKIE OBSHCHESTVA   For. Rus. des. Balkars
           KABARDY   ("Five Mountain Societies
                            of Kabarda").   In   the
pre-Soviet   period the Balkars were divided into five
tribal societies. They lived in the mountainous part of
the area then called Kabarda. From this situation the
Balkars became known as the Five Mountain Societies of
Kabards. They were also called Mountain Tatars. SEE
Balkar.

Q

QABARD (QABARDIAN, QABARDIN,   Alt. spel. and des.
           QABARDINIAN)   Kabard. SEE Kabard.

QABARTAI (QABARTAY)   Alt. spel. Kabartai; alt. des.
                        Kabard. SEE Kabard.

QACHA (QACHIN)   Alt. spel. Kacha. SEE Kacha, Khakass.

QADJAR (QADZHAR)   Alt. spel. Kadzhar. SEE Kadzhar,
                      Azerbaidzhan.

QAIBAL   Alt. spel. Kaibal; alt. des. Koibal. SEE
           Koibal, Khakass.

QAIDAQ (QAITAQ)   Alt. des. and spel. Kaitak. SEE
                    Kaitak, Dargin.

QAJAR   Alt. spel. Kadzhar. SEE Kadzhar, Azerbaidzhan.

QALCHA   Alt. spel. Kalcha. SEE Kalcha, Kirgiz.

163 Qaraqalpaq

QALMUQ (QALMYK)   Alt. des. and spel. Kalmyk. SEE
Kalmyk.

QAMASA SAMODI (SAMOED,   Alt. des. and spel. Kamasa
SAMOIED, SAMOYED)   Samoyed. SEE Kamasa Samoyed,
Koibal, Khakass.

QAMASIN SAMODI (SAMOED,   Alt. des. and spel. Kamasa
SAMOIED, SAMOYED)   Samoyed. SEE Kamasa Samoyed,
Koibal, Khakass.

QAPUCHA (QAPUCHIN)   Alt. spel. Kapucha; alt. des.
Bezheta. SEE Bezheta, Andi-Dido
Peoples, Avar.

QARA NOGAI (NOGAY,   Alt. spel. Kara Nogai. SEE Kara
NOGHAI, NOGHAY)   Nogai, Nogai.

QARA QIRGHIZ (QIRGIZ,   Alt. spel. Kara Kirgiz; for.
QYRGHYZ, QYRGYZ)   des. Kirgiz. SEE Kara Kirgiz,
Kirgiz.

QARA TATAR   Alt. spel. Kara Tatar. SEE Kara Tatar,
Tatar.

QARACHAI (LI)(LY)   Alt. spel. and des. Karachai. SEE
Karachai.

QARACHAY (LI)(LY)   Alt. spel. and des. Karachai. SEE
Karachai.

QARADASH (LI)(LY)   Alt. spel. and des. Karadash. SEE
Karadash, Turkmen.

QARAGASH (LI)(LY)   Alt. spel. and des. Karagash. SEE
Karagash, Astrakhan Tatar, Tatar.

QARAIM (QARAIT, QARAITE)   Alt. spel. and des. Karaim.
SEE Karaim, Jew.

QARALPAQ   Alt. spel. Karalpak; alt. des. Karakalpak.
SEE Karakalpak.

QARANOGAI   (QARANOGAY,   Alt. des. Kara Nogai. SEE
QARANOGHAI, QARANOGHAY)   Kara Nogai, Nogai.

QARAPAPAH (QARAPAPAKH,   Alt. des. and spel.
QARAPAPAQ)   Karapapakh. SEE Karapapakh,
Meskhetian, Azerbaidzhan.

QARAQAIDAQ (QARAQAITAQ)   Alt. spel. Karakaidak,
Karakaitak; alt. des.
Kaitak. SEE Kaitak, Dargin.

QARAQALPAQ   Alt. spel. Karakalpak. SEE Karakalpak.

QARAQAYDAQ (QARAQAYTAQ)   Alt.   spel.   Karakaidak, Karakaitak; alt. des. Kaitak. SEE Kaitak, Dargin.

QARAQIRGHIZ (QARAQIRGIZ, QARAQYRGHYZ, QARAQYRGYZ)   Alt. des. Kara Kirgiz; for. des. Kirgiz. SEE Kirgiz.

QARASA SAMODI (SAMOED, SAMOIED, SAMOYED)   Alt. des. and spel. Karasa Samoyed. SEE Karasa Samoyed, Ent.

QARASHI   Alt. spel. Karashi; alt. des. Karagash. SEE Karagash, Astrakhan Tatar, Tatar.

QARASIN SAMODI (SAMOED, SAMOIED, SAMOYED)   Alt. des. and spel. Karasa Samoyed. SEE Karasa Samoyed, Ent.

QARATA   Alt. spel. Karata. SEE Karata, Andi-Dido Peoples, Avar.

QARATAI (QARATAY)   Alt. spel. Karatai. SEE Karatai, Mordvinian.

QARIN TATAR   Alt. des. Kara Tatar. SEE Kara Tatar, Tatar.

QARIM (I)   Alt. spel. Karym. SEE Karym, Russian.

QARYM (Y)   Alt. spel. Karym. SEE Karym, Russian.

QASHGAR (LIK)(LUK)(LYK)   Alt. spel. and des. Kashgar. SEE Kashgar, Uigur.

QASHQAR (LIK)(LUK)(LYK)   Alt. spel. and des. Kashgar. SEE Kashgar, Uigur.

QASIMOV TATAR   Alt. spel. Kasimov Tatar. SEE Kasimov Tatar, Tatar.

QASOQ   Alt. des. Kasog. SEE Kasog, Azerbaidzhan.

QAYBAL   Alt. des. Koibal. SEE Koibal, Khakass.

QAYDAQ (QAYTAQ)   Alt. des. and spel. Kaitak. SEE Kaitak, Dargin.

QAZAQ   1-Alt. des. Kazakh. SEE Kazakh.
2-Alt. des. Kasog. SEE Kasog, Azerbaidzhan.

QAZAN TATAR   Alt. spel. Kazan Tatar; alt. des. Tatar. SEE Kazan Tatar, Tatar.

QAZANLIK (QAZANLUK, QAZANLYK)   Alt. des. Kazan Tatar.
                                SEE Kazan Tatar, Tatar.

QAZI QUMUH (QUMUKH,   Alt. spel. and des. Kazi Kumukh;
           QUMUQ)   for. des. Lak. SEE Lak.

QAZIQUMUH (QAZIQUMUKH,   Alt. des. Kazi Kumukh; for.
           QAZIQUMUQ)   des. Lak. SEE Lak.

QIPCHAQ (QIPSHAQ)   Alt. spel. and des. Kypchak. SEE
                     Kypchak, Uzbek.

QIRGHIZ   Alt. spel. Kirgiz. SEE Kirgiz.

QIRGHIZ QAISAQ (QAYSAQ,   Alt. des. and spel. Kirgiz
        QAZAKH, QAZAQ)   Kazakh; for. des. Kazakh.
                          SEE Kazakh.

QIRGIZ   Alt. spel. Kirgiz. SEE Kirgiz.

QIRGIZ QAISAQ (QAYSAQ,   Alt. des. and spel. Kirgiz
        QAZAKH, QAZAQ)   Kazakh; for. des. Kazakh.
                         SEE Kazakh.

QIRIM TATAR   Alt. des. Crimean Tatar. SEE Crimean
               Tatar, Tatar.

QIRIMCHAQ   Alt. des. Krymchak. SEE Krymchak, Jew.

QIZIL   Alt. spel. Kyzyl. SEE Kyzyl, Khakass.

QOIBAL   Alt. spel. Koibal. SEE Koibal, Khakass.

QONDOMA TATAR   Alt. spel. Kondoma Tatar; for. alt.
                 des. Shor. SEE Shor.

QOYBAL   Alt. spel. Koibal. SEE Koibal, Khakass.

QRIM TATAR   Alt. des. Crimean Tatar. SEE Crimean
              Tatar, Tatar.

QRIMCHAQ   Alt. spel. Krymchak. SEE Krymchak, Jew.

QRIZ (QRYZ)   Alt. spel. Kryz. SEE Kryz, Shahdag
               Peoples, Azerbaidzhan.

QUBACHI   Alt. spel. Kubachi. SEE Kubachi, Dargin.

QUBAN ABHAZ (ABKHAZ)   Alt. spel. Kuban Abkhaz; for.
                        alt. des. Abaza. SEE Abaza.

QUBAN NOGAI (NOGAY,   Alt. spel. Kuban Nogai; alt.
      NOGHAI, NOGHAY)   des. Ak Nogai. SEE Ak Nogai,
                        Nogai.

QUMANDA (QUMANDIN)   Alt. spel. Kumanda. SEE Kumanda,
                       Altai.

QUMUQ (QUMYQ)   Alt. spel. Kumyk. SEE Kumyk.

QUNDROV TATAR   Alt. spel. Kundrov Tatar. SEE Kundrov
                  Tatar, Astrakhan Tatar, Tatar.

QURAMA   Alt. spel. Kurama. SEE Kurama, Uzbek.

QURD (QURMANDJ, QURMANDZH,   Alt. spel. and des. Kurd.
      QURMANJ, QURT)   SEE Kurd.

QWANADI (N)   Alt. spel. Kwanadi; alt. des. Bagulal.
                SEE Bagulal, Andi-Dido Peoples, Avar.

QWANALI (QWANALIN,   Alt. spel. Kwanali; alt. des.
         QWANALY)   Andi. SEE Andi, Andi-Dido
                       Peoples, Avar.

QYPCHAQ (QYPSHAQ)   Alt. spel. Kypchak. SEE Kypchak,
                      Uzbek.

QYRGHYZ   Alt. spel. Kirgiz. SEE Kirgiz.

QYRGHYZ QAISAQ (QAYSAQ,   Alt. des. and spel. Kirgiz
        QAZAKH, QAZAQ)   Kazakh; for. des. Kazakh.
                             SEE Kazakh.

QYRGYZ   Alt. spel. Kirgiz. SE Kirgiz.

QYRGYZ QAISAQ (QAYSAQ,   Alt. des. and spel. Kirgiz
       QAZAKH, QAZAQ)   Kazakh; for. des. Kazakh. SEE
                            Kazakah.

QYZYL (QYZL)   Alt. spel. and des. Kyzyl. SEE Kyzyl,
                 Khakass.

R

RAANDALIST   Alt. des. Livonian ("coast dwellers"). SEE
               Livonian, Latvian.

RACHA   Self des. Rach'veli; oth. des. Rachin(tsy) One
          of the numerous Kartvelian ethnographic groups
that went into the formation of the Georgians. They
speak a distinct (Racha) dialect of Georgian. The Racha
are Eastern Orthodox in religion, and live, primarily,
in the region of the upper Rioni River in the Georgian

SSR. SEE Georgian.

RACHIN   Alt. des. Racha. SEE Racha, Georgian.

RANDAL   Alt. des. Raandalist; alt. des. Livonian.
            SEE Raandalist, Livonian, Latvian.

ROM   Self and alt. des. Gypsy. SEE Gypsy.

ROMANIAN   Self des. Roman; Rus. des. Rumyn(y); oth.
              des. Romanian. The different spellings of
Romanian (Romanian or Rumanian) represent more than
just alternatives in spelling. They are politically
important. Romanian (with an o) refers to connections
with Rome (the West), whereas Rumanian (with a u)
refers to connections with Byzantium (the East).
Whereas the Romanians themselves insist on the o
spelling, the Soviets insist on using the u (Rumyny for
the people, Rumyniya for the country). ETHN: The
Romanian population represents a relatively small group
of Romanians that found themselves citizens of the USSR
after World War II when the Soviet Union formally
annexed a part of Romania (Moldavia and the Bukovina).
The Romanians in the Bukovina lived interspersed among
Ukrainians and the Soviets attached it to the Ukrainian
SSR (Chernovits Oblast). Most of the Romanians in the
USSR live in this region. Some also live in the
Moldavian SSR. LANG: The Romanians speak local dialects
of the Romanian language (in Moldavia, Moldavian) which
belongs to the Romance branch of the Indo-European
language family. Romanian is not officially a
recognized language of the USSR and the Soviet
Romanians use either Moldavian or Ukrainian as their
literary languages. POP: 128,792 (1979); 119,292
(1970); 106,366 (1959); 4,651 (1926). The Romanians of
Moldavia are Eastern Orthodox in religion. Prior to the
incorporation of the Bukovina into the USSR after World
War II the Romanians living there were mixed Uniate and
Eastern Orthodox in religion. After World War II the
Uniate Church was abolished and the Romanians, like the
Uniate Ukrainians and Belorussians, officially became
Eastern Orthodox in religion. The Romanians live,
primarily, in the Ukraine (especially in the Bukovina)
and Moldavia in areas adjacent to Romania. SEE MAP 6.

ROMEOI (ROMEOS)   Des. of the Greek speaking Greeks of
                     the USSR. The non-Greek (Turkish)
                     speaking Greeks are called Urum. SEE
                     Pontic Greek, Greek.

RUMANIAN   Alt. des. Romanian. SEE Romanian.

RUMYN (Y)   Rus. and oth. des. Romanian. SEE Romanian.

RUSAKI   Alt. des. Krieviņi. SEE Krieviņi, Latvian.

RUSHAN   Self des. Rykhen. ETHN: The Rushan are one of
          the six Pamir Peoples. Until the late 1930s
each of these peoples was considered a distinct ethnic
group. Since that time they have been classified as
Tadzhiks. LANG: The Rushan language belongs to the
Shugnano-Rushan group of the East Iranian division of
the Iranian branch of the Indo-European language
family. Rushan is mutually intelligible with, and
sometimes considered a dialect of Shugnan. Rushan is
comprised of two dialects Rushan and Khuf. The speakers
of the Khuf dialect have often been considered a
distinct ethnographic group. The Rushan are usually
tri-lingual (Rushan, Shugnan, and Tadzhik). Rushan is
not written and Tadzhik serves as the literary language
of the Rushans. POP: The Rushans are Ismaili Moslem in
religion. They are being assimilated by the Tadzhiks.
The Rushan live, primarily, along the Pyandzh River
from the village Darmor-Akht to Lower Khuf. SEE Pamir
Peoples, Tadzhik.

RUSIN (RUSNAK, RUSNIAK,   Alt. spel. and des. Carpatho-
       RUSNYAK)   Rusin. SEE Carpatho-Rusin,
                          Ukrainian.

RUSSIAN   Self des. Russkiy; oth. des. Great Russian
          (Veliko-Russkiy). The term Great and Little
(Veliko and Malo) Russia and Russian derive from the
Byzantine (and Roman) system of geographical
nomenclature. Those areas closer to Byzantium were
called Little or Lesser, as the exact extent of the
territory was known. The areas beyond that (presumed to
be larger) was designated Great or Greater. The pair
Lesser and Greater are not related to value judgements,
importance, or relative power. This terminology was
applied to the Russians (Great Russians) and the
Ukrainians (Little Russians). Although the term Little
Russians (Malo Rusy) is no longer officially used, the
Soviets have maintained the term Great Russian (Veliko
Rusy) for the Russians. ETHN: The Russians are the
numerically largest and dominant ethnic group in the
USSR. They comprise roughly one half the entire
population of the USSR today. It was around this group
that the Russian Empire and its heir, the Soviet Union,
was formed. The Russians are mixed in origin. Although
basically East Slavic in origin, a large component of
Slavicized Finns, and to a lesser extent other peoples
(Siberians, Turks, Balts, etc.), went into the
formation of the Russians. Much of this early
Russification resulted from the conversion of
surrounding peoples (most notably various Finnic
peoples) to Eastern Orthodoxy, and the expansion of the
Russians' states — Muskovy, Novgorod, Imperial Russia,
and today the Soviet Union. Also important in this
process was intermarriage between early Russian
hunters, explorers, and settlers with other peoples.

The process of Russification continues at a great pace today. Many Finnic peoples (Karelians, Izhora, Veps, and Mordvinians) are declining in population as a result of this process, as are many Siberian peoples. Russification of the closely related Eastern Orthodox Ukrainians and Belorussians also continues at a rapid rate. It is of interest to note that the Russians have had little to no success in assimilating the Moslem peoples of the USSR (with the sole exception of the Tatars who live in scattered communities among the Russians, and even here the rate of assimilation has been relatively low), and the Georgians. The rates of assimilation among the Moldavians, Estonians, Latvians, and Lithuanians are also quite low. Among the Russians many culturally distinct groups exist as the result of isolation, cultural borrowing from other peoples, ethnic mixing, or groups who have isolated themselves for religious reasons. Among these are the: Meshcheryak, Kerzhak, Bukhtarman (Kamenshchik), Semeiki, Polyak, Starozhily, Russkoustin, Markov, Yakutyan, Kamchadal, Karym, Kolymchan, Zatundren, Pomory, Polekh, Sayan, and Ural groups, as well as the various Russian Cossack and religious groups that retained, and often still retain, their identities. LANG: Russian belongs to the Eastern division of the Slavic branch of the Indo-European language family. Russian is extremely uniform and has no dialect divisions. There are, however, numerous minor differences in pronunciation (speech) found in different areas. These speech differences are divided into two groups: northern and southern. A Slavonic-Russian literary language has existed since the 11th cent. Modern Russian, however, dates back to the late 18th cent. It has always been written in the Cyrillic script, albeit different forms over time. The last major alphabet reform was carried out just after the revolution. The Russian literary language is used by virtually all Russians and is the national language of the USSR (all Soviet students must study it). POP: 137,397,089 (1979); 129,015,140 (1970); 114,113,579 (1959); 77,791,124 (1926). Besides natural reproduction, assimilation (Russification) of other Soviet peoples (and in particular Ukrainians and Belorussians) has accounted for a significant part of the growth of the Russian population. In the late 1920s the Kuban Cossacks were officially reclassified from Ukrainian to Russian, thereby increasing the Russian population at that time alone by between two and three million. The Russians are predominantly Eastern Orthodox in religion, and Eastern Orthodoxy has historically been the official religion of the Russians. There were, however, many Old Believer groups and other sects (e.g. Molokan), and now there appears to be a growth of Western Evangelical (Baptist, Seventh Day Adventist, Jehovah's Witnesses, etc.) movements

among many Russians. The Russians live, primarily, in
the RSFSR, the eastern Ukraine, and northern
Kazakhstan. Russian settlements are found throughout
the USSR.

RUSSKIY   Rus. des. Russian. SEE Russian.

RUSSKOUSTIN (TSY)   The Russkoustin are a group of
                     Russians who settled in the
village of Russkoe Uste on the Indigirka River in the
Polar region. There they mixed with local Chuvans and
Yukagirs and adopted elements of their culture. They
maintained the Russian language and identity; however,
culturally they are more similar to the local Siberian
peoples. They engage, primarily, in fishing, hunting,
breeding dogs and, to some extent, reindeer. They are
similar to the Markov who live in the village of
Markovo on the Anadyr River. SEE Russian, Chuvan,
Yukagir.

RUSYN   Alt. des. Carpatho-Rusin. SEE Carpatho-Rusin,
         Ukrainian.

RUTHENIAN   The term Ruthenian is an Anglicized form
             of the word Rusin. This term was
originally applied by the Greco-Romans to the East-
Slavic peoples of the Byzantine rite. It originally
referred to members of the Eastern Orthodox religion;
however, from the end of the 16th cent. it had come to
be used to refer predominantly to the members of the
Uniate Church (those who maintained the Byzantine rite
but who accepted Papal authority) under Polish-
Lithuanian or Hungarian rule. These peoples are now
designated Ukrainians and Belorussians in the USSR. The
designation Ruthenian (Rusin or Rusyn) survives mainly
in emigrant Ruthenian communities in the West. SEE
Carpatho-Ruthenian, Ukrainian, Belorussian.

RUTUL   No general ethnic self des. in the pre-Soviet
         period. The term Rutul derives from the clan
federation (Rutul Magal) to which all of the Rutuls
(and many Lezgins) belonged. ETHN: The Rutul are one of
the numerically small ethnic groups of southern
Dagestan. The Rutuls lived under a very strong cultural
and linguistic influence of the Azerbaidzhans (and to
a lesser extent the Lezgins) and up until the 1930s
were being assimilated by them. LANG: Rutul belongs to
the Samurian group of the northeast division of the
Caucasian language family. The Rutul language is not
written and Russian (formerly Azeri and Lezgin) serves
as the literary language of the Rutuls. Although
Russian is the official literary language of the
Rutuls, knowledge of Lezgin and Azeri are far more
widespread among the Rutuls than is Russian. POP:
15,032 (1979); 12,071 (1970); 6,732 (1959); 10,495

(1926). The sharp decline of the Rutul population between 1926 and 1959 was the result of the assimilation of the majority of Rutuls living in the Azerbaidzhan SSR. The Rutuls are Sunni Moslem in religion. They live, primarily, in a compact area in southern Dagestan and in two contiguous villages in northern Azerbaidzhan. SEE MAP 6.

S

SAAMI (SABMI)   Alt. and self des. Lapp. SEE Lapp.

SAGAI   Self des. Sagai. One of the five teritorial divisions of the Khakass. Each of these groups was formerly considered a distinct ethnic group. The Sagai are of complex origin. Nineteen seoks (clan units) went into the formation of the Sagai: eleven of Shor origin [Sebecha, Sai, Aba, Chetti Puri (Chettiber), Koby, Kyzylgaya, Karga (Tag and Sug Karga), Shor (Sor), Kyy, Tom and Tayas]; two of Yenisei Kirgiz (Orkhon Turkic) origin (Kyrgyz and Pyuryut; and six of Siberian (Old Uigur) Turkic origin [Sagai (Yus and Tom Sagai), Ichige, Turan, Choda, Irkit, and Saryg]. The Sagai were formed by the consolidation of these various groups around the Sagai. The Sagai speak the Sagai dialect of Khakass. Although officially Eastern Orthodox in religion, their religion is a mixture of shamanist-animist and Eastern Orthodox beliefs. They live, primarily, in the steppeland bounded in the west by the Kuznets Alatau Spur and in the east by the Kamyshta and Abakan Rivers in the Khakass AO. SEE Khakass.

SAGAY   Alt. spel. Sagai. SEE Sagai, Khakass.

SAIAN   Alt. spel. Sayan. SEE Sayan, Russian.

SALIR   Alt. spel. Salyr. SEE Salyr, Turkmen.

SALYR   Self des. Salyrly. The Salyr are one of the major tribal-territorial divisions of the Turkmen. In the pre-Soviet period they were each considered distinct peoples. The Salyr speak the Salyr dialect of Turkmen. They live, primarily, in the central part of Chardzhou Oblast in the Turkmen SSR. SEE Turkmen.

SAMAGAR   Alt. des. Samogir. SEE Samogir, Nanai.

SAMEH (SAMEK, SAMELATS)   Alt. des. Lapp. SEE Lapp.

SAMODI (N)   Alt. des. Samoyed; for. des. of Nenets, Ent(sy), Nganasan. SEE Nenets, Ent, Nganasan.

SAMODI (N) TAVGI   Alt. des. Tavgi Samoyed; for. des. of Nganasan. SEE Nganasan.

SAMOED   Alt. spel. Samoyed; for. des. of Nenets, Ent(sy), Nganasan. SEE Nenets, Ent, Nganasan.

SAMOED TAVGI   Alt. des. Tavgi Samoyed; for. des. of Nganasan. SEE Nganasan.

SAMOEDIC PEOPLES   Alt. spel. Samoyedic Peoples. SEE Samoyedic Peoples.

SAMOGIR   The Samogir are a clan of Evenk or Manchu origin that merged with, and was assimilated by, the Nanai. They maintain a distinct Samogir identity and were listed separately in the 1926 census (pop: 551). SEE Nanai.

SAMOGIT   Alt. des. Žemaičiai. SEE Žemaičiai, Lithuanian.

SAMOGITIAN   Alt. des. Samogit; alt. des. Žemaičiai. SEE Žemaičiai, Lithuanian.

SAMOIED   Alt. des. Samoyed; for. des. of Nenets, Ent(sy), Nganasan. SEE Nenets, Ent, Nganasan.

SAMOIED TAVGI   Alt. des. Tavgi Samoyed; for. des. of Nganasan. SEE Nganasan.

SAMOIEDIC PEOPLES   Alt. spel. Samoyedic Peoples. SEE Samoyedic Peoples.

SAMOYED   1-For. des. (pre-1930s) of the Nenets. The Nenets were listed as Samoyeds in the 1926 census. SEE Nenets. The term Samoyed was traditionally applied to the Nenets of the European and Ob North, while the term Yurak was appled to the Nenets of the Yenisei North. Contrary to popular Russian belief, the word Samoyed does not mean "self eater," but may refer to the Nenets' occupation. It is etymologically related to the term Saam, as in the alt. and self des. of Lapps. SEE Nenets.
2-For. des. (19th cent.) of the Ent and Nganasan. SEE Ent, Nganasan.
3-Alt. des. Samoyedic Peoples. SEE Samoyedic Peoples.

SAMOYED TAVGI   For. des. of Nganasan; SEE Nganasan.

SAMOYEDIC PEOPLES   Col. des. of the various peoples
                      who speak languages belonging to
the Samoyedic division of the Uralian branch of the
Uralo-Altaic language family. This language group is
comprised of two divisions: northern and southern. The
northern group is comprised of Nenets, Ent, and
Nganasan. The languages of these peoples are
not mutually intelligible, although aspects of their
cultures are similar. The Selkup language is distinct
from the other surviving Samoyedic tongues. The
distribution of Samoyedic peoples has diminished
greatly in the past few centuries. Many southern
Samoyeds either died of epidemics introduced by Russian
(and other) hunters, traders, and settlers, or as a
result of warfare with each other or neighboring
peoples. Some fled into the northern tundra. Their
population has also diminished as a result of
assimilation by the Russians or neighboring Siberian
peoples. Nonetheless, there were approximately 30,960
northern Samoyeds in 1979.

SAMURIAN PEOPLES   Col. des. for the peoples speaking
                     languages that belong to the
Samurian division of the northeast branch of the
Caucasic language family. This is the linguistically
most heterogeneous group within this language family.
All of the languages within the Samurian group are
distinct (none are mut~ally intelligible with any of
the others). The peoples in this group include the:
Lezgins, Rutuls, Aguls, Tabasarans, Tsakhurs, Udi
(Udin), and the Shahdag peoples (Dzhek, Khinalug, and
Budug). The Dzhek are sometimes further divided into
Dzhek, Kryz, and Gaput peoples (speaking relatively
similar dialects of the Dzhek language). With the sole
exceptions of the numerically small Budug (who are
Shiite Moslem in religion) and Udi (who are Eastern
Orthodox and Armeno-Gregorian in religion) all of these
peoples are Sunni Moslem in religion. The Udi and
Shahdag peoples represent small remnants of once
numerically more important peoples who were assimilated
(and are still being assimilated) by the Azerbaidzhans.
The Azerbaidzhans have also assimilated many Lezgins,
Rutuls, and Tsakhurs who lived in Azerbaidzhan. All of
the Samurian peoples have been strongly influenced
culturally and linguistically by the Azerbaidzhans, and
have to varying degrees been under strong assimilation
pressure by the Azerbaidzhans. At the present among all
of the Samurian peoples the knowledge of Azeri is
widespread and Azeri serves as a lingua franca among
them. The Samurian peoples live, primarily, in southern
Dagestan and contiguous northern Azerbaidzhan. With the

exception of the Udi (and sometimes the Shahdag peoples) the Samurian peoples have also been known collectively as Southern Dagestani.

SAMURZAKAN Oth. des. Samurzakan Abkhaz. The Samurzakan are one of the three divisions of the Abkhaz (Samurzakan, Abzhui, and Bzyb-Gudaut). They speak a distinct dialect of Abkhaz which is heavily influenced by Mingrelian. The Samurzakan Abkhaz have been under a strong influence by the Mingrelians and were being assimilated by them. In much of the literature this has mistakenly been referred to as the Georgianization of the Abkhaz. The Samurzakan live, primarily, along the Inguri River in the southeastern part of the Abkhaz ASSR in northwestern Georgia. SEE Abkhaz.

SARIK Alt. spel. Saryk. SEE Saryk, Turkmen.

SART The exact origin of the term Sart is still debated. Some maintain that it is an old ethnic name from a group (Yaksart) who lived along the Syr Darya, which was formerly called Yak-Sart. Others, that is was a term used to designate settled peoples as opposed to nomads and was not an ethnic term. Others, that it comes from a designation for Turkic peoples who lost their tribal identities. Still others that it derives from a word meaning merchant, and was used somewhat pejoratively for urban merchants in Central Asian cities. ETHN: The term Sart was generally applied to the Uzbeks who had settled among the Tadzhiks in the urban areas of Central Asia, had lost their tribal identities, and who had adopted the culture of, and merged with, the local Tadzhiks. The exact component of Tadzhikified Uzbeks and Uzbekified Tadzhiks is unknown. The Sarts were equally fluent in Tadzhik and Uzbek, regardless of ethnic (if any) affiliation. The Sarts live, primarily, in the main cities of Central Asia (Samarkand, Bukhara, Khiva, etc.). SEE Uzbek, Tadzhik.

SART KALMUK Alt. des. Sart Kalmyk. SEE Sart Kalmyk, Kirgiz.

SART KALMYK The Sart Kalmyks are a group of Kalmyks who settled in the Issyk-Kul region of Kirgizia in 1884. There, they adopted Islam (Sunni) and began to shift over to the Kirgiz language. In 1959 approximately 2,400 people identified themselves as Sart Kalmyks, of whom 1,845 considered Kirgiz their native language (their population in 1926 was registered as 2,793). Although they are merging with the Kirgiz they have maintained many Mongolic (Kalmyk) cultural and linguistic traits. SEE Kirgiz.

SART ÖZBEK (ÖZBEQ)   Alt. des. Sart Uzbek; alt. des.
                      Sart. SEE Sart, Uzbek, Tadzhik.

SART QALMUQ   (QALMYQ)   Alt. des. and   spel. Sart
                         Kalmyk.   SEE   Sart Kalmyk,
                         Kirgiz.

SART UZBEK   Alt. des. Sart. SEE Sart, Uzbek, Tadzhik.

SARTOL   The Sartol are a group of Khalkha-Mongols
          from Mongolia who migrated to Siberia where
          they were assimilated by the Buryats. SEE
          Buryat.

SARYK   Self des. Saryqly. The Saryk are one of the
         major   tribal-territorial   divisions of the
Turkmen. In the pre-Soviet period each of these groups
was considered a distinct ethnographic group. The Saryk
speak the Saryk dialect of Turkmen.   They live,
primarily, in the basin of the middle Murgab River in
the Turkmen SSR. SEE Turkmen.

SAVAKKO   Alt. des. Savakot. SEE Savakot, Finns of
           Leningrad Oblast.

SAVAKOT   The Savakot are a group of Finns (from the
           Savo region) whose ancestors migrated to the
area called Ingria (Ingermanland) in Leningrad Oblast
in the 17th cent. They are one of the two divisions of
the Finns of Leningrad Oblast (Savakot and Ayramoiset).
The Savakot are Lutheran in religion. They live,
primarily, on the southern coast of the Finnish Gulf,
south of the Kovasha River. SEE Finns on Leningrad
Oblast.

SAYAN (Y)   The Sayan are an ethnographic group of
              Russians who live, primarily, in Kursk
Oblast. They differ only slightly in language and
culture from the Russians, having mixed with the local
population. SEE Russian.

SELENGA   The Selenga are one of   the   many
           geographical divisions of the Buryats.
One of the main trading forts of Buryatia was
Seleginsk. SEE Buryat.

SELENGIN   Alt. des. Selenga. SEE Selenga, Buryat.

SELKUP   Self des. Sel'kup; for. des. Ostyako-Samoyed.
          ETHN: The Selkup speak a southern Samoyedic
language, and are culturally influenced by the Kets of
western Siberia. Most Selkup are southern Samoyed, with
some Ket influence. The Selkup are divided into two
cultural groups: Taz Turukhan or northern (the tundra
dwelling Selkup); and Narym or southern (the forest

dwelling Selkup). In the past, the Taz Turukhan Selkups were considered to be comprised of two distinct divisions [Taz and Turukhan (Baisha or Baikha Ostyak)]. Among the Narym Selkups two distinct dialects are spoken, Tym and Ket. Formerly, the Tym and Ket speakers were considered distinct ethnographic divisions of the Narym. Assimilation by the Russians has been strong among the Selkups, especially among the Narym. Virtually all Narym speak Russian, and many have completely given up the Selkup language. LANG: Selkup belongs to the southern division of the Samoyedic group of the Uralian branch of the Uralo-Altaic language family. Selkup is comprised of three distinct dialects: Taz (spoken by the Taz Turukhan Selkups), Tym, and Ket. The Selkup language is not written and Russian serves as the literary language of the Selkups. Virtually all Selkups speak Russian. POP: 3,565 (1979); 4,282 (1970); 3,768 (1959); 1,630 (1926). In 1926 the Selkups were listed in the census as Ostyako-Samoyeds. The decline in the population of Selkups between 1970 and 1979 was largely the result of assimilation by the Russians. The Selkup are shamanist-animist in religion. They live, primarily, in the Yamalo-Nenets AO and Tomsk Oblast. SEE MAP 15.

SEMEIKI   The Semeiki are a group of Russian Old Believers who fled to Poland in the 17th-18th cents. In the mid-18th cent. they were expelled from Poland. They then migrated to the Transbaikal region (Buryatia) of south-central Siberia. In this region they became known as Semeiki as they lived in large strongly cohesive family groups (from sem'ya, the Russian word for family). SEE Russian.

SEMEYKI   Alt. spel. Semeiki. SEE Semeiki, Russian.

SEMIGALLIAN   Alt. des. Zemgalieši. SEE Zemgalieši, Latvian.

SETU   Oth. Rus. des. Poluvertsy; oth. des. Setukesian. The Setu are an eastern tribe of Estonians who converted to Eastern Orthodoxy. As such they were more heavily influenced by the Russians than the Lutheran Estonians and adopted many cultural and linguistic traits from the Russians. Many have been assimilated by the Russians. They speak a distinct dialect of Estonian. The Setu live around the region of Lake Peipus on the Estonian-Russian border. SEE Estonian.

SETUKESIAN   Alt. des. Setu. SEE Setu, Estonian.

SEVERO KAVKAZ (TSY)   Rus. des. North Caucasians. SEE North Caucasians.

SEVERO OSETIN (TSY)   Rus. des. North Ossetian. SEE
                         North Ossetian, Ossetian.

SHAHDAG PEOPLES   Col. des. for the Caucasic peoples
                     who live in the region of Mount
Shahdag in northern Azerbaidzhan. This group is
comprised of the Khinalug, Budug, and Dzhek peoples.
The latter group is sometimes divided into the Dzhek,
Gaput, and Kryz (based on the dialects of Dzhek)
peoples. All but the Budug (who are Shiite Moslem) are
Sunni Moslem in religion. All of these peoples are
being assimilated by the Azerbaidzhans. SEE Khinalug,
Budug, Dzhek, Azerbaidzhan.

SHAHDAGH PEOPLES   Alt. spel. Shahdag Peoples. SEE
                     Shahdag Peoples, Azerbaidzhan.

SHAHSEVEN   The Shahseven are a semi-nomadic
               ethnographic group of Azerbaidzhans who
live in the southern region of the Azerbaidzhan SSR
near the Iranian border. The majority of Shahseven live
across the border in northwestern Iran. The term
Shahseven derives from the Azeri "lover of the Shah"
(of Iran). They formed a group that was loyal to the
rulers of the Iranian Empire. The Shahseven are Shiite
Moslem in religion. SEE Azerbaidzhan.

SHAKHDAG (SHAKHDAGH) PEOPLES   Alt. spel. Shahdag
                                 Peoples. SEE Shahdag
                                 Peoples, Azerbaidzhan.

SHAKHSEVEN   Alt. spel. Shahseven. SEE Shahseven,
                Azerbaidzhan.

SHAPSUG   Self des. Shapsugh. Until the 1860s, when
             the majority of Circassians emigrated to
Turkey, the Shapsug tribe was the numerically largest
of the western (Adygei) Circassian tribes. Each of
these tribes was formerly considered a distinct people.
They are now classified as Adygei. The Shapsug lived,
primarily, along the Black Sea coast between the Dzhuba
(Pshad) and Shakhe (Lesser Shapsug) Rivers, and to the
southeast on the slopes of the Caucasus Mountains in
the western North Caucasus. Between the late 1920s-30s
the Shapsug were given an autonomous region of their
own (the Shapsug AO) and were classified as a distinct
ethnic group. Since that time they have been classified
as Adygei. SEE Adygei, Circassian.

SHAPSUGH   Alt. spel. Shapsug. SEE Shapsug, Adygei,
             Circassian.

SHELGA   Alt. des. Chuvan. SEE Chuvan, Yukagir.

SHENSI   Alt. des. Shensi Dungan. SEE Shensi Dungan,
           Dungan.

SHENSI DUNGAN   One of the two divisions of the
                   Dungans of the USSR. These divisions
are based on the province of origin and the dialect of
Chinese   spoken by them.   The Shensi Dungan   came
originally from Shensi province in China and speak the
Shensi dialect of Chinese. The other group are the
Hansu Dungans who originated in Hansu province and
speak the Hansu dialect. The Dungans are Sunni Moslem
in religion. The Shensi Dungans live, primarily, in the
Chu valley of eastern Kazakhstan. SEE Dungan.

SHKHARAWA (SHQARAWA)   Alt. des. Ashkharawa. SEE
                         Ashkharawa, Abaza.

SHOR   No self des. in the pre-Soviet period;
         contemporary self des. Shor; for. des. (18-
19th cents.) Mrassa, Kondoma, or Kuznets Tatar; oth.
des. Mountain Shor. ETHN: The Shors are of complex
origin. They are the descendants of Turkified Ugrian,
Samoyedic, and Kettic speaking groups (clans and
tribes). Many Shor tribes also went into the formation
of the Sagai division of the Khakass and into the
formation of the Altai. The Shors were formed by the
consolidation of the various Shor groups around the
largest of the Shor tribes (the Shor). In the pre-
Soviet period each of these tribes (Shor, Aba Kizhi,
etc.) was considered a distinct people. LANG: The Shor
language belongs to the Old Uigur sub-group of the
eastern division of the Turkic branch of the Uralo-
Altaic language family. The Shor literary language was
established in the mid-1920s using the Cyrillic script.
It was changed in 1930 to the Latin and in the late
1930s back to the Cyrillic. Although Shor has the
status of being a literary language, little   is
published in this language and Russian serves as the
main literary language of the Shors. POP: 16,033
(1979); 16,494 (1970), 15,274 (1959); 12,601 (1926).
Although officially eastern Orthodox in religion, the
religion of the Shors is a mixture of shamanist-animist
and Eastern Orthodox beliefs. A Shor ethnic autonomy
was created in 1925 [The Mountain Shor (Gorno-Shorskiy)
National Rayon] but it was abolished in 1939 as the
Shor were only a small minority in that territory. The
Shors live, primarily, on the slopes of the Kuznets
Alatau along the middle Tom, Kondoma, and Mrassa Rivers
in the Kuzbass.

SHUGHNAN (SHUGHNANI,   Alt. spel. and des. Shugnan. SEE
         SHUGNI)   Shugnan, Pamir Peoples, Tadzhik.

SHUGNAN   Self des. Khunini; oth. des. Shugni. The
           Shugnan are the numerically largest and
most widespread of the Pamir peoples. The Shugnan are
closely related culturally to the Mountain Tadzhiks.
The Shugnan language belongs to the Shugnano-Rushan
group of the Eastern Iranic division of the Iranian
branch of the Indo-European language family. The
speakers of the Badzhui dialect of Shugnan are often
considered a distinct ethnographic group. The Shugnan
language serves as a lingua franca for all of the Pamir
peoples. An attempt was made in the late 1920s to
establish a Shugnan literary language to be used by all
of the Pamir peoples. This attempt was dropped in the
early 1930s and Tadzhik was adopted as the literary
language of all of these peoples. The Shugnan, like the
other Pamir peoples, are being assimilated by the
Tadzhiks. The Shugnan are Ismaili Moslem in religion.
They live, primarily, in the Gunt, Shahdara, and
Pyandzh valleys in the Gorno-Badakhshan AO in
southeastern Tadzhikistan. SEE Pamir Peoples, Mountain
Tadzhik, Tadzhik.

SHUGNANI (SHUGNI)   Alt. spel. and des. Shugnan. SEE
                     Shugnan, Pamir Peoples, Tadzhik.

SHWAN   Alt. des. Svanetian. SEE Svanetian, Georgian.

SIBERIAN PEOPLES   Alt. des. Peoples of Siberia. SEE
                    Peoples of Siberia.

SIBERIAN TATAR   Alt. des. West Siberian Tatar. SEE
                  West Siberian Tatar, Tatar.

SIBIRIAK   Alt. spel. Sibiryak. SEE Sibiryak, Russian,
            Ukrainian, Belorussian.

SIBIRYAK   Col. des. of the Russians, Ukrainians, and
            Belorussians who settled Siberia in the
pre-Soviet period. Those who migrated to Siberia during
the Soviet period are called Novoseltsy (New
Settlers). SEE Russian, Ukrainian, Belorussian.

SLOVAK   Self des. Slovak. ETHN: There is a relatively
          small number of Slovaks in the USSR. They are
the descendants of either Slovaks who migrated to the
Russian Empire during the late 19th and early 20th
cents. or of those that found themselves in Soviet
controlled territory after the incorporation of the
Czechoslovakian province of Ruthenia at the end of
World War II and did not return to Czechoslovakia. In
culture and language they differ only slightly from
those living in Czechoslovakia. The culture and
language of the Slovaks living in Ruthenia were
influenced by the Hungarians and Carpatho-Rusin
Ukrainians of that region. LANG: The Slovak language

belongs to the Western division of the Slavic branch of
the Indo-European language family. The Slovaks of the
USSR speak an eastern dialect of Slovak that has been
strongly influenced by both Hungarian and Ukrainian.
According to the 1979 census more Slovaks considered
Hungarian their native language than Slovak, and
virtually all of the remaining Slovaks speak Hungarian
as well. Slovak is not an officially recognized
language of the USSR and Hungarian, and to a lesser
extent Ukrainian, serves as the literary language of
the Slovaks. POP: 9,409 (1979); 11,658 (1970); 14,674
(1959). In 1926 the population figures for both Czechs
and Slovaks were given together (27,123). The decline
in the Slovak population of the USSR is the result,
primarily, of assimilation of the Slovaks by the
Hungarians, and to a lesser extent by the Ukrainians.
The Slovaks of the USSR were mainly Uniate in religion.
They live, primarily, in the western part of the
Ukraine near the border of Czechoslovakia.

SOIOT   Alt. spel. Soyot. SEE Soyot, Buryat.

SOLON   The Solon are a Tungusic tribe that has been
         assimilated by the Buryats. They now form one
         of the territorial divisions of the Buryats.
         SEE Buryat.

SOUTH OSET (OSETIAN,   Alt. des. and spel. South
      OSETIN, OSSET)   Ossetian; Alt. des. Tualläg.
                        SEE Tualläg, Ossetian.

SOUTH OSSETIAN (OSSETIN)   Alt. des. Tualläg. SEE
                            Tualläg, Ossetian.

SOYOT   Oth. des. Tunka Soyot. The Soyot are a group
         of Tuvinians who have been partially
assimilated by the Buryats. The Soyot form one of the
territorial divisions of the Buryats. Pop: 229 (1926).
The Soyots live, primarily, in Oka Aimak Rayon in the
Buryat-Mongol ASSR in south-central Siberia. SEE
Buryat.

STAROZHILY   Self and Rus. des. Starozhily (literarlly
              Old Inhabitants). The term Starozhily is
applied to those Russians from Central Russia (and
their descendants) who migrated to, and settled, in
Siberia in the 16th-17th cents. They are spread over a
vast area and vary in culture, speech, and customs from
region to region. Only a few groups of Starozhily have
maintained their separate identities. Most notable are:
the Bukhtarman or Kamenshchik; the Polyaki, who
migrated to Siberia by way of Poland and settled in the
Altai; and the Semeiki (a division of the Polyaki) who
settled in the Transbaikal region (Buryatia). The
Starozhily were, primarily, Old Believers. SEE Russian.

STAVROPOL TRUHMEN   (TRUKHMEN,   Alt. des. Trukhmen. SEE
          TURKMAN,   TURKMEN,   Trukhmen, Turkmen.
          TURKOMAN, TURKOMEN)

SUDAVI   Alt. des. Yatvig. SEE Yatvig, Lithuanian,
          Belorussian.

SURGUT OSTIAK   Alt. spel. Surgut Ostyak; for. des.
          of Khant. SEE Khant.

SURGUT OSTYAK   For. des. of Khant. SEE Khant.

SUVAL   Alt. des. Suvalkiečiai. SEE Suvalkiečiai,
          Lithuanian.

SUVALKECHAI   Alt. (Rus) spel. Suvalkiečiai. SEE
   (SUVALKECHAY)   Suvalkiečiai, Lithuanian.

SUVALKECHIAI   Alt.   spel.   Suvalkiečiai.   SEE
          Suvalkiečiai, Lithuanian.

SUVALKIEČIAI   Self des.   Suvalkiečiai (sing.
                    Suvalkietis); oth. des. Užnemuniečiai
(sing. Užnemunietis); Rus. des. Zaneman(tsy). The
Suvalkiečiai are a group of Lithuanians that live in
the area to the southwest of the Nemunas River
(Zanemanye or Suvalkiya). The Suvalkiečiai are
sometimes divided into two sub-groups: Kapsai (sing.
Kapsas) ("eastern") and Zanavykai (sing. Zanavykas)
("western"). The Suvalkiečiai are one of the
geographical groups of Lithuanians that is based on
former Baltic tribal divisions of the Lithuanians. SEE
Lithuanian.

SUVALKI   Alt. des. Suvalkiečiai. SEE Suvalkiečiai,
          Lithuanian.

SVAN   Alt. des. Svanetian. SEE Svanetian, Georgian.

SVANETIAN   Self des. Shwan, Mushwan; oth. des.
              Svan(y), Swan. ETHN: The Svanetians are
one of the Kartvelian peoples of the Georgian SSR. They
are culturally related to the Mingrelians and the
Georgians (albeit linguistically distinct), and are
being assimilated by the Georgians. Until the 1930s the
Svanetians were considered a distinct ethnic group.
Since that time they have been classified as Georgians.
The Svanetians have also assimilated (in the late 19th
cent.) a group of Jews living in Svanetia (Lakhamul).
It is not clear whether these were Georgian (or other)
Jews who had migrated to the area, or were Svanetians
who had adopted Judaism. SEE Lakhamul. LANG: The
Svanetian language forms an independent group of the
Kartvelian (southern) division of the Caucasic
language family. Svanetian is comprised of four closely

related dialects: Upper and lower Bal (spoken in the Inguri region); Lashkh; and Lentekh (in the Tskhenis-Tskali region). Svanetian is not written and Georgian serves as the literary language of the Svanetians. POP: 13,218 (1926); 15,756 (1897). The Svanetians are Eastern Orthodox in religion. They live, primarily, in two valleys south of Mount Elbrus (that of the upper Tskhenis-Tskali and its tributary the Kheledula, and that of the upper Inguri River). in the northern part of the Georgian SSR. SEE Georgian.

SWAN   Alt. des. Svanetian. SEE Svanetian, Georgian.

T

TABARASAN   Alt. des. Tabasaran. SEE Tabasaran.

TABASARAN   Self des. Tabasaran Zhvi, Tabarasan Zhvi; oth. des. Tabarasan. ETHN: The Tabasaran are one of the Samurian peoples of southern Dagestan. Until the late 1920s and early 1930s the Tabasarans were being assimilated by the Azerbaidzhans (and to a lesser extent by the Lezgins with whom they frequently intermarried). LANG: The Tabasaran language belongs to the Samurian group of the northeast division of the Caucasic language family. Tabasaran is comprised of two radically different (non-mutually intelligible) dialects: northern (Khanag) and southern (Tabasaran). The Tabasaran literary language was established in 1932 on the basis of the Tabasaran dialect (with additions from Khanag). This literary language used the Latin script and was changed in 1938 to the Cyrillic. The creation of this literary language was part of a major policy aimed at preventing the Turkification (by the Azerbaidzhans) of the Dagestani peoples. Virtually all Tabasarans are bilingual (Tabasaran and Azeri) and many tri- or multi-lingual (Lezgin and/or Russian). POP: 75,239 (1979); 55,188 (1970); 34,700 (1959); 31,983 (1926). The Tabasaran are Sunni Moslem in religion. They live, primarily, in southwestern Dagestan in the basins of the upper Rubas and Chirakh Rivers, in the eastern North Caucasus. SEE MAP 6.

TABUNUT   The Tabunut are one of the five major tribal divisions of the Buryats. They live, primarily, on the right bank of the Selenga River between the Chikoi and Uda Rivers. SEE Buryat.

TADJIK   Alt. spel. Tadzhik. SEE Tadzhik.

TADJIK CHAGATAI (CHAGATAY,   Alt.   spel.   Chagatai
        CHAGHATAI, CHAGHATAY)   Tadzhik; alt. des.
                                  Chagatai. SEE Chagatai,
                                  Tadzhik.

TADZHIK   Self des. Todzhik. ETHN: The Tadzhiks are
            the descendants of the old Iranian (ie. pre-
Turkic) population of Central Asia. In the past the
term Tadzhik referred to "settled people" as opposed to
the nomadic or semi-nomadic groups. At that time it
also referred to the settled Uzbeks. This term later
came to refer exclusive to the Iranian-Tadzhiks. The
Tadzhiks are divided into two distinct culture groups:
the lowland Tadzhiks (who are similar in culture to the
settled Uzbeks) and the Mountain Tadzhiks (who are
similar in culture to the Pamir peoples and the Iranian
mountaineers of northern Afghanistan). There are also
two ethnographic groups of Tadzhiks who maintain
distinct identities: Chagatai and Kharduri. The origins
of these two groups is not known. The Tadzhiks are also
in the process of assimilating a number of Iranian and
non-Iranian peoples that live in the Tadzhik SSR (and
to a lesser extent in the Uzbek SSR). Among these
groups are the six Pamir peoples (Shugnan, Rushan,
Bartang, Yazgul, Ishkashim, Wakhan), the Yagnob,
Galcha, Khazara (Berber), Central Asian Arab, and
others. LANG: The Tadzhik language belongs to the
western division of the Iranian branch of the Indo-
European language family. It is closely related to
Persian. Tadzhik is comprised of four major dialect
groups: northern (Samarkand-Bukhara, Fergana,
Pendzhikent, and the dialect of the Central Asian
Jews), central (upper Zeravshan); southern (Badzkhshan,
Rog, Kulyab), and southeastern (Darwaz). The Tadzhiks
formerly used classical Persian as their literary
language. Since the late 19th-early 20th cents. a
distinct Tadzhik literary form arose based on the
northern (Samarkand-Bukhara) dialect. It originally
used the Arabic script, was changed in 1929 to the
Latin, and in 1939 to the Cyrillic. POP: 2,897,697
(1979); 2,135,883 (1970); 1,396,839 (1959); 978,680
(1926). With the exception of the Pamir peoples
(Ismaili Moslems) the Tadzhiks are Sunni Moslem in
religion. They live, primarily, in the Tadzhik SSR and
adjacent areas in the Uzbek, Turkmen, and Kirgiz SSRs,
and in scattered settlements throughout the Uzbek SSR
(in particular in the major cities). SEE MAP 8.

TADZHIK CHAGATAI   Alt. des. Chagatai. SEE Chagatai,
                     Tadzhik.

TADZHIK CHAGATAY (CHAGHATAI,   Alt. spel. Tadzhik
                   CHAGHATAY)   Chagatai; alt. des.
                                      Chagatai SEE
                                      Chagatai, Tadzhik.

TAJIK   Alt. spel. Tadzhik. SEE Tadzhik.

TAJIK CHAGATAI   (CHAGATAY,   Alt.   spel.   Tadzhik
       CHAGHATAI, CHAGHATAY)   Chagatai;   alt.   des.
                                      Chagatai. SEE Chagatai,
                                      Tadzhik.

TALISH (TALUSH)   Alt. spel. and des. Talysh. SEE
                    Talysh, Azerbaidzhan.

TALYSH   Self des.   Talush,   Toyshon. ETHN: The Talysh
          are the   remnants of a once more populous
nation. They are the descendants of the old Iranian
groups that lived in the area of what is now
Azerbaidzhan.   The Talysh were assimilated by the
Azerbaidzhan Turks that migrated into this area. The
Talysh of the USSR have been almost completely
assimilated by the Azerbaidzhans (a similar process is
taking place among the Talysh of northwestern Iran).
LANG: Talysh belongs to the northwest division of the
Iranian branch of the Indo-European language family.
Attempts were made in the 1930s to establish a Talysh
literary language (1932-1939), however, it was soon
abandoned and Azeri serves as the literary language of
the Talysh. POP: In 1959 10,616 individuals declared
Talysh their native language, although no Talysh were
listed as a distinct ethnic group in the census. In
1926 80,629 individuals were listed as Talysh speakers
(only 77,323 individuals were listed as ethnic Talysh
in that year). Talysh is spoken today in the USSR only
by the elderly Talysh. The young speak Azeri and
consider themselves Azerbaidzhans. The Talysh are,
primarily, Sunni Moslem in religion (with a sizable
Shiite minority). Although they were formerly
widespread throughout southern Azerbaidzhan the
remaining Talysh live, primarily, in southeastern
Azerbaidzhan along the border of Iran. SEE
Azerbaidzhan.

TAPANTA   Until the mid-19th cent. the Tapanta were
           one of the two divisions of the Abaza
(Tapanta and Ashkharawa). The Tapanta were comprised of
the Loov, Biberdoa, Dudaru, Klych, Kyach, and
Dzhantemir tribes. The Tapanta dialect forms the basis
of the Abaza literary language. Unlike the Ashkharawa
dialect Tapanta is not mutually intelligible with
Abkhaz. SEE Abaza.

TARA TATAR   Self des. Tarlyk; oth. des. Irtysh
              Tatar. The Tara Tatars are one of the
territorial divisions of the West Siberian Tatars. They
speak the Tara dialect of Tatar and use the standard
Tatar literary language. POP; 11,517 (1926). Since the
1930s the Tara Tatars have been listed as Tatars. The
Tara Tatars are Sunni Moslem in religion. They live,
primarily, in Tarskiy Rayon in Omsk Oblast along the
Tara and Irtysh Rivers, in western Siberia. SEE West
Siberian Tatar, Tatar.

TARANCHI   Self des. Taranchy. The Taranchi are a
            group of Uigurs from Eastern Turkestan
(China) who migrated to the Ili region of Kazakhstan in
the 18th cent. The term Taranchi is an Uigur word
meaning farmer, which the Taranchi applied to
themselves as an ethnonym along with Uigur. Until the
1930s they (like the Kashgars) were considered a
distinct ethnic group. Since that time they have been
classified as Uigurs. POP: 53,010 (1926). SEE Uigur.

TARANCHY   Alt. spel. Taranchi. SEE Taranchi, Uigur.

TARLIK (TARLUK, TARLYK)   Alt. des. Tara Tatar. SEE
                           Tara Tatar, West Siberian
                           Tatar, Tatar.

TAT   Self des. Tat; oth. des. Tati. The Tats, like
       the Talysh, are the remnants of a once more
populous nation. They are the descendants of Old
Iranian groups that formerly inhabited northern
Azerbaidzhan. They were assimilated by the Azerbaidzhans
(Turks), and to a lesser extent by the Armenians. The
Tats are divided into three distinct culture groups:
Moslem (the vast majority), Armeno-Gregorian, and
Jewish Tats. Only the former two (the Moslem and
Armeno-Gregorian) have been classified in the Soviet
period as Tats. The Jewish Tats are classified as Jews
and statistically appear as either Mountain Jews
(Gorskie Evrei) or Jews (Evrei). SEE Mountain Jews.
Over the past few centuries the Moslem Tats have been
assimilated by the Azerbaidzhans and the Christian Tats
by the Armenians. LANG: Tat belongs to the southwest
division of the Iranian branch of the Indo-European
language family. Only the dialect of Tat spoken by the
Mountain Jews (which has many borrowings from Hebrew
for religious terminology) is written. An attempt was
made in the early 1920s to create a Tat literary
language based on the dialect of the Moslem Tats but
this was soon abandoned and Azeri serves as the
literary language of the Moslem Tats. Until the 1950s
Armenian served as the literary language of the Armeno-
Gregorian Tats; however, this was officially changed to
Russian. It is presumed that the Tats that appear in
the 1959, 1970, and 1979 censuses are Christian Tats

from Baku that had not been assimilated by the
Armenians. POP: 22,441 (1979); 17,109 (1970); 11,463
(1959); 28,705 (1926). In 1897 95,056 native speakers
of Tat (which includes the Mountain Jews) were recorded
in the census. The Tats are mixed Shiite Moslem and
Armeno-Gregorian in religion. Although formerly
widespread throughout central and coastal Azerbaidzhan,
the remaining Tats live in and around the city of Baku.
SEE Azerbaidzhan.

TAT JEW   Alt. des. Mountain Jew. SEE Mountain Jew,
           Jew.

TAT (SKIY) EVREI   Rus. alt. des. Mountain Jew. SEE
                    Mountain Jew.

TAT (SKIY) EVREY (IEVREI,   Alt. spel. Tat(skiy) Evrei;
YEVREI, YEVREY)   Rus. alt. des. Mountain
                   Jew. SEE Mountain Jew.

TATAR   Self des. Tatar, plus many local designations
         based on territorial divisions. The term Tatar
in the pre-Soviet period (and in particular in the
16th, 17th, 18th, and early 19th cents.) was mistakenly
applied indiscriminately to many non-Tataric peoples as
well as to the Tatars themselves. It was used at
various times in a general linguistic sense to
designate various Turkic peoples, in a general
religious sense to designate various Moslem peoples,
and sometimes in an ethno-racial sense to designate
peoples that appeared "oriental." Thus, historically,
such peoples as the Azerbaidzhans, Balkars, and various
Siberian peoples (Altai, Khakass, etc.) were at times
called Tatars. ETHN: The Tatars are the descendants of
various Kypchak speaking tribes that migrated westward
from southern Siberia in the 10th-13th cents. and mixed
with local groups (Finnic and Slavic in the Volga and
Crimean regions, Bolgar in the Volga region, Caucasic
in the eastern North Caucasus, and Siberian groups in
southern Siberia). Those groups that maintained
dialects of Kypchak and who adopted Sunni Islam became
known as Tatars. By the 16th cent. the term Tatar
became basically synonymous with the Golden Horde and
its various branches and territorial divisions (Kazan,
Crimean, Nogai, and West Siberian). In its strictest
sense the term Tatar has come to designate exclusively
the Kazan Tatars and their descendants (who lived
scattered throughout the Russian Empire). It was also
applied directly to the Crimean Tatars, the Nogai
Tatars of Astrakhan, and to the West Siberian Tatars
(Tara, Tobol, Baraba, Tom, etc.). Under the influence
of the Eastern Orthodox Church of Kazan a number of
Tatars converted to Eastern Orthodoxy. They were
formerly known as Kryashen (Christianized) Tatars.
Until the late 1930s the Kryashen had their own

literary language which used the Cyrillic script. There
was also a group of Mordvinians (Meshchera) who were
being assimilated by the Tatars (Mishars) that came to
be known as Tatars. Both of these groups were
considered distinct ethnic groups until the 1930s when
they were classified as Tatars. The Tatars are divided
into a number of territorial groups which still
maintain distinct identities. The most important of
these are the Volga (Kazan) (the largest and most
important), Crimean (who were deported in 1944 to
Central Asia), Astrakhan (including the Kundrov and
Karagash), Lithuanian, West Siberian (including the
Tara, Tyumen, Tobolsk and Baraba), Kara, and Glazov
Tatars. Prior to the Soviet period the Tatars were in
the process of assimilating the closely related
Bashkirs, and to varying extents the other peoples of
the Middle Volga (Mari, Chuvash, Udmurts, and
Mordvinians). The Soviets maintained the Tsarist policy
of supporting the other peoples of the region, by
creating ethnic autonomies and by developing or
creating distinct literary languages for the Bashkirs,
Chuvash, Mari, Mordvinians, and Udmurts. LANG: Tatar
belongs to the Kypchak-Bolgar group of the Kypchak
division of the Turkic branch of the Uralo-Altaic
language family. Tatar is one of the oldest literary
languages in use in the USSR. The Tatars have had a
literary language since as early as the 11th-12th
cents. (using the Uigur and Mongol literary languages).
A distinct Tatar literary language based on the dialect
of Kazan developed during the 16th cent. using the
Arabic script. With the conversion of the Kryashen in
the 17th-18th cents. a distinct Kryashen literary
language arose using the Cyrillic script. In 1928 the
Tatar literary language was changed to the Latin and
in 1940 to the Cyrillic (at which time the Kryashen
literary language was abolished). The contemporary
Tatar literary language is based on the Kazan dialect
with elements from Mishar. Until the late 19th-early
20th cent. the Tatar literary language was the literary
language of the Tatars, Bashkirs, Kazakhs, and northern
Kirgiz, as well as being widespread among the other
peoples of the Volga, southwestern Siberia, and the
North Caucasus. The Crimean Tatars, however, had their
own literary language until their deportation in 1944.
Some publishing in Crimean Tatar has been permitted
since the 1960s. POP: 6,317,468 (1979); 5,930,670
(1970); 4,967,701 (1959); 2,916,536 (1926). Except for
the Kryashen (Easten Orthodox) the Tatars are Sunni
Moslem in religion. The Tatars live throughout the
USSR, with major concentrations in the Middle Volga,
Uzbekistan, and Kazakhstan. SEE MAP 11.

TATAR OF TRANSCAUCASIA   For. alt. des. Azerbaidzhan.
                            SEE Azerbaidzhan.

TAULU   Turk. and alt. des. Mountaineers. SEE
           Mountaineers.

TAVAS   Alt. des. Chuvash. SEE Chuvash.

TAVGI SAMODI (SAMOED,   Alt. des. and spel. Tavgi
    SAMOIED, SAMOYED)   Samoyed; alt. des. Nganasan.
                            SEE Nganasan.

TAVLIN (TSY)   Rus. des. Mountaineers. This term
           derives from the Turkic term Taulu
           (Mountaineer). SEE Mountaineer.

TAZ SELKUP   The Taz Selkup are one of the two groups
            that together form the northern, Tundra,
or Taz Turukhan Selkup. The Taz speak a distinct sub-
dialect and have, at times, been considered a distinct
ethnographic group of Selkups. SEE Taz Turukhan Selkup,
Selkup.

TAZ TURUHAN SELKUP   Alt. spel. Taz Turukhan Selkup.
                        SEE Taz Turukhan Selkup, Selkup.

TAZ TURUKHAN SELKUP   Des. of the northern (Tundra)
                        Selkups. The Taz   Turukhan
Selkups are culturally distinct from the Narym Selkups
(forest dwelling) and speak a distinct (Taz) dialect.
The Taz Turukhan are comprised of two closely related
groups that in the past were sometimes considered
distinct   ethnographic groups of Selkups (Taz and
Turukhan). They live, primarily, in the Yamalo-Nenets
AO in northwestern Siberia. SEE Selkup.

TEKE   Self des. Tekeli; oth. des. Tekin(tsy). The
        Teke are the largest of the major tribal-
territorial   divisions of the Turkmen (comprising
approximately 35% of the Turkmen population). Each of
these tribal-territorial groups was formerly considered
distinct   peoples.   The Teke were famous for the
production of carpets (Bukharan or Teke carpets). Many
Teke, especially those who lived in the vicinity of
Bukhara, migrated to Afghanistan during the Basmachi
rebellion   (1920s) against the incorporation of
Turkestan into the Soviet state. Although Turkmen has
been written since the Middle Ages it was not
standardized until the mid-late 19th cent. at which
time it was written in the Arabic script and based on
the Teke dialect of Turkmen. It was changed in 1928-29
to the Latin script and in 1940 to the Cyrillic. The
Teke live, primarily, in the basins of the Murgab and
Tedzhen   Rivers and the foothill oases along the
northern slopes from the Kopet Dagh to Kyzyl-Armavat on
the west and Zangezur Karakum on the north. SEE
Turkmen.

TEKIN   Alt. des. Teke. SEE Teke, Turkmen.

TELENGIT   For. des. Uryankhai Kalmyk. The Telengit
        are a Turkic speaking tribe that went into
the formation of the Tuvinians and the Altai. They form
one of the tribal-territorial divisions of the southern
Altai (for. col. des. Mountain or Biy Kalmyk). In the
18th cent. the Telengit were called Uryankhai or
Uryankhai Kalmyks. This was a misnomer as they were
Turkic and not Kalmyk (Mongolic) in origin. POP: 3,415
(1926). Until the 1930s the Telengit were considered a
distinct group. Since that time they have been
classified as Altai. SEE Altai.

TELESI   Alt. spel. Telesy. SEE Telesy, Altai.

TELESY   The Telesy are a Turkic tribe that went into
        the formation of the Altai. The Telesy form
one of the tribal-territorial groups of the southern
Altai (for. col. des. Mountain or Biy Kalmyk). The
designation of the Telesy as Kalmyk was a misnomer as
they were Turkic and not Kalmyk (Mongolic) in origin.
Until the 1930s the Telesy were considered a distinct
group. Since that time they have been classified as
Altai. SEE Altai.

TELEUT   For. des. White or Frontier Kalmyk. The
        Teleut are a Turkic tribe that went into the
formation of the Altai. The Teleut form one of the
tribal-territorial groups of the southern Altai (for.
col. des. Mountain or Biy Kalmyk). The designation of
the Teleut as Kalmyk was a misnomer as they were Turkic
and not Kalmyk (Mongolic) in origin. The Teleut were
formerly considered a distinct group. Since the 1930s
they have been classified as Altai; however, they have
requested to obtain official recognition as a distinct
"Teleut" ethnic group. SEE Altai.

TEMIRGOI   Oth. des. Kemirgoi, Chemgui. The Temirgoi
        are one of the ten major tribal divisions
of the Adygei. Each of these was formerly considered a
distinct people. They are now classified as Adygei. The
majority of Temirgoi, along with the other Abazgo-
Circassians emigrated to Turkey in the mid-1860s. The
Temirgoi dialect forms the basis of the contemporary
Adygei literary language. This literary language was
established in 1927 using the Latin script and was
changed in 1938 to the Cyrillic. The Temirgoi live,
primarily, between the lower Laba and Belaya Rivers in
the western North Caucasus. SEE Adygei, Circassian.

TEMIRGOY   Alt. spel. Temirgoi. SEE Temirgoi, Adygei,
        Circassian.

TENGUSHEV (ERZIA, ERZYA) Alt. des. Tengushev
Mordvinian. SEE Tengushev
Mordvinian, Mordvinian.

TENGUSHEV MORDOVIAN Alt. des. Tengushev Mordvinian.
(MORDVA, MORDVIN) SEE Tengushev Mordvinian,
Mordvinian.

TENGUSHEV MORDVINIAN The Tengushev Mordvinians are
the descendants of a group of
Erzya Mordvinians who, in the 17th cent., settled in
two villages (Drakino and Kazhlodka) near Tengushev, in
the Moksha part of the Mordvinian region. They have
maintained their Erzya identity, but culturally have
adopted many Moksha elements. They speak a transitional
dialect between Erzya and Moksha, and form a
transitional group between the Erzya and Moksha
Mordvinians (whose languages are not mutually
intelligible). SEE Mordvinian.

TEPTER (TEPTIAR) Alt. des. and spel. Teptyar. SEE
Teptyar, Bashkir.

TEPTYAR The Teptyars are the descendants of a group
of Tatars and Mishars who settled in
Bashkiria in the 17th-18th cents. There, they formed a
privileged class (Tepter). Although they became
linguistically and culturally Bashkirized, as a result
of their strong social identification they maintained a
distinct identity. Until the 1930s they were considered
a distinct ethnic group. Since that time they have been
classified as Bashkirs. POP: 27,387 (1926). The Teptyar
are Sunni Moslem in religion. They live, primarily, in
the Bashkir ASSR in the Middle Volga region. SEE
Bashkir.

TERIUHAN MORDOVIAN (MORDVA, Alt. des. and spel.
MORDVIN, MORDVINIAN) Teryukhan Mordvinian. SEE
Teryukhan Mordvinian,
Mordvinian.

TERIUKHAN MORDOVIAN (MORDVA, Alt. des. and spel.
MORDVIN, MORDVINIAN) Teryukhan Mordvinian. SEE
Teryukhan Mordvinian,
Mordvinian.

TERYUHAN MORDOVIAN (MORDVA, Alt. des. and spel.
MORDVIN, MORDVINIAN) Teryukhan Mordvinian. SEE
Teryukhan Mordvinian,
Mordvinian.

TERYUKHAN MORDOVIAN Alt. des. and spel. Teryukhan
(MORDVA, MORDVIN) Mordvinian. SEE Teryukhan
Mordvinian, Mordvinian.

TERYUKHAN MORDVINIAN   The Teryukhan Mordvinians are a
                        small group of Mordvinians who
live in Gorkiy Oblast, not far from the city of Gorkiy.
Until the mid 1920s many of the Teryukhan Mordvinians
(mainly the elderly) still spoke Mordvinian, but by the
middle of the 20th cent. they had been completely
assimilated by the Russians. They both consider
themselves to be Russians and speak Russian as their
native language. SEE Mordvinian.

TIIN   The Tiin are a sub-group of the Kettic speaking
         Yara. They went into the formation of the Kacha
         division of the Khakass. SEE Kacha, Khakass.

TIM (KARAKON) (OSTIAK,   Alt. des. of Tym Selkup. SEE
             OSTYAK)   Tym Selkup Narym Selkup,
                         Selkup.

TIN   Alt. spel. Tiin.   SEE Tiin, Kacha, Khakass.

TINDAL   Alt. des. Tindi. SEE Tindi, Andi-Dido
          Peoples, Avar.

TINDI   Self des. Idaraw Hekwa; oth. des. Tindal,
         Idera, Iderin(tsy). ETHN: Until the early
1930s the Tindi, as well as the other Andi-Dido
peoples, were considered distinct ethnic groups. Since
that time they have been classified as Avars. LANG: The
Tindi language belongs to the Andi group of the Avaro-
Andi-Dido division of the northeast branch of the
Caucasic language family. Until the 1930s the Tindi
language was considered a distinct language. Since that
time it has been classified as a dialect of Avar. The
Tindi language is not written and Avar serves as the
literary language of the Tindi. POP: 3,812 (1926). The
Tindi are Sunni Moslem in religion. They, like the
other Andi-Dido peoples, are being assimilated by the
Avars. They live in highland southwestern Dagestan. In
1944 many Tindi moved to Vedeno Rayon in the Dagestan
ASSR. SEE Andi-Dido Peoples, Avar.

TIUMEN TATAR   Alt. spel. Tyumen Tatar. SEE Tyumen
                Tatar, West Siberian Tatar, Tatar.

TIURK (I)   Alt. spel. Tyurk(i). SEE Tyurk,
             Azerbaidzhan, Turk, Turk of Fergana and
             Samarkand, Uzbek.

TIURK OF FERG(H)ANA AND   Alt. spel. Turk of Fergana
             SAMARKAND   and Samarkand. SEE Turk of
                           Fergana and Samarkand,
                           Uzbek.

TIVER (IAN)   A group of Roman Catholic Ukrainians who
               still maintained an old Slavic tribal
designation as late as the mid-19th cent. In 1861 their
population, along with the Uglich, was 8,398. They
lived around Proskuriv in the Podilya (Podolia) region
of the western Ukraine. They have since been totally
assimilated by the Ukrainians. SEE Ukrainian.

TIVER(TSY)   Rus. des. Tiver. SEE Tiver, Ukrainian.

TOBOL TATAR   Self des. Toboluk. The Tobol Tatars are
               one of the territorial divisions of the
Tatars. The Tobol Tatars are one of the Tatar groups
that forms the West Siberian Tatars. They speak the
Irtysh dialect of Tatar and use the standard Tatar
(Kazan Tatar) literary language. POP: 32,102 (1926).
Since the 1930s they have been listed as Tatars. The
Tobol Tatars are Sunni Moslem in religion. They live in
the environs of the city of Tobolsk in western Siberia.
SEE West Siberian Tatar, Tatar.

TOBOLIK   (TOBOLIQ, TOBOLUK,   Alt. des. Tobol Tatar.
   TOBOLUQ, TOBOLYK, TOBOLYQ)   SEE Tobol Tatar, West
                                 Siberian Tatar, Tatar.

TODJAN   Alt. spel. Todzhan. SEE Todzhan, Tuvinian,
          Tofalar.

TODZHAN   Self des. Todzhan; oth. des. Tuba (pl.
           Tubalar) or Tof (pl. Tofalar). The Todzhan
are a small group of northeastern Tuvinians (numbering
in the hundreds) who resettled in Irkutsk Oblast among
the Tofalars. These Tuvinians adopted the culture and
language of the Tofalars and associate with them. They
now call themselves, and are called by the Tofalars
and other neighboring peoples, Tofalars (Tubalar). The
main difference between the Todzhans and Tofalars is
that the Todzhans have been little influenced by the
Russians, whereas the Tofalars have been strongly
influenced by them. SEE Tuvinian, Tofalar.

TOF   Alt. des. Tofalar. SEE Tofalar.

TOFALAR   1-Self des. Tubalar (sing. Tuba) or Tofalar
           (sing. Tof); for. des. Karagas. ETHN: The
Tofalars are a numerically small Turkic speaking ethnic
group of south-central Siberia. They are closely
related ethnically, culturally, and linguistically to
the Tuvinians (and in particular to the Todzhan
Tuvinians who live among the Tofalars and speak the
Tofalar language). The only significant difference
between the Tofalars and the Todzhans is that the
Todzhans strongly resisted the influence of the
Russians, whereas the Tofalars were strongly influenced
by them. The Tofalars are being assimilated by the

Russians. Many Tofalars also went into the formation
(in the 19th cent.) of the Tubalar division of the
Northern Altai. LANG: The Tofalar language belongs to
the Old Uigur group of the eastern division of the
Turkic branch of the Uralo-Altaic language family.
Tofalar is not written and Russian serves as the
literary language of the Tofalars. POP: 620 (1979); 586
(1959); 2,829 (1926). In 1926 the Tofalars were listed
as Karagass in the census. The Tofalar population was
not listed separately in the 1979 census (the
numerically smallest group listed, the Izhora, had a
population 748). The Tofalar population was decimated
during the period of settlement and collectivization
(late 1920s - early 30s). This accounted for a
significant part of the decline in the Tofalar
population between 1926 and 1959. In addition, there
has been a significant decline due to assimilation by
the Russians. Probably any increase in Tofalar
population would reflect an increase in the Todzhan-
Tuvinan population (who are not distinguished in the
census from Tofalars) rather than that of the Tofalars
themselves. The Tofalars formerly roamed over a
relatively extensive area on the northern slopes of the
Eastern Sayan Mountains. SEE Todzhan.
      2-Alt. des. Todzhan. SEE Todzhan, Tuvinian,
      Tofalar.

TOJAN   Alt. spel. Todzhan. SEE Todzhan, Tuvinian,
      Tofalar.

TONGUS   1-A self des. used by the Mongolized,
      Buryatized, and Yakutized Evenks. Among all
of these peoples one finds tribal or clan groups of
Evenk origin called Tongus. SEE Evenk.
      2-Alt. des. Tungus; for. des. Evenk. SEE
      Evenk.

TORGOUT   The Torgout are one of the three major
      divisions ·(tribal-territorial groups based
on former military ulus divisions) of the Kalmyks. The
majority of Torgout were killed on the Great Migration
to Mongolia in the 18th cent. The Torgout today are a
relatively small remnant of a once important group. The
Torgout live, primarily, in the southeastern part of
the Kalmyk ASSR. SEE Kalmyk.

TRANSBAIKAL BURIAT   Alt. spel. Transbaikal Buryat.
      SEE Transbaikal Buryat, Buryat.

TRANSBAIKAL BURYAT   Col. des. for the Buryats that
      live east of Lake Baikal. SEE
      Buryat.

TRANSBAYKAL BURYAT   Alt. spel. Transbaikal Buryat.
      SEE Transbaikal Buryat, Buryat.

TRANSCAUCASIAN   PEOPLES   Alt.   des.   Peoples   of
Transcaucasia. SEE Peoples
of Transcaucasia.

TRANSCAUCASIAN TATAR   For. alt. des. Azerbaidzhan.
SEE Azerbaidzhan.

TRUHMEN (OF STAVROPOL)   Alt. spel. Trukhmen. SEE
Trukhmen, Turkmen, Nogai.

TRUKHMEN   Oth. des. Trukhmen (Turkmen) of Stavropol.
ETHN: The Trukhmen are the descendants of
Turkmen   from   the   Mangyshlak   Peninsula   region   of
Turkmenistan who settled in the Nogai steppe in the
North Caucasus in the 17th cent. They have been
strongly influenced by the Nogai in that region, and in
the past were being assimilated by them. LANG: The
dialect of Turkmen spoken by them has been strongly
influenced by Nogai and Russian. It differs greatly
from the Turkmen dialects of Turkmenistan. The Trukhmen
use the Nogai and Russian literary languages (not
Turkmen). POP: 4,533 (1926). In the 1926 census the
Trukhmen were listed as Turkmen. The Trukhmen are being
assimilated   by   the Nogai.   They are Sunni Moslem in
religion. They live, primarily, in Stavropol Krai in
the steppe region of the North Caucasus. SEE Turkmen,
Nogai.

TRUKHMEN   OF   STAVROPOL   Alt.   des.   Trukhmen.   SEE
Trukhmen,   Turkmen,   Nogai.

TSAHUR   Alt. spel. Tsakhur. SEE Tsakhur.

TSAKHUR   Formerly no general self des. as an ethnic
group, but rather identified by village
(aul); contemporary self des. Tsakhighali (from the
village Tsakhur). ETHN: The Tsakhurs are one of the
numerically small Samurian peoples of southern Dagestan
and contiguous northern Azerbaidzhan. The Tsakhurs were
formerly   being   heavily   assimilated   by   the
Azerbaidzhans. The Soviet regime fosters the continuing
assimilation of the Tsakhurs of Azerbaidzhan; however,
it opposes the similar assimilation of them by the
Azerbaidzhans in Dagestan itself. The Tsakhurs continue
to be under strong Azerbaidzhan influence and virtually
all are at least bilingual (Tsakhur and Azeri). LANG:
The Tsakhur language belongs to the Samurian division
of the northeast branch of the Caucasic language
family. The situation regarding the literary language
of the Tsakhurs is complex. The Tsakhurs in
Azerbaidzhan have continued to use the Azeri literary
language. As part of the policy to stop further
Turkification (by the Azerbaidzhans) of the southern
Dagestanis, an attempt was made in 1932 to create a

Tsakhur literary language for these Tsakhurs living
in the Dagestan ASSR. This attempt was soon dropped
(1938-39) and Avar was made the official literary
language of the Tsakhurs of Dagestan. This policy was
changed in the 1950s and Russian is now the official
literary language of the Tsakhurs of Dagestan. The
Tsakhurs of Dagestan continue to be bilingual (Tsakhur
and Azeri), and many are also fluenct in Avar and/or
Russian. POP: 13,478 (1979); 11,103 (1970); 7,321
(1959); 19,085 (1926). The sharp decline in the Tsakhur
population between 1926-1959 was the result, primarily,
of the assimilation of the Tsakhurs of Azerbaidzhan by
the Azerbaidzhans. The Tsakhurs are Sunni Moslem in
religion. They live, primarily, on the southwestern
border of Dagestan and in adjacent areas in
Azerbaidzhan (Belokany Rayon). SEE
MAP 6.

TSES   Alt. spel. Tsez; alt. des. Dido. SEE Dido,
Andi-Dido Peoples, Avar.

TSES PEOPLES   Alt. spel. Tsez Peoples; alt. des. Dido
Peoples. SEE Dido Peoples, Andi-Dido
Peoples, Avar.

TSEZ   Alt. des. Dido. SEE Dido, Andi-Dido Peoples,
Avar.

TSEZ PEOPLES   Alt. des. Dido Peoples. SEE Dido
Peoples, Andi-Dido Peoples, Avar.

TSIGAN   Alt. spel. Tsygan; Rus. and alt. des. Gypsy.
SEE Gypsy.

TSIGAN(E) SREDNEI AZII   Alt. spel. Tsygan(e) Srednei
Azii; Rus. des. Gypsy of
Central Asia. SEE Gypsy of
Central Asia, Gypsy.

TSOVA TUSH (IN)   Alt. des. Batsbi. SEE Batsbi,
Georgian.

TSYGAN (E)   Rus. and alt. des. Gypsy. SEE Gypsy.

TSYGAN(E) SREDNEI AZII   Rus. des. Gypsy of
Central Asia. SEE Gypsy
of Central Asia, Gypsy.

TUAL (TSY)   Alt. des. Tualläg. SEE Tualläg, Ossetian.

TUALLÄG   Self des. Tualläg; oth. des. Tual(tsy), South
Ossetian. ETHN: The Tualllägs are the
descendants of the Iranian Ossetians who migrated south
of the Great Caucasian chain under pressure from Turkic
and Mongolic invaders of their former territory in the

North Caucasian steppe areas. They differ from the Iron
(Eastern   Orthodox North Ossetians)   in that   their
language and culture have been strongly influenced by
the Georgians among whom they live. The Tuallägs are
also being assimilated by the Georgians. LANG: The
Tualläg dialect of Ossetian has been strongly
influenced in vocabulary by the Georgian language. The
Tualläg dialect is close to (and mutually intelligible
with) the Iron dialect and the Tuallägs use the Iron
Ossetian literary language (and also Georgian). SEE
Ossetian.

TUBALAR   1-Self des. Tubalar (sing. Tuba). The
Tubalars are a group of Tofalars that went
into the formation of the Altai. They form one of the
tribal-territorial divisions (Tubalar) of the northern
group of the Altai (for. col. des. Chernevyy Tatar).
SEE Chernevyy Tatar. Altai.
            2-Alt. des. Tofalar. SEE Tofalar.
            3-Alt. des. Todzhan. SEE Todzhan, Tuvinian,
            Tofalar.

TÜMEN TATAR   Alt. spel. Tyumen Tatar. SEE Tyumen
                Tatar, West Siberian Tatar, Tatar.

TUNDRA ENISEI (ENISEY) SAMODI   Alt.   des. and spel.
   (SAMOED, SAMOIED, SAMOYED)   Tundra Enisei Samoyed;
                                 alt.   des.   Khantaika
                                 Samoyed. SEE Khantaika
                                 Samoyed, Ent.

TUNDRA ENT   Alt. des. Khantaika Samoyed.   SEE
                Khantaika Samoyed, Ent.

TUNDRA IENISEI SAMODI (SAMOED,   Alt.   des. and spel.
        SAMOIED, SAMOYED)   Tundra Enisei Samoyed;
                                 alt.   des.   Khantaika
                                 Samoyed. SEE Khantaika
                                 Samoyed, Ent.

TUNDRA IURAK   Alt. spel. Tundra Yurak; for. des.
                 Tundra Nenets. SEE Tundra Nenets,
                 Nenets.

TUNDRA NENETS   Des. of the Tundra   dwelling
                   (northern) Nenets [as opposed to
the Khandeyar (forest or southern Nenets)]; for des.
Tundra Yurak. The Tundra Nenets are the more numerous
of the two Nenets groups. The Nenets literary language,
which was established in 1932 (in the Cyrillic script),
is based on the Bolshaya Zemlya dialect of Tundra
Nenets. The Tundra Nenets live, primarily, along the
Arctic coast in the Yamalo-Nenets, Taimyr (Dolgano-
Nenets), and Nenets AOs. SEE Nenets.

TUNDRA YENISEI (YENISEY) SAMODI   Alt. des. and spel.
    (SAMOED, SAMOIED, SAMOYED)   Tundra Enisei Samoyed;
                                 alt.   des.   Khantaika
                                 Samoyed. SEE Khantaika
                                 Samoyed, Ent.

TUNDRA YURAK   For. des. Tundra Nenets. SEE Tundra
                 Nenets, Nenets.

TUNG-AN   Alt. (Chinese) des. Dungan. SEE Dungan.

TUNGUS   For. des. Evenk. The Evenk were listed as
           Tungus in the 1926 census. Northern Tungus
is also used to refer to the Evenk, Even, and Negidal.
SEE Evenk, Even, and Negidal.

TUNGUSIC PEOPLES   Col. des. for the peoples who speak
                     languages   that   belong   to   the
Tungusic division of the Tunguso-Manchu branch of the
Uralo-Altaic language family. This group is comprised
of three ethnically, culturally, and linguistically
related peoples. The Tungusic languages are all, to
varying degrees, mutually intelligible. The Tungusic
peoples are the: Evenk (including the Birar, Orochen,
Manegir,   and   Tongus groups — all of   whom   were
considered distinct ethnic groups until the 1930s),
Even, and Negidal. The Tungusic peoples were formerly
more numerous and widespread; however, over the past
few centuries they have been assimilated by the
surrounding   peoples   (Russians,   Buryats,   Yakuts,
Yukagirs, Koryaks, and the various Manchu peoples). SEE
Even, Evenk, Negidal.

TUNKA SOIOT   Alt. spel. Tunka Soyot; alt. des. Soyot.
                SEE Soyot, Tuvinian, Buryat.

TUNKA SOYOT   Alt. des. Soyot. SEE Soyot, Tuvinian,
                Buryat.

TURFAN (LIK)(LUK)LYK)   Alt. des. Turpan. SEE Turpan,
                          Uigur.

TURK   1-Des. of the Turks of Turkey [oth. des.
         Osman(li) Turk].
         2-For. (pre-1930s) des. Azerbaidzhan. SEE
         Azerbaidzhan.
         3-Alt. des. Meskhetian. SEE Meskhetian.
         4-Alt. des. Turks of Fergana and Samarkand.
         SEE Turks of Fergana and Samarkand.
         5-A Turkic speaking group of people in the
         villages of Firyuz and Germab in Turkmenistan
who are culturally similar to the Kurds and are
associated with them. In the 1959 and subsequent
censuses they were listed as Kurds, although they speak
a Turkic language and identify themselves as Turks. SEE

Kurd.
6-Des. of a speaker of any of the Turkic
languages. SEE Turkic Peoples.

TURK OF FERGANA AND SAMARKAND   Self des. Türki; Rus.
des. Tyurki. A group
of semi-nomadic Uzbeks who maintain their distinct
tribal identities (Karluk, Kaltatai, Barlas, etc.).
They are descendants of the pre-Uzbek Turkic nomads of
Uzbekistan and have not yet been totally assimilated by
the Uzbeks. POP: 537 (1926). SEE Uzbek. The Turks of
Fergana and Samarkand are Sunni Moslem in religion.
They live, primarily, in Fergana and Samarkand Oblasts
in the Uzbek SSR. SEE Uzbek.

TURK OF FERGHANA AND SAMARKAND   Alt. spel. Turk of
Fergana and Samarkand.
SEE Turk of Fergana
and Samarkand, Uzbek.

TURKESTANI   Col. des. for the inhabitants of the area
referred to in the 19th-early 20th
cents. as Turkestan. This territory is roughly
concomitant with the four republics of Central Asia
(Uzbekistan, Tadzhikistan, Turkmenistan, and Kirgizia).
The Turkestani peoples include the: Uzbeks, Tadzhiks,
Yagnobs, Pamir peoples, Turkmen, Kirgiz, and
Karakalpaks. Sometimes the minority groups living in
this area (Beluchi, Kurds, Central Asian Jews, Uigurs,
Dungans, etc.) and the southern Kazakhs (those living
within the borders of Turkestan) were also included in
this collective category.

TURKIC PEOPLES   Col. des. of the peoples of the USSR
that speak languages that belong to
the Turkic branch of the Uralo-Altaic language family.
Linguistically the Turkic peoples of the USSR are
grouped into five major divisions: Kypchak, Karluk,
Oguz, Bulgar, and Eastern. The Kypchak division is
comprised of three groups: Kypchak-Bulgar (Tatar and
Bashkir); Kypchak-Oguz or Polovetsian (Crimean Tatar,
Kumyk, Karachai, and Balkar); and Kypchak-Nogai
[Kazakh, Kirgiz, Karakalpak, Nogai, the languages
spoken by the southern Altai (Altai, Telengit, Telesy,
and Teleut) and some of the Uzbek dialects]. The Karluk
division is comprised of two major groups (Uzbek and
Uigur). The Uzbeks around Khiva are sometimes
classified as a distinct linguistic group as their
dialect is mixed with Oguz and Kypchak elements. The
Oguz division is comprised of three groups: Oguz-
Turkmen (Turkmen and Trukhmen); Oguz-Seldzhuk (Azeri
and Turkish); Oguz-Bulgar (Gagauz). The Bulgar group is
comprised of the Chuvash, whose exact relationship
within the Turkic language family has not yet been
established. The Eastern group is comprised of two
groups: Orkhon-Turkic (there are no longer any

surviving groups of Orkhon speakers — all having been
assimilated by other groups); and Old Uigur [the
languages spoken by the northern Altai groups (Tubalar,
Chelkan, and Kumanda), Khakass, Tuvinian, Tofalar,
Yakut, and Shor]. The Turkic peoples of the USSR are
also divided along religious lines. Most are Sunni
Moslem (Uzbeks, Karakalpaks, Kirgiz, Kazakhs, Bashkirs,
Tatars, Turkmen, Kumyk, Nogai, Balkar, Karachai, and
Crimean Tatars). The Azerbaidzhans are, primarily,
Shiite Moslem in religion (with a substantial Sunni
minority). The Chuvash, Kryashen (Christian Tatars),
and Nagaibak (Christian Bashkirs) are Eastern Orthodox
in religion. The Tuvinians are Buddhist in religion, and
the various other Siberian Turkic peoples (Yakuts,
Dolgans, Khakass, Altai, Shors, and Tofalars) are
basically shamanist-animist (with varying degrees of
borrowings from Eastern Orthodoxy). Until the 18th
cent. the Turkic peoples occupied a continuous
territory from the Crimea in the west, to the lands of
the Tuvinians in the east, to the tundra in the north,
and to the borders of Iran, Afghanistan, and China in
the south.

TURKMAN   Alt. des. Turkmen. SEE Turkmen.

TURKMAN OF STAVROPOL   Alt. des. Trukhmen. SEE Trukhmen,
             Turkmen.

TURKMEN   Self des. Türkmen; oth. des. Turkoman. ETHN:
             The Turkmen are one of the major peoples of
Central Asia. The Turkmen are the descendants of early
Oguz-Turkic invaders who migrated to Central Asia
during the 8th-10th cents. These Oguzic invaders
assimilated many of the Iranian and pre-Oguzic Turkic
tribes of the area. Although they are culturally more
closely related to the other peoples of Central Asia
(and in particular to the nomadic and semi-nomadic
Karakalpaks, and southwestern Kazakhs), the Turkmen are
linguistically more closely related to the
Azerbaidzhans. The Turkmen are divided into major
tribal-territorial groups, each of which speaks a
distinct dialect of Turkmen, and each of which was
considered a distinct people in the pre-Soviet period.
The Turkmen still maintain strong tribal divisions and
loyalties. The main Turkmen tribes are the: Teke (who
alone account for roughly 35% of the total Turkmen
populaton), Yomud, Ersari, Salyr, Saryk, Göklen,
Choudor, Ali-Ili (Alili), Karadash, and Emreli. In the
17th-18th cents. a group of Turkmen from the Mangyshlak
Peninsula migrated to the Nogai Steppe in the North
Caucasus. They are now known as Trukhmen (or Turkmen)
of Stavropol Krai. The Turkmen are also in the process
of assimilating the Beluchi and Kurds who live in the
Turkmen SSR. LANG: Turkmen belongs to the Oguz division
of the Turkic branch of the Uralo-Altaic language

family. There are many dialects of Turkmen which
correspond to the Turkmen tribal-territorial divisions.
Although the Turkmen language has been written since
the Middle Ages, the modern Turkmen literary language
dates back to the late 18th-early 19th cents. when it
was formalized. This modern Turkmen literary language
is based on the dialect of the Teke tribe. It was
originally written in the Arabic script, changed in
1928-29 to the Latin script, and in 1940 to the
Cyrillic. POP: 2,027,913 (1979); 1,525,284 (1970);
1,001,585 (1959); 763,940 (1926). The Turkmen are Sunni
Moslem in religion. They live, primarily, in the
Turkmen SSR, and in scattered settlements in adjacent
areas in Uzbekistan and Tadzhikistan. SEE MAP 1.

TURKMEN OF STAVROPOL   Alt. des. Trukhmen.   SEE
Trukhmen, Turkmen.

TURKOMAN   Alt. des. Turkmen. SEE Turkmen.

TURKOMAN OF STAVROPOL   Alt. des. Trukhmen.   SEE
Trukhmen, Turkmen.

TURPAN   Self des. Turpanlyk (Turfanlyk). The Turpan
           are a group of Uigurs who migrated to the
Russian Empire in the 18th cent. from the town of
Turfan in Chinese (Eastern) Turkestan. Although they
call themselves Uigurs, they also maintian the self
des. Turpanlyk. SEE Uigur.

TURQOMAN   Alt. des. Turkmen. SEE Turkmen.

TURQOMAN OF STAVROPOL   Alt. des. Trukhmen.   SEE
Trukhmen, Turkmen.

TURUHAN SELKUP   Alt. spel. Turukhan Selkup.   SEE
Turukhan Selkup, Taz Turukhan
Selkup, Selkup.

TURUKHAN SELKUP   Oth. des. Baikha (Baisha) Ostyak.
           The Turukhan Selkups are one of the
two groups of Selkups (Taz and Turukhan) who comprise
the northern (Taz Turukhan) group of Selkups. They
speak the Turukhan sub-dialect of the Taz dialect of
Selkup, and they live, primarily, in the Tundra zone of
the Yamalo-Nenets AO along the Turukhan and Yelogui
Rivers. SEE Taz Turukhan Selkup, Selkup.

TUSH (IN)   Alt. des. Tushetian. SEE Tushetian,
              Georgian.

TUSHETIAN   Self des. Tushuri; oth. des. Tush(in). The
              Tushetians are one of the numerous
Kartvelian ethnographic groups that went into the
formation of the Georgians. The Tushetians should not

be confused with the Batsbi (Tsova Tush) who are a
group of Veinakh speaking peoples that migrated to the
area of Tushetia from the North Caucasus. The
Tushetians speak a distinct (Tushetian) dialect of
Georgian. They are Eastern Orthodox in religion, and
live, primarily, in the Tushetia region of Georgia. SEE
Georgian.

TUVA TODJAN   Alt. spel. Tuva Todzhan; alt. des.
                   Todzhan. SEE Todzhan, Tuvinian, Tofalar.

TUVA TODZHAN   Alt. des. Todzhan. SEE Todzhan,
                   Tuvinian, Tofalar.

TUVA TODJAN   Alt. spel. Tuva-Todzhan; alt. des.
                   Todzhan. SEE Todzhan, Tuvinian, Tofalar.

TUVAN (TUVIN)   Alt. des. Tuvinian. SEE Tuvinian.

TUVINIAN   Self des. Tuva; oth. des. Tuva, Tuvan,
               Tuvin. ETHN: The Tuvinians are of mixed
origin. Although they are basically a group of
linguistically Turkified Mongols, a number of Turkic,
Samoyedic, and Kettic groups also went into the
formation of this people. The Tuvinian territory was
formally incorporated into the USSR in 1944, although
it had become a client state (Tanu-Tuva, or the Tuvan
Peoples Republic) of the Soviet Union in 1921.
Traditional pastoral Tuvinian culture survives in the
more remote mountainous region of Tuvinia. Many
Tuvinians have been assimilated by, and gone into the
formation of, other Siberian peoples. The Soyots are a
group of Tuvinians that were assimilated by the
Buryats; the Beltir are a group of Tuvinian origin that
forms one of the five territorial divisons of the
Khakass; and the Todzhans are a group that has been
linguistically and culturally assimilated by the
Tofalars (Tubalars). LANG: The Tuvinian language
belongs to the Old Uigur group of the Eastern division
of the Turkic branch of the Uralo-Altaic language
family. It is closely related (albeit to varying
degrees) to Shor, Khakass, the northern group of Altai,
Yakut, and Tofalar. The Tuvinians formerly used the
classical Mongol and Tibetan literary languages. The
modern Tuvinian literary language was established in
1930 using the Latin script and was changed in 1943 to
the Cyrillic. POP: 166,082 (1979); 139,388 (1970);
100,145 (1959). The Tuvinians are predominantly
Buddhist in religion, with some shamanist-animist
beliefs. They live, primarily, in the Tuvinian AO in
south-central Siberia. SEE MAP 15.

TYM KARAKON OSTIAK   For. alt. des. Tym Selkup. SEE Tym
         (OSTYAK)   Selkup, Narym Selkup, Selkup.

TYM KARAKON SELKUP   Alt. des. Tym Selkup. SEE Tym
Selkup, Narym Selkup, Selkup.

TYM OSTYAK   For. des. Tym Selkup. SEE Tym Selkup,
Narym Selkup, Selkup.

TYM SELKUP   Oth. des. Tym Karakon Selkup. The Tym
Selkups are one of the two divisions of
the Narym (southern or forest dwelling) Selkups. They
speak a distinct dialect of Selkup and are sometimes
considered, on that basis, to be a distinct group. The
other division is the Ket Selkup who also speak a
distinct dialect. SEE Narym Selkup, Selkup.

TYUMEN TATAR   Self des. Tümen Tatar. The Tyumen
Tatars are one of the territorial
divisions of the Tatars. They are one of the Tatar
groups known collectively as West Siberian Tatars. They
speak a distinct dialect of Tatar, although they use
the standard Tatar (Kazan Tatar) literary language.
POP: 22,636 (1926). Since the 1930s they have been
listed as Tatars. The Tyumen Tatars are Sunni Moslem in
religion. They live, primarily, in the vicinity of
Tyumen in western Siberia. SEE West Siberian Tatar,
Tatar.

TYURK (I)   Rus. and alt. des. Turk. SEE Turk.

TYURK (I) OF FERGANA   Alt. des. Turk of Fergana and
    AND SAMARKAND   Samarkand. SEE Turk of Fergana
                         Fergana and Samarkand, Uzbek.

U

UBIH (UBIKH, UBYH)   Alt. spel. Ubykh. SEE Ubykh,
Circassian.

UBYKH   Self des. Ubykh. ETHN: The Ubykh are
ethnically and culturally closely related to
the Abaza, and to a lesser extent, the western
Circassian tribes. In March of 1864 the entire Ubykh
population chose to emigrate to Turkey rather than live
under Russian rule. It is estimated that at the time of
their emigration there were approximately 30,000 Ubykh.
The Ubykh were formerly divided into five tribes:
Vardane, Sasshe, Kizhe, Subashi, and Alani. LANG: The
Ubykh language forms an independent group of the

Abazgian division of the Abazgo-Circassian (western)
branch of the Caucasic language family. Although
related to both Abaza and Abkhaz, Ubykh is not mutually
intelligible with either of them. During the time that
the majority of the Abazgo-Circassians emigrated to
Turkey (the 1860s) the entire Ubykh population
emigrated. They now live in Turkey where they are
called Abkhaz (as are the Abaza and Abkhaz). The Ubykh
are Sunni Moslem in religion. They formerly lived on
the Black Sea coast between the Shakhe and Khosta
(Khamysh) Rivers, in the territory between the Shapsug
(Adygei) and Abkhaz peoples. SEE Circassian.

UDEE   Alt. des. Udegei. SEE Udegei.

UDEGEI   Self des. Udee, Udekhe; oth. des. Udekhe.
           ETHN: The Udegei occupy a transitional
position, culturally and linguistically, between the
Manchu and Tungusic peoples. Udegei is the closest of
the Manchu languages to the Tungusic languages. LANG:
Udegei forms an independent group in the Manchu
division of the Tunguso-Manchu branch of the Uralo-
Altaic language family. The other group is comprised of
the Nanai, Ulchi, Orok, and Orochi (who are considered
by many linguists and ethnographers to be territorial
divisions of one Nani people, speaking closely related
dialects of one Nani language). Udegei is not written
and Russian serves as the literary language of the
Udegei. POP: 1,551 (1979); 1,469 (1970); 1,444 (1959);
1,357 (1926). In the 1926 census the Udegei were listed
as Udekhe. The Udegei are shamanist-animist in religion
with elements of Chinese beliefs. The Udegei live on
both slopes of the Sikhote Alin Mountains, scattered
over a large territory in Primorskiy and Khabarovsk
Krais, south of the Amur River. SEE MAP 6.

UDEGEY (UDEHE, UDEKHE)   Alt. spel. and des. Udegei.
                           SEE Udegei.

UDI   Self des. Udi; oth. des. Udin, Uti(n), Utii(n).
        ETHN: The Udi are the descendants of the
earliest known inhabitants of what is today
Azerbaidzhan. The Udi were once far more widespread and
numerous. Over the past two millennia they have been
assimilated by the Iranians (the ancestors of the
Tats), Turks (Azerbaidzhans), and Armenians that have
settled in their territory. In the 18th-early 19th
cents. the Udi were divided into two religious groups:
the majority had adopted Shiite Islam from the
Azerbaidzhans, and a minority had become Armeno-
Gregorian Christians under the influence of the
Armenians. The Moslem Udi were being assimilated by the
Azerbaidzhans, and the Christian Udi by the Armenians.
In the early 1920s a group of Udi resettled in Georgia
where they became Eastern Orthodox, and fell under

strong Georgian cultural and linguistic influence. By the mid to late 20th cent. the only remaining Udi were the Armeno-Gregorian Udi of Azerbaidzhan and the Udi of Georgia. Virtually all Moslem Udi have become Azerbaidzhans. LANG: The Udi language belongs to the Samurian division of the northeast branch of the Caucasic language family. Udi is not written. Until the 1950s the Moslem Udi used the Azeri literary language, the Armeno-Gregorian Udi the Armenian, and the Eastern Orthodox Udi (those of the Georgian SSR) the Georgian. In the 1950s the Soviets adopted a policy of introducing only Russian as a language of instruction and as a literary language among the Christian minorities in the Azerbaidzhan SSR (Tats and Udi). This policy severely weakened the Armenian influence on these two peoples. POP: 6,863 (1979); 5,919 (1970); 3,678 (1959); 2,455 (1926). The Udi of Azerbaidzhan are primarily Armeno-Gregorian in religion (with a Shiite Moslem minority), and those of the Georgian SSR are Eastern Orthodox in religion. The Udi live in the villages of Vartashen and Nidzh in Azerbaidzhan, and in the village Oktembri in eastern Georgia.

UDIN (Y)   Rus. and alt. des. Udi. SEE Udi.

UDMORT   Alt. des. Udmurt. SEE Udmurt.

UDMURT   Self des. Udmurt, Udmort; for. des. Votyak.
The Udmurts are culturally and linguistically closely related to the Komi and the Komi Permyaks. Regarding their religion, the Udmurts share with the Mari a strong adherence to their shamanist-animist beliefs. Depending on the degree of contact with other peoples, Udmurts in different areas have also adopted elements of the religions of the surrounding peoples. Those in close contact with the Russians and Chuvash have adopted many Eastern Orthodox beliefs, while those in contact with Tatars or Bashkirs have adopted Islamic ones. Those having little contact with other peoples, or those living among the Mari, have retained the Udmurt shamanist-animist religion. Among the Udmurts there is a distinct ethnographic group, the Besermyan. The Besermyan are the descendants of a group of Volga-Bolgars who were assimilated by the Udmurts. In their dialect of Udmurt they maintain many Turkic (Chuvash and Tatar) elements. LANG: Udmurt belongs to the Permian group of the Finnic division of the Uralian branch of the Uralo-Altaic language family. Udmurt is closely related to (and to some degree mutually intelligible with) Komi and Komi Permyak. The Udmurt language is comprised of two closely related dialects: northern and southern. The Udmurt literary language is based on a local speech that occupies a transitional position between the two dialects. The first work appeared in Udmurt in 1910, but Udmurt did not become a

regularized literary language until 1920. Udmurt has always been written in the Cyrillic script. POP: 713,696 (1979); 704,328 (1970); 624,794 (1959); 504,187 (1926). In the 1926 census the Udmurts were listed as Votyak. The religion of the Udmurts is basically shamanist-animist with borrowings (regionally) from Eastern Orthodoxy and Islam. The Udmurts live, primarily in the Udmurt ASSR, with scattered settlements in the Tatar, Mari, and Bashkir ASSRs, and Kirov and Perm Oblasts. SEE MAP 9.

UGLICH (I)   A group of Roman Catholic Ukrainians who maintained an old Slavic tribal designation as late as the mid-19th cent. In 1861 the population of the Uglich, along with the Tiver, was 8,398. They lived around Proskuriv in the Podilya (Podilia) region of the western Ukraine. They have since been totally assimilated by the Ukrainians. SEE Ukrainian.

UGOR (UGORIAN, UGRI)   Alt. des. Ugrian Peoples. SEE Ugrian Peoples.

UGRIAN PEOPLES   Col. des. for the peoples of the USSR that speak languages belonging to the Ugrian division of the Uralian branch of the Uralo-Altaic language family. Linguistically these peoples are divided into two groups: Ob-Ugrian and Magyar. Ob-Ugrian is comprised of the Khant(y) and Mansi who are closely related culturally, ethnically, and linguistically to each other. They live, primarily, in the basin of the Ob River and its tributaries in northwestern Siberia. The religions of these two peoples are a mixture of shamanist-animist with Eastern Orthodox borrowings. The Hungarians comprise the Magyar group. The Hungarians of the USSR speak an eastern dialect of Hungarian. These Hungarians, however, are, by and large, Magyarized Ukrainians and Slovaks, and are primarily Uniate in religion (unlike the majority of Hungarians who are Catholic or Protestant) with a substantial Catholic minority. The Hungarians are only distantly related linguistically to the Ob-Ugrians, are only remotely related ethnically, and not at all related culturally. SEE Khant, Mansi, Hungarian.

UGRO-RUSIN (RUSSIAN, RUSYN   Alt. des. Carpatho-Rusin.
        RUTHENIAN)   SEE Carpatho-Rusin, Ukrainian.

UHRO-RUSIN (RUSSIAN, RUSYN   Alt. des. Carpatho-Rusin.
        RUTHENIAN)   SEE Carpatho-Rusin, Ukrainian.

UIGHUR   Alt. spel. Uigur. SEE Uigur.

UIGUR   Self des. Uigur (since 1921); prior to 1921 no
           common self des. as an ethnic group, but
rather self des. according to place of origin or mode
of livelihood: Qashqarlyq (Kashgarlik), Turpanliq,
Aqsuluq (Aksuluk),   Yarkanlik, Taranchi. ETHN: The
Uigurs of the USSR are the descendants of Uigur
migrants from Chinese Turkestan between the 18th and
20th cents. The majority migrated to Central Asia in
the mid-18th cent. and migrated as entire village
groups. They also settled in these groups, and
therefore, maintained self designations based on these
place names of origin [Aksuluk (those from Aksu),
Yarkenlik (those from Yarkend), Kashgarlik (those from
Kashgar), Turpanlik (those from Turfan)]. The Uigurs
who settled in the Ili region in the 18th cent. as
farmers adopted the self designation Taranchi ("farmer"
in Uigur). The common designation Uigur was formally
adopted by a group of representatives of Uigurs in
Tashkent in 1921. The Uigurs of the USSR are divided
into two distinct culture groups: those of the Fergana
Valley (in Uzbekistan) and those of the Semirechie
region (in Kazakhstan). The Uigurs of the Semirechie
region have retained both their Uigur culture and
language, whereas those of the Fergana region have been
strongly influenced by the Uzbeks. Many Uigurs of the
Fergana region have lost the Uigur language and culture
and have adopted those of the culturally and
linguistically related Uzbeks. Many have been totally
assimilated by them. In the early and mid-20th cent.
there were two minor waves of immigration from Chinese
Turkestan (Uiguristan). These newer immigrants refer to
themselves as Uigurs and have maintained both the Uigur
language and culture. LANG: The Uigur language belongs
with Uzbek to the Karluk division of the Turkic branch
of the Uralo-Altaic language family. Most Uigurs of the
USSR speak the northern dialect of Uigur, whereas the
majority of the Uigurs of China speak the southern
dialect. Although the Uigurs have had a written
language since the 11th cent., the modern Uigur
literary language used by the Uigurs of the USSR dates
back only to 1946 when an Uigur literary language was
established based on the northern dialects. It
is written in the Cyrillic script. The literary Uigur
language of China is based on the southern dialect and
uses the Latin (formerly the Arabic) script. Prior to
the establishment of the Uigur literary language in the
USSR, the Soviet Uigurs used either the Uzbek, Kazakh,
or Tatar literary languages. POP: 210,612 (1979);
173,276 (1970); 95,208 (1959); 108,570 (1926). In 1926
the Uigurs were listed under three separate listings
[Taranchi (pop: 53,010), Uigur (pop: 42,550), and
Kashgar (pop: 13,010)]. The marked decline in the Uigur
population between 1926-1959 was primarily the result
of the assimilation of many of the Fergana Uigurs by
the Uzbeks. It is difficult to assess the extent of

this assimilation process as there was a simultaneous
immigration of Uigurs from China at that time. The
rapid rise in population among the Uigurs resulted from
a combination of a rather high rate of natural increase
and a substantial immigration from Chinese Turkestan
(Sinkiang Province). The Uigurs are Sunni Moslem in
religion. They live, primarily, in southeastern
Kazakhstan, eastern Uzbekistan (especially around
Andizhan), and in the main cities of Kirgizia. The
majority of Uigurs live in Sinkiang Province of China.
SEE MAP 12.

UKRAIN(TSY)   Rus. des. Ukrainian. SEE Ukrainian.

UKRAINIAN   Self des. Ukraintsy; for. des. Malorussy
               (Little or Lesser Russians). The term Malo
(Little) Rus, as opposed to Veliko (Great) Rus, derives
from the Byzantine system of ethno-geographical
nomenclature. Those areas closer to Byzantium were
called Little or Lesser, as the exact extent of the
territory was known. The area beyond that (presumed to
be larger) was designated Great or Greater. The pair
Lesser and Greater are not related to value judgements,
importance, or relative power. ETHN: The term Ukraina
(frontier territory or borderland) was first used in
the 12th cent. and referred only to a relatively small
area of the Ukraine (Galicia-Dniestr region). By the
17th cent, with the incorporation of much of the
Ukraine into the Polish-Lithuanian state, the term
Ukraina came to be used for all of the Ukraine. At that
time the term meaning borderland or frontier referred
to the Ukraine as a frontier of Poland-Lithuania and
not of Muskovy. As a result of diverse physical-
geographical conditions, numerous partitions between
other states, and ethnic contact with neighboring
peoples (Russians, Belorussians, Tatars, Romanians,
Poles, Slovaks, Hungarians, and Circassians) the
Ukrainian culture varies greatly from region to region.
Ukrainians are divided into three major ethnographic
groups: Central-Eastern (or Southeastern), Northern,
and Western (or Southwestern). The dialects of
Ukrainian roughly follow this ethnographic division.
The Central-Eastern group is further divided into three
sub-groups or sub-regions: the Middle Dniepr (Kiev,
Poltava, and the southern part of Chernigov Oblast),
Slobodskaya Ukraina, and the southern steppe. It was in
the Middle Dniepr that the modern Ukrainian nation was
formed. In this region the culture of the Ukrainians
both preserved many early Slavic Ukrainian culture
traits and adopted many others from the steppe nomads
(Tatars) and in the southeast from the Circassians. In
this region the Ukrainian population was Eastern
Orthodox in religion and strongly tied to Russia on
religious and cultural grounds. Animal husbandry and
grain farming in the steppe was important in the daily

lives of these Ukrainians. It was in this group that the Ukrainian Cossacks developed. SEE Cossack. The Northern group (including the northern parts of Suma, Kiev, Zhitomir, Rovno, Volyn, and Chernigov Oblasts) was far less influenced by the Tatars and Circassians, and more so by the Russians and Belorussians. Within this group there is a distinct ethnographic group of Ukrainians (Polishchuk) whose culture and language have been heavily influenced by the Belorussians among whom they live (in the Polesie marshes). They are also Eastern Orthodox in religion. In this region dairying, forestry, grain farming in the mixed forest, and raising flax were very important. The Western group is culturally distinct from the other two and forms a culturally transitional group between the Eastern and Western Slavs, and between the Ukrainians and the Poles, Hungarians, Slovaks, and Romanians. This group is found in the Ukrainian areas of Galicia, Bukovina, Transcarpathia, Volynia, and Podolia. These Ukrainians were culturally strongly influenced by the Poles, Romanians, Hungarians, and to a lesser extent the Slovaks. In religion they were primarily Uniate, with an Eastern Orthodox minority. These Ukrainians were forest dwellers (woodsmen) and semi-nomadic shepherds, as well as grain farmers and raisers of cattle and pigs. In the far western part of this region three ethnographic groups of Ukrainians are found: Hutsuls, Boiki, and Lemki (col. des. Carpatho-Rusins). SEE Carpatho-Rusin. In the past few centuries the Ukrainians have been under strong assimilation pressure by the Russians (in the north and east), Poles (in the northwest), and by the Hungarians (among the Carpatho-Rusins in the west). Both Tsarist and Soviet authorities have strongly sponsored the Russification of the ethnically, linguistically, and culturally related Ukrainians. At different times the Russian and Soviet governments have suppressed the Ukrainian language and culture in attempts to Russify these people. In the late 1920s the Kuban Cossacks were reclassified from Ukrainian to Russian. This resulted in a sharp decline (by between two and three million) in the Ukrainian population. The Ukrainians also suffered great losses of life during the period of collectivization (in the millions). The Ukrainian population was again decimated during World War II and the period of incorporation of the Western Ukraine into the Soviet Union after the War. Given the similar rates of natural increase among the Russians and Ukrainians the impact of the Russification of, and losses of life among, the Ukrainians can best be shown by comparing their relative populations in 1926 and 1979. In 1926 there were approximately 78,000,000 Russians and 31,000,000 Ukrainians (one must also consider that an additional Ukrainian population numbering in the millions was at that time not part of the USSR and does

not appear in this figure of 31,000,000— the total
Ukrainian population being in the vicinity of
35,000,000). In 1979 their relative populations were
approximately 137,000,000 Russians and 42,000,000
Ukrainians. A significant part of the increase of the
Russian population has resulted from the Russification
of Ukrainians. LANG: The Ukrainian language belongs to
the Eastern division of the Slavic branch of the Indo-
European language family. It is relatively closely
related to Russian and Belorussian (the other languages
in this group). There are three major dialect divisions
of Ukrainian: Southeastern, Northern, and Southwestern
(Western). These are roughly concomitant with the
ethnographic divisions of the Ukraine. Each of these
dialects has a number of sub-dialects. Although a
Ukrainian literary language arose in the 14th cent.
(and was highly developed), it was subsequently
submerged by Russian and Polish. The modern Ukrainian
literary language was established in the 19th cent.,
is based on the central (Kiev) dialect, and is written
in the Cyrillic script. In addition to this literary
language, other Ukrainian literary forms arose in
various parts of Galicia (using a Polish orthography
and based on a Galician dialect) and Transcarpathian
Ukraine (based on the Ruthenian dialect, and using the
Hungarian orthography, or the Cyrillic script). POP:
42,347,387 (1979); 40,753,246 (1970); 37,252,430
(1959); 31,194,976 (1926). The majority of Ukrainians
are Eastern Orthodox in religion. In the Western
Ukraine, however, the Uniate Church was widespread. The
Ukrainians live, primarily, in the Ukrainian SSR, with
significant communities scattered throughout the USSR,
especially in Siberia and northern Kazakhstan. SEE MAP
1.

UKRAINIAN GERMAN   The Germans of the Ukraine migrated
                     to the Ukraine (primarily in the
lower Dniepr region) during the reign of Catherine the
Great. During and after World War II they were either
killed or evacuated eastward (deported) to northern
Kazakhstan or southern Siberia, or retreated with the
German armies. The Ukrainian Germans were, primarily,
Lutheran or Mennonite in religion. There are few
Germans in the Ukraine at the present time. SEE German.

ULCHI   Self des. Nani; for. des. Mangu (1850-1880);
          oth. des. Olchi. ETHN: The Ulchi are one of
the Manchu peoples col. called Nani. The status of the
Ulchi as a distinct ethnic group is still debated. The
Ulchi, Nanai, Orok, and Orochi all consider themselves
to be one Nani people speaking one Nani language. Many
ethnographers consider these four peoples to be
territorial divisions of one Nani people as well.
Although linguistically the Ulchi are a Manchu people,
culturally they are more closely related to the

neighboring Nivkhi. The Ulchi, like the other Manchu
peoples, are being linguistically and culturally
assimilated by the Russians among whom they live. LANG:
The Ulchi language forms with Nanai, Orok, and Orochi
the Nani group of the Manchu division of the Tunguso-
Manchu branch of the Uralo-Altaic language family.
These four are actually dialects of one Nani language,
and all are mutually intelligible. Ulchi is not written
and Russian serves as the literary language of the
Ulchi. POP: 2,552 (1979); 2,448 (1970); 2,055 (1959);
723 (1926). In the 1926 census the Ulchi were listed as
Olchi. The religion of the Ulchi is a mixture of
shamanist-animist, Eastern Orthodox, and Chinese
beliefs. The Ulchi live, primarily, along the lower
reaches of the Amur River in Khabarovsk Krai in
southeastern Siberia. SEE Nani, Manchu Peoples, MAP 6.

UNANGAN (UNANGUN)   Self des. and alt. des. Aleut. SEE
                    Aleut.

UNGA   Oth. des. Ungin(tsy). One of the numerous
        territorial divisions of the Buryats. SEE
        Buryat.

UNGIN   Alt. des. Unga. SEE Unga, Buryat.

ÜPÖ CHEREMISS   For. des. Üpö Mari. SEE Üpö Mari,
                 Mari.

ÜPÖ MARI   For. des. Üpö Cheremiss; oth. des. Eastern
            Mari. The Üpö Mari are one of the three
ethnographic divisions of the Mari. The Üpö Mari live,
primarily, in the Bashkir and Tatar ASSRs and in
Sverdlovsk Oblast. The religion of the Üpö Mari is
predominantly shamanist-animist (as are the Highland
and Lowland Mari) with many Islamic adoptions. The
dialect spoken by the Üpö Mari is similar to that of
the Kozhla (Olyk) Mari with whom they share a common
literary language (Lowland Mari). The Üpö Mari have
been influenced strongly by the Tatars, and their
culture and language have many Tatar elements. SEE
Mari.

URAL (TSY)   The Ural(tsy) are an ethnographic group
              of Russians who live in the Karakalpak
ASSR and Kazakhstan along the Amu-Darya and Syr-Darya
Rivers, and on islands in the Aral Sea. They are the
descendants of Ural Cossacks who were later excluded
from this Cossack unit and were sent to the area around
the Aral Sea and the lower Amu- and Syr-Darya regions
in the 19th cent. They are basically fisherman. The
Ural are a group of Russian Old Believers in religion.
SEE Russian.

URALIAN PEOPLES   Col. des. of the peoples whose
                     languages belong to the Uralian
branch of the Uralo-Altaic language family. The Uralian
peoples are linguistically divided into three major
divisions: Finnic, Ugrian, and Samoyedic. The Finnic
peoples are divided into five groups: Balto-Finnic
(Western Finnic), which is comprised of two groups
[northern (including the Finns, Izhora, Karelians, and
Veps), and southern (including the Estonians, Vod, and
Livonians)]; Lapp (Saami); Mordvinian (including the
Erzya and Moksha Mordvinians, and the Meshchera); Mari;
and Permian (including the Udmurts, Komi, and Komi
Permyaks). The Ugrians are divided into two groups: Ob-
Ugrian (comprised of the Khant and Mansi) and Magyar
(Hungarian). The Samoyedic peoples are divided into two
groups: northern (including the Nenets, Ents, and
Nganasans) and southern (Selkup).

URANGHAI (URANGHAY) SAHA   Alt. spel. Urangkhai Sakha;
                             for. alt. des. Yakut. SEE
                     Yakut.

URANGKHAI SAKHA   For. alt. des. of Yakut. SEE Yakut.

URANGKHAY SAKHA   Alt. spel. Urangkhai Sakha; for.
                     alt. des. of Yakut. SEE Yakut.

URIANHAI (URIANHAY) (KALMUK,   Alt. spel. and des.
     KALMYK, QALMUQ, QALMYQ)   Uryankhai; for. des. of
                                Telengit. SEE Telengit,
                                Altai, Tuvinian.

URIANKHAI (URIANKHAY) (KALMUK, Alt. spel. and des.
     KALMYK, QALMUQ, QALMYQ)   Uryankhai; for. des. of
                                Telengit. SEE Telengit,
                                Altai, Tuvinian.

URUM   Self des. Urumchi. The term Urum derives from
        the Turkish word for the Roman (Byzantine)
Empire (Rum), and its people (Rum millet). The term
Urum has come to refer to those Greeks from Turkey who
had given up the Greek language and who had become
Turkish speakers. Those Greeks who had retained the
Greek language are called Romeos (pl. Romeoi), the Greek
word for a Roman (Byzantine) citizen. The Urum use the
literary language of the areas in which they live in
the USSR (usually Russian or Georgian) and not Greek.
SEE Greek.

URUMCHI   Alt. des. Urum. SEE Urum, Greek.

URUSBI (EVTSY)   For. alt. des. of Karachai; oth. des.
                    Uruspi (evtsy). The term Urusbi is
derived from the village of Urusbi, which was a major
Karachai village in the 19th cent. SEE Karachai.

URUSPI (EVTSY)   Alt. des. Urusbi; for. alt. des. of
                 Karachai. SEE Urusbi, Karachai.

URYANHAI (URYANHAY) (KALMUK,   Alt. spel. and des.
    KALMYK, QALMUQ, QALMYQ)   Uryankhai; for. des. of
                                Telengit. SEE Telengit,
                                Altai, Tuvinian.

URYANKHAI   For. (18th - early 19th cent.) des. of
                Telengit. SEE Telengit, Altai, Tuvinian.

URYANKHAI (URYANKHAY) (KALMUK,   Alt. spel. and des.
    KALMYK, QALMUQ, QALMYQ)   Uryankhai; for. des. of
                                  Telengit. SEE Telengit,
                                  Altai, Tuvinian.

UTI (UTII, UTIIN, UTIN)   Alt. des. Udi. SEE Udi,
                           Azerbaidzhan.

UYGHUR (UYGUR)   Alt. spel. Uigur. SEE Uigur.

UZBEK   Self des. Özbek. ETHN: The Uzbeks are the most
         numerous of the Turkic and Islamic peoples of
the USSR. The Uzbek nation was formed by the merging
over centuries of settled Iranian (basically Tadzhik)
and nomadic Turkic groups. Although the cultural
background of the Uzbeks derived primarily from the
settled Iranian group, the language that prevailed was
that of the Turks. There are three culturally distinct
groups of Uzbeks: Sart, Türki, and Kypchak. The Sarts
are the settled Uzbeks who are culturally
indistinguishable from the Tadzhiks. They have no
tribal divisions. The majority of Uzbeks are Sart. The
Türki are the descendants of the Turkic tribes that
inhabited Central Asia prior to the invasion of the
proto-Uzbeks in the 15th cent. They have maintained
their tribal identities (Karluk, Kaltatai, Barlas,
etc.) and are collectively called Türki (Tyurki) or
Turks of Fergana and Samarkand. In the 1926 census they
were listed as Tyurki (pop: 537). They are also related
to Iranians but with some Mongoloid (Turkic) elements.
The Kypchak are the nomadic or semi-nomadic groups of
Uzbeks who form a transitional group both culturally
and linguistically between the Uzbeks and Kazakhs. They
have maintained their tribal identities (Kypchak,
Kungrat, Mangyt, Kurama, etc.). Although they are also
related to the Iranians, they display a strong
Mongoloid racial element. The Uzbeks are in the process
of assimilating these formerly nomadic and semi-nomadic
Turkic tribal groups. In the 1926 census two of these
groups were listed separately: Kurama (pop. 50,079) and
Kypchak (pop. 33,502). The Uzbeks have also assimilated
many Karakalpaks, Tadzhiks, Uigurs, and other Central
Asian Islamic peoples. LANG: The Uzbek language belongs
with Uigur to the Karluk (Chagatai) division of the

Turkic branch of the Uralo-Altaic language family. The
Uzbek language is comprised of a number of distinct
dialect groups: Karluk, Oguz, and Kypchak, each having
a number of sub-dialects. The dominant dialect group is
the Karluk (or Chagatai) group. Karluk dialects are
spoken in the main urban centers of Uzbekistan. Of
these the central dialects, as a result of a strong
Iranian influence, have lost vowel harmony. The
southern Karluk dialects, on the other hand, still
maintain vowel harmony. The dialects spoken around
Khiva (Khwarezm) are basically Oguzic (a result of
Turkmen influence) with a strong Kypchak element. The
dialects of the Kypchak nomads are basically Kypchak
(rather than Karluk). The first literary Turkic
language of Uzbekistan (pre-Uzbek) was based on a
Karluk dialect (10th-11th cent.). A new literary
language was introduced in the 12th cent. and was used
until the 15th (i.e., until the arrival of the Uzbek
invaders). This was based on an Oguz language similar
to Turkmen. Since the 15th cent. the literary Turkic
language of Uzbekistan has been based on a Karluk
(Chagatai) dialect. Until the time of the revolution
Persian (Tadzhik) was used as frequently as Chagatai
among the Turkic Uzbeks. Virtually all of the Sart
Uzbeks were bilingual. Many still are (Uzbek and
Tadzhik). During the Soviet period not only has the
script been changed (until 1928 the Arabic script was
used, changed in 1928 to the Latin, and in 1940 to the
Cyrillic), but the literary dialect has shifted
frequently. Between 1922-1929 various literary forms
based on local dialects were employed. In 1929 the
Kipchak dialect of the town of Turkestan in southern
Kazakhstan became the official literary Uzbek language.
In 1934 it was replaced by the dialect of Tashkent. A
particular problem has existed in the development of an
Uzbek literary language as the many dialects (and sub-
dialects) of Uzbek are so radically different from each
other. Uzbek is also spoken by many Tadzhiks, Kirgiz,
Turkmen, Karakalpaks, Central Asian Jews, Uigurs, and
Kazakhs. POP: 12,455,978 (1979); 9,195,093 (1970);
6,015,416 (1959); 3,904,622 (1926). In 1926 the Türki,
Kurama, and Kypchak were listed separately [Uzbek pop.
including these groups 3,988,740 (1926)]. The Uzbeks
are Sunni Moslem in religion. They live, primarily, in
the Uzbek SSR and adjacent territories in Tadzhikistan,
Turkmenistan, Kazakhstan, and Kirgizia. SEE MAP 10.

UZBEQ   Alt. spel. Uzbek. SEE Uzbek.

UŽNEMUNIEČIAI   Alt. des. of Suvalkiečiai. SEE
                      Suvalkiečiai, Lithuanian.

V

VAD   Alt. des. Vod. SEE Vod.

VADEEV   NGANASAN   The Vadeev Nganasan are   the
                      descendants of a group of Evenks
who migrated to the Taimyr Peninsula in   the mid-18th
cent. where they were assimilated by the Nganasan. SEE
Nganasan.

VAHAN   (VAKHAN)   Rus. and alt. des. Wakhan. SEE
                     Wakhan, Pamir Peoples, Tadzhik.

VELIKO RUS (SKIY)   Rus. des. Great Russian; Rus. alt.
                     des. Russian. The term Veliko
(Great) Rus, as opposed to Malo (Little) Rus, derives
from the Byzantine system of ethno-geographical
nomenclature. Those areas closer to Byzantium were
called Little or Lesser, as the exact extent of the
territory was known. The area beyond that (presumed to
be larger) was designated Great or Greater. The pair
Greater and Lesser are not related to value judgements,
importance, or relative power. SEE Russian.

VENGER (TSY) (VENGRY)   Rus. des. Hungarian. SEE
                          Hungarian.

VEPS   Self des. Vepsä (among the southern Veps) or
                    Lyudinikad (among the northern and central
Veps.); for. des. Chud, Chudin, Lyydinik; for. Rus.
des. Chukhar(y), Chukhon(tsy), Kaivan(y); oth. des.
Vepsya. ETHN: The Veps are closely related ethnically,
culturally, and linguistically to the Karelians. The
Veps were formerly more numerous and widespread;
however, in the past few centuries they have been
assimilated by the Russians. The Veps, as a result of
Russian immigration into their territory and the
Russification of the majority of their population, now
live in three non-contiguous territories: northern,
central, and southern. The northern Veps live on the
southwestern shore of Lake Onega in the Karelian ASSR;
the southern Veps live in the northern part of
Efimovskiy Rayon in Leningrad Oblast; and the central
Veps live in villages scattered between these other two
in Vologda and Leningrad Oblasts. Only the southern
Veps refer to themselves as Veps. The others call

themselves Lyudinikad (Lyudinik) which is also the
analogous name of part of the Karelian population (to
whom the Veps are related). LANG: The Veps language
belongs to the northern sub-group of the Baltic group
of the Finnic division of the Uralian branch of the
Uralo-Altaic language family. Veps is comprised of
three dialects which correspond to the three
territorial divisions. The northern dialect is mutually
intelligible with Karelian. Veps is not written and
Russian serves as the literary language of the Veps.
Virtually all Veps speak Russian, and many (roughly
half) no longer speak Veps. POP: 8,094 (1979); 8,281
(1970); 16,374 (1959); 32,785 (1926). The continuous
decline of the Veps population, like that of the
Karelians, mainly results from their assimilation by
the Russians.

VIDZEMIAN   Alt. des. Vidzemieši. SEE Vidzemieši,
              Latvian.

VIDZEMIEŠI   Self des. Vidzemieši (sing. Vidzemietis);
              oth. des. Vidzemnieki (sing. Vidzemnieks),
Vidzemian. The Vidzemieši are the inhabitants of the
Vidzeme region of Latvia (one of the four traditional
provinces of Latvia). SEE Latvian.

VIDZEMIETIS (VIDZEMNIEKI,   Alt. des. Vidzemieši. SEE
            VIDZEMNIEKS)   Vidzemieši, Latvian.

VIRIAL   Alt. spel. Viryal. SEE Viryal, Chuvash.

VIRYAL   The Viryal are one of the two ethnic
           divisions (Viryal and Anatri) of the
Chuvash. The Viryal are often referred to as Upper
Chuvash (the Anatri, Lower Chuvash). The Anatri dialect
forms the basis of the Chuvash literary language. The
Viryal live, primarily, in the northern and
northwestern parts of the Chuvash ASSR in the Middle
Volga region. SEE Chuvash.

VOD Self des. Vad'd'alaiset; for. Rus. des. Vad',
     Vozhan(e), Chud' (which they also applied to other
Finnic peoples); oth. des. Vot, Votes. ETHN: The Vod
are ethnically and linguistically closely related to
the Estonians. The ancestors of the Setu (Estonians)
and the Livonians were probably Vod. The Vod were
formerly more numerous and widespread in the region
between the Narva and Neva Rivers. Since contact with
Novgorod (11th-12th cents.) the Vod have been steadily
Slavicized by the Russians. Their total assimilation
will have been completed within a few years, if it has
not already been accomplished. LANG: The Vod language
belongs to the southern group of the Baltic division of
the Finnic branch of the Uralo-Altaic language family.
It is mutually intelligible with Estonian. Vod was

never written and Russian served as the literary language of the Vod. POP: 23 (1959); 705 (1926). The Vod were Eastern Orthodox in religion.

VOGUL   For. des. of Mansi. The Mansi were listed as Vogul in the 1926 census. SEE Mansi.

VOJAN   Alt. spel. Vozhan; alt. des. Vod. SEE Vod.

VOLGA GERMAN   The Volga Germans migrated to the Volga region during the reign of Catherine the Great. At the onset of World War II the entire Volga German population, which lived, primarily, in the Volga German ASSR, was deported to northern Kazakhstan and southwestern Siberia. At that time (1939) the German autonomy was abolished and education and publishing in the German language ceased. Unlike the Germans of the Baltic region, Bessarabia, and the Ukraine the Volga Germans could not retreat with the German armies at the end of the War. They still live, primarily, in the cities of northern Kazakhstan. Since the early 1970s some limited publishing has been resumed in German for the Germans of Kazakhstan. In addition, since the early 1970s the Soviets have been allowing a slow, but steady, emigration of Germans to Germany. The Volga Germans were, primarily, Lutheran and Mennonite in religion. SEE German.

VOLGA FINNS   Col. des. of the Finnic speaking peoples of the Volga region. Included in this group are the Mari, Udmurt, and Mordvinian peoples. At times the Komi and Komi Permyaks are also included in this group (although traditionally they are not). SEE Mari, Udmurt, Mordvinian.

VOLGA TATAR   Self des. Tatar, Qazan Tatar (Kazan Tatar), Mishar (the Mishar division of the Tatars); oth. des. Kazan Tatar. The Volga Tatars are the most numerous and important of the numerous Tatar territorial groups. The Volga Tatars today are divided into three culture groups: Tatar (Kazan Tatar), Mishar, and Kryashen. The Mishars are a group of Tatarized Meshchera (Mordvinians) who still maintain a number of Volga Finnic culture and linguistic traits. The Kryashen are a group of Tatars that accepted Eastern Orthodoxy, (i.e., became Christians) and developed close cultural ties with the Russians. Until the 1930s each of these groups was considered a distinct ethnic group. Since that time the Kryashen and Mishar populations have been classified as Tatars. Among the Volga Tatars two dialects of Tatar are spoken: western (Mishar), and central (Kazan). The western dialect forms the basis of the Tatar literary language. SEE Tatar.

VOLGA TURK   Col. des. of the peoples of the Volga
              region whose languages belong to the
Turkic branch of the Uralo-Altaic language family.
These peoples are divided into two groups: the Tatars
and Bashkirs, and the Chuvash. The Tatars and Bashkirs
are closely related culturally (both are Sunni Moslem),
ethnically, and linguistically (Bashkir is in actuality
an eastern dialect of Tatar and is mutually
intelligible with Tatar). The Chuvash are a culturally
and linguistically distinct people. The Chuvash
language belongs to the Bolgar division of the Turkic
language branch (unlike Tatar and Bashkir which belong
to the Kypchak division), and they are Eastern Orthodox
in religion. SEE Tatar, Bashkir, Chuvash.

VOT (VOTES)   Alt. des. Vod. SEE Vod.

VOTIAK   Alt. spel. Votyak; for. des. of Udmurt. SEE
          Udmurt.

VOTYAK   For. des. of Udmurt. The Udmurts were listed
          as Votyaks in the 1926 census. SEE Udmurt.

VOZHAN (E)   For. Rus. des. Vod. SEE Vod.

W

WAHAN   Alt. spel. Wakhan. SEE Wakhan, Pamir Peoples,
         Mountain Tadzhik, Tadzhik.

WAKHAN   Self des. Khik.; Rus. and oth. des.
          Vakhan(tsy). The Wakhan are one of the six
peoples that comprise the group of ethnic groups known
as the Pamir peoples. The Wakhan language forms the
Wakhan group of the eastern division of the Iranian
branch of the Indo-European language family. The
Wakhan, like the other Pamir peoples, are Ismaili
Moslem in religion. Also like the other Pamir peoples
they are being assimilated by the Tadzhiks. Until the
late 1930s-early 1940s each of the six Pamir peoples
was considered a distinct ethnic group. They are now
classified as ethnographic groups of Tadzhiks. The
Wakhan language is not written and Tadzhik serves as
the literary language of the Wakhan. They live,
primarily, in the highest valleys at the sources of the
Pyandzh, Darshai, Boibar, and Pamir Rivers in the
Gorno-Badakhshan AO in southeastern Tadzhikistan, near

the border of Afghanistan. A substantial number of
Wakhan also live on the Afghan side of the border. SEE
Pamir Peoples, Mountain Tadzhik, Tadzhik.

WEST SIBERIAN TATAR   Col. des. of the four Tatar
                       territorial groups of Tatars
that live in western Siberia [Tobol, Tyumen, Tara
(Ishim), and Baraba Tatars]. All of these groups are
linguistically and culturally similar to the Volga
(Kazan) Tatars, and they use the Tatar literary
language. Each speaks a distinct dialect of Tatar. The
West Siberian Tatars are also Sunni Moslem in religion.
The Tobol Tatars live near the city of Tobolsk; the
Tyumen Tatars live near the city of Tyumen; the Tara
Tatars live along the Irtysh and Tara Rivers in Tarskiy
Rayon (Omsk Oblast); and the Baraba Tatars live in the
Baraba Steppe in Novosibirsk Oblast. The Tatars who
live around Tomsk (Tom or Tomsk Tatars) are often
considered a distinct group of West Siberian Tatars. In
1926 each of these groups (with the exception of the
Tom Tatars) was listed separately in the census: Tobol
Tatar (32,102), Tyumen Tatar (22,636), Tara Tatar
(11,517), and Baraba Tatar (7,528). In 1926 11,659
Bukharans were incorrectly registered as Tatars in the
census. Each of these territorial groups is divided
into a number of tribes and clans which still maintain
their distinct identities. SEE Tatar.

WESTERN FINNIC PEOPLES   Alt. des. Balto-Finnic
                          Peoples. SEE Balto-Finnic
                          Peoples.

WHITE KALMUK (KALMYK,   Alt. des. Porubezhnyy Kalmyk;
  QALMUQ, QALMYQ)   for. des. of Teleut. SEE
                          Teleut, Altai.

WHITE NOGAI (NOGAY,   Alt. des. Ak Nogai. SEE Ak
  NOGHAI, NOGHAY)   Nogai, Nogai.

WHITE RUSSIAN   Eng. alt. des. Belorussian. SEE
                 Belorussian.

WHITE RUTHENIAN   For. Eng. alt. des. Belorussian.
                   SEE Belorussian.

Y

YAGE   Alt. des. Yage Dungan. SEE Yage Dungan, Dungan.

YAGE DUNGAN   The Yage Dungans are a relatively small
                group of Dungans who migrated to the
Russian Empire (to   the   villages   of Aleksandrovka,
Sokuluk, and Chilik in Kazakhstan) from the towns of
Lanchzhou and Inchuan in China. They speak the Ninsya-
Lanchzhou dialect of Chinese, which is a transitional
dialect between Hansu and Shensi dialects (the majority
of Dungans in the USSR are originally from   the
provinces   of Hansu and Shensi and speak   these
dialects). The Yage Dungans are a culturally distinct
group, and the term Yage carries a somewhat pejorative
meaning (refugee, run-away). SEE Dungan.

YAGNOB   Self des. Yaghnob. ETHN: The Yagnobs are the
           descendants   of   the   Sogdian   (Iranian)
population of Central Asia. They represent a small
group that has not yet been totally assimilated by the
Tadzhiks. The Sogdians went into the formation of the
Uzbek and Tadzhik populations. The Yagnobs are not one
of the Pamir peoples, and should not be confused with
them. LANG: The Yagnob language belongs to the eastern
division of the Iranian branch of the Indo-European
language family. Yagnob is not written and Tadzhik
serves as the literary language of the Yagnobs. All are
bilingual (Yagnob and Tadzhik). POP: 1,829 (1926).
Until the late 1930s the Yagnobs were considered a
distinct ethnic group. Since that time they have been
classified as an ethnographic group of Tadzhiks. The
Yagnobs are Sunni Moslem in religion. They live,
primarily, along the upper reaches of the Yagnob River
in Tadzhikistan. SEE Tadzhik.

YAKUT   Self des. Sakha; for. self des. Urangkhai
          Sakha. ETHN: The dominant theory on the origin
of the Yakuts is that they are a group of Turkic
speaking peoples from around the region of Lake Baikal
who were forced to move northward by the ancestors of
the Mongolic Buryats in the 13th-14th cents. There they
mixed with, or replaced the Tungusic and Paleoasiatic
peoples of that area. Judging by tribal and clan names
a number of Mongolic tribes have also gone into the
composition of the Yakuts. The Yakuts are divided into

two culturally distinct groups: northern and southern
(the majority). The northern Yakut culture is similar
to the hunting, fishing, and reindeer breeding cultures
of the Tungus and Yukagirs, whereas the southern Yakuts
still emphasize cattle breeding. At times the northern
Yakuts have been referred to as Tungus, even though
they speak Yakut, and call themselves Yakuts (Sakha).
The Yakuts have assimilated many of the surrounding
peoples and Yakut serves as a lingua franca among many
Dolgans, Yukagirs, Evenks, and Evens. The Dolgans have
gone over completely to speaking Yakut. The Yakutyan(e)
should not be confused with the Yakuts. The Yakutyan(e)
are a group of Russians who lived along the Lena River,
who mixed with local Yakuts, and adopted the Yakut
culture but kept their Russian identity and language.
They are considered an ethnographic group of Russians.
Another group of Russians settled along the Kolyma
River where they mixed with local Yakuts. These people
are called Kolymchan(e). The Kolymchan(e), unlike the
Yakutyan(e), gave up the Russian language and culture
and became totally Yakutized. They, however, still
consider themselves Russians, and are classified as an
ethnographic group of Russians. LANG: The Yakut
language belongs to the Old Uigur group of the Eastern
division of the Turkic branch of the Uralo-Altaic
language family. The Yakut language is related to Shor,
Tuvinian, Khakass, Tofalar, and the dialects of the
northern group of Altai. Yakut is not divided into
dialects, and the few local speech differences are
insignificant. The Yakut literary language was created
in 1905 and has always been written in the Cyrillic
script. POP: 328,018 (1979); 296,244 (1970); 233,344
(1959); 240,709 (1926). The decline in population among
the Yakuts between 1926-1959 was the result, primarily,
of heavy losses in lives during the period of
collectivization. The religion of the Yakuts is a
mixture of Eastern Orthodox and shamanist-animist
beliefs. The Yakuts live, primarily, in the Yakut ASSR,
and adjacent areas of eastern Siberia. SEE MAP 4.

YAKUTIAN(E)   Alt. spel. Yakutyan(e). SEE Yakutyan(e),
               Russian, Yakut.

YAKUTYAN(E)   The Yakutyan are an ethnographic group
               of Russians of mixed Russian and Yakut
origin who live along the Lena River. They speak
Russian and consider themselves Russians, although
their culture is heavily influenced by Yakut. SEE
Russian, Yakut.

YARA   Oth. des. Yarin. The Yara, like the Yasta, are
        a Kettic speaking group that went into the
formation of the Kacha division of the Khakass. SEE
Kacha, Khakass.

YARIN   Alt. des. Yara. SEE Yara, Kacha, Khakass.

YARKENDLIK (YARKENDLYK)   Alt. des. Yarkenlik. SEE
                                 Yarkenlik, Uigur.

YARKENLIK   Self des. Yarkenlik; oth. des. Yarkendlik.
              The Yarkenlik are a group of Uigurs whose
ancestors migrated to Central Asia from the town of
Yarkend in Chinese Turkestan in the mid-18th cent.
Until the early 20th cent. the various Uigur groups
identified themselves according to the place of origin
of their ancestors in China. SEE Uigur.

YARKENLYK   Alt. spel. Yarkenlik. SEE Yarkenlik, Uigur.

YASTA   Oth. des. Yastin. The Yasta, like the Yara,
          are a Kettic speaking group that went into the
formation of the Kacha division of the Khakass. SEE
Kacha, Khakass.

YATVIG (IAN)   Oth. des. Yatvyag(ian), Yatving(ian),
                 Sudavi. The Yatvigs are a group of
Balts (closely related to the Lithuanians) who lived
mainly in the central part of southern Grodno Gubernya
in Belorussia. In 1861, 30,927 people designated
themselves as Yatvigs. They were Eastern Orthodox in
religion, and presumably speakers of Belorussian. Since
that time they have been totally assimilated by the
Belorussians. SEE Belorussian.

YATVING (YATVINGIAN, YATVYAG,   Alt. des. Yatvig. SEE
         YATVYAGIAN)   Yatvig, Belorussian.

YAZGHULEM (YAZGHULYIAM,   Alt. spel. and des. Yazgulem.
         YAZGHULYAM, YAZGUL)   SEE Yazgulem, Pamir Peoples,
                                 Tadzhik.

YAZGULEM   Self des. Zgamig; oth. des. Yazgul,
             Yazgulyam. The Yazgulem are one of the six
Pamir peoples. The Yazgulem language forms the Yazgulem
group of the Eastern division of the Iranian branch of
the Indo-European language family. Yazgulem is not
written and Tadzhik serves as the literary language of
the Yazgulem. The Yazgulem, like the other Pamir
peoples, are Sunni Moslem in religion. Until the late
1930s-early 1940s each of the Pamir peoples was
considered a distinct ethnic group. Since that time
they have been classified as ethnographic groups of
Tadzhiks. The Yazgulem are being assimilated by the
Tadzhiks. They live, primarily, along the Yazgulyam
River in Vanch Rayon in the Gorno-Badakhshan AO in
southeastern Tadzhikistan near the border with
Afghanistan. Many Yazgulem live on the other side of
the border. SEE Pamir Peoples, Mountain Tadzhik,
Tadzhik.

YAZGULIAM (YAZGULYAM)   Alt. des. Yazgulem. SEE Yazgulem, Pamir Peoples, Mountain Tadzhik, Tadzhik.

YAZID   Alt. des. Yezid. SEE Yezid, Kurd.

YAZVA   Alt. des. Yazva Komi Permyak. SEE Yazva Komi Permyak, Komi Permyak.

YAZVA KOMI PERMIAK   Alt. spel. Yazva Komi Permyak. SEE Yazva Komi Permyak, Komi Permyak.

YAZVA KOMI PERMYAK   Oth. des. Yazvin, Yazvin(skiy) Komi Permyak; for. des. Yazva (Yazvin) Zyryan. The Yazva are one of the two ethnic sub-divisions of the Komi Permyaks (Yazva and Zyuzda Komi Permyak) who live outside the Komi Permyak AO. The Yazva live, primarily, in the basin of the Yazva River (a tributary of the Vishera). They speak a distinct sub-speech of Komi (not of Komi Permyak). Some are also Russian Old Believer in religion. In 1959 their population was approximately 4,000. SEE Komi Permyak.

YAZVA ZIRIAN (ZIRYAN, ZYRIAN)   Alt. spel. Yazva Zyryan; for. des. Yazva Komi Permyak. SEE Yazva Komi Permyak, Komi Permyak.

YAZVA ZYRYAN   For. des. Yazva Komi Permyak. SEE Yazva Komi Permyak, Komi Permyak.

YAZVIN(SKIY) KOMI PERMYAK (ZIRIAN, ZIRYAN, ZYRIAN, ZYRYAN)   Alt. des. Yazva Komi Permyak. SEE Yazva Komi Permyak, Komi Permyak.

YENISEI   For. des. of Ket and Ent. SEE Ket, Ent.

YENISEI OSTIAK   Alt. spel. Yenisei Ostyak; for. des. of Ket. SEE Ket.

YENISEI OSTYAK   For. des. of Ket. SEE Ket.

YENISEI SAMODI (SAMOED, SAMOIED)   Alt. des. and spel. Yenisei Samoyed; for. des. Ent. SEE Ent.

YENISEI SAMOYED   For. des. of Ent. SEE Ent.

YENISEI TATAR   For. des. of Khakass. SEE Khakass.

YENISEY   Alt. spel. Yeinisei; for. des. of Ket and Ent. SEE Ket, Ent.

YENISEY OSTYAK   Alt. spel. Yenisei Ostyak; for. des.
                 of Ket. SEE Ket.

YENISEY SAMODI (SAMOED,   Alt. des. and spel. Yenisei
              SAMOYED)   Samoyed; for. des. Ent. SEE
                          Ent.

YENISEI TATAR   Alt. spel. Yenisei Tatar; for. des.
                 of Khakass. SEE Khakass.

YEZID   The Yezids are a religious division of the
           Kurds. The Yezid religion is considered a
heretical sect by the Sunni Moslems and as such the
Yezids   were   persecuted in many   Middle   Eastern
countries.   They have maintained many elements of
Zoroastrianism (including fire worship). As a result of
such persecution in Turkey·in the 19th cent. many Yezid
Kurds   migrated   to Russian controlled   areas   of
Transcaucasia (Armenia and Georgia). Unlike the Sunni
and Shiite Moslem Kurds, the Yezids are not being
assimilated by other Islamic peoples among whom they
live.   Until the 1930s the Yezids were considered a
distinct ethnic group and appear as Yezids in the 1926
census (pop: 14,523). Since that time they have been
classified as an ethnographic group of Kurds and appear
as Kurds in statistical publications. SEE Kurd.

YOMUD   Oth. des. Yomut. The Yomud are one of the
           major tribal-territorial divisions of the
Turkmen (they are the third largest and account for
roughly 14% of the total Turkmen population). In the
pre-Soviet period they were each considered distinct
peoples. The Yomud speak a distinct dialect of Turkmen
(Yomud).   They   live,   primarily,   in a continuous
territory to the east of the Caspian Sea. The border of
their territory is roughly a line running from the
southwest to the northeast from the Atrek River to
Kyzyl Arvat to Kunya Urgench. SEE Turkmen.

YOMUT   Alt. des. Yomud. SEE Yomud, Turkmen.

YUGO OSET(IN)   Rus. des. South Ossetian; alt. des.
                 Tualläg. SEE Tualläg, Ossetian.

YUGRI (YUGRY)   For. alt. des. Ugrian Peoples. SEE
                 Ugrian Peoples, Hungarian, Khant,
                 Mansi.

YUIT   Alt. and for. des. of Eskimo. This was the
          official designation of the Eskimoes of the
USSR between 1931-38. The term Yuit is derived from the
Eskimo self des. Yogyt.

YUITI (YUITY)   Alt. des. Yuit; for. alt. des. Eskimo.
                 SEE Eskimo.

YUKAGHIR   Alt. des. Yukagir. SEE Yukagir.

YUKAGIR   Formerly no collective self des. (by clan);
contemporary self des. Odul (derived from
Tundra Yukagir self des. Odul); for. alt. des. Odul.
ETHN: The Yukagir are one of the numerically small
Paleoasiatic peoples of northeastern Siberia. They were
formerly more numerous and widespread; however, as a
result of epidemics and assimilation by neighboring
peoples (Yakut, Even, Chukchi, and Russian) their
population has declined markedly since the 18th cent.
The Omok and Anaul are two groups of Yukagirs that are
now extinct as a result of epidemics in the 19th cent.
Traditional Yukagir occupations were hunting and
fishing, with little time spent breeding reindeer. The
Yukagirs are divided into two culturally and
linguistically distinct groups. One group lives in the
upper Kolyma region in Sredne-Kanskiy Rayon in Magadan
Oblast and Verkhne-Kolymskiy Rayon in the Yakut ASSR.
The other lives along the forest edge in the Tundra in
the basin of the Chukochei River in the lower reaches
of the Kolyma and Alazeya Rivers. The languages spoken
by these two groups are not mutually intelligible.
LANG: The Yukagir language is classified as a
Paleoasiatic language. It is comprised of two non-
mutually intelligible dialects (actually two distinct
languages), neither of which is written. Russian and
Yakut serve as the literary languages of the Yukagirs.
Virtually all Yukagirs are at least bilingual. The
Yukagirs of the upper Kolyma region speak Yakut and
Yukagir. Those of the Tundra region speak Even, and
often also Chukchi and Yakut. Many in both groups can
also speak Russian. POP: 835 (1979); 615 (1970); 442
(1959); 443 (1926); 2,350 (1859). The Yukagir
population declined markedly between 1859 and 1926 as a
result of epidemics and assimilation. The Yukagirs are
shamanist-animist in religion. They live, primarily, in
Magadan Oblast and the northeastern part of the Yakut
ASSR. SEE Paleoasiatic Peoples, MAP 5.

YURAK   For. des. of Nenets. In the pre-Soviet period
the term Yurak was commonly used as a
designation of the Nenets in the Yenisei north, while
the term Samoyed was used for the Nenets in the
European and Ob North. In 1926 2,104 Nenets were listed
as Yurak. SEE Nenets.

YURAK-SAMODI (SAMOED,   Alt. des. and spel. Yurak-
SAMOIED, SAMOYED)   Samoyed; for. des. of Nenets.
SEE Nenets.

YURAK SAMOYED   For. des. of Nenets. SEE Nenets.

Z

ZAKARPATTSY   Ukrainian alt. des. Carpatho-Rusin. SEE
                 Carpatho-Rusin, Ukrainian.

ZAKARPATO-RUS (RUSIN,   Rus. alt. des. Zakarpatsko-
            RUSYN)   Rusin(y) (Carpatho-Rusin). SEE
                          Carpatho-Rusin, Ukrainian.

ZAKARPATSKO-RUS (RUSIN,   Rus. des. Carpatho-Rusin.   SEE
              RUSYN)   Carpatho-Rusin, Ukrainian.

ZAN   1-Alt. des. Laz. SEE Laz, Georgian.
         2-Alt. col. des. Megrelo-Laz. SEE Megrelo-Laz,
         Georgian.

ZANAVYKIAI   The Zanavykiai form the western division
                of the Suvalkiečiai (the Kapsai form the
eastern division). They live in the area to the
southwest of the Nemunas (Rus.- Neman) River in the
region of Lithuania called Suvalkiya (Rus.- Zanemane).
SEE Suvalkiečiai, Lithuanian.

ZANEMAN(E)   Rus. des. Suvalkiečiai. SEE Suvalkiečiai,
                Lithuanian.

ZATUNDREN(E)   The Zatundren(e) are an ethnographic
                  group of Russians who live in the
northern Tundra along the Dudinka and Khatanga Rivers.
They are of mixed Russian and Dolgan origin. Although
they were culturally and linguistically assimilated by
the   Dolgans (they speak Dolgan as their native
language), they have maintained a Russian identity. SEE
Russian.

ŽEMAIČIAI   Self des. Žemaičiai (sing. Žemaitis);
               Rus. des. Zhmud; oth. des. Zhemait(i),
Zhemoit, Samogit(ian). The Žemaičiai (lowlanders) are
one of the two major divisions of the Lithuanians
(Žemaičiai and Aukštaičiai). It now refers to the
inhabitants of western Lithuania. The Žemaičiai form a
distinct culture group of Lithuanians. The Žemaičiai,
like the Aukštaičiai (highlanders), are sometimes
considered distinct ethnographic groups of Lithuanians.
SEE Lithuanian.

ŽEMAITI   (ŽEMAITIS)   Alt.   des.   Žemaičiai   (sing.
                            Žemaitis).   SEE   Žemaičiai,
                            Lithuanian.

ZEMGAL (ZEMGAĻI,   ZEMGALIAN)   Alt.   des.   Zemgalieši.
                            SEE Zemgalieši, Latvian.

ZEMGALIEŠI   Self des. Zemgalieši (sing. Zemgalietis);
              oth. des. Zemgal(ian), Zemgaļi, Zemgalis.
The Zemgalieši are the inhabitants of Zemgale, one of
the four traditional provinces of Latvia.   They are
sometimes considered a distinct ethnographic group of
Latvians. SEE Latvian.

ZEMGALIETIS (ZEMGALIS)   Latvian sing. des. Zemgalieši.
                          SEE Zemgalieši, Latvian.

ZEREHGERAN (ZEREKHGERAN)   Alt. des. Zirekhgeran; for.
                           alt. des. of Kubachi. SEE
                           Zirekhgeran, Kubachi,
                           Dargin.

ZHEMAIT (ZHEMAITI, ZHEMAITY,   Alt. des. Žemaičiai.
         ZHEMAYTY, ZHEMOIT)   SEE Žemaičiai,
                                  Lithuanian.

ZHID   For. Rus. des. (now pejorative) of Jew. SEE Jew.

ZHMUD (ZHMUT)   Rus. and alt. des. Žemaičiai. SEE
                  Žemaičiai, Lithuanian.

ZIREKHGERAN   For. alt. des. of Kubachi. The term
                Zirekhgeran is derived from the Persian
"maker of chainmail."   The Kubachi were renowned
throughout the Middle East as makers of fine jewelry,
daggers, and chainmail. SEE Kubachi, Dargin.

ZIRIAN   Alt. spel. Zyryan; for. des. Komi and Komi
          Permyak. SEE Komi, Komi Permyak.

ZIRIAN IJEM (IJMI, IZHEM,   Alt. des. Izhmi. SEE Izhmi,
            IZHMI)   Komi.

ZIUZDA   Alt. spel. Zyudza; alt. des. Zyuzda Komi
          Permyak. SEE Zyuzda Komi Permyak,   Komi
          Permyak.

ZIUZDA KOMI PERMIAK   Alt. spel. Zyuzda Komi Permyak.
                       SEE Zyuzda Komi Permyak, Komi
                       Permyak.

ZIUZDA ZIRIAN (ZYRIAN)   Alt. spel. Zyuzda Zyryan;
                          for. des. of Zyuzda Komi
                          Permyak. SEE Zyuzda Komi
                          Permyak, Komi Permyak.

ZIUZDIN (SKI) KOMI PERMIAK   Alt. spel. and for. des.
     (ZIRIAN, ZYRIAN)   Zyuzda Komi Permyak. SEE
                                  Zyuzda Komi   Permyak,
                                  Komi Permyak.

ZYRIAN   Alt. spel. Zyryan. For. des. of Komi and Komi
           Permyak. SEE Komi, Komi Permyak.

ZYRIAN IJEM (IJMI, IZHEM)   Alt. des. and spel. Zyryan
                                  Izhmi; for. des. of Komi
                                  Izhmi; alt. des. Izhmi. SEE
                                  Izhmi, Komi.

ZYRYAN   For. des. Komi and Komi Permyak. SEE Komi,
           Komi Permyak.

ZYRYAN IJEM (IJMI, IZHEM)   Alt. des. and spel. Zyryan
                                  Izhmi; for. des. of Komi
                                  Izhmi; Alt. des. Izhmi.
                                  SEE Izhmi, Komi.

ZYRYAN IZHMI   For. des. of Komi Izhmi; alt. des.
                 Izhmi. SEE Izhmi, Komi.

ZYUZDA   Alt. des. Zyuzda Komi Permyak. SEE Zyuzda
           Komi Permyak, Komi Permyak.

ZYUZDA KOMI PERMYAK   Oth. des. Zyuzdin(skiy) Komi
                        Permyak; for. des. of Zyuzda
(Zyuzdin) Zyryan. The Zyuzda Komi Permyak are one of
the two ethnographic groups of Komi Permyaks (Zyuzda
and Yazva Komi Permyak) who live outside the Komi
Permyak AO. They live in Zyuzdinskiy Rayon in Kirov
Oblast. The Zyuzda Komi Permyak speak a dialect that is
transitional between Komi and Komi Permyak. In 1959
their population was approximately 7,000. SEE Komi
Permyak.

ZYUZDA ZIRYAN   Alt. spel. Zyuzda Zyryan; for. des.
                  Zyuzda Komi Permyak. SEE Zyuzda Komi
                  Permyak, Komi Permyak.

ZYUZDA ZYRYAN   For. des. of Zyuzda Komi Permyak. SEE
                  Zyuzda Komi Permyak, Komi Prmyak.

ZYUZDIN (SKIY) KOMI PERMYAK   Alt. des. and for. des.
     (ZIRYAN, ZYRYAN)   Zyuzda Komi Permyak. SEE
                                  Zyuzda Komi   Permyak,
                                  Komi Permyak.

List of Maps

Map Index

Map 1

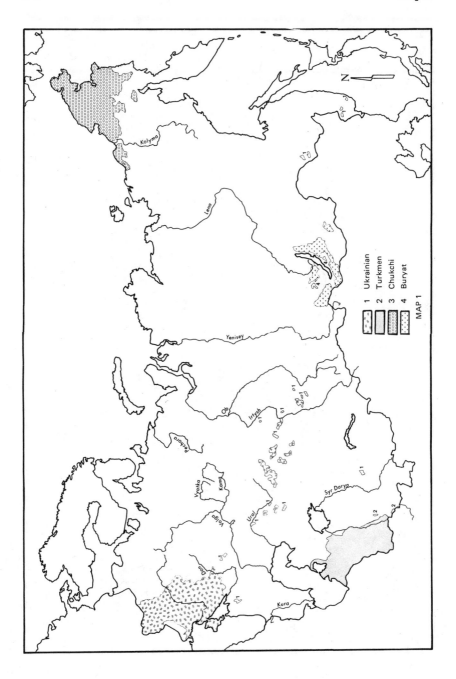

1 Ukrainian
2 Turkmen
3 Chukchi
4 Buryat

MAP 1

Map 2   232

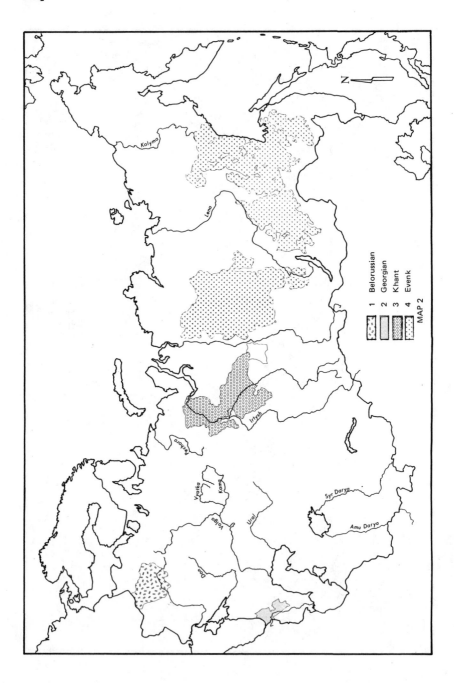

Map 3

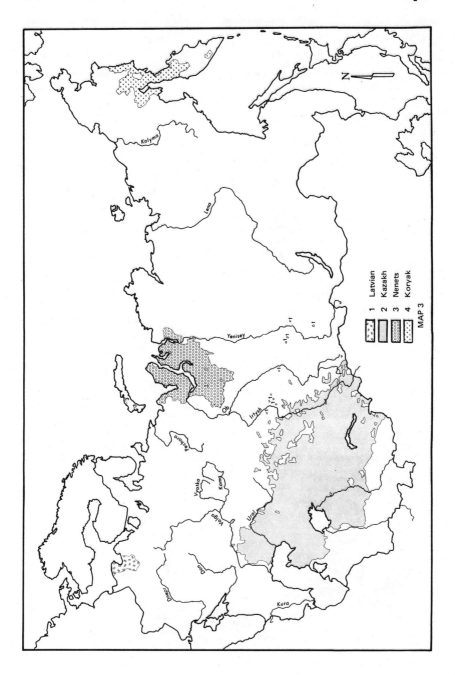

Map 4

234

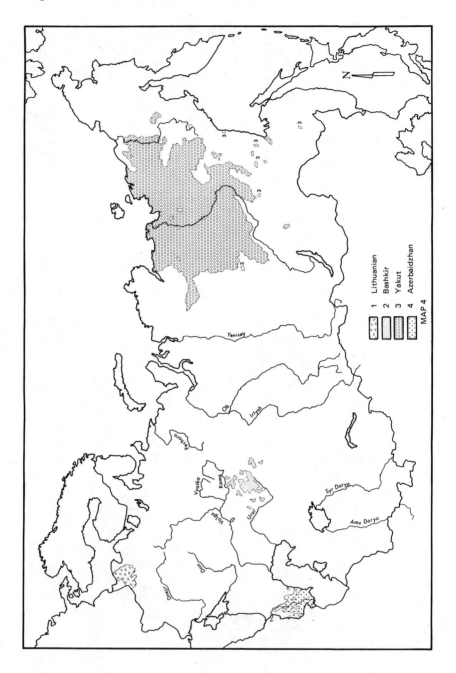

Lithuanian
Bashkir
Yakut
Azerbaidzhan

1
2
3
4

MAP 4

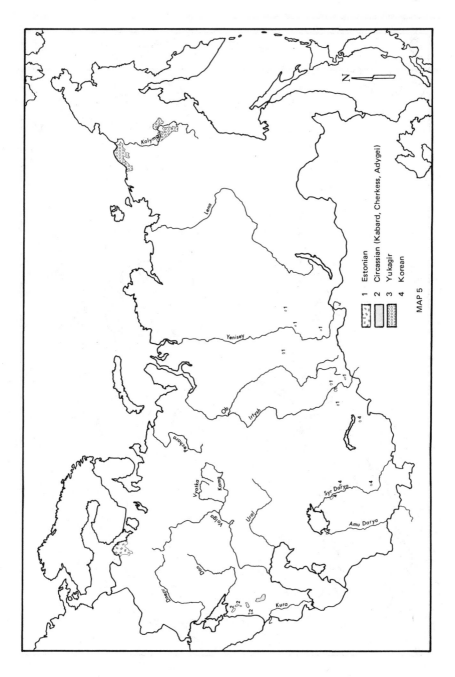

Estonian
Circassian (Kabard, Cherkess, Adygei)
Yukagir
Korean

1 2 3 4

MAP 5

Map 6

236

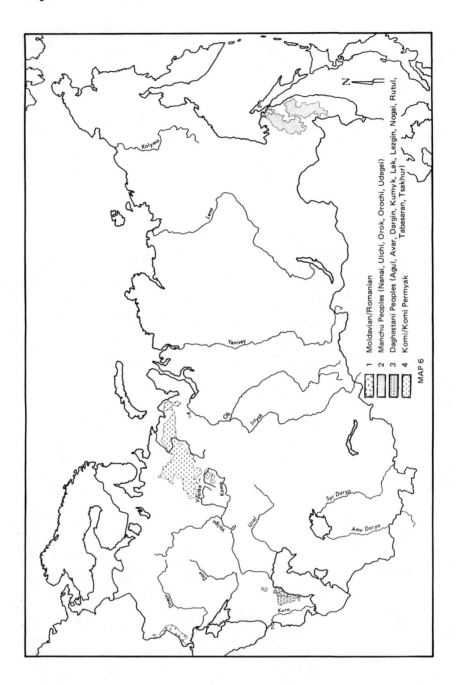

MAP 6

1 Moldavian/Romanian
2 Manchu Peoples (Nanai, Ulchi, Orok, Orochi, Udegei)
3 Daghestani Peoples (Agul, Avar, Dargin, Kumyk, Lak, Lezgin, Nogai, Rutul, Tabasaran, Tsakhur)
4 Komi/Komi Permyak

Map 7

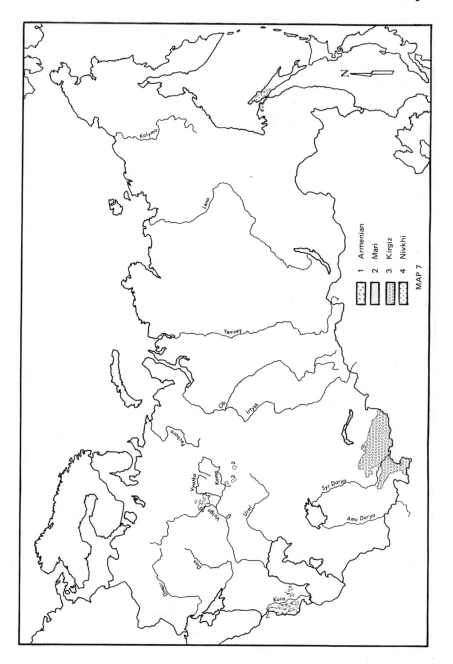

Map 8

238

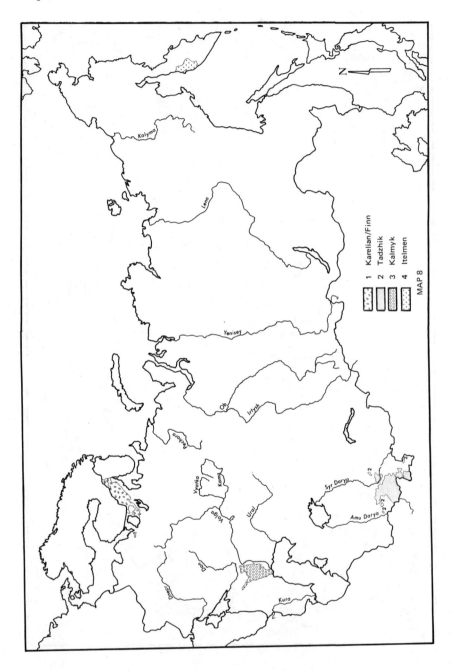

MAP 8

1 Karelian/Finn
2 Tadzhik
3 Kalmyk
4 Itelmen

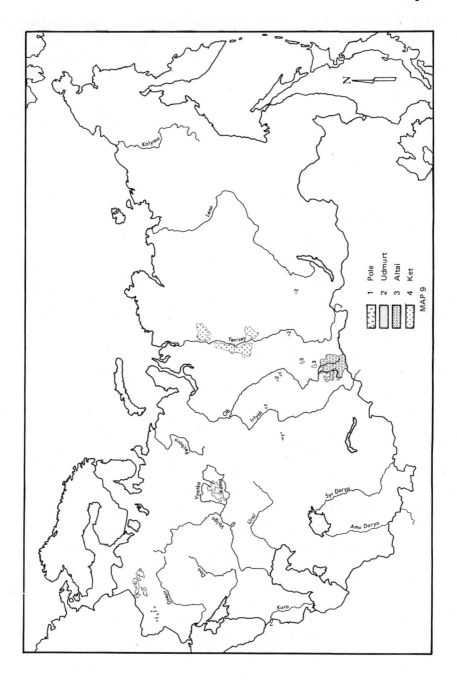

Map 10 240

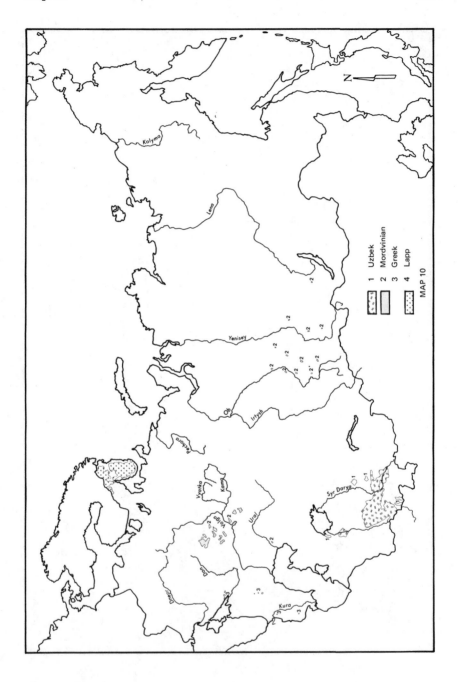

MAP 10

1 Uzbek
2 Mordvinian
3 Greek
4 Lapp

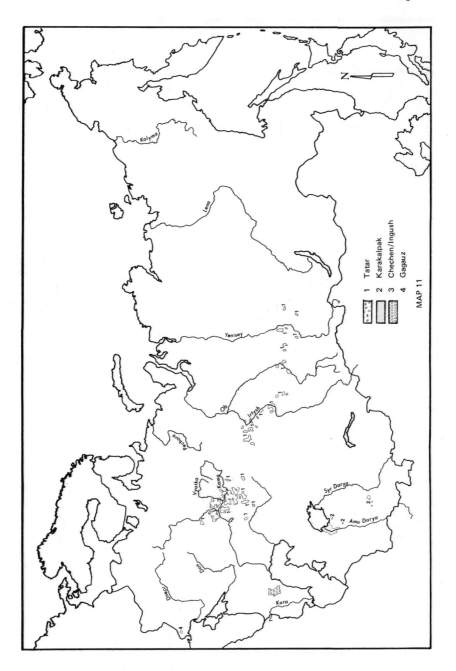

MAP 11

1 Tatar
2 Karakalpak
3 Chechen/Ingush
4 Gagauz

Map 12 242

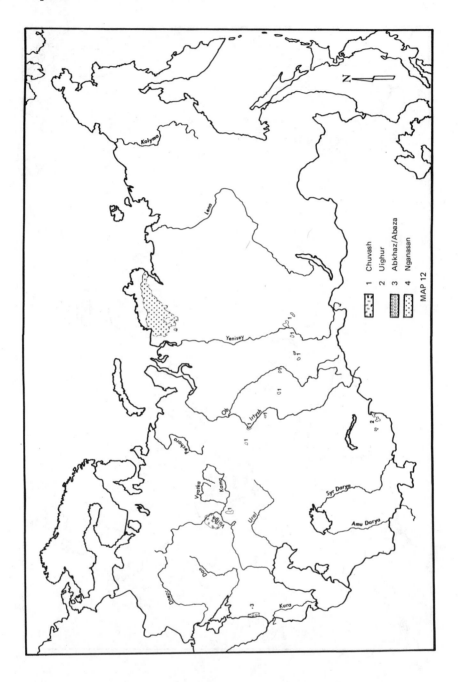

Legend:
1 Chuvash
2 Uighur
3 Abkhaz/Abaza
4 Nganasan

MAP 12

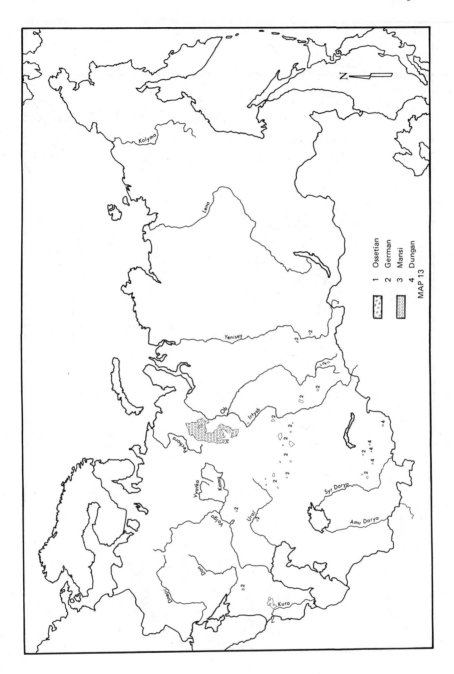

1 Ossetian
2 German
3 Mansi
4 Dungan

MAP 13

Map 14 244

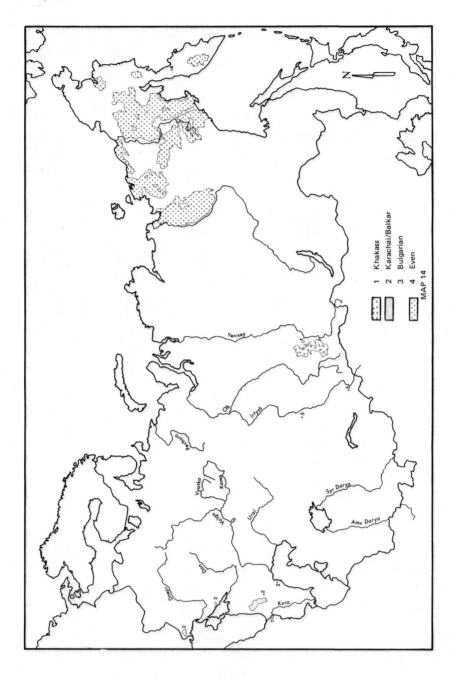

1 Khakass
2 Karachai/Balkar
3 Bulgarian
4 Even

MAP 14

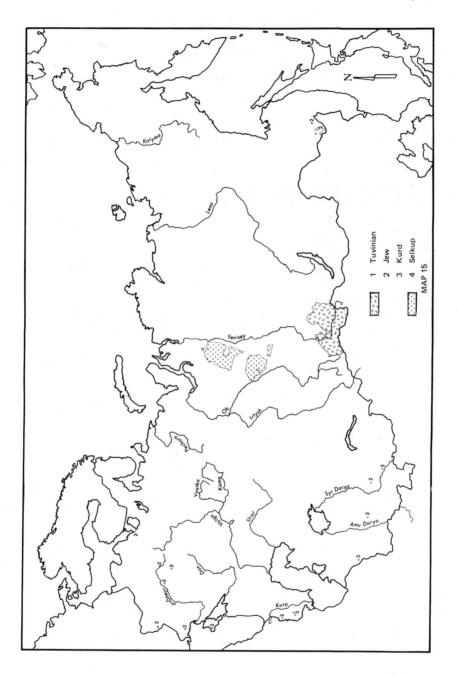

MAP 15

1 Tuvinian
2 Jew
3 Kurd
4 Selkup

About the Author

Ronald Wixman earned a bachelor's degree at Hunter College of the City University of New York, a master's at Columbia University, and a doctorate at the University of Chicago. He is currently associate professor of geography at the University of Oregon. Professor Wixman is the author of *Language Aspects of Ethnic Patterns and Processes in the North Caucasus*, a great many published articles, and numerous entries in the 3rd edition of *The Encyclopedia of Islam*.